Ethics in Psychotherapy and Counseling

李聰

Kenneth S. Pope

Melba J. T. Vasquez

Ethics in Psychotherapy and Counseling

A Practical Guide

Second Edition

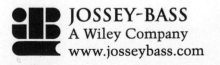

JOSSEY-BASS
A Wiley Company
www.josseybass.com

Published by Jossey-Bass
A Wiley Imprint
989 Market Street, San Francisco, CA 94103-1741   www.josseybass.com

Readers should be aware that Internet Web sites offered as citations and/or sources for further information may have changed or disappeared between the time this was written and when it is read.

Jossey-Bass books and products are available through most bookstores. To contact Jossey-Bass directly call our Customer Care Department within the U.S. at 800-956-7739, outside the U.S. at 317-572-3986, or fax 317-572-4002.

Jossey-Bass also publishes its books in a variety of electronic formats. Some content that appears in print may not be available in electronic books.

Library of Congress Cataloging-in-Publication Data

Pope, Kenneth S.
    Ethics in psychotherapy and counseling: a practical guide/Kenneth S. Pope, Melba
J. T. Vasquez.—2nd ed.
        p.   cm.
    Includes bibliographical references and index.
    ISBN 0-7879-4306-1 (alk. paper)
        1. Counselors—Professional ethics.   2. Psychotherapists—Professional ethics.
3. Counseling—Moral and ethical aspects.   4. Psychotherapy—Moral and ethical
aspects.   5. Counselor and client.   I. Vasquez, Melba Jean Trinidad.   II. Title.
    BF637.C6P59   1998
    174'.915—dc21
                                                                                            98-11798
                                                                                            CIP

Printed in the United States of America
SECOND EDITION
PB Printing   10 9

⸺ Contents

For Alan, Alison, Gary, Janet, Karen, Laura, Paula, Patti, Phil, Pete, and Tom, whose courage, love, and kindness have meant more than they will ever know
—*Ken Pope*

To Ofelia Vasquez Philo, the late Joe Vasquez, Jr., and Jim H. Miller—*my models of integrity*
—*Melba Vasquez*

⟿ Preface

Ethics are an essential guide for the work of psychotherapy and counseling. They are a process through which we awaken, enhance, inform, expand, and improve our ability to respond effectively to those who come to us for help.

Although they may be reflected in the formal standards of a professional association, in the civil or criminal law, or in the administrative guidelines of licensing or certification boards, ethics are not static codes. Such codes can call our attention to important values and mark off some of the extreme areas of unacceptable behavior, but they cannot do our questioning, thinking, feeling, and responding for us. Such codes can never be a substitute for the active process by which the individual therapist or counselor struggles with the sometimes bewildering, always unique constellation of questions, responsibilities, contexts, and competing demands of helping another person.

We wrote this book to serve as a resource for that active, occasionally lonely, but potentially exciting process. *Ethics in Psychotherapy and Counseling* is based upon the premise that ethics are neither vague and lofty aspirations unrelated to the daily practicalities of the helping professions nor unvarying and coercive rules that preempt professionals' decisions and control their actions.

Solidly rooted in the research tradition, psychology is the only profession to use an empirical approach to creating its ethical standards. In 1948, the American Psychological Association (APA) surveyed all its members to ask what ethical challenges they faced in their day-to-day work. The responses identified over one thousand dilemmas that, carefully analyzed, became the basis of the APA's first ethical standards. As noted in this book, this empirical approach to ethics was replicated over fifty years later, with interesting results (see Chapter Two).

APA's approach emphasized what is obvious to any therapist or counselor: Ethics must be practical. Clinicians confront an almost unimaginable diversity of situations, each with its own shifting questions, demands, and responsibilities. Every clinician is unique in important ways. Every client is unique in important ways. Ethics that are out of touch with the practical realities of clinical work, with the diversity and constantly changing nature of the therapeutic venture, are useless.

We wrote this book as a resource for those who are practicing, learning, or teaching psychotherapy. It grew out of our own work in those three roles.

To create a resource that would be genuinely helpful to beginning and experienced clinicians, we examine ethics not only as they are reflected in the formal professional codes but also as they are manifested in the actual work of the therapist. This book acknowledges and examines the complex interplay—and sometimes stark conflicts—among the needs of the client, values of the therapist, formal ethical standards, and legal obligations. Attention is devoted to the external factors and complexities that can make recognizing and fulfilling ethical responsibilities seem so difficult and to those internal, very human tendencies that we all share, by which we deny, avoid, or distort the ethical implications of our behavior.

AUDIENCE

We wrote this book primarily for individuals who are doing, learning, or teaching therapy or counseling. Although this text identifies ethical issues as they occur in actual practice and suggests possible approaches, it also provides a variety of open-ended vignettes and questions to prompt discussion in ethics courses, clinical supervision and consultation, staff meetings, continuing education programs, and workshops. We created this book as a resource not only for those in institutional settings (students and teachers in university courses or internships, staff and trainees in clinics, hospitals, and managed care facilities) but also for those in independent practice. We hope that these "do-it-yourself" vignettes and questions will help independent practitioners by prompting or facilitating the formation of both formal and informal networks in which such questions are openly, candidly, and regularly discussed. Unfortunately, those of us in independent practice can easily become unnecessarily isolated from our colleagues and thus cut off from useful, frequent discussion of ethical challenges and questions.

There is another reason for including these open-ended vignettes and questions: They emphasize the view that ethical awareness, deliberation, and behavior do not involve passive obedience or adherence to inflexible lists of "do's and don't's." The process is active and personal. Each therapist must struggle to create an ethical response to an individual client with individual needs within the context of a unique and constantly changing situation. All of us (except those who are omniscient, omnipotent, or sociopathic) feel overwhelmed at times because the work we have chosen to do and the responsibilities we have chosen to assume involve the hard questions, irreducible complexity, and frequently conflicting demands of human experience. Our work influences, sometimes in an extremely direct, profound, and immediate way, the lives of clients who may be hurting, unhappy, vulnerable, and perhaps in crisis. None of us is free from encountering unexpected, unfamiliar clinical situations for which there are no clear answers. What is crucial is that we continue our active involvement in the process of informed ethical awareness, questioning, analysis, and struggle.

A NOTE ON TERMINOLOGY

This book addresses ethical issues encountered by psychologists functioning as *therapists* and *counselors.* For the sake of brevity and convenience, we have often used one term or the other rather than both in a given sentence. Similarly, some psychologists identify those to whom they provide services as *clients;* others use the term *patients.* Again, for the sake of brevity and convenience, we have used these terms interchangeably throughout the book.

ACKNOWLEDGMENTS

We are indebted to the many individuals who contributed, directly or indirectly, to this book. We are grateful to all, but space limitations allow us to mention only a few by name. Ursula Delworth, Gerald Koocher, and Janet Sonne carefully reviewed a draft manuscript during preparation of the first edition and offered valuable suggestions for improving it. Sandra Haber and Karen Zager, who served as editors of the APA Division 42's Independent Practitioner, helped to improve certain portions of this book that appeared previously in that journal. Finally, we greatly appreciate the exceptionally capable and generous help we have received from Rebecca McGovern and Xenia Lisanevich of Jossey-Bass Publishers in preparing the first edition, and from Alan Rinzler, Katie Levine, Margaret Sebold, Joanne Clapp Fullagar, and Paula Goldstein of Jossey-Bass Publishers and Rachel Anderson of Satellite Publishing Services in preparing the second edition.

Norwalk, Connecticut   KENNETH S. POPE
May 1998

Austin, Texas   MELBA J. T. VASQUEZ
May 1998

Ethics in Psychotherapy and Counseling

CHAPTER ONE

Helping Without Hurting

Enhancing Ethical Awareness

P sychotherapy and counseling hold out the promise of help for people who are hurting and in need. When the process works as it is supposed to, lives can be changed in lasting and profound ways. Clients can gain awareness and understanding of themselves and their lives. They can confront traumas and tragedies and come to terms with these events in a way that will not leave them numb or paralyzed. They can become happier and more fulfilled or at least less miserable. They can learn new behaviors as well as how to teach themselves new behaviors. They can learn to trust or to trust more wisely. They can become more aware of what values they affirm, what makes their life meaningful. They can develop a sense of well-being and become better able, as Freud noted, to love and to work.

Our ethics acknowledge the great responsibilities inherent in the promise and process of our profession. They reflect the fact that if we do not fulfill these responsibilities with the greatest care, people may be hurt.

ETHICS AND RESPONSIBILITY

Our work as therapists and counselors may make a crucial difference in whether a client loses hope and commits suicide or continues to live, whether a battered spouse is able to find a safe environment or remains in a potentially lethal setting, or whether a teenager developing anorexia receives adequate help or starves to death, to name but a few examples. Even therapists at the beginning of their careers are aware that such focused and dramatic examples tell only part of the story. So many people who come to us for help face much more elusive, mundane, and sometimes seemingly trivial problems, yet the arduous, risky, and frequently discouraging course of their therapy may play a key role in their struggle to lead more meaningful, more effective, more personally fulfilling lives.

Few therapists take this responsibility lightly. Few are able to set aside their concern about a suicidal client between sessions. Few sit unmoved while a client is recounting, often with great emotion, a traumatic event that has just come into awareness after a long period of forgetfulness.

This very human ability to be moved by the dilemmas and struggles of another human being and the sense of responsibility we feel regarding our attempts to help, at times feel like a tremendous weight upon our shoulders. Our work can evoke anxiety and a sense of great uncertainty (Pope & Tabachnick, 1993). Unfortunately, it can also make us more vulnerable to additional sources of stress inherent in our attempts to help (Pope & Tabachnick, 1994).

One additional source of stress for some of us is that there is no by-the-book, one-size-fits-all guide to responding to a client's clinical needs. Whether increasing the number of weekly sessions from two to four during a crisis would help or hurt (or, less likely, have no net effect) is a decision that must be made on the basis of professional judgment regarding the individual situation of the client. Whether providing a stressed client with imagery techniques designed to reduce stress would ultimately be more helpful for a given client (helping the client to become less distressed and therefore more functional) or possibly harmful (facilitating the client's adjustment to an abusive work or home environment) is a question to which there is no instantly clear and universally accepted answer. The inescapable responsibility of rendering careful, informed, professional judgments regarding issues of enormous complexity can, especially when we are feeling stress from other sources, be a burden.

Another source of stress for some of us is the fear that we will be held accountable, after the fact, by formal review agencies. Some agencies, such as local, state, and national professional ethics committees, focus specifically on the ethical aspects of our work. Others, such as state licensing boards and the civil courts, seek to enforce professional standards of care that may embody ethical principles and responsibilities. Many of us tend to react to the possibility of facing a formal complaint with something approaching panic.

The advent of managed care has increased the concern of some therapists about being held accountable after the fact. For example, capitation contracts provide a certain amount of money to cover all services provided to a group of patients. The agency responsible for providing services to that group of patients, having estimated the average number of sessions they will need to provide to each patient, must therefore limit the total number of sessions they provide to that group to remain profitable. There may be strict guidelines limiting the number of sessions that may be provided in light of a patient's condition, diagnosis, prognosis, or other factors, and there may be informal yet powerful pressure to terminate early and quickly. Even if a clinician follows the agency's formal procedures in deciding whether to provide services to a covered patient and, if so, for how long, the clinician may later face charges before an ethics committee, licensing board, or malpractice court for patient abandonment, improper denial of treatment, or similar issues (see, for example, Caudill & Pope, 1995). The stress experienced by the clinician may involve not only concern for being held accountable by a formal review agency but also a concern about the patient's welfare and perhaps even survival in light of limited resources. One national study found that 86 percent of the participating therapists had experienced fear that a client may need clinical resources that are unavailable (Pope & Tabachnick, 1993).

Still another source of stress can be the process of learning or supervising therapy and counseling. As supervisors, we may be uncomfortable with how the supervisee responds to the client (if they respond differently from how we would), with our obligation to evaluate the supervisee's work, and with the demands of our role as teacher and mentor. As supervisees, we may be doubtful of our ability to assume clinical responsibilities (especially when they involve suicidal or homicidal risks), fearful of making mistakes, frustrated by differences in values or theoretical orientation between ourselves and our supervisor, and concerned that if we are completely truthful in describing to our supervisor what we actually thought, felt, and did with our clients, we might be advised to look for another line of work.

The following six fictional scenarios were created for a series of ethics and malpractice workshops. None of the hypothetical vignettes found here or throughout this book is based on an actual or specific case (and none of the individuals is based upon an actual clinician or patient), but all the scenarios represent the kinds of challenges faced by therapists and counselors. In these scenarios, each clinician was attempting to do his or her best. Readers may disagree over whether the clinician met the highest or even minimal ethical standards, and such disagreements can form the focus of classroom, case conference, supervision, or related discussions. In at least one or two instances, you may conclude that what the clinician did was perfectly reasonable and perhaps even showed courage and sensitivity. In some cases, you may feel that significant relevant information is missing. But in each instance, the professional's actions (or failures to act) become the basis of one or more formal complaints.

Life in Chaos

Mr. Alvarez, a thirty-five-year-old professor of physics, has never before sought psychotherapy. He shows up for his first appointment with Dr. Brinks. Mr. Alvarez says that his life is in chaos. He was granted full professor status about a year ago; about one month after that, his wife suddenly left him to live with another man. He became very depressed. About four months ago, he began to become anxious and to have trouble concentrating. He feels he needs someone to talk to so that he can figure out what happened. Mr. Alvarez and Dr. Brinks agree to meet twice every week for outpatient psychotherapy.

During the first few sessions, Mr. Alvarez says that he feels relieved that he can talk about his problems, but he remains very anxious. During the next few months, he begins talking about some traumatic experiences in his early childhood. He reports that he is having even more trouble concentrating. Dr. Brinks assures him that this is not surprising, that problems concentrating often become temporarily worse when a patient starts recovering painful memories. She suggests that they begin meeting three times a week, and Mr. Alvarez agrees.

One month later, Mr. Alvarez collapses, is rushed to the hospital, but is dead upon arrival. An autopsy reveals that a small but growing tumor had been pressing against a blood vessel in his brain. When the vessel burst, he died.

Months after Mr. Alvarez's death, Dr. Brinks is served notice that the state ethics committee is opening a formal case against her based upon a complaint filed by Mr. Alvarez's relatives. Furthermore, she is being sued for malpractice. The ethics complaint and the malpractice suit allege that she was negligent in diagnosing Mr. Alvarez in that she had failed to take any step to rule out organic causes for Mr. Alvarez's difficulty concentrating, had not applied any of the principles and procedures of the profession of psychology to identify organic impairment, and had not referred Mr. Alvarez for evaluation by a neuropsychologist or to a physician for a medical examination.

Psychotherapists and counselors in ethics and malpractice workshops (who would probably *not* constitute a random sample of practicing psychologists) who have reviewed this scenario have tended to conclude that Dr. Brinks may have been functioning beyond the range of her competence (see Chapter Five) and that she violated some of the fundamental standards of assessment (see Chapter Nine).

Evaluating Children

Ms. Cain brings her two children, ages four and six, to Dr. Durrenberger for a psychological evaluation. She reports that they have become somewhat upset during the last few months. They are having nightmares and frequently wet their beds. She suspects that the problem may have something to do with their last visit with their father, who lives in another state.

Dr. Durrenberger schedules three sessions in which he sees Ms. Cain and her two children together and three individual sessions with each of the children. As he is preparing his report, he receives a subpoena to testify in a civil suit that Ms. Cain is filing against her exhusband. She is suing for custody of her children. During the trial, Dr. Durrenberger testifies that the children seem, on the basis of interviews and psychological tests, to have a stronger, more positive relationship with their mother. He gives his professional opinion that the children would be better off with their mother and that she should be given custody.

Mr. Cain files an ethics complaint, a civil suit, and a licensing complaint against Dr. Durrenberger. One basis of his complaint is that Dr. Durrenberger had not obtained informed consent to conduct the assessments. When Mr. and Ms. Cain had divorced two years previously, the court had granted Mr. Cain legal custody of the children but had granted Ms. Cain visitation rights. (Ms. Cain had arranged for the assessments of the children during a long summer visit.) Another basis of the complaint was that Dr. Durrenberger had made a formal recommendation regarding custody placement without making any attempt to interview or evaluate Mr. Cain. Mr. Cain's attorney and expert witnesses maintained that no custody recommendation could be made without interviewing both parents.

Although laws regarding rights of custodial and noncustodial parents differ from state to state, participants in ethics and malpractice workshops tend to conclude that Dr. Durrenberger had not fulfilled his ethical (and in many states, legal) responsibility to obtain adequate informed consent from the relevant parent (see Chapter Eight) and that he had failed to conduct an adequate assessment to justify his conclusion (see Chapter Nine).

The Fatal Disease

When George, a nineteen-year-old college student, began psychotherapy with Dr. Hightower, he told the doctor that he was suffering from a fatal disease. Two months into therapy, George felt that he trusted his therapist enough to tell her that the disease was AIDS.

During the next eighteen months, much of the therapy focused on George's losing battle with his illness and his preparations to die. After two stays in the hospital for pneumonia, George informed Dr. Hightower that he knew he would not survive his next hospitalization. He had done independent research and talked with his physicians, and he was certain that if pneumonia developed again, it would be fatal due to numerous complications and that death was likely to be long and painful. George said that when that time came, he wanted to die in the off-campus apartment he had lived in since he came to college—not in the hospital. He would, when he felt himself getting sicker, take some illicitly obtained drugs that would ease him into death. Dr. Hightower tried to dissuade him from this plan, but George refused to discuss it and said that if Dr. Hightower continued to bring up the subject, he would quit therapy. Convinced that George would quit therapy rather than discuss his plan, Dr. Hightower decided that the best course of action was to offer caring and support—rather than confrontation and argument—to a patient who seemed to have only a few months to live.

Four months later, Dr. Hightower was notified that George had taken his life. Within the next month, Dr. Hightower became the defendant in two civil suits. One suit, filed by George's family, alleged that Dr. Hightower, aware that George was intending to take his own life, did not take reasonable and adequate steps to prevent the suicide, that she had not notified any third parties of the suicide plan, had not required George to get rid of the illicit drugs, and had not used hospitalization to prevent the suicide. The other suit was filed by a college student who had been George's lover. The student alleged that Dr. Hightower, knowing that George had a lover and that he had a fatal, sexually transmitted disease, had a duty to protect the lover. The lover alleged ignorance that George had been suffering from AIDS.

This scenario has been one of the most agonizing and controversial for the psychotherapists and counselors who consider it at ethics and malpractice workshops. Some believe that Dr. Hightower acted in the most humane, sensitive, and ethical manner; others believe that she was wrong to accept, without more vigorous challenge, George's decision to take his own life. In this sense, it illustrates the dilemmas we face when confronted with a suicidal individual (see Chapter Fourteen). It also illustrates how issues such as confidentiality (see Chapter Thirteen) have been challenged when a specific third party, or the public more generally, is perceived to be put at risk by a client.

Many would argue that the main goal of therapy when suicide is an issue is to defuse the potentially lethal situation. According to this stance, we have a professional duty to take appropriate affirmative measures to prevent patients from harming themselves, a duty that may include in extreme cases seeking a civil commitment of the patient. There has been increasing attention to an alternate view, however, in which the clinician may respect and accept the client's autonomy to such a degree that even the client's decision to commit suicide is respected and accepted. Some would accord this "right to die" to any client; others would recognize it only in certain extreme situations (for example, the client suffers from a painful and terminal disease). Some would draw the line at accepting a client's decision to commit suicide and taking no steps to interfere with the client's self-destructive acts; others would consider actively assisting the person to die. These agonizing, controversial issues have become especially difficult for some who provide mental health services to those with AIDS (see, for example, Pope & Morin, 1990), as in this vignette. As is so often the case, the ethical and clinical issues are interwoven with legal standards. Some states have considered and continue to consider legislation related to the issue of assisted suicide, and such legislation has been reviewed by the Supreme Court (Burt, 1997; Gostin, 1997).

The Mechanic

Ms. Huang, whose family had moved from mainland China to the United States fifteen years ago, is a forty-five-year-old automobile mechanic. She agreed, at the strong urging of her employer, to seek psychotherapy for difficulties that seem to affect her work. She has been showing up late at her job, has often phoned in sick, and frequently appears distracted. She complains to her new therapist, Dr. Jackson, of the difficulties of coping both with psychomotor epilepsy, which has been controlled through medication, and with her progressive diabetes, for which she is also receiving medical care.

Although she has no real experience treating those from the Chinese culture or those with chronic medical conditions such as epilepsy, Dr. Jackson begins to work with Ms. Huang. She meets with her on a regular basis for three months, but never feels that a solid working alliance is developing. After three months, Ms. Huang abruptly quits therapy. At the time, she has not paid for the last six sessions.

Two weeks later, Dr. Jackson receives a request to send Ms. Huang's treatment records to her new therapist. Dr. Jackson notifies Ms. Huang that she will not forward the records until the bill has been paid in full.

Some time later, Dr. Jackson is notified that she is the complainee in an ethics case opened by the Ethics Committee of the American Psychological Association (APA) and that she has been sued for malpractice. The complaints allege that Dr. Jackson had been practicing outside of her areas of competence because she had received no formal education or training and had no supervised experience in

treating people from the Chinese culture or those with multiple serious and chronic medical diseases. The complaints also alleged that
Ms. Huang had never adequately understood the nature of treatment,
as evidenced by the lack of any written informed consent. Finally, the
complaints alleged that "holding records hostage" for payment violated Ms. Huang's welfare and deprived her subsequent therapist
of having prompt and comprehensive information necessary to Ms.
Huang's treatment.

Participants in ethics and malpractice workshops who are asked to
assume the role of an ethics committee to review this scenario tend to
conclude that Dr. Jackson was acting without adequate competence
(see Chapter Five) to treat someone from a different culture (see
Chapter Twelve) or with a chronic medical condition, had not obtained adequate consent (see Chapter Eight), and had misused the
power of her role as therapist in refusing to disclose records because
of an unpaid bill (see Chapter Three).

The Internship

Dr. Larson is executive director and clinical chief of staff at the
Golden Internship Health Maintenance Organization (HMO). For
one year, he closely supervises an excellent postdoctoral intern,
Dr. Marshall. The supervisee shows great potential, working with a
range of patients who respond positively to her interventions. After
completing her internship and becoming licensed, Dr. Marshall goes
into business for herself, opening an office several blocks from
Golden Internship Health Maintenance Organization. Before terminating her work at the HMO, Dr. Larson tells Dr. Marshall that she
must transfer all patients to other center therapists. All of the patients
who can afford her fee schedule, however, decide to continue in therapy with Dr. Marshall at her new office. The patients who cannot
afford Dr. Marshall's fee schedule are assigned to new therapists at
the center. Dr. Larson hires an attorney to take legal action against
Dr. Marshall, asserting that she unethically exploited the HMO by
stealing patients and engaging in deceptive practices. He files formal
complaints against her with both the state licensing board and the
APA Ethics Committee, charging that she had refused to follow his
supervision in regard to the patients and pointed out that he, as the
clinical supervisor of this trainee, had been both clinically and legally
responsible for the patients. He refuses to turn over the patients'

charts to Dr. Marshall or to certify to various associations to whom she has applied for membership that Dr. Marshall has successfully completed her internship.

Dr. Marshall countersues, claiming that Dr. Larson is engaging in illegal restraint of trade and not acting in the patients' best interests. The patients, she asserts, have formed an intense transference and an effective working alliance with her; to lose their therapist would be clinically damaging and not in their best interests. She files formal complaints against Dr. Larson with the licensing board and the APA Ethics Committee, charging that his refusal to deliver copies of the patients' charts and to certify that she completed the internship violates ethical and professional standards.

Some of the patients sue the HMO, Dr. Larson, and Dr. Marshall, charging that the conflict and the legal actions (in which their cases are put at issue without their consent) have been damaging to their therapy.

Workshop participants have tended to conclude that both Dr. Larson and Dr. Marshall have behaved unethically in terms of misusing their power (see Chapter Three), failing to clarify in advance the conclusion of Dr. Marshall's work with the patients (see Chapter Seven), and neglecting to address these issues adequately in the supervisory contract (see Chapter Fifteen).

Staying Sober

Mr. Edwards is alcoholic, having drunk heavily for four years prior to the therapy. His therapist, Dr. Franks, uses a psychodynamic approach but also incorporates behavioral techniques specifically designed to address the drinking problem.

Two months into therapy, when it becomes apparent that outpatient psychotherapy alone is not effective, Mr. Edwards agrees to attend Alcoholics Anonymous (AA) meetings as an adjunct to his therapy. During the next nine months of therapy, Mr. Edwards generally remains sober, suffering only two relapses, each time falling off the wagon for a long weekend.

Now, a year into therapy, Mr. Edwards suffers a third relapse. He comes to the session having just had several drinks. During the session, Dr. Franks and Mr. Edwards conclude that some of the troubling material that has been emerging in the therapy had led Mr. Edwards to begin drinking again. At the end of the session, Mr. Edwards feels that he has gained some additional insight into why he drank. He decides to go straight from the session to an AA meeting.

One month later, Dr. Franks is notified that he is being sued. On his way from the therapy session to the AA meeting, Mr. Edwards had run a red light and had killed a mother and her child who were crossing the street. The suit alleged that the therapist knew or should have known his patient to be dangerous and should have taken steps to prevent him from driving until his alcoholism no longer constituted a danger to the public.

Although workshop participants tend to fault Dr. Franks for not adequately assessing his client's condition and the danger that the client's driving in that condition would constitute for the public (see Chapter Nine), there was a common empathetic response, as with many of the other scenarios. Clinicians tended to identify with the fictional Dr. Franks and thought, "There, but for the grace of God, go I." Struck by the enormous complexity and responsibilities the clinicians face in these scenarios, we wonder whether we would do any better if we were in their places and whether we are doing any better in our own practices (our failures of responsibility perhaps being in different areas, though just as serious).

Each scenario tends to bring home the reality that formal mechanisms of accountability act to protect clients from unethical and potentially harmful practices (see Chapter Two) but may also increase the stress that we feel at the possibility that one day we may be the subject of a formal complaint.

Yet another source of stress for some of us is the sense that, in some areas at least, the responsibilities to which we are held accountable do not seem matched by our abilities and resources. For example, society (through the courts) may hold us accountable for predicting and preventing homicide. But accurately predicting whether someone will or will not kill seems to be beyond the capacity of mental health professionals, or anyone else, for that matter (see Chapter Nine).

Amid all this responsibility, complexity, uncertainty, and stress, remaining alert to the ethical aspects of our work in a consistent and meaningful manner can seem overwhelming.

ETHICS AND DENIAL

If staying alert to ethical aspects and fulfilling the ethical responsibilities of our work overwhelm us, or if we are personally overwhelmed by other factors so that we are unable to be ethically responsible, all of us are vulnerable to denial and other ways of dismissing, distorting, or discounting ethical questions as they threaten to become prominent. We all have our favored ways of making uncomfortable ethical challenges disappear, perhaps by transforming them almost magically into something else, perhaps by attacking the client or colleague who raises the ethical question, perhaps by viewing ourselves as helpless, as compelled by necessity to act in a way that we suspect may be unethical. Take a few minutes to conduct a private self-assessment of the degree to which these forms of ethical denial may have infiltrated your own practice as a therapist, counselor, supervisor, or trainee.

For the therapist, counselor, supervisor, or trainee, professional ethics represent at least three basic tasks (discussed more fully in Chapter Three). First, professional ethics involve acknowledging the reality and importance of the individuals whose lives we affect by our professional actions. Second, they involve understanding the nature of the professional relationship and professional interventions. Third, they involve affirming accountability for our behavior.

A moment of active and honest self-assessment can give us at least a general sense of the degree to which we are accomplishing these tasks effectively, regardless of whether we are graduate students, interns, new licensees, seasoned veterans, or supervisors.

Are the people whom we serve real to us? To what extent do we misuse valid diagnostic and classification systems in a way that diminishes clients? Do we think, for example, of three people to whom we are providing services not so much as individuals but as the two schizophrenics and the one borderline? To what extent do we view them as somehow inferior humans because they are clients? If we are in independent practice, have we begun thinking of our clients less as individuals to be helped than as sources of payment for office overhead? Do we recognize and act in accordance with their rights (see, e.g., Appendix B; American Psychological Association, 1997)?

To what extent do we maintain an adequate awareness of the nature and implications of the professional relationship and of our professional interventions? Have we become insensitive to the trust with which so many of our clients invest their relationship to us, of the degree to which they count on us for hope and help? Have we begun to blur the professional boundaries so that certain clients are no longer sure whether they are our clients or our business partners, friends, dining companions, fellow poker or tennis players, or lovers?

To what extent do we hold ourselves accountable not only for what we do but also for what we fail to do as professionals? Do we tend to shift all responsibility onto the bureaucracy of the organization for which we work? Do we assume because we have not been subject to any formal complaint procedures that therefore we have been behaving in an ethically exemplary manner? Do we attempt to use the complexity of our work as a cloak to conceal the responsibilities that we have failed to fulfill?

This general self-assessment may be supplemented with a more specific assessment of the degree to which we use common fallacies and rationalizations to justify our unethical behavior and to quiet a noisy conscience. These attempts to disguise unethical behavior might be termed *ethical substandards,* although they are in no way ethical and many are so far beneath the standards of the profession that "sub-" becomes an understatement. They can make even the most hurtful and reprehensible behaviors seem ethical, or at least insignificant. All of us, at one time or another, probably have endorsed at least some of them—and all of us could probably extend the list. If some excuses seem absurd and humorous to us, we probably have not yet had to resort to using those particular rationalizations. At some future moment of great stress or exceptional temptation, those funny absurdities may gain considerable plausibility if not a comforting certitude. Such substandards we commonly use to justify the unjustifiable include the following:

1. It's not unethical as long as you don't talk about ethics. The principle of general denial is at work here. As long as neither you nor your colleagues mention ethical aspects of practice, no course of action could be identified as unethical.

2. It's not unethical as long as you don't know a law, ethical principle, or professional standard that prohibits it. This substandard encompasses two principles: specific ignorance and specific literalization. The principle of specific ignorance states that even if there is, say, a law prohibiting an action, what you do is not illegal as long as you are unaware of the law. The principle of literalization states that if you cannot find specific mention of a particular incident anywhere in legal, ethical, or professional standards, it must be ethical. In desperate times, when the specific incident is unfortunately mentioned in the standards and

you are aware of it, it is still perfectly ethical as long as the standard does not mention your theoretical orientation. Thus if the formal standard prohibits sexual involvement with patients, violations of confidentiality, or diagnosis without actually having met the client, a behavioral, humanistic, or psychodynamic therapist may legitimately engage in these activities as long as the standard does not explicitly mention behavioral, humanistic, or psychodynamic therapy.

3. It's not unethical as long as you can name at least five other clinicians—right off the top of your head—who do the same thing. (There are probably countless thousands more whom you don't know about or whom you could name if you just had the time.)

4. It's not unethical as long as none of your clients has ever complained about it.

5. It's not unethical as long as your client wanted you to do it.

6. It's not unethical as long as your clients' condition (probably borderline) made them so difficult to treat and so troublesome and risky to be around that they elicited whatever it was you did (not, of course, to admit that you actually did anything).

7. It's not unethical as long as you weren't really feeling well that day and thus couldn't be expected to perform up to your usual level of quality.

8. It's not unethical as long as a friend of yours knew someone who said that an ethics committee somewhere once issued an opinion that it's OK.

9. It's not unethical as long as you're sure that legal, ethical, and professional standards were made up by people who don't understand the hard realities of psychological practice.

10. It's not unethical as long as you're sure that the people involved in enforcing standards (for example, licensing boards, administrative law judges, expert witnesses) are dishonest, or stupid, or extremist, or unlike you in some significant way. Or conspiring against you.

11. It's not unethical as long as it results in a higher income or more prestige.

12. It's not unethical as long as it's more convenient than doing things another way.

13. It's not unethical as long as no one else finds out—or if whoever might find out probably wouldn't care anyway.

14. It's not unethical as long as you're observing most of the other ethical standards. This means that everyone can, by fiat, nullify one or two ethical principles as long as the other more important standards are observed. In a pinch, it's OK to observe a majority of the standards. In a real emergency, it's acceptable simply to have observed one of the ethical principles in some situation at some time in your life. Or to have thought about observing it.

15. It's not unethical as long as there's no intent to do harm.

16. It's not unethical as long as there is no body of universally accepted, scientific studies showing, without any doubt whatsoever, that exactly what you did was the sole cause of harm to the client. This view was vividly and succinctly stated by a member of the Texas pesticide regulatory board charged with protecting Texas citizens against undue risks from pesticides. In discussing chlordane, a chemical used to kill termites, one member said, "Sure, it's going to kill a lot of people, but they may be dying of something else anyway" ("Perspectives," 1990, p. 17).

17. It's not unethical as long as you don't intend to do it more than once.

18. It's not unethical as long as no one can prove you did it.

19. It's not unethical as long as you're an important person. The criteria for importance generally include being rich, well known, extensively published, tenured, having a large practice, possessing substantial malpractice liability coverage, or knowing personally someone who, in retrospect, thought APA's purchase of *Psychology Today* was a good idea.

20. It's not unethical as long as you're busy. After all, given your work load and responsibilities, who could reasonably expect you to obtain informed consent from all your clients, keep your chart notes in a secured area, be thorough when conducting assessments, or follow every little law?

Even if these self-serving defenses, rationalizations, and phony justifications fail to protect us from at least some sense that we are engaging in unethical behavior, memory may take care of the discomfort. At the end of Woody Allen's film *Crimes and Misdemeanors,* the doctor played by Martin Landau talks about a monumental event in his life: His mistress had threatened to make public their affair; he had arranged to have her murdered. He speaks with obvious fascination of how he had expected the event to haunt him for the rest of his life. However, he had found that each day the memory had bothered him a little less; the memory faded and ceased to carry any impact. He was, in fact, far happier than he had ever been. (Spiegel [1997] wrote of the capacity to expunge memories of having committed heinous crimes.)

Cognitive psychology has demonstrated the amazing degree to which our memories become altered to fit the schemas (or images) we have of ourselves. Interested readers may want to read Neisser's (1981) fascinating account of the workings of John Dean's memory. During the Watergate hearings, Dean appeared to have a remarkably accurate and detailed memory—virtually photographic. Neisser compared Dean's testimony about conversations with President Nixon to the actual tapes of those conversations, which were only released later. The memory errors were systematic: Dean's memory had distorted events to make himself appear better, more important. Our selective and malleable memory is always available to ensure that ethical unease about a particular incident can fade.

ETHICAL AWAKENING

We use the ethical substandards and other mechanisms of denial to dull and quiet our concerns, to lull our conscience, ethical judgment, and sensitivity to sleep. At least occasionally, ethical responsibilities can make such demands on our integrity and can become so pressing, troubling, and painful that we seek any avenue of escape. We want to get rid of the responsibility or at least of the awareness of the responsibility.

But the necessity of awakening ourselves to the ethical aspects of each new clinical situation remains constant. There is no realistic or legitimate way to spare ourselves the continuing process of examining, identifying, and attempting to address the ethical challenges of our work. Our shared and very human vulnerability to denial and the other strategies we use to protect ourselves from this process (at the expense of our clients, our work, and ourselves) is a major focus of this book. In addressing various topics, the book highlights some of the maneuvers by which we commonly try to avoid acknowledging and fulfilling our ethical responsibilities.

BASIC ASSUMPTIONS

This book does not attempt to provide an encyclopedic discussion of all ethical aspects of every topic related to psychotherapy and counseling, nor does it attempt to provide a set of easy-to-use "answers" to apply reflexively whenever an ethical question arises. Rather, it presents an approach to ethics in the early chapters and focuses in the latter chapters on a few of the major areas of practice such as assessment, working with suicidal clients, and supervision.

The approach presented in this book involves the following basic assumptions:

1. Ethical awareness is a continuous, active process. Fatigue, stress, and routine are some of the factors that, along with the substandards listed above, can make it likely that we will fail to notice important ethical aspects of our work. It is crucial that we practice continued alertness to the ethical implications of what we do.

2. Awareness of the ethics codes, the legal framework for mental health practice, and other formal standards is crucial to competence in the area of ethics, but the formal standards (discussed in Chapter Two) are not a substitute for an active, deliberative, and creative approach to fulfilling our ethical responsibilities. They prompt, guide, and inform our ethical consideration; they do not preclude or serve as a substitute for it. There is no way that the codes and principles can be effectively followed or applied in a rote, thoughtless manner. Each new client, whatever his or her similarities to previous clients, is a unique individual. Each situation also is unique and is likely to change significantly over time. The explicit codes and principles may designate numerous possible approaches as clearly unethical. They may identify with greater or lesser degrees of clarity the types of ethical concerns that are likely to be especially significant, but they cannot tell us how these concerns will manifest themselves in a particular clinical situation. They may set forth essential tasks that we must fulfill, but they cannot tell us how we can accomplish these tasks with a unique client facing unique problems.

3. Awareness of the scientific and professional literature on the current and evolving research and theory in the area of clinical psychology is likewise crucial to competence in the area of ethics (see for

example, Chambless et al., 1998), but the claims emerging in the literature can never be passively and reflexively accepted. A necessary response to such claims is active, careful, informed, persistent, and comprehensive questioning. This process of questioning is illustrated in detail in Chapter Six.

4. Despite what might be hinted at by the seeming authority, finality, and tone of some scientific and professional writings, psychotherapy and counseling are carried out by fallible human beings. The attempt to respond helpfully to a unique client's needs is made by another unique human being. In too many cases, our training may have neglected this aspect of our work. In the course of our work as clinicians, we may feel sexual attraction, fear, anger, or even hate, to name but a few examples of human responses. Our competence as clinicians includes emotional as well as intellectual competence: our awareness of our selves as individuals and how our personal responses may help or hurt a client. Chapter Five ("The Human Therapist") explores these issues.

5. Clinicians repeatedly encounter ethical dilemmas for which a clear ethical response is elusive. The therapist is confronted by needs that don't match resources, by conflicting values and responsibilities, by situations whose meaning varies sharply depending on the context in which it is viewed, by limits in the degree to which science is currently able to understand certain conditions or identify effective interventions, by the therapist's own feelings or other reactions that seem to block or sidetrack an effective response. There is no legitimate way to avoid these struggles. Clinicians must be prepared to examine these dilemmas actively as a normal and expected part of their work. Chapters Seven through Fifteen end with a set of scenarios, each with a series of questions for readers to consider, to encourage an active approach to such dilemmas.

Because the formal ethical codes and related means of accountability play a significant role—as noted in basic assumption 2 above—in prompting, guiding, and informing our ethical deliberations, we turn our attention to them in Chapter Two.

Ethical and Legal Codes and Complaints

Historical, Actuarial, and Empirical Foundations

A s psychotherapists and counselors, we are members of the mental health profession. Exactly what we have to profess has been the subject for debate from the beginning. We have always had difficulty defining what we do.

The Boulder Conference conducted one of the most intense efforts to define psychotherapy so it could be effectively taught to clinical and counseling psychologists. Carl Rogers, president of the American Psychological Association (APA) in 1947, had appointed David Shakow to chair a committee on defining and teaching psychotherapy. The Shakow report, adopted at the 1947 APA convention, resulted in the Boulder Conference two years later. On August 28, 1949, the recorder for the Boulder task force for defining psychotherapy and setting forth criteria for adequate training provided the following summary: "We have left therapy as an undefined technique which is applied to unspecified problems with a nonpredictable outcome. For this technique we recommend rigorous training" (Lehner, 1952, p. 547)

Since the Boulder Conference, many other conferences and various groups have attempted to define the process of psychotherapy.

Forces external to the profession have also influenced our practices. For example, insurance companies tend to require specific kinds of diagnoses for reimbursement. Managed care often requires demonstration by the therapist of medical necessity and a specific kind of treatment plan. Such organizations may severely limit the number of authorized sessions. How we think about, how we engage in, and how we deal with the business aspects of the practice of psychotherapy continues to be challenging.

MECHANISMS OF ACCOUNTABILITY

Difficulties in defining domains and activities, however, do not release any profession from the primary responsibility of setting forth its ethics. The hallmark of a profession is the recognition that the work its members carry out influences, sometimes in an extremely direct, profound, and immediate way, the lives of their clients. The powerful nature of this influence makes the customary rules of the marketplace (often resting on variations of the principle "Let the buyer beware") inadequate (see Chapter Three). Society asks that the profession set forth a code to which the members of the profession agree to be held accountable. At its heart, this code calls for the professional to protect and promote the welfare of clients and to avoid letting the professional's self-interests place the client at risk for harm. In addition to the fundamental code of ethics, there may be a code or statement of the rights of patients (see, for example, American Psychological Association, 1997; Appendix B) or the ethics as applicable in a specific setting such as managed care organizations (see, for example, National Academies of Practice, 1997; Appendix C).

Perhaps because society would never put complete trust in professions to enforce their own standards, and perhaps because the professions have demonstrated that they, at least occasionally, are less than vigorous, scrupulous, and effective in governing their own behavior, society has established additional means for attempting to ensure that professions meet minimal standards as they carry out their work, and that those who are served by professionals are protected from the iatrogenic harm that can result from incompetent, negligent, and unscrupulous practitioners.

Four major mechanisms hold psychotherapists and counselors formally accountable to an explicit set of professional standards: professional ethics committees, state licensing boards, civil (for example, malpractice) courts, and criminal courts. Each of these four mechanisms uses a different formulation of standards, though there may be substantial overlap. Behavior may be clearly unethical and yet not form the basis for criminal charges.

In some cases, psychotherapists and counselors may feel an agonizing conflict among these sets of standards. They may, for example, feel that the law compels them to act in a way that violates the welfare of the client and the clinician's own sense of what is ethical. A national survey of psychologists found that a majority (57 percent) of the respondents had intentionally violated the law or a similar formal standard because, in their opinion, not to do so would have injured the client or violated some deeper value (Pope & Bajt, 1988). The actions reported by two or more respondents included refusing to report child abuse (21 percent), illegally divulging confidential information (21 percent), engaging in sex with a patient (9 percent), engaging in nonsexual dual relationships (6 percent), and refusing to make legally required warnings regarding dangerous patients (6 percent).

That almost one out of ten of the participants reported engaging in sex with a client (see Chapter Ten) using the rationale of patient welfare or deeper moral value highlights the risks, ambiguities, and difficulties of evaluating the degree to which our own individual behavior is ethical. Pope and Bajt (1988) reviewed the attempts of philosophers and the courts to address the issue of the individual deciding to go against the law. On the one hand, for example, the U.S. Supreme Court emphasized that in the United States no one could be considered higher than the law: "In the fair administration of justice no man can be judge in his own case, however exalted his station, however righteous his motives, and irrespective of his race, color, politics, or religion" (*Walker* v. *City of Birmingham*, 1967, pp. 1219–1220).

On the other hand, however, courts endorsed Thoreau's (1849/1960) injunction that if a law "requires you to be the agent of injustice to another, then . . . break the law" (p. 242). The California Supreme Court, for example, tacitly condoned violation of the law only when the principles of civil disobedience are followed: "If we were to deny to every person who has engaged in . . . nonviolent civil disobedience . . . the right to enter a licensed profession, we would deprive the community of the services of many highly qualified persons of the highest moral courage" (*Hallinan* v. *Committee of Bar Examiners of State Bar*, 1966, p. 239).

A profound decision that confronts each of us is whether to, in essence, take the law into our own hands or to affirm Edmund Burke's

(1790/1961) axiom: "One of the first motives to civil society, and which becomes one of its fundamental rules, is, that no man should be judge in his own cause" (p. 71). "Neither stance may seem acceptable to psychologists who believe that compliance with a legal or professional obligation would be harmful, unjust, or otherwise wrong. Absolute compliance connotes a just following orders' mentality all too ready to sacrifice personal values and client welfare to an imperfect system of rules and regulations. Selective noncompliance connotes an association of people who have anointed themselves as somehow above the law, able to pick and choose which legal obligations and recognized standards they will obey" (Pope & Bajt, 1988, p. 828).

As Pope and Bajt note, civil disobedience (Gandhi, 1948; King, 1958, 1964; Plato, 1956a, 1956b; Thoreau, 1849/1960; Tolstoy, 1894/1951) is useful in many contexts for resolving this dilemma. The individual breaks a law considered to be unjust and harmful but does so openly, inviting the legal penalty both to demonstrate respect for the system of law and to call society's attention to the supposedly unjust law. Counselors and therapists, however, often find this avenue of openness unavailable because of the requirement of confidentiality (see Chapter Thirteen). If we, as a profession and as individual practitioners, are to address the possible conflicts between the law and the welfare of our clients, one of the initial steps is to engage in frequent, open, and honest discussion of the issue. The topic must be addressed in our graduate courses, internship programs, case conferences, professional conventions, and informal discussions with our colleagues.

The various mechanisms by which psychotherapists and counselors are held accountable for their actions can be a source of confusion for our clients, who often lack adequate information about these mechanisms. They may, for example, incorrectly believe that a professional ethics committee has the authority to revoke a license or that a licensing board has the power to expel a practitioner from a professional organization such as the American Psychological Association. The following sections describe the four major mechanisms of accountability.

PROFESSIONAL ETHICS COMMITTEES

Professional associations of therapists and counselors are voluntary organizations; membership is not a state or federal requirement for the practice of the profession. One can, for example, be licensed (by the state) and practice as a psychologist without being a member of the American Psychological Association or any other association. An association, through its ethics committee, holds its members accountable to the ethical principles it sets forth in the code it has developed. To illustrate how such a code is developed, we focus on the American Psychological Association, which currently has about 87,000 full members, an additional 62,500 student affiliates, 3,500 international affiliates, and 2,000 high school teacher affiliates (personal communication, APA Membership Office, May 8, 1998).

Founded in 1892 and incorporated in 1925, the APA first formed a Committee on Scientific and Professional Ethics in 1938. As complaints were brought to its attention, this committee improvised solutions on a private, informal basis. There was no formal or explicit set of ethical standards, so all of the committee's work was, of necessity, done on the basis of consensus and persuasion.

One year later, the committee was charged with determining whether a formal code of ethics would be useful for the organization. In 1947, the committee decided that a formal code of ethics would indeed be useful, stating, "The present unwritten code is tenuous, elusive, and unsatisfactory" ("A Little Recent History," 1952, p. 425). The board of directors established a Committee on Ethical Standards to determine what methods to use in drafting the code. Chaired by Edward Tolman, the committee included John Flanagan, Edwin Ghiselli, Nicholas Hobbs, Helen Sargent, and Lloyd Yepsen (Hobbs, 1948).

Some members strongly opposed the development of an explicit set of ethical standards, and many of their arguments appeared in *American Psychologist*. Calvin Hall (1952), for example, wrote that any code, no matter how well formulated, "plays into the hands of crooks. . . . The crooked operator reads the code to see how much he can get away with, and since any code is bound to be filled with ambiguities and omissions, he can rationalize his unethical conduct by pointing to the code and saying, 'See, it doesn't tell me I can't do this,' or 'I can interpret this to mean what I want it to mean'" (p. 430). Hall endorsed accountability, but he believed that it could be enforced without an elaborate code. He recommended that the application form for APA membership contain this statement: "As a psychologist, I agree to conduct myself professionally according to the common rules of decency, with the understanding that if a jury of my peers decides that I have violated these rules, I may be expelled from the association" (pp. 430–431). Hall placed most of the responsibility upon graduate schools. He recommended that "graduate departments of psychology, who have the power to decide who shall become psychologists, should exercise this power in such a manner as to preclude the necessity for a code of ethics" (p. 431).

An Empirical Approach to Ethics

The Committee on Ethical Standards determined that because empirical research was a primary method of psychology, the code itself should be based upon such research and should draw upon the experience of APA members. As Hobbs (1948, p. 84) wrote, the method would produce "a code of ethics truly indigenous to psychology, a code that could be lived." The board of directors accepted this recommendation, and a new committee was appointed to conduct the research and draft the code. Chaired by Nicholas Hobbs, the new committee included Stuart Cook, Harold Edgerton, Leonard Ferguson, Morris Krugman, Helen Sargent, Donald Super, and Lloyd Yepsen (APA Committee on Ethical Standards for Psychology, 1949).

In 1948, all 7,500 members of the APA were sent a letter asking each member "to share his experiences in solving ethical problems by describing the specific circumstances in which someone made a decision that was ethically critical" (APA Committee on Ethical Standards for Psychology, 1949, p. 17). The committee received reports of over 1,000 critical incidents. During the next years, the incidents with their accompanying comments were carefully analyzed, categorized, and developed into a draft code.

The emergent standards, along with the illustrative critical incidents, were published in *American Psychologist* (APA Committee on Ethical Standards for Psychology, 1951a, 1951b, 1951c). The standards were grouped into six major sections:

1. Ethical standards and public responsibility

2. Ethical standards in professional relationships

3. Ethical standards in client relationships

4. Ethical standards in research

5. Ethical standards in writing and publishing

6. Ethical standards in teaching

The draft generated considerable discussion and was revised several times. Finally, in 1953, it was formally adopted as the *Ethical Standards of Psychologists* (American Psychological Association, 1953).

In 1954, information on the complaints that the committee had handled for the past dozen years (during most of which there had been no formal code of ethics) was published in *American Psychologist* ("Cases and Inquiries," 1954). During this period, the ethical principles most frequently violated were

- Invalid presentation of professional qualifications (cited forty-four times)
- Immature and inconsiderate professional relations (twenty-three)
- Unprofessional advertisement or announcement (twenty-two)
- Unwarranted claims for tests or service offered, usually by mail (twenty-two)
- Irresponsible public communication (six)

The most recent version of the ethical principles (American Psychological Association, 1992), the Ethical Principles of Psychologists and Code of Conduct, consists of an introduction, a preamble, six general principles, and specific ethical standards. The preamble and general principles, which include competence, integrity, professional and scientific responsibility, respect for people's rights and dignity, concern for others' welfare, and social responsibility, are aspirational goals to guide psychologists toward the highest ideals of psychology. The specific ethical standards are enforceable rules for conduct.

The APA Ethics Committee adjudicates cases reported to them about member violations. Processing complaints is the main activity of the Ethics Committee (APA Ethics Committee, 1997). The Ethics Committee is required by the bylaws of the APA to report on the number and types of complaints investigated on an annual basis.

The most recent report of the Ethics Committee described loss of licensure as the most frequent reason for complaints being processed (37 percent); a large number of cases are processed by the Ethics Committee secondary to actions taken by state licensure boards, felony convictions, expulsion from state associations, and malpractice (APA Ethics Committee, 1997). Primary and multiple categories are listed in cases opened in 1996. The report noted that the multiple issues per allegations reported are important because a primary category relates to the basis on which APA is processing the case rather than to the underlying behavior, and a secondary category is always assigned. Thus, sexual misconduct (see Chapter Ten) is the primary underlying behavior in 63 percent of the cases in the category "loss of licensure."

The following are major and subcategories of cases opened in 1996.

Dual relationships continue to be a major category of alleged violations, including the subcategories of sexual misconduct, adult (two primary cases, nineteen multiple cases); sexual misconduct, minor (two multiple cases); and nonsexual dual relationship (five primary cases, nine multiple cases).

The next major category of reported allegations, *inappropriate professional practice,* listed the following subcategories: child custody, ten primary cases, ten multiple cases; confidentiality, four primary cases, six multiple cases; test misuse, one primary case, four multiple cases; insurance/fee problems, five multiple cases; outside competence, one primary case, two multiple cases; and inappropriate professional relations, one primary case, one multiple case.

The category *inappropriate research, teaching, or administrative practice* included subcategories in which allegations were reported, including discrimination, three primary cases, three multiple cases; termination/supervision, two primary cases, three multiple cases; and improper research techniques, one primary case, one multiple case.

The category *inappropriate public statements* included allegations in one subcategory: false, fraudulent, or misleading, three primary cases, four multiple cases.

The Empirical Approach Half a Century Later

As noted above, many of the pioneers in the APA noted reasons that an empirical approach would be useful in constructing an ethics code. But a critical incident survey of APA members could also serve another purpose. Although the actuarial data of ethics committees, licensing boards, and civil and criminal courts can reveal trends in ethical or legal violations as they are established by review agencies, empirical critical incident studies can reveal ethical dilemmas and concerns as they are encountered in day-to-day practice by the broad range of psychologists (that is, not just those who are subject to formal complaint).

The APA critical incident study undertaken in the 1940s was replicated in the 1990s and published in the American Psychologist (Pope & Vetter, 1992). A random sample of 1,319 APA members were asked to describe incidents that they found ethically challenging or troubling. Responses from 679 psychologists described 703 incidents in twenty-three categories, as follows.

CATEGORY	n	PERCENT
Confidentiality	128	18
Blurred, dual, or conflictual relationships	116	17
Payment sources, plans, settings, and methods	97	14
Academic settings, teaching dilemmas, and concerns about training	57	8
Forensic psychology	35	5
Research	29	4
Conduct of colleagues	29	4
Sexual issues	28	4
Assessment	25	4
Questionable or harmful interventions	20	3
Competence	20	3
Ethics (and related) codes and committees	17	2
School psychology	15	2
Publishing	14	2
Helping the financially stricken	13	2
Supervision	13	2
Advertising and (mis)representation	13	2
Industrial-organizational psychology	9	1
Medical issues	5	1
Termination	5	1
Ethnicity	4	1

CATEGORY	*n*	PERCENT
Treatment records	4	1
Miscellaneous	7	1

Here is a sampling of some of the ethical concerns as described by the participants in this anonymous survey.

> *Confidentiality:* "The executive director of the Mental Health Clinic with which I'm employed used his position to obtain and review clinical patient files of clients who were members of his church. He was [clerical title] in a . . . church and indicated his knowledge of this clinical (confidential) information would be of help to him in his role as [clerical title]."

> *Confidentiality:* "Having a psychologist as a client who tells me she has committed an ethical violation and because of confidentiality I can't report it."

> *Confidentiality:* "One of my clients claimed she was raped; the police did not believe her and refused to follow up (because of her mental history). Another of my clients described how he raped a woman (the same woman)."

> *Blurred, dual, or conflictual relationships:* "I live and maintain a . . . private practice in a rural area. I am also a member of a spiritual community based here. There are very few other therapists in the immediate vicinity who work with transformational, holistic, and feminist principles in the context of good clinical training that 'conventional' people can also feel confidence in. Clients often come to me because they know me already, because they are not satisfied with the other services available, or because they want to work with someone who understands their spiritual practice and can incorporate its principles and practices into the process of transformation, healing, and change. The stricture against dual relationships helps me to maintain a high degree of sensitivity to the ethics (and potentials for abuse or confusion) of such situations but doesn't give me any help in working with the actual circumstances of my practice. I hope revised principles will address these concerns!"

> *Blurred, dual, or conflictual relationships:* "Six months ago a patient I had been working with for three years became romanti-

cally involved with my best and longest friend. I could write no less than a book on the complications of this fact! I have been getting legal and therapeutic consultations all along, and continue to do so. Currently they are living together and I referred the patient (who was furious that I did this and felt abandoned). I worked with the other psychologist for several months to provide a bridge for the patient. I told my friend soon after I found out that I would have to suspend our contact. I'm currently trying to figure out if we can ever resume our friendship and under what conditions." [Note: This latter example is one of many that demonstrate the extreme lengths to which most psychologists are willing to go to ensure the welfare of their patients.]

Payment sources, plans, settings, and methods: "A seven-year-old boy was severely sexually abused and severely depressed. I evaluated the case and recommended six months treatment. My recommendation was evaluated by a managed health care agency and approved for ten sessions by a nonprofessional in spite of the fact that there is no known treatment program that can be performed in ten sessions on a seven-year-old that has demonstrated efficacy."

Payment sources, plans, settings, and methods: "Much of my practice is in a private hospital which is in general very good clinically. However, its profit motivation is so very intense that decisions are often made for $ reasons that actively hurt the patients. When patients complain, this is often interpreted as being part of their psychopathology, thus reenacting the dysfunctional families they came from. I don't do this myself and don't permit others to do so in my presence—I try to mitigate the problem—but I can't speak perfectly frankly to my patients and I'm constantly colluding with something that feels marginally unethical."

Payment sources, plans, settings, and methods: "A managed care company discontinued a benefit and told my patient to stop seeing me, then referred her to a therapist they had a lower fee contract with."

Academic settings, teaching dilemmas, and concerns about training: "I employ over 600 psychologists. I am disturbed by the fact that those psychologists with marginal ethics and competence were so identified in graduate school and no one did anything about it."

Forensic psychology: "A psychologist in my area is widely known, to clients, psychologists, and the legal community, to give whatever testimony is requested in court. He has a very commanding "presence" and it works. He will say anything, adamantly, for pay. Clients/lawyers continue to use him because if the other side uses him, that side will probably win the case (because he's so persuasive, though lying)."

Forensic psychology: "Another psychologist's report or testimony in a court case goes way beyond what psychology knows or his own data supports. [The quandary is] how or whether I should respond."

Forensic psychology: "I find it difficult to have to testify in court or by way of deposition and to provide sensitive information about a client. Although the client has given permission to provide this information, there are times when there is much discomfort in so doing."

Research: "I am co-investigator on a grant. While walking past the secretary's desk I saw an interim report completed by the PI [principal investigator] to the funding source. The interim report claimed double the number of subjects who had actually entered the protocol."

Research: "I have consulted to research projects at a major university medical school where 'random selection' of subjects for drug studies was flagrantly disregarded. I resigned after the first phase."

Research: "Deception that was not disclosed, use of a data videotape in a public presentation without the subject's consent (the subject was in the audience), using a class homework assignment as an experimental manipulation without informing students."

Conduct of colleagues: "As a faculty member, it was difficult dealing with a colleague about whom I received numerous complaints from students."

Conduct of colleagues: "At what point does 'direct knowledge' of purportedly unethical practices become direct knowledge which I must report—is reporting through a client 'direct' knowledge?"

Conduct of colleagues: "I referred a child to be hospitalized at a nearby facility. The mother wanted to use a particular psychiatrist. . . . When I called the psychiatrist to discuss the case, he advised me that, since he was the admitting professional, he'd assume full responsibility for the case. . . . He advised how he had a psychologist affiliated with his office whom he preferred to use."

Conduct of colleagues: "I see foster children who have little control over their lives and case workers who have little time/interest in case management. How can I maintain good professional relationships with those who don't function up to their duties?"

Conduct of colleagues: "A director of the mental health center where I worked was obviously emotionally disturbed and it impacted on the whole center—quality of service to clients, staff morale, etc. He would not get professional help or staff development assistance."

Conduct of colleagues: "The toughest situations I and my colleague seem to keep running into (in our small town) are ones involving obvious (to us) ethical infractions by other psychologists or professionals in the area. On three or more occasions he and I have personally confronted and taken to local boards . . . issues which others would rather avoid, deal with lightly, ignore, deny, etc., because of peer pressure in a small community. This has had the combined effect of making me doubt my reality (or experience), making me wonder why I have such moral compunctions, making me feel isolated and untrusting of professional peers, etc."

Sexual issues: "A student after seeing a client for therapy for a semester terminated the therapy as was planned at the end of the semester, then began a sexual relationship with the client . . . I think APA should take a stronger stance on this issue."

Sexual issues: "I currently have in treatment a psychiatrist who is still in the midst of a six-year affair with a patient. He wishes to end the affair but is afraid to face the consequences."

Sexual issues: "My psychological assistant was sexually exploited by her former supervisor [who] threatened her with not validating her hours for licensure if she didn't service his needs."

LICENSING BOARDS

Each of the fifty states has its own set of administrative laws and regulations setting forth criteria for obtaining authorization to practice as (or, in some states, to identify oneself as) a psychotherapist or counselor. The states also set forth administrative standards of practice to ensure the safety and well-being of clients. In some cases, these administrative standards may embody ethical principles, but not always. (For example, some may set forth the relatively mundane obligation to pay an annual licensing fee.) Formal licensing actions are how therapists and counselors are held accountable to these standards of practice. Violation of these standards may lead to the suspension or revocation of the practitioner's license or certification.

The data reviewed here concerning licensing disciplinary actions were collected by the Association of State and Provincial Psychology Boards (ASPPB) from actions reported to the ASPPB disciplinary data system by ASPPB member boards (personal correspondence, Association of State and Provincial Psychology Boards, Central Office, "Reported Disciplinary Actions for Psychologists August 1983– July 1997."). The data are abstracted from the ASPPB Disciplinary Data Reports from August, 1983 to July, 1997.

For at least two major reasons, the percentages that follow provide only the roughest estimations of the causes of disciplinary actions. First, as Dr. Pat Bricklin, ASPPB president in 1988, stressed in authorizing the presentation of these percentage data, certain paths toward resolution of licensing complaints—for example, a licensee may unilaterally surrender a license to evade formal action by the board— may not be represented in the reports (Pat Bricklin, personal communication, September 8, 1988). Second, different states categorize the basis of disciplinary actions in different ways, some of them more vague than others ("ethical violations" or "unprofessional conduct," for example). We counted each disciplinary action only once; when more than one cause of action was given, we tried to select the most salient or informative basis. Although not all states indicated whether a dual relationship was sexual in nature, it was clear that most dual relationship violations involved sexual intimacies.

The disciplinary actions taken by licensing boards were based on violations in the following areas:

- 35 percent: sexual or dual relationship with patient
- 28.6 percent: unprofessional, unethical, or negligent practice
- 9.5 percent: fraudulent acts
- 8.6 percent: conviction of crimes
- 4.9 percent: inadequate or improper supervision

- 4.1 percent: impairment
- 3.9 percent: breach of confidentiality
- 3.4 percent: improper or inadequate record keeping
- 2.5 percent: fraud in application for licensure
- 0.7 percent: failure to comply with continuing education requirements

CIVIL STATUTES

Each state has its own legislation and accumulated case law setting forth professional standards; violation of them can serve as the basis of malpractice suits against psychotherapists and counselors. Because the states differ in their legal standards, an act that one state may require may violate the legal standards in another state. In addition, some clinicians who work in federal institutions, such as Veterans Administration Medical Centers, may be subject to federal standards.

What are the primary reasons clinicians are sued? The data we review here, which are provided by the American Psychological Association's Insurance Trust (APAIT), are the most recent incidence data available; the data reported were gathered from 1976 to 1991 (personal correspondence, American Psychological Association's Insurance Trust, Central Office, "Harris's Characterization of APAIT Incidence Data" October 2, 1997). Data on the monetary percentages associated with these statistics were not available. The following include a breakdown in order of percent of total claims.[1]

1. *Sexual impropriety.* This category continues to account for the largest percentage, 20 percent, of the total number of claims. Dual relationships, particularly sexual dual relationships, account for the largest share of formal complaints against psychologists, whether those complaints are filed with the civil courts, licensing boards, or ethics committees. It is especially appalling to note that a sizable number of patients who are sexually victimized by their therapists are minors, some as young as three years old (see Chapter Ten). Sexual improprieties can occur not only between psychologists and their patients but also between psychologists and their students or supervisees (see Chapter Fifteen).

2. *Incorrect treatment.*   Incompetence in the choice or implementation of the treatment plan accounts for 14 percent of the total claims against psychologists.

To a great degree, these cases may frequently be understood as psychologists undertaking work in areas for which they are not qualified by education, training, and experience (see Chapter Five). First, there are cases in which psychologists seek to change specialties—for example, from clinical to industrial-organizational or from experimental to counseling—without undertaking adequate formal education in the new specialty. It is important for APA members to be aware of the two policy statements regarding what is often called "retreading."At its January 23–25, 1976 meeting, the Council of Representatives of the APA formally adopted the following "Policy on Training for Psychologists Wishing to Change Their Specialty." (Note particularly items 4 and 5.)

1. We strongly urge psychology departments currently engaged in doctoral training to offer training for individuals, already holding the doctoral degree in psychology, who wish to change their specialty. Such programs should be individualized, since background and career objectives vary greatly. It is desirable that financial assistance be made available to students in such programs.

2. Programs engaging in such training should declare so publicly and include a statement to that effect as a formal part of their program description and/or their application for accreditation.

3. Psychologists seeking to change their specialty should take training in a program of the highest quality and, where appropriate, exemplified by the doctoral training programs and internships accredited by the APA.

4. With respect to subject matter and professional skills, psychologists taking such training must meet all requirements of doctoral training in the new specialty, being given due credit for relevant course work or requirements they have previously satisfied.

5. It must be stressed, however, that merely taking an internship or acquiring experience in a practicum setting is not, for example, considered adequate preparation for becoming a clinical, counseling, or school psychologist when prior training had not been in the relevant area.

6. Upon fulfillment of all formal requirements of such training program, the students should be awarded a certificate indicating the successful completion of preparation in the particular specialty, thus according them due recognition for their additional education and experience.

7. This policy statement shall be incorporated in the guidelines of the Committee on Accreditation so that appropriate sanctions can be brought to bear on university and internship training programs which violate paragraphs 4 and/or 5 of the above.

In reaffirming and extending its previous policy, the Council of the APA, at its January 22–24, 1982 meeting, adopted the following policy: "The American Psychological Association holds that respecialization education and training for psychologists possessing the doctoral degree should be conducted by those academic units in regionally accredited universities and professional schools currently offering doctoral training in the relevant specialty, and in conjunction with regularly organized internship agencies where appropriate. Respecialization for purposes of offering services in clinical, counseling, or school psychology should be linked to relevant APA approved programs."

In addition to ensuring that they meet the education and training standards for functioning within their specialty area, clinical and counseling (as well as school and industrial-organizational) psychologists can benefit from carefully reviewing the relevant Specialty Guidelines (American Psychological Association, 1981) for their particular specialty.

Second, there are cases in which psychologists, while functioning within their legitimate specialty area (for example, clinical or counseling), attempt to work with specific populations (rape survivors, incest perpetrators, the chronically ill) or to use specific techniques (hypnotism, biofeedback, implosive therapy) for which they are inadequately prepared in terms of their education, training, and experience. Research indicates that approximately 25 percent of psychologists acknowledge providing services outside their areas of competence, at least on a rare basis (Pope, Tabachnick & Keith-Spiegel, 1987).

3. *Loss from evaluation.* Individual claims to have suffered a loss as a result of an improper evaluation accounted for 11 percent of the total claims made against psychologists. Practitioners need to use

exceptional care in assessing candidates for various positions; for example, high-stress jobs such as police work.

4. *Breach of confidentiality or privacy.*   This category accounts for 7 percent of the total claims in malpractice suits against psychologists. As noted previously, violations of confidentiality constitute the fifth most frequent cause of violations in ethics cases and the seventh most frequent cause of licensing disciplinary actions. (For additional discussion of confidentiality issues, see Chapter Thirteen.)

5. *Diagnosis: failure to, or incorrect.*   This category accounts for 7 percent of the total claims. (For discussion of diagnostic and assessment issues, see Chapter Nine.)

6. *Other.*   This mysterious category accounts for 6 percent of the total claims.

7. *Suicide of patient.*   Patients taking their own lives account for 5 percent of the total number of cases (see Chapter Fourteen).

8. *Defamation: libel/slander.*   This category accounts for 4 percent of the total claims.

9. *Countersuit for fee collection.*   This category accounts for 4 percent of the total claims.

10. *Violation of civil rights.*   This category accounts for 3 percent of the total claims.

11. *Loss of child custody or visitation.*   This category accounts for 3 percent of the claims filed.

12. *Failure to supervise properly.*   This category accounts for 2 percent of the total claims filed. Independent practitioners need to stay aware that they are responsible for the services provided by psychological assistants or clinical supervisees who are working under their license.

13. *Improper death of patient or others.*   This category accounts for 2 percent of the total claims.

14. *Violation of legal regulations.*   This category accounts for 2 percent of the total suits filed against psychologists.

15. *Licensing or peer review.*   This category accounts for 2 percent of the total claims.

16. *Breach of contract.*   This cause of action accounts for 1 percent of total claims.

17. *Failure to cure/poor results.*   This category accounts for 1 percent of total claims.

18. *Failure to treat.*   This category accounts for 1 percent of total claims.

19. *Abandonment.* This cause of action accounts for 1 percent of the claims.

20. *Improper referral.* This category accounts for 1 percent of the claims.

21. *Failure to warn/refer.* This category accounts for 1 percent of the claims.

22. *Assault and battery.* This cause of action accounts for 1 percent of the total claims.

23. *Undue influence.* This cause of action accounts for 1 percent of the total claims filed against psychologists.

CRIMINAL STATUTES

Each state also has its own set of criminal laws, generally set forth in the penal code. Although we were unable to locate any reliable actuarial data concerning psychotherapists convicted of crimes, one of the most frequently mentioned areas involves fraud, particularly related to third-party billings. Donald Bersoff, then attorney representing the APA, emphasized the importance of conforming to all rules and regulations regarding billing practices for third-party coverage, both public and private, and noted that therapists currently serving time in prison could attest to the significance of violating those rules and regulations (see Ethics Committee of the American Psychological Association, 1988b).

Over the past decade, various states have enacted laws regarding therapist sexual misconduct in an attempt to curb this behavior (see Chapter Ten). Although many of the laws are civil reporting laws and injunctive relief statutes, about fifteen states have enacted criminal statutes regarding psychotherapist-patient sexual contact (see Pope, 1994). The underlying rationalization for criminalization of the behavior is that sexual contact between professional and patient threatens public safety and has been shown to be harmful. This legislation is designed to serve as a forceful strategy to reduce the incidence of sexual misconduct by psychotherapists.

CONCLUSION

Exceptional caution is appropriate in attempts to generalize, compare, or interpret the actuarial data presented in this chapter regarding complaints to ethics committees, licensing boards, and malpractice courts. Various types of actual violations, as the research indicates, may only very rarely lead to a formal complaint with a criminal court, civil court, licensing board, or ethics committee. Certain types of violation may be difficult to prove. Formal complaints may be informally resolved and thus not be reflected in archival data. And, as noted earlier, ways of classifying complaints can vary significantly.

Nevertheless, the general trends apparent in the archival data as well as the data from critical incident studies reviewed here may be useful to us. They can call our attention to aspects of our own practice in which there is room for improvement. They can also suggest possible topics for which we might want to take continuing education courses. These data, then, can provide a resource for us as individuals and as a helping profession seeking to maintain the high standards and integrity of our work and to minimize possible harm to those whom we serve.

Exceptional caution is also warranted in considering these mechanisms of accountability and their relationship to ethical behavior. All of us may experience some tendency to confuse at some level ethical behavior with that which does not bring us before one of these review agencies. Our sense of what is ethical runs through a reductionistic mill and becomes, in the worst-case scenario, "avoiding detection" or "escaping accountability." Much that we may do that is unethical may never come to light and may never trigger inquiry by one of these mechanisms of accountability.

As noted in Chapter One, the principles articulated by our profession, licensing boards, and civil and criminal courts should not serve to inhibit careful ethical deliberation but more appropriately provide us with a framework and serve as a catalyst to provoke the painstaking ethical consideration of the situation that confronts us. This careful and continuing consideration involves setting aside misconceptions about the nature of our work (Chapter Four), honestly assessing our own competence and abilities to address the situation safely and effectively (Chapter Five), and questioning the claims made about the relevant research and theory (Chapter Six). Evaluating these aspects of our work, ourselves, and the research and theory often allows us to focus more clearly on the crucial concepts of trust, power, and caring, the subjects of Chapter Three.

Note

1. Note that the APAIT data warrant caution in interpretation. When a suit involved multiple violations, only a "main" violation was coded. Violations cited in amended complaints may not have been included. Finally, ratings of a main violation may be unreliable (B. Bennet, personal communication, March 29, 1998).

Trust, Power, and Caring

The ethical responsibilities of psychotherapists are founded upon the recognition that therapy involves trust, as well as power and caring.

TRUST

Societies grant therapists professional status in acknowledgment of the fiduciary relationship between therapist and client. The social order expects or requires therapists not to exploit the trust with which it invests them and their enterprise; the social order depends on independent therapists to fulfill the trust for the benefit of individual clients as well as for the social order. (Many ethical dilemmas result when the benefit of the individual client is in actual or apparent conflict with the benefit of the social order, or when the benefit of the client is in actual or apparent conflict with the benefit of those therapists who wish to assume the benefits but not the costs or responsibilities of the professional role.) In return for assuming a role in which the safety, welfare, and ultimate benefit of clients is to be held as a "sacred trust," therapists are entitled to the privileges and power due professionals.

This concept of trust is crucial for understanding the context in which clients approach and enter into a working relationship with psychotherapists. Clients rightfully expect, or at least desperately hope, that their trust in the therapist is not misplaced. Many, if not most, clients have deep fears that their trust may be betrayed. In some cases, these clients have often struggled painfully with issues of trust. In other cases, clients may be unaware of how their concerns about the trustworthiness of others have affected their ability to love, work, and enjoy life; the issues of trust may emerge gradually during the course of therapy.

The trust underlying therapy is illustrated by the following phenomenon: A client may walk into the consulting room of an absolute stranger and begin disclosing personal information that no one else will be permitted to hear. Therapists may ask questions that would be unwarranted, intrusive, and offensive were anyone else to ask them. Acknowledging and respecting the powerful nature of the private, sensitive, and sometimes secret information that patients tell their therapists, all states recognize some form of professional confidentiality and therapist-patient privilege: Therapists are prevented—with some specific exceptions—from disclosing to third parties what clients tell their therapists during the course of therapy.

In its reliance on trust as fundamental, therapy is similar to surgery. Surgery patients allow themselves to be physically opened up in the hope that their condition will improve. They must trust that surgeons will not take advantage of their vulnerable state to cause harm or exploit. Similarly, therapy patients undergo a process of psychological opening up in the hope that their condition will improve. They must trust that therapists will not take advantage, harm, or exploit.

Freud (1952) originally noticed this similarity. He wrote that the newly developed "talking therapy" was "comparable to a surgical operation" (p. 467) and emphasized that "the transference especially . . . is a dangerous instrument. . . . [I]f a knife will not cut, neither will it serve a surgeon" (p. 471). Recognizing and respecting the potential harm that could result from psychotherapy was, according to Freud, fundamental: "[I]t is grossly to undervalue both the origins and the practical significance of the psychoneuroses to suppose that these disorders are to be removed by pottering about with a few harmless remedies. . . . [P]sychoanalysis . . . is not afraid to handle the most dangerous forces in the mind and set them to work for the benefit of the patient" (Freud, 1963, p. 179). Therapists must never ignore, handle carelessly, or exploit clients' trust that the therapist will do nothing that knowingly and needlessly places them at risk for deep, pervasive, and lasting harm.

When therapists betray their clients' trust, the betrayal of trust alone can cause pervasive and lasting damage. Mann and Winer, discussing the ways that exploitation of trust can harm patients, quote Adrienne Rich: "When we discover that someone we trusted can be trusted no longer, it forces us to reexamine the whole instinct and concept of trust. For a while, we are thrust back into some bleak, jutting ledge . . . in a world before kinship, or naming, or tenderness exist; we are brought close to formlessness" (quoted in Mann & Winer, 1991, p. 325).

For each individual client, the issue of trust is not a conceptual abstraction of the type suggested by philosophical discussions of "fiduciary relationships" established to preserve and benefit the "social order." Trust is a deeply personal experience that defines the therapist-client relationship and provides a context for a sometimes bewildering diversity of hopes, hurts, failures, realizations, vulnerabilities, questions, and possibilities of change that can constitute the process of psychotherapy.

POWER

The trust bestowed upon the psychotherapist by society and by individual clients is a source of power—for example, the power to assume and to attempt to fulfill or manipulate, exploit, and betray the trust. But it is also a recognition of the many levels of power inherent in the role of therapist. The manifestations of the therapist's power range from the superficial to the profound, from temporary to enduring.

Power Conferred by the State

There is power inherent in the states' establishment of licensure as a requirement. Licensed professionals are permitted to engage in certain activities that are prohibited to others who do not possess the license. With the consent of patients, surgeons can cut human beings wide open and remove internal organs, anesthesiologists can render them unconscious, and psychiatrists—and in some instances, psychologists—can administer mind- or mood-altering drugs to them, all with the legal approval and authority vested by the state. Individuals will disrobe and willingly (well, somewhat willingly) submit to all manner of indignities when undergoing a comprehensive medical examination; they will allow the licensed physician to do things to them that no one else would be permitted to do. In a similar manner, clients will open up to a therapist, will allow the therapist to explore extremely private aspects of the client's history, fantasy life, hopes, and fears. Therapists are allowed by clients to hear the most personal secrets, material shared with literally no one else. Therapists are allowed to make inquiries that might provoke a slap in the face if asked by anyone else.

The states recognize the importance of protecting clients against the intentional or unintentional misuse of this power to invade the privacy of the person. (Metaphorically, psychotherapy, like surgery, is an "invasive procedure," although in both cases the client or patient consents to the invasion.) Except in a very few instances, most involving some sort of likely danger to a third party, therapists are required to keep confidential what they have learned about their clients through the professional relationship. The client's freely given informed consent must be obtained before a therapist can reveal confidential information to third parties. That therapists hold such private information about their clients gives them considerable power in relation to their clients.

In licensing therapists, the states also invest them with the power of state-recognized authority to influence drastically the lives of their clients. Therapists are given the power to make decisions (though subject to judicial review) regarding the civil liberties of their clients. Some therapists are given the power to determine whether an American citizen constitutes an immediate danger to the life of another individual and therefore should be held against his or her will in an institution for observation or treatment. Alan Stone (1978), professor of law and medicine at Harvard University and a former president of the American Psychiatric Association, points out that the United States has incarcerated more of its citizens against their will for mental health purposes than any other country, that this process reached its peak in the 1950s when one out of every 300 citizens was held involuntarily in a mental institution, and that the abuse of this power has led to extensive reforms and formal safeguards.

The Power to Name and Define

Therapists possess, to a limited but substantial extent, the power of naming and defining. To diagnose someone is to exercise power. In reporting one of the most widely cited psychological research studies, "On Being Sane in Insane Places," in the journal *Science,* Rosenhan (1973) wrote, "Such labels, conferred by mental health professionals, are as influential on the patient as they are on his [sic] relatives and friends, and it should not surprise anyone that the diagnosis acts on all of them as a self-fulfilling prophesy. Eventually, the patient himself accepts the diagnosis, with all of its surplus meanings and expectations, and behaves accordingly" (p. 254; see also Langer & Abelson, 1974; Mednick, 1989; Murphy, 1976; Pope, 1996; Pope, Butcher & Seelen, 1993; Reiser & Levenson, 1984; Chapter Nine of this book). The potential power of diagnosis and other forms of clinical naming to affect how individuals are perceived is illustrated in Caplan's (1995) description of psychiatrist Bruno Bettelheim's analysis of student protesters: "In the turbulent 1960s, Bettelheim . . . told the United States Congress of his findings: Student anti-war protesters who charged the University of Chicago with complicity in the war machine had no serious political agenda; they were acting out an unresolved Oedipal conflict by attacking the university as a surrogate father" (p. 277).

The Power of Testimony

Therapists also possess state-recognized authority to influence the lives of their clients through their testimony as experts in the civil and criminal courts and through similar judicial or administrative proceedings. Testimony by a therapist may determine whether someone convicted of murder will receive the death penalty or will be paroled. Testimony by a therapist may influence whether a parent is granted custody or visiting rights to his or her child. Testimony by a therapist may influence a jury in deciding whether a defendant was capable of committing a crime, was likely to have committed it, was legally sane at the time the crime was committed, or is likely to commit similar crimes in the future. Testimony by a therapist may also influence a jury to believe that a very young child was sexually molested or that the child fantasized the event (or was coached to make a false allegation as part of a custody dispute). And testimony by expert witnesses in personal injury suits may lead a jury to believe that the plaintiff is an innocent victim of a needless trauma who is suffering severe and chronic harm, or that the same plaintiff is a chronic liar, a gold-digger, or a malingerer who is feigning or at least exaggerating dramatic symptoms.

The Power of Knowledge

The role of psychotherapist involves power beyond what a license establishes. There is power derived from knowledge. Psychotherapists formally study human behavior and the factors that influence motivation, decision, and action. They learn methods for promoting change. Acknowledgment and respect for this aspect of power is essential to avoid the subtle ways in which it may be used to manipulate and exploit clients.

The Power of Expectation

The process of psychotherapy itself elicits, creates, and uses forms of power. Virtually all therapies recognize the importance of the client's expectation that the therapist's interventions will be able to induce beneficial change. One aspect of this expectation is sometimes termed the *placebo effect,* a factor that must be taken into account when conducting research into the possible efficacy of various interventions. Thus the client's investment of the therapist with power to occasion change can become a significant facet and resource of the change process itself.

The therapist frequently becomes invested with other important meanings as well. Psychodynamic theory, for example, describes a process termed *transference:* clients transfer feelings, attachments, or styles of relationship associated with figures from their past (such as parents) onto the therapist. The client may react toward the therapist as if he or she were the client's mother or father. Deep feelings such as love, rejection, shame, guilt, longing for approval, dependence, panic, and neediness—each perhaps representing the unfinished business of development, or traumatic experiences needing understanding and healing—originally experienced within an early formative relationship may emerge in the therapist-client relationship in ways that tend to shock and overwhelm the client.

Therapists' potential to elicit such profound feelings—simply by serving as a therapist—and to "feel" to the client as though the therapist were a figure from the client's past (with the client frequently functioning as if he or she were at an earlier stage of development) represent the sometimes surprising aspects of therapists' power to affect their clients.

Actively Establishing Power

In some approaches, the therapist may be active in establishing specific forms of power. For example, a family therapist may assertively "unbalance" the equilibrium and alliances among family members. A behavior therapist may create a hospital ward or halfway house in which "desirable" behaviors bring forth a rewarding response from the staff (perhaps in the form of tokens that can be exchanged for goods or privileges) and "undesirable" behaviors bring forth an aversive response; the power of the therapist and staff is used to control, or at least influence, the client's behavior.

Psychologist Laura Brown (1994) describes another domain of the therapist's power: "The therapist also has the power to engage in certain defining behaviors that are real and concrete. She sets the fee; decides the time, place, and circumstances of the meeting; and determines what she will share about herself and not disclose. Even when she allows some leeway in negotiating these and similar points, this allowance proceeds from the implicit understanding that it is within the therapist's power to give, and to take away, such compromises" (p. 111).

An Inherent Power Differential

The power differential is inherent in psychotherapy. Although certain approaches to therapy have emphasized egalitarian ideals in which therapist and client are "equal," such goals are viewed only within a narrowly limited context of the relationship. In truly equal relationships, in which there is no appreciable power differential, there is no designation of one member as "therapist" in relation to the other member, there is no fee charged by one member to the other for the relationship (nor are bills submitted to third parties such as insurance companies for reimbursement), there is no designation of the activity as "professional" (and thus falling within the scope of a professional liability policy), there is no use by one member of a license to work with the other, and so on. A defining attribute of the professional is the recognition, understanding, and careful handling of the considerable power inherent in the role.

CARING

Both the individual client and society recognize the diverse powers of the professional role and place their trust in professionals to use those powers to benefit—never to harm or exploit—those who seek help from the therapist. The trust that society and the individual client give must be matched by the caring of the therapist. Only within a context of caring—specifically, caring about the client's well-being—are the therapist's professional status and powers justified. Historically, charging high fees did not create or define professional status, nor did spending long years in training or reaching a high level of expertise. The central, defining characteristic of the professional was an ethic of placing the client's welfare foremost and not allowing professional judgment or services to be drawn off course by one's own needs.

The touchstone for the approaches discussed in this book is caring for and about people whom professional interventions are meant to serve. The concept of caring as we use it in this book is not relegated to a passive, empty sentimentality. Rather, caring involves a responsiveness to the legitimate needs of a client and a recognition that the client must never be exploited or abused (although the therapist's personal wants and needs might seem to justify, and both the therapist's powers and the client's vulnerabilities might facilitate tempting forms of exploitation and abuse). Caring also involves actively assuming the full array of professional responsibilities to act in ways that legitimately benefit and do not needlessly endanger the client and a diligence in carrying out these professional duties.

Unfortunately, this concept may not receive adequate attention in graduate training programs, as Sarason (1985) points out:

> On the surface, trainees accept the need for objectivity—it does have the ring of science, and its importance can be illustrated with examples of the baleful consequences of "emotional over-involvement"—but

internally there is a struggle, as one of my students put it, "between what your heart says you should say and do and what theory and your supervisor say you should say and do." Many trainees give up the struggle but there are some who continue to feel that in striving to maintain the stance of objectivity they are robbing themselves and their clients of something of therapeutic value. The trainee's struggle, which supervisors gloss over as a normal developmental phase that trainees grow out of, points to an omission in psychological-psychiatric theories. Those theories never concern themselves with caring and compassion. What does it mean to be caring and compassionate? When do caring and compassion arise as feelings? What inhibits or facilitates their expression? Why do people differ so widely in having such feelings and the ways they express them? It is, of course, implicit in all of these theories that these feelings are crucial in human development, but the reader would be surprised how little attention is given to their phenomenology and consequences (positive and negative) [p. 168; see also Pope, 1990b; Pope, Sonne & Holroyd, 1993; Pope & Tabachnick, 1993, 1994].

The powers of the therapist must be governed by an ethic of caring for those whom the therapist serves. Caring whether their powers will ultimately benefit or harm their clients helps therapists to maintain an awareness of the consequences, meanings, and implications of their acts and to assume appropriate and realistic responsibility for those acts. Caring about what happens to clients is one of the strongest foundations for the myriad formal rules and regulations that are society's attempt to hold the therapist accountable, but it also encourages therapists to look beyond those explicit generalities. The professional attitude of caring is incompatible with a goal of meeting the lowest possible standards, doing as little as possible to get by, or using explicit regulations to resist, obscure, and evade professional responsibilities.

Although few of us would set as a goal "meeting the lowest possible standards," certain assumptions, which many of us have held at some time during our careers, about the nature of therapy and counseling seem to encourage neglect of our ethical responsibilities. These assumptions are discussed in Chapter Four.

Common Misperceptions That Interfere with Ethical Practice

Some beliefs about the nature of psychotherapy or ethics can, in their more extreme forms, make it more difficult for us to recognize and consider the ethical aspects of our work. Six of these beliefs are discussed in this chapter.

PSYCHOTHERAPY AS SCIENTIFIC TECHNOLOGY

Many practitioners consider psychotherapy to be a science or at least a scientifically based technology (see, for example, Singer, 1980). One of the great strengths of those who develop psychotherapeutic theory and methods is their willingness to adopt a scientific approach to their work: to define their terms and concepts clearly, to formulate their hypotheses in such a way that they can be verified or contradicted, to avoid overreliance upon appeals to tradition or authority, to disseminate their findings in peer-reviewed journals that enable their findings to be evaluated independently by disinterested professionals prior to any attempts to gain fame and fortune in the popular media, and to acknowledge explicitly competing theories and contradictory data. This eagerness—or at least willingness—to be guided by empirical data that are systematically, carefully, and objectively gathered and evaluated tends to distinguish scientifically based psychotherapy from popular methods of helping people with their problems such as past-life regression and channeling.

The risk is that some therapists may believe that their interventions constitute a scientific technology that is "value free" so that ethical analysis is not generally applicable or useful. This belief takes many forms. Most commonly, neither scientific research nor the resulting technologies are held to be, in and of themselves, ethical or unethical. The discovery of atomic energy and the development of technologies for releasing the "power of the atom" are viewed as ethically neutral. The technologies can be used to send cancer into remission or to obliterate a city. By extension, both the research scientists and the technologists are functioning within an ethically neutral sphere as long as they are functioning as scientists and technologists. According to this view, only those who are choosing the uses to which the research findings and resultant technologies will be put are engaging in activities subject to ethical scrutiny.

By analogy, therapists are believed to be developing and providing technologies relevant to human experience and behavior. It is the individual client who must assume responsibility for seeking the benefits of this technology and attempting to gain use of it in particular ways for his or her life (for example, to attempt to alter one's sexual orientation). It would be presumptuous, authoritarian, and oppressive for the therapist to nullify the client's freedom of choice and range of opportunities. In summary, this view holds that the therapist only provides an array of ethically neutral human technologies; the client decides to seek a particular technology for a particular goal. According to this "scientific" approach, the client must bear the ethical responsibility for the uses to which the technology of psychotherapy is put; the therapist is merely a conduit for the technology.

PSYCHOTHERAPY AS MYSTERY

Some therapists may emphasize the miraculous nature of life itself, the mystery of human experience, and the ultimately impenetrable enigma of existence. For them, the psychotherapist's attempts to understand and intervene in a client's life must rest within, depend on, and gain meaning from some form of philosophical skepticism such as that resulting from the line of British empiricists (for example, Hume), religious faith that attempts to symbolize and articulate the mystery, existentialism that attempts to confront and wrest meaning from the absurdity of ontological principles, or some other framework that views all human endeavors (such as psychotherapy) as possible or meaningful only in their relationship to an outlook focusing on the ultimate mystery of human life and experience.

A great strength of many of these approaches to therapy is their high level of respect for the client. The client is someone who can never be understood completely and can never be pigeonholed or taken for granted. Such approaches recognize and value the uniqueness of each client. Any tendencies to reduce clients to the status of labels, jargon, or variables are resisted. The special worth of the individual is held as primary. Clients may view such therapists as more approachable. Such therapists may communicate more warmth and convey less of the stereotype of the cold scientist in the white lab coat.

The risk is that an *exclusive* focus on the mystery of life may preclude or discourage a careful examination of the therapist's behavior and its implications, and of the degree to which the therapist is fulfilling the responsibilities of his or her role. If assertions are carelessly made that all life is unpredictable, therapists may tend to decline any responsibility for the negative consequences of their behaviors (because the outcomes would be, within this framework, unpredictable).

In the most extreme cases, therapists may come to believe that their work is beyond understanding or accountability. The therapist can take at least implicit credit for anything positive that happens while attributing the negative outcomes to fate, chance, and forces beyond human understanding. The therapist may become the stereotype of a guru.

PSYCHOTHERAPY AS BUSINESS

For those therapists who charge money for their services (whether in the form of fees from clients and insurance coverage or of wages or salary from an employer), therapy is at least in part a business. Therapists attempt to determine how much their services are worth, how much therapists providing comparable services are earning, how much clients (or organized systems of care or other employing institutions) are willing or able to afford, and how much they, as therapists, need or want to earn.

Many therapists have begun to adopt practices from the world of business to increase their revenue. They may conduct publicity and networking campaigns, employ sophisticated billing and bill-collection procedures, and rely on the professional guidance of attorneys, accountants, public relations specialists, and business consultants. The degree to which the business aspects of providing psychotherapeutic services have become of increasing interest to therapists is reflected in the increasing percentage of space in professional association newsletters and in programs at professional conventions devoted to this topic.

This explicit attention to the financial aspects of our profession is relatively new. Older volumes that presented and reviewed psychotherapy research tended to ignore the subject entirely, prompting one contributor to comment, "As a footnote, I would like to remark that if a Martian read the volumes reporting the two psychotherapy conferences and if he read all the papers of this conference it would never occur to him that psychotherapy is something done for money. Either therapists believe money is not a worthwhile research variable or money is part of the new obscenity in which we talk more freely about sex but never mention money" (Colby, 1968, p. 539).

Similarly, Mintz (1971) once termed fees a "tabooed subject," suggesting that "a varied set of guidelines" concerning fee payment has "functioned to inhibit therapists from inquiring too closely into the financial side of psychotherapeutic practice and the actual effects it may have on the therapeutic enterprise" (p. 37). The pendulum seems to have swung forcefully the other way, and the financial aspects of psychotherapy are now discussed much more openly.

A strength of this trend is that the actual nature of the therapeutic relationship is more clearly and candidly defined. Therapists who charge for their services are forced to forgo a phony pose of "someone who just wants to help." Therapists who would otherwise claim to be offering unconditional acceptance and positive regard must acknowledge that the therapeutic process is in fact conditional upon payment of a fee or the approval of the managed care system's case reviewer. Therapists find it more difficult to gloss over both their complex motives in functioning as psychotherapists and the multilayered nature of the therapeutic relationship. Acknowledging, working through, and integrating the therapist's motivations for functioning as a therapist are beneficial if not essential steps in establishing an authentic, or unhypocritical, professional status and in understanding the therapeutic relationship.

The risk is that an overly exclusive focus on psychotherapy as business may obscure or erode the professional nature and ethical principles of the endeavor. The complexities of a business enterprise become an absorbing world, and the sometimes intense pressure not only to survive but also to thrive in the competition for clients and their revenue can make serious attention to ethical aspects of the business seem an undesirable luxury, a distraction from the responsibilities of ensuring that the business flourishes, or a quaint but dangerous inability to face up to "the real world." Virtually anything—including ethical principles—that would interfere with the generation of profit is reflexively rejected. Good business principles may somehow come to replace good ethical principles. Especially when the source of highly valued revenue is an institution—for example, when an insurance company or governmental agency pays part or all of the fee for large populations of clients—individual therapists may come to accept whatever standards and procedures the institution imposes even when such acceptance seems to lead to actions that violate professional prerogatives and ethics. For example, a president of the American Psychiatric Association noted some of the business practices within his profession that seemed, at a minimum, to blur the commitment to attend to the clinical needs of the patient: "payments to increase the length of stay of patients in hospitals. . . . Fifty dollars for each admission. Fifty dollars if you talk a patient out of leaving the hospital. Fifty dollars if you interfere with a patient's leaving against medical advice" (Fink, 1989, p. 1101; for other examples, see Pope, 1990a).

Fink's quote in the previous paragraph emphasizes pressures to ensure that patients acquire more services and longer terms of service. It is ironic that whereas some clinicians face such pressures, others face pressures to ensure that patients receive fewer services or shorter terms of service. For these clinicians, some of the most difficult ethical issues focus not so much on providing too much care (as in Fink's discussion of indemnity insurance and direct payment models) but rather too little (under capitation and other organized systems of care). Capitation contracts (which provide a lump sum of money for a group of potential clients, rather than a certain amount per person, thus requiring the providers to estimate what the number of sessions they can provide per person and still be profitable) may have a tendency to pressure psychotherapists to terminate early and quickly. Those providers who have agreed by contract to provide services for significantly lower fees may then be reluctant to provide the best services for those particular populations. Although some believe that quality care, accessible service, and cost-effectiveness are simultaneously possible, others believe that managed care's focus on cutting mental health expenses has resulted in cutting of essential services and quality of care (see, for example, Miller, 1996). "The Ethical Guidelines for Professional Care in a Managed Care Environment" (National Academies of Practice, 1997; see Appendix C) provides a clear statement of ethical responsibilities in responding to such pressures: "[I]t is unethical to compromise a patient's needs and quality care concerns to satisfy financial objectives. The patient's right to appropriate care must not be diluted by economic pressures (p. 2)."

If therapy is misconceived as *solely* business, the language of ethics may still be used but only in the service of business principles. Having an explicit ethics code or discussions about ethics may be viewed as good public relations, good employee motivators, the necessary evil of complying with the demands of external regulatory agencies— in brief, good business. The challenge, as concerns extent of coverage, capitation rates, amount of client co-payment, and so on, is to ensure that the realities of business ethics are recognized and respected, but not at the expense of clinical ethics. Moffic (1997, p. 135) suggested four of the possible ways that the ethics of health care and business can interact:

> *Both healthcare and business ethics win* if we maintain the profit margin we've chosen and there is some overall improvement in the quality of care while unnecessary harm (actual and potential) to patients and providers is assiduously avoided.
>
> *Business ethics win but healthcare ethics lose* if managed care companies produce large savings or profits for themselves and the payers, but there is a reduction of overall quality of care so that large numbers of patients suffer needlessly and good clinicians are prevented from participation in the system.
>
> *Healthcare ethics win but business ethics lose* if clinicians endeavor to provide the ideal and best treatment (psychoanalysis and long-term hospitalization is [sic] potentially available to all) and bad clinicians are ignored, so that healthcare costs continue to rise, some patients get dramatically better, and some patients don't improve or worsen despite extensive treatment.

Both sides lose if payers decide they can no longer afford to support mental healthcare, so that only the rich can try to find the good clinicians and bare warehousing is available for the poor.

ETHICS AS ADHERENCE TO LEGAL AND ADMINISTRATIVE STANDARDS

Similar to the increasing interest in business aspects is the increasing interest in the legal regulation of psychotherapists and psychotherapy. Over the past few decades, states have adopted licensing or certification requirements for an increasing number of disciplines that provide therapy or counseling. The administrative regulations specifying the requirements for obtaining and renewing a license, the scope of mandatory or prohibited professional activities, and the disciplinary procedures for therapists who violate the requirements are becoming increasingly complex. In addition to these licensing or certification regulations are statutory injunctions in the criminal, evidence, and related codes regarding issues such as privilege and mandatory reporting of certain information obtained during professional activities. Civil suits filed against therapists can, upon appeal, establish precedents of case law (which interprets and supplements legislation) that further serve to regulate the behavior of psychotherapists. Again, the increasing role that such legal regulation plays in the professional life of the psychotherapist is reflected in the growing attention paid to such matters in professional newsletters and conventions.

A benefit of such legal regulation of the psychotherapies is that it forces professionals to confront the issue of what is permissible and impermissible professional behavior. Therapists are participants in this legal process in diverse roles, such as members of licensing boards and expert witnesses in civil suits helping the judge and jury to understand the prevailing standards of conduct. Therapists are discouraged from the tendency to consider themselves as beyond accountability or questioning because of their professional status or expertise (see Chapter Two).

A risk in the emphasis on legal standards is that adherence to minimal legal standards, which in some cases entails finding ways around those standards, can become a substitute for ethical behavior. This trend has become increasingly prevalent in the political arena. A politician or political appointee holding a position of great public trust may face incontrovertible evidence that he or she engaged in behavior that betrayed that trust. When no other defense or justification is available, the individual will insist that nothing wrong was done because no law was broken. (Even such desperate defenses hit a snag when it turns out that a law was broken; in those cases the individual stresses that there was a "technical violation of the law.") Thus an overly exclusive focus upon legal standards can discourage ethical awareness and sensitivity. It is crucial to realize that ethical behavior is more than simply avoiding violation of legal standards and that one's ethical and legal duties may, in certain instances, be in conflict.

ETHICS AS RARE DRAMATIC CONFLICT

It is often the intensely dramatic ethical conflict that grabs headlines in the popular media and professional newsletters. The following hypothetical scenarios, both from the forensic setting, illustrate these vividly charged conflicts.

The client is a serial killer of numerous children. He has been convicted and sentenced to death. During all phases of the trial, he has claimed privilege and refused to let the therapist whom he has recently seen disclose any of the therapeutic discussions. Only the therapist knows, based upon what the killer has told her, the names of many missing children whom her client killed and where their bodies are hidden. (All these disclosures came after the fact; the state had no legislation that required or permitted the therapist to disclose this information.) Parents of literally hundreds of missing children are desperate to find out whether their child was among the murdered and, if so, where they can recover the body. Should the therapist violate both the law and her agreement with the client by disclosing this information?

A therapist working in the prison system is assigned a prisoner who is on death row. The execution has been delayed because the prisoner has been evaluated as incompetent due to a mental disorder. The therapist, after the first two sessions, determines that the prisoner is suffering from an extreme stress reaction (understandable in light of the death sentence), which has elicited a psychosis. If the therapist's intervention is effective, the client will be put to death; if the therapist's intervention is ineffective, the client will live. What should the therapist do?

Such instances, when they are publicly reported, tend to galvanize intense interest and concern. They highlight the inescapable ethical

conflicts that clinical work entails as well as the profound consequences (sometimes a matter of life or death) of the ethical decisions
that therapists make.

A possible risk, however, is that we may focus our ethical awareness and concern almost exclusively on such dramatic situations. As
a result, we may overlook the numerous, less dramatic, but no less
significant ethical decisions that each of us—no matter what our setting, clientele, or approach—faces in our day-to-day clinical work.

ETHICS AS MINDLESS RULE FOLLOWING

In our graduate training, we are given sets of ethical standards or
principles developed by the profession and are urged to take them to
heart. We read them, discuss them, and try to think how we can put
all the "do's and don't's" into practice.

Such codes are of enormous importance. They tell clinicians,
clients, and the public what sorts of behaviors are and are not permissible, desirable, or mandatory. They help identify important areas
of ethical concern. They set forth standards to which the professional
agrees to be held accountable (see Chapter Two).

A risk is that we may come to view ethics as simply the obedient
and unthinking following of a certain set of "do's and don't's." As we
noted in the Preface and Chapter One, ethics codes, standards, or
rules can never legitimately serve as a substitute for a thoughtful,
creative, and conscientious approach to our work. They can never
relieve us of the responsibility to struggle with competing demands,
multiple perspectives, evolving situations, and the prospect of uncertain consequences—that is to say, life as it is lived, in all its complexity. The studies of how individuals respond to ethical dilemmas,
how they decide what course to take, how they evaluate their own
behavior and the behavior of others, and how they construe and
make attributions regarding the outcomes demonstrate the complex
interactions among the individual, the specific dilemma, formal and
implicit values and principles, and the context (L. S. Brown, 1990,
1994; J. C. Gibbs & Schnell, 1985; Gilligan, 1982; Gilligan, Ward,
Taylor & Bardige, 1988; Hamilton, Blumenfeld & Kushler, 1988;
Kelman & Hamilton, 1989; Kohlberg, 1969; Lickona, 1976; Mednick, 1989; Milgram, 1974; Shaver & Drown, 1986; Smith & Whitehead, 1988).

Ethics codes, standards, or rules serve best to awaken us to potential pitfalls but also to opportunities, to guide and inform our

attempts to help without hurting. They cannot do our work for us. If we—rather than lists of "do's and don't's"—have the responsibility for responding ethically to our clients (in a way that does justice to the power, trust, and caring inherent in our work), we must possess at least a basic competence to perform our work. That competence is the subject of the next chapter.

CHAPTER FIVE

The Human Therapist

When clients put their trust in us as professionals, one of their most fundamental expectations is that we will be competent. Society, through the courts and licensing boards, also holds us to this standard.

Clients, of course, may have a variety of unrealistic—sometimes virtually magical—expectations. They may hope, for example, that we will be able to assess and intervene with certainty and without error, that we will be able to guarantee results, and that we will be able to meet all of their needs. Unfortunately, some clinicians may suffer from such delusions and may encourage these beliefs in their clients. One of the fundamental purposes of this chapter is to provide a simple reminder that as therapists, we are all human and imperfect, with weaknesses and blind spots that accompany the strengths and insights. The opening chapters of this book have set aside inadequate views of ethics such as the rote application of various rules and presented an approach to ethics in which professional codes, administrative directives, legislative requirements, and other "givens" mark the beginning of a process of questioning in which therapists strive to arrive at the most ethical response to a unique client with unique needs and resources in a unique context. Chapter Six provides an example of the range, depth, and detail inherent in this questioning.

This complex process of questioning must be carried out by fallible human beings, subject at times to tiredness, discouragement, frustration, anger, fear, and the feeling of being overwhelmed. This chapter is a reminder that therapists must not only possess the demonstrable intellectual competence (knowing about and knowing how) but also what might be called *emotional competence* (Pope & Brown, 1996).

COMPETENCE AS AN ETHICAL AND LEGAL RESPONSIBILITY

Although the omniscient, omnipotent, and error-free clinician is a myth, therapists and counselors have an ethical and legal responsibility to offer clients a basic and adequate competence. In psychotherapy and counseling, *competence* is complex and difficult to define. Licensing boards and the civil courts sometimes specify the defining criteria for discrete areas of practice. More often, however, they tend to require simply that in whatever area of therapy and counseling the clinician is practicing, he or she should possess *demonstrable* competence. When demonstrable competence is formally and explicitly required, the clinician is prevented from merely asserting competence; evidence of the competence must be produced. Generally, this evidence comes in the form of the clinician's formal education, professional training, and carefully supervised experience.

The competence requirement is frequently established in the ethical, legal, and professional standards governing the work of therapists. For example, article 8 ("Rules of Professional Conduct"), section 1396 of California Title 16 declares, "The psychologist shall not function outside his or her particular field or fields of competence as established by his or her education, training, and experience." Section 1.6 of the *Specialty Guidelines for the Delivery of Services* (American Psychological Association, 1981, p. 7) states, "Clinical psychologists limit their practice to their demonstrated areas of professional competence." Ethical standard 1.04a of the APA's "Ethical Principles of Psychologists and Code of Conduct" (1992, p. 1600) states, "Psychologists provide services, teach, and conduct research only within the boundaries of their competence, based on their education, training, supervised experience, or appropriate professional experience."

To affirm the crucial importance of competence as an ethical requirement is to recognize that the power (see Chapter Three) implicit and invested in the therapist's role cannot be handled in a careless, ignorant, or thoughtless manner. The complex, hard-to-define nature of therapy may tend to obscure the reasonableness and necessity of this requirement. It becomes more vivid by analogy to other fields. A physician who is an internist or general practitioner may do excellent work, yet who among us would want that physician to perform coronary surgery or neurosurgery on us if the physician does not have adequate education, training, and supervised experience in these forms of surgery? A skilled professor of linguistics may have a solid grasp of a variety of Indo-European languages and dialects and yet be completely unable to translate a Swahili text.

COMPETENCE AND CONFLICT

Given the encouragement of clients who may hold exaggerated beliefs about our talents, it may be difficult for us to acknowledge that we simply are not competent to intervene in a particular situation. It may be particularly difficult if we do not want to disappoint or alienate a valued source of referrals who has referred a client to us or if we desperately need new clients to cover office overhead and feel that we cannot afford to turn away potential business. Organized systems of care may make it difficult to turn away a client who has been assigned to us. Nevertheless, extensive education, training, and supervised experience in working with adults does not qualify us to work with children; solid competence in providing individual counseling or psychotherapy does not qualify us to lead a therapy group; and expertise in working with individuals suffering from profound depression does not qualify us to work with individuals suffering from developmental disorders.

At times, the complexity of the situation requires exceptional care and skill in determining how to respond most effectively and ethically to a client's needs while remaining within one's areas of competence. For example, a counselor may begin working with a client on issues related to depression, an area in which the counselor has had considerable education, training, and supervised experience. But much later the therapeutic journey leads into a problem area—bulimia, for example—in which the counselor has no or very limited expertise. As another example, a client initiates psychotherapy to deal with what seems like moderately severe difficulty concentrating at work. Soon, however, it becomes apparent that the client is suffering from agoraphobia. Can the counselor ethically presume that the course on anxieties and phobias that he or she took ten years ago in graduate school is sufficient to address the problem competently? The counselor faces the decision about whether he or she has the time, energy, and commitment necessary for consultation to provide the most up-to-date treatment for agoraphobia or whether it will be necessary to refer the client to someone who is a specialist or at least competent to work with someone suffering from agoraphobia.

Clinicians who work in isolated or small communities may face this dilemma frequently. If the therapist or counselor is the only practitioner in an area, he or she probably will frequently encounter unfamiliar problems. Fulfilling the ethical responsibility of competence is especially difficult for these practitioners. They are constantly attending workshops and consulting long distance with a variety of experts to ensure that their clients are receiving competent care.

Despite the clear ethical and legal mandates to practice only with competence, therapists and counselors may suffer lapses. A national survey of psychologists, for example, found that almost one-fourth of the respondents indicated that they had practiced outside their area of competence either rarely or occasionally (Pope, Tabachnick & Keith-Spiegel, 1987).

INTELLECTUAL COMPETENCE: KNOWING ABOUT AND KNOWING HOW

Intellectual competence involves "knowing about." In their graduate training, internships, supervised experience, continuing education, and other contexts, therapists and therapists-in-training learn the kind of information about empirical research, theories, interventions, and other topics that is required for their work. They learn to question the information, to evaluate its validity and relevance for particular situations and populations. They learn to form and test hypotheses about assessment and interventions.

Part of intellectual competence is learning which clinical approaches, strategies, or techniques show evidence or promise of effectiveness. If clinical methods are to avoid charlatanism, hucksterism, and well-meaning ineffectiveness, they must *work* (at least some of the time). Thus the supposed competence of the practitioner has little meaning if his or her methods lack competence. In his provocative article "The Scientific Basis of Psychotherapeutic Practice: A Question of Values and Ethics," Singer (1980) emphasized the importance of clinicians' remaining knowledgeable concerning the emerging research basis of the methods they use. (The following chapter presents a case study in the comprehensive questioning necessary to evaluate whether our approaches rest on a solid empirical base.) Intellectual competence also involves learning what approaches have been shown to be invalid or perhaps even harmful. Stricker (1992) wrote: "[A]lthough it may not be unethical to practice in the absence of knowledge, it is unethical to practice in the face of knowledge. We all must labor with the absence of affirmative data, but there is no excuse for ignoring contradictory data" (p. 564)

Another aspect of intellectual competence is recognizing what we do not know. We may know about depression in adults but not about depression in children. We may be familiar with the culture of one Asian population but not of others. We may understand the degree to which the MMPI-II is useful in assessing malingering but not whether it is useful in assessing leadership abilities.

Intellectual competence also involves knowing how to do certain clinical tasks. This aspect of competence is gained through carefully supervised experience. Knowing how to do psychotherapy is not something one can adequately learn solely from reading a book or sitting in a classroom.

Emotional Competence: Knowing Oneself

Emotional competence reflects therapists' acknowledgment and respect for themselves as unique, fallible human beings. It involves self-knowledge, self-acceptance, and self-monitoring. Therapists must know their own emotional strengths and weaknesses, their needs and resources, their abilities and limits for doing clinical work.

Psychotherapy often provides the occasion for strong emotional reactions for both therapist and client. To the degree that therapists are unprepared or otherwise unable to experience the emotional stresses and strains of therapy, their well-intentioned efforts may prove unhelpful and perhaps even harmful.

Behavior	Study 1[a]	Study 2[b]	Study 3[c]
Disclosing details of current personal stresses to a client		38.9%	
Crying in the presence of a client	56.5%		
Telling a client that you are angry at him or her	89.7%		77.9%
Raising your voice at a client because you are angry at him or her			57.2%
Having fantasies that reflect your anger at a client			63.5%
Feeling hatred toward a client			31.2%
Telling clients of your disappointment in them	51.9%		
Feeling afraid that a client may commit suicide			97.2%
Feeling afraid that a client may need clinical resources that are unavailable			86.0%
Feeling afraid because a client's condition gets suddenly or seriously worse			90.9%
Feeling afraid that your colleagues may be critical of your work with a client			88.1%
Feeling afraid that a client may file a formal complaint against you			66.0%
Using self-disclosure as a therapy technique	93.3%		
Lying on top of or underneath a client			0.4%
Cradling or otherwise holding a client in your lap			8.8%
Telling a sexual fantasy to a client			6.0%
Engaging in sexual fantasy about a client	71.8%		
Feeling sexually attracted to a client	89.5%		87.3%
A client tells you that he or she is sexually attracted to you			73.3%
Feeling sexually aroused while in the presence of a client			57.9%
A client seems to become sexually aroused in your presence			48.4%
A client seems to have an orgasm in your presence			3.2%

Table 5.1.   Intense Emotion in Therapy.

[a] Study 1: A national survey of 1,000 psychologists with a 46% return rate (Pope, Tabachnick, & Keith-Spiegel, 1987).

[b] Study 2: A national survey of 4,800 psychologists, psychiatrists, and social workers with a 49% return rate (Borys & Pope, 1989).

[c] Study 3: A national survey of 600 psychologists with a 48% return rate (Pope & Tabachnick, 1993).

Source: Copyright © 1987, 1989, 1993 by the American Psychological Association. Adapted with permission.

Table 5.1 presents relevant research findings about intense emotions experienced in therapy. The numbers indicate the percentage of therapists in each study who reported at least one instance of each behavior. Readers who have had experience as therapists or patients may wish to compare their own experience to these findings.

Therapists, of course, bring something to the work they do. Each therapist has a unique personal history. Table 5.2 presents national survey results showing therapists' self-reports of their experiences of various kinds of abuse during childhood, adolescence, and adulthood. Note that these results suggest that perhaps almost one-third of male therapists and over two-thirds of female therapists experience at least one of these forms of abuse over their lifetimes.

Type of Abuse	Percentage of Men	Percentage of Women
Abuse during childhood or adolescence		
Sexual abuse by relative	5.84	21.05
Sexual abuse by teacher	0.73	1.96
Sexual abuse by physician	0.0	1.96
Sexual abuse by therapist	0.0	0.0
Sexual abuse by non-relative (other than those previously listed)	9.49	16.34
Nonsexual physical abuse	13.14	9.15
At least one of the above	26.28	39.22
Abuse during adulthood		
Sexual harassment	1.46	37.91
Attempted rape	0.73	13.07
Acquaintance rape	0.0	6.54
Stranger rape	0.73	1.31
Nonsexual physical abuse by a spouse or partner	6.57	12.42
Nonsexual physical abuse by an acquaintance	0.0	2.61
Nonsexual physical abuse by a stranger	4.38	7.19
Sexual involvement with a therapist	2.19	4.58
Sexual involvement with a physician	0.0	1.96
At least one of the above	13.87	56.86
Abuse during childhood, adolescence, or adulthood	32.85	69.93

Table 5.2.   Percentage of Male and Female Therapists Reporting Having Been Abused.

Source: The table summarizes a national study by Pope & Feldman-Summers (1992). Copyright © 1992 by the American Psychological Association. Adapted with permission.

Such experiences can affect emotional competence. It is important not to assume a one-size-fits-all theory about how any particular form of abuse (or any other experience) may affect an individual therapist. (There is no research supporting the notion that all those who have a history of abuse are more competent or less competent as therapists, or that those who have no history of abuse are more or less competent as therapists. Each instance must be evaluated on an individual basis, with the full range of available information and without stereotypes.) What is important is for therapists to be aware of how such events affect them, and the degree to which such experiences may affect the emotional competence of the therapist.

Emotional competence also involves a process of constant questioning of the self: Do the demands of the work or other factors suggest that the therapist himself or herself needs therapy in order to maintain or restore emotional competence? Table 5.3 presents the results of a national study of therapists as therapy patients. Eighty-four percent of the therapists in this study reported that they had been in personal therapy. Only two of them indicated that the therapy was not helpful, but about a fifth (22 percent) reported that their own therapy had included what they believed to be harmful aspects (regardless of whether it also included positive aspects).

This research suggests that most therapists experience, at least once, intense emotional distress. Over half (61 percent), for example, reported experiencing clinical depression. Over a fourth (29 percent) reported suicidal feelings, and 4 percent reported attempting suicide. About 4 percent reported having been hospitalized (Pope & Tabachnick, 1994). Readers may wish to consider their own experiences in light of these findings.

Emotional competence is no less important than intellectual competence, and it is for that reason that we have included, beginning with Chapter Seven, specific clinical scenarios at the end of each chapter. These scenarios describe hypothetical situations that might be encountered by readers of this book. Each is followed by a handful of questions designed to give readers practice in the process of questioning, which is explored in detail in Chapter Six. The first question in each sequence is a variant of "What do you feel?" An honest recognition of the emotional response to clinical situations is an important aspect of emotional competence.

To the extent that these scenarios and questions form the basis of class or group discussion in graduate school courses, internships,

Item	0	1	2	3	4
In your own personal therapy, how often (if at all) did your therapist (N = 400):					
Cradle or hold you in a nonsexual way	73.2	2.7	8.0	8.8	6.0
Touch you in a sexual way	93.7	2.5	1.8	0.3	1.0
Talk about sexual issues in a way that you believe to be inappropriate	91.2	2.7	3.2	0.5	1.3
Seem to be sexually attracted to you	84.5	6.2	3.5	3.0	1.5
Disclose that he or she was sexually attracted to you	92.2	3.7	1.0	1.3	0.8
Seem to be sexually aroused in your presence	91.2	3.7	2.2	0.8	1.3
Express anger at you	60.7	14.3	16.8	5.7	1.8
Express disappointment in you	67.0	11.3	14.8	4.7	1.3
Give you encouragement and support	2.5	0.8	6.2	21.8	67.5
Tell you that he or she cared about you	33.7	6.7	19.5	21.8	16.3
Make what you consider to be a clinical or therapeutic error	19.8	18.0	36.2	19.0	5.5
Pressure you to talk about something you didn't want to talk about	57.5	7.5	21.3	8.8	4.0
Use humor in an appropriate way	76.7	8.8	10.0	2.2	1.5
Use humor in an inappropriate way	5.2	2.5	12.5	35.0	43.5
Act in a rude or insensitive manner toward you	68.7	13.0	12.0	4.0	1.5
Violate your rights to confidentiality	89.7	4.5	2.7	1.3	1.8
Violate your rights to informed consent	93.2	3.2	1.3	0.3	0.3
Use a course of psychotropic medication as part of your treatment	84.7	7.0	3.0	3.0	1.5
Use hospitalization as part of your treatment	96.2	1.8	0.5	0.5	1.0
In your own personal therapy, how often (if at all) did you (N = 400):					
Feel sexually attracted to your therapist	63.0	8.0	14.0	7.5	6.5
Tell your therapist that you were sexually attracted to him or her	81.5	6.2	5.5	3.0	2.7
Have sexual fantasies about your therapist	65.5	8.0	12.8	7.0	5.2
Feel angry at your therapist	13.3	9.5	32.7	28.5	15.0
Feel that your therapist did not care about you	49.5	13.0	19.0	12.3	5.5
Feel suicidal	70.0	8.5	9.5	8.3	3.0
Make a suicide attempt	95.5	2.5	1.0	0.0	0.0
Feel what you would characterize as clinical depression	38.5	15.8	16.0	16.5	12.5

Table 5.3. Therapists as Therapy Patients.

Codes: 0 = never, 1 = once, 2 = rarely (2–4 times), 3 = sometimes (5–10 times), 4 = often (over 10 times).

Source: The table summarizes a national survey by Pope & Tabachnick (1994). Copyright © 1994 by the American Psychological Association. Adapted with permission.

in-service training, continuing education workshops, or other group settings, their value may be in direct proportion to the class's or group's ability to establish a genuinely safe environment in which participants are free to disclose responses that may be politically incorrect, "emotionally incorrect," or otherwise at odds with group norms or with what some might consider the "right" response. Only if participants are able to speak honestly with each other about responses that they might be reluctant to speak about in other environments, and to discuss such responses with mutual respect, will the task of confronting these questions be likely to prove helpful in developing emotional competence.

Learning to discuss these sensitive topics and individual responses with others is important not only in developing our own emotional competence but also in developing resources for maintaining our competence throughout our careers. Our colleagues constitute a tremendous resource for helping us to avoid or correct mistakes, to identify stress or personal dilemmas that are becoming overwhelming, and to provide fresh ideas, new perspectives, and second and third opinions. A national survey of psychologists found that therapists rated informal networks of colleagues as the most effective resource for prompting effective, appropriate, and ethical practice (Pope, Tabachnick & Keith-Spiegel, 1987). Informal networks were seen as more valuable in promoting ethical practice than laws, ethics committees, research, continuing education programs, or formal ethical principles. We can provide an invaluable resource for each other when engaged in the process of careful questioning, which is the foundation of both ethics and clinical work and the topic of the next chapter.

CHAPTER SIX

Asking Questions

A Case Study in Questioning Claims from the Recovered Memory Controversy

P erhaps no chapter is more important to this book's approach than this chapter on questioning. There is no shortage of formal ethical standards and civil, criminal, and administrative legislation and case law governing the practice of therapy. But as emphasized in Chapter Two and elsewhere throughout this book, these documents do not and cannot replace active, informed, creative deliberation. This deliberation is a process of continuous questioning.

Note: Much of the material in this chapter was originally presented as the award address for the American Psychological Association's Award for Distinguished Contributions to Public Service at the 103rd Annual Convention of the American Psychological Association in New York, NY, in August 1995, and later appeared as "Memory, Abuse, and Science: Questioning Claims About the False Memory Syndrome Epidemic," by Kenneth S. Pope (*American Psychologist*, September 1996, pp. 957–974) and "Science As Careful Questioning: Are Claims of a False Memory Syndrome Epidemic Based on Empirical Evidence?" by Kenneth S. Pope (*American Psychologist*, September 1997, pp. 997–1006). This material, which is copyrighted by the American Psychological Association, is used with APA's permission.

Vignettes with questions are presented within some of the chapters and at the end of Chapters Seven through Fifteen as examples of one form of this questioning. Yet the questioning about aspects of helping a particular person does not occur in a vacuum. It occurs within the broader, more complex context of questioning claims about diagnostic categories, interventions, research findings, and standards of care. To provide a case study in such questioning, this chapter focuses on a specific set of claims about recovered memories of abuse. The general topic of abuse has brought forth numerous claims. For example, it has been claimed that "it is not unlikely that *more than half of all women* are survivors of childhood sexual trauma" (Blume, 1990, p. iv; italics in original). When such claims—which, if valid, have important implications for clinical work and public policy— emerge in widely selling books or other forums, it is important that they be met with neither reflexive acceptance nor rejection but with active questioning. It is essential to question such claims in the context of the available empirical data, especially when there is no general population research reported in a peer-reviewed scientific or professional journal that supports this claim.

Preceding chapters (the section "Ethics and Denial" in Chapter One; Chapter Four, "Common Misperceptions that Interfere with Ethical Practice") have described some of the all-too-human capacities to avoid this process of questioning. These strategies of avoidance are no less common in regard to the kind of questioning exemplified in this chapter. The claims at issue address fundamental aspects of diagnosis, intervention, and the standard of care. They address whether all clinicians who suspect child abuse on the basis of presenting symptoms are committing malpractice, whether a client's recovered memories are an infallible indicator of therapist malpractice, whether therapists must consider all recovered memories of abuse to be false, whether therapists should be restricted in the kinds of books they may give to patients, whether therapists have caused an epidemic, and whether dissent or questioning of points of view regarding recovered memories should be excluded from scientific meetings. Nevertheless, it may be tempting to take the position that we as therapists have no ethical responsibility for questioning such claims and that such claims have no relevance to our work and the ethics of our work. We may wish to ignore them, reflexively accept them, or reflexively reject them—any alternative to struggling with them through careful, active, informed questioning.

This book's approach is not to provide a simplified set of supposed answers, set forth an easy cookbook approach to the ethics of clinical work, or support a sense of certitude, but rather to suggest that an essential task of health care providers is this process of careful, informed, and comprehensive questioning. We must question our own assumptions, biases, and perspectives, not just once during initial training, but throughout our careers. We must also question claims about diagnoses, interventions, and the standard of care, no matter how prestigious or popular the source. The APA's "Ethical Principles of Psychologists and Code of Conduct" (1992), standards 1.04, "Boundaries of Competence," 1.05, Maintaining Expertise," and 1.06, "Basis for Scientific and Professional Judgments," speak to the responsibilities we have in undertaking study and questioning to ensure appropriate and competent treatment of clients.

Complex factors may shape the process by which clinical and counseling psychologists engage in this questioning. These factors may influence whether various claims about diagnosis, therapy, the standard of care, and other clinical issues encounter or elude careful scrutiny. Such factors include not only the human tendencies of denial and avoidance mentioned above, but also prevailing scientific paradigms, historical contexts, and the bandwagon effect. They can influence the degree to which people are inclined, willing, and free to question certain claims. These factors are themselves a legitimate and important focus of active questioning.

We've chosen claims about false memories of abuse to use as an example for many reasons. One reason is that the original 1991 edition of this book emphasized the fallibility and malleability of memory, citing published studies of memory distortion and even emphasizing how therapists' memories tend to ease aside awareness of ethically questionable behavior [for example, "Our selective and malleable memory is always available to ensure that ethical unease about a particular incident can fade" (p. 17)]. The original edition also emphasized the harm that results when unvalidated measures are put forth to establish that child abuse has occurred. Since that first edition was published, however, a set of prominent claims about false memories and child abuse has emerged. This relatively recent set of claims holds that many therapists—for reasons as diverse as well-meaning naiveté, greed, incompetence, and zealotry—suggest a history of childhood sexual abuse to clients who have no actual abuse history. According to the claims, clients who uncritically accept these suggestions and come to believe illusory memories of abuse with great conviction, suffer from an iatrogenic disorder termed *false memory syndrome*. This psychopathology, which according to Kihlstrom (1996) resembles a personality disorder, has allegedly manifested sufficient numbers of cases to reach epidemic proportions. In the short span of time since the 1992 founding of the False Memory Syndrome Foundation (FMSF), claims about false memory syndrome—a condition that the Foundation identified and named—and related phenomena have had a profound impact on issues germane to ethical and competent psychological science and practice. FMSF noted its own "success" as reflected in the "institutionalization of this information in psychology textbooks, in reference works, in novels, in television dramas, and in hundreds of scholarly papers" (P. Freyd, 1996). The American Psychological Association approved FMSF as a sponsor of continuing education programs for psychologists ("American Psychological Association Approves," 1995). The false memory syndrome concept is addressed in appellate decisions (e.g., *State* v. *Warnberg*, 1994).[1] A recent article in *Columbia Journalism Review* has noted the popular media's frequently uncritical acceptance of these claims (Stanton, 1997; see also Bowman and Mertz, 1996a; Herman, 1994; Landsberg, 1996a, 1996b).

Although it is unusual that a lay advocacy group could produce adequate scientific evidence to support its discoveries and claims, FMSF highlights the contributions of its Scientific and Professional Advisory Board. FMSF emphasizes not only that "board members make substantial donations to the Foundation both in time and money" but also that "it is the presence of the Advisory Board that has given our efforts credibility" ("FMSF Advisory Board Meeting," 1993, p. 3). The FMSF Scientific and Professional Advisory Board includes distinguished and prominent members in the fields of psychology, psychiatry, sociology, and cognitive science (False Memory Syndrome Foundation, 1996a). Their contributions of time, money, reputations, and credibility to the goals and work of FMSF may represent a significant if not crucial factor in the Foundation's success. The Scientific and Professional Advisory Board's implicit endorsement of the false memory syndrome diagnosis may help explain why such FMSF claims are so vividly reflected in the professional literature, expert testimony, and the popular media. If widely accepted, claims about a false memory syndrome epidemic traced to therapeutic malpractice may influence diagnosis and treatment for many people, the access or lack of access that individuals have to various services, and the clinical, forensic, and public response to those who report memories of childhood abuse (Pope & Brown, 1996).

This chapter suggests questions that may be useful for evaluating the evidence that purportedly established the validity of claims about false memory syndrome and their policy implications. The questions are meant to be illustrative of the questioning process that is an essential responsibility of therapists. The chapter also proposes that scholarly examination of some methods used to promote these claims (for example, diagnosis and characterization of those who disagree) might reveal factors influencing the degree to which these claims are critically examined. Are the methods used to promote these claims creating a context in which such claims are unlikely to be examined critically, freely, and comprehensively? This form of questioning, which involves careful attention to context, is also an essential responsibility of therapists.

REVIEW OF THE LITERATURE: MEMORY THEORY PRIOR TO THE FALSE MEMORY SYNDROME FOUNDATION AND FALSE MEMORY SYNDROME

The notion that psychology tended to view memory as a near-perfect recording device until the last several years finds no historical support. A review of the literature reveals a long history of exploring how, rather than whether, memory could be fallible, malleable, and suggestible. Psychology's fascination with memory's imperfections dates back at least to the founding of the APA, which provides a vivid example. Writing a history of the Association's first thirty-eight years, Fernberger (1932) described the memorable meeting on July 8, 1892 among APA organizers Stanley Hall, George Fullerton, Joseph Jastrow, William James, George Ladd, James Cattell, and Mark Baldwin. A decade later, he described his attempts to verify accounts of that meeting, including his contacting of two of the alleged participants (Cattell and Jastrow), both of whom denied having attended. He concluded, "There is really no evidence that the meeting was ever actually and physically held" (Fernberger, 1943, p. 35).

Two years before this supposed meeting, William James (1890) wrote the following:

False memories are by no means rare occurrences in most of us. . . .
Most people, probably, are in doubt about certain matters ascribed to

their past. They may have seen them, may have said them, done them, or they may only have dreamed or imagined they did so. . . . The most frequent source of false memory is the accounts we give to others of our experiences. Such accounts we almost always make both more simple and more interesting than the truth. We quote what we should have said or done rather than what we really said or did; and in the first telling we may be fully aware of the distinction. But ere long the fiction expels the reality from memory and reigns in its stead alone. This is one great source of the fallibility of testimony meant to be quite honest. . . . It is next to impossible to get a story of this sort accurate in all its details, although it is the inessential details that suffer most change (pp. 373–374).

Muensterberg's (1908) studies of how people imperfectly remember experimentally staged events, Bird's (1927) demonstration of how postevent information can influence recollection, and Barlett's (1932) analysis of how telling a story from memory (as in the game of "gossip" or "telephone") reveals distortions are but a few examples of the rich and diverse history of research in this area.

The fallibility of memory and even perception itself, which furnishes so much of memory's content, result in part from their creative action. Long before Hubel and Wiesel (1962a, 1962b, 1979) investigated the neurophysiological construction of perceptions, Koffka (1935) reviewed extensive studies of how stimulus properties, contextual forces, and observer variables could bring forth misperceptions such as Wertheimer's (see Boring, 1950) "phenomenal movement" (or "phi-phenomenon"), the classic optical illusions, and the phantom limb phenomenon. The mind did not passively receive and store perfect perceptual representations; it actively constructed representations of varying correspondence with external events and continued to work on the constructions. In rejecting the static, passive, storehouse model of perception, memory, and mind, Koffka (1935) emphasized, "what a strange store-house we find it to be! Things do not simply fall into those places into which they are being thrown, they arrange themselves in coming and during their time of storage according to the many ways in which they belong together. And they do more; they influence each other, form groups of various sizes and kinds, always trying to meet the exigencies of the moment (p. 518)."

He concluded that "we are in full agreement with Barlett, who says: 'In fact, if we consider evidence rather than presupposition, remembering appears to be far more decisively an affair of construction rather than one of mere reproduction'" (p. 656). The mind, memory, and perception have each emerged this century not as "static, not a large storage bin [or] a passive blank slate [but rather as] an organ of activity, process, and ongoing work" (Pope & Singer, 1978a, p. 106; see also Pope & Brown, 1996; Pope & Singer, 1978b, 1980).

FALSE MEMORY SYNDROME: CLAIMS OF A SCIENTIFICALLY VALIDATED SYNDROME AND EPIDEMIC

Memory's imperfection provides a context for the FMSF's claims about the supposed syndrome it appeared to discover and helped to institutionalize. According to proponents of this reputed new syndrome, sufficient cases have been diagnosed to constitute an epidemic. These claims of a mental health epidemic provide an opportunity to consider questions that can be useful in evaluating purported scientific discoveries, evidence, and conclusions. The definition of false memory syndrome found in the literature published by the FMSF was written by John Kihlstrom, who has served as an FMSF Scientific and Professional Advisory Board member. Kihlstrom (1994, p. 2) claimed that there is a

> False Memory Syndrome—a condition in which a person's identity and interpersonal relationships are centered around a memory of traumatic experience which is objectively false but in which the person strongly believes. Note that the syndrome is not characterized by false memories as such. We all have memories that are inaccurate. Rather, the syndrome may be diagnosed when the memory is so deeply engrained that it orients the individual's entire personality and lifestyle, in turn disrupting all sorts of other adaptive behaviors. The analogy to personality disorder is intentional. False Memory Syndrome is especially destructive because the person assiduously avoids confrontation with any evidence that might challenge the memory. Thus it takes on a life of its own, encapsulated, and resistant to correction. The person may become so focused on the memory that he or she may be effectively distracted from coping with the real problems in his or her life. (See also Kihlstrom, 1996; also cited in False Memory Syndrome Foundation, 1995a, 1995b, 1995c, 1997.)

Methodology for Assessing an "Entire Personality and Lifestyle"

How did those who validated false memory syndrome assess whether that false memory actually "orients the individual's entire personality and lifestyle?" Assessing whether there are aspects of the individual's personality or lifestyle that remain consistent and unchanged (that is, not oriented to the objectively false "memory") would present a considerable challenge even to the most skilled and experienced clinicians. Disclosing the methodology for making this determination would allow careful examination of the assumptions, evidence, and reasoning that support the research and would encourage replication and additional research into false memory syndrome.

Claims of False Memory Syndrome's Similarity to Personality Disorders

It is not clear how similar this new disorder is to the recognized personality disorders to which it is explicitly analogized by Kihlstrom, or whether this analogy simply makes explicit the notion that the same sort of severe pathology presumed present in the classic personality disorders is present in the alleged false memory syndrome. The *Diagnostic and Statistical Manual of Mental Disorders* (4th ed.; *DSM-IV*; American Psychiatric Association, 1994), for example, states that "a Personality Disorder is an enduring pattern of inner experience and behavior that deviates markedly from the expectations of the individual's culture, is pervasive and inflexible, has an onset in adolescence or early adulthood, is stable over time, and leads to distress or impairment" (American Psychiatric Association, 1994, p. 629).

Does defining false memory syndrome to resemble recognized personality disorders imply that onset does not occur beyond early adulthood? Does it suggest that, whereas the syndrome becomes manifest in adulthood, its foundation—like the foundation of recognized personality disorders—rests on earlier weaknesses or dysfunction in the individual? Wakefield and Underwager (1994), for example, noted that "Gardner sees the women who make false allegations based on recovered memories as very angry, hostile, and sometimes paranoid. He believes that all will have demonstrated some type of psychopathology in earlier parts of their lives" (p. 333). The *Philadelphia Inquirer* quoted Wakefield's description of those who recover memories: "The adult children who 'remember' sexual abuse decades after they say it happened are . . . 'not just anybody. They are women who already have problems, such as personality disorder, and they're likely to be unusually suggestible'" (Sifford, 1991, p. 12).

Thousands of Empirically Documented Cases

Within about a year of the founding of FMSF, which identified and named a new syndrome, proponents began to claim that the syndrome was widespread. FMSF Scientific and Professional Advisory Board member Martin Gardner (1993) wrote that among the purposes of the FMSF was "to seek reasons for the FMS epidemic" (p. 375). In the process of researching the problem, FMSF made the following statement: "FMSF is first a research organization that is documenting the extent of this phenomenon. There is a standard procedure that is followed for phone interviews. We currently have in our files hundreds and hundreds of 'Maybe's.' Maybe's are names that are given to us as families that are affected by false memory syndrome but for whom we do not have the standard documentation information. Unless we have complete and standard documentation, we do not add these people to the count of affected families" (False Memory Syndrome Foundation, 1993, p. 7). Two of the founding Scientific and Professional Advisory Board members cited as validating evidence for false memory syndrome "the empirical data the FMS Foundation has from 12,000 families" (Wakefield & Underwager, 1994, p. 98).

The FMSF's research evidence allegedly "points with high certainty towards a false memory syndrome that meets the requirements for a syndrome contained in the *DSM-III-R* and the *DSM-IV*. The thousands of instances that contain those common elements are likely to be more support for this syndrome than for any other that has been accepted as a legitimate classification category" (Wakefield & Underwager, 1994, p. 99).

Expert witnesses, therapists, policy makers, reporters, the courts, graduate courses, and continuing education programs could thus cite a growing literature accepting and helping institutionalize the notion that false memory syndrome was not only a scientifically validated disorder caused by psychotherapy, but that the number of documented cases was exceptionally large. For instance, Goldstein and Farmer (1993) asserted, "Now we know that false memory syndrome is an iatrogenic disease created by therapy gone haywire. We know that False Memory Syndrome has reached epidemic proportions" (p. 9). By 1996, FMSF distributed an information sheet and order form (for its video *False Memory Syndrome*) in which it claimed that "False Memory Syndrome [is] a devastating phenomenon that has affected tens of thousands of individuals and families worldwide" (False Memory Syndrome Foundation, 1996b).

It would be helpful for FMSF and its Scientific and Professional Advisory Board to describe the research protocols or other formal procedures by which false memory syndrome has been adequately validated as a syndrome and by which it was determined that it has affected tens of thousands of individuals and families. Clearly stating operationalized procedures such as how reported memories of abuse are found to be "objectively false" in any study that documents the widespread nature of false memory syndrome would allow the independent analysis, verification, and replication that is the hallmark of psychological scientific empiricism. It is possible that the impressive names, prestige, offices, and affiliations of the Scientific and Professional Advisory Board may have, however unintentionally, led fellow scientists, the courts, the popular media, and others to accept— without customary skepticism, care, and examination of alternative hypotheses—the methodology and arrays of primary data relevant to the notion of false memory syndrome and other FMSF assertions as scientifically validated.

It is worth emphasizing that some therapists engage in incompetent, unethical, or well-meaning but misguided behaviors, sometimes with disastrous consequences for patients (see, for example, Pope, 1990d, 1994; Pope & Bouhoutsos, 1986; Pope, Simpson, & Weiner, 1978). In some instances, these behaviors include using unvalidated, misleading, or bizarre methods for assessing whether a patient was sexually abused as a child (as previously noted, the use of unvalidated measures to establish that child abuse had occurred was discussed in the first edition of this book). Such facts alone, however, are an insufficient basis for claims that there "is an iatrogenic disease created by therapy" and that this "False Memory Syndrome has reached epidemic proportions" (Goldstein & Farmer, 1993, p. 9). The scientific evidence that supposedly validates claims about this so-called syndrome, its causes, and its epidemic proportions needs to be made available and carefully examined.

Informed-Consent Issues in Research
Validating False Memory Syndrome

Research involving human participants usually involves the informed consent of the participants. For those independently evaluating or attempting to replicate studies seeming to validate the existence and widespread occurrence of false memory syndrome, it would be useful if the procedures for obtaining informed consent—if consent was obtained—from people who were diagnosed as suffering from false memory syndrome were disclosed. It appears possible, on the basis of reading the materials generated by the FMSF, that some might not consider interviewing or clinically assessing the people supposedly afflicted by false memory syndrome to be an essential component of a study of the validity and occurrence of the syndrome. If, for this reason, the informed consent of or even direct contact with people diagnosed with false memory syndrome has been considered unnecessary in documenting specific cases or the extent of the phenomenon, it would be useful for FMSF and its Scientific and Professional Advisory Board to report any available scientific data about the ability to diagnose false memory syndrome without meeting the person alleged to have the disorder. If the person reporting the so-called memory does not participate in the research, how do researchers conclude that the memory is objectively false (rather than simply subjectively judged to be false by those who have been accused)? How do researchers determine that the center of a person's identity and interpersonal relationships is a particular false memory without even meeting the person? How do they examine all aspects of personality without interviewing, evaluating, or even knowing the person?

Independent Examination of the
Primary Data and Methodology

Independent examination of the primary data and methodology used to establish the validity and reliability of a new psychological diagnosis, prior to its application to large numbers of people, is an essential scientific responsibility. Diagnoses lacking validity may attract proponents if distorting influences like confirmation bias, illusory correlation, and false consensus have not been eliminated from the validation studies and subsequent use. However, once set forth as a scientifically valid, established, and institutionalized category, a readily diagnosed formal psychological syndrome gains immense power to influence others. As Rosenhan wrote: "Such labels, conferred by mental health professionals, are as influential on the patient as they are on his [sic] relatives and friends, and it should not surprise anyone that the diagnosis acts on all of them as a self-fulfilling prophesy. Eventually, the patient himself [sic] accepts the diagnosis, with all of its surplus meanings and expectations, and behaves accordingly" (1973, p. 254; see also D. Brown, 1995b; Langer & Abelson, 1974; Mednick, 1989; Murphy, 1976; Pope, Butcher, & Seelen, 1993; Reiser & Levenson, 1984).

The Cause of False Memory Syndrome: Trauma Memories Implanted in Therapy

To explain why people who had never been abused would accuse parents or others of sexually abusing them, false memory syndrome proponents have tended to assert that therapists implanted the memories. For example, False Memory Syndrome Foundation (1995b) claimed "that certain psychotherapeutic techniques, theories and practices have led many people to falsely believe they were sexually abused as children" (p. 1). Seeking research evidence that specific therapist behaviors cause harm poses a dilemma: Investigators cannot randomly assign patients to conditions hypothesized to cause injury. Typically, studies attempt to correct for the absence of random assignment by selecting appropriate comparison groups, matching patients on relevant variables, and using measures that are likely to create maximum sensitivity and specificity to the phenomenon at issue. For example, research assessing whether therapists' sexual behaviors were associated with specific patient symptoms might compare a group of patients who had engaged in sex with a therapist with matched (in regard to demographics, etc.) groups of patients who had not engaged in sex with a therapist and of patients who had engaged in sex with a physician who was not a therapist (for reviews of such research, see Pope, 1994; Pope, Sonne, & Holroyd, 1993; Chapter Ten). In this instance, researchers have tended instead to attempt to demonstrate that false memories of events described as traumatic can be implanted in other contexts, and to generalize from these findings to what must occur in psychotherapy.

Loftus's widely cited experiment in which older family members apparently implanted memories in fourteen-year-old Chris, eight-year-old Brittany, and three other participants has been claimed as the "proof" (Loftus & Ketcham, 1994, p. 99) that implanting traumatic memories is possible. When challenged with the assertion, "But it's just not possible to implant in someone's mind a complete memory with details and relevant emotions for a traumatic event that didn't happen," Loftus responded: "But that's exactly what we did in the shopping mall experiment" (Loftus & Ketcham, 1994, p. 212). Proponents described this experiment as demonstrating the creation of an extensive false memory. Lynn and Nash (1994) reported that "Loftus and Coan were able to implant an extensive autobiographical memory" (p. 198). Lindsay and Read (1994) claimed that "Loftus and Coan . . . demonstrated that people can be led to create detailed and extended 'recollections' of childhood that never occurred" (p. 289). The popular press echoed a similar theme, arguing, for example, that the most practical significance about the lost-in-the-shopping-mall study is that "it buttresses an alternative explanation for the source of recovered memories that True Believers purport to have repressed. Namely, that the memories have been implanted by some type of suggestion; they are false" (Boss, 1994, p. 12).

Among the kinds of questions that might be useful in evaluating claims about implanting "a complete memory with details and relevant emotions for a traumatic event that didn't happen" based on this research are the following:

1. Does the trauma specified in the lost-in-the-mall experiment seem comparable to the trauma forming the basis of false memory syndrome? Loftus (1993) described the implanted traumatic event in the shopping-mall experiment as follows: "Chris was convinced by his older brother Jim, that he had been lost in a shopping mall when he was five years old" (p. 532). Does this seem, for example, a reasonable analogy for a five-year-old girl being repeatedly raped by her father? Pezdek (1995; see also Pezdek, Finger, & Hodge, 1996, 1997) has suggested that this may not be the case. In attempting to arrive at a more analogous situation—that of a suggested false memory of a rectal enema—her experimental attempts at implantation of a suggestion had a 0 percent success rate.

2. What is the impact of the potentially confounding variables in claiming the shopping-mall experiment to be a convincing analogue

of therapy (Loftus, 1993; Loftus & Ketcham, 1994)? Is it possible that the findings are an artifact of this particular design?; for example, that the older family member claims to have been present when the event occurred and to have witnessed it, a claim the therapist can never make. To date, replications and extensions of this study have tended to use a similar methodology; that is, either the older family member makes the suggestions in his or her role as the experimenter's confederate, or the experimenter presents the suggestion as being the report of an older family member, thus creating a surrogate confederate.

3. Has this line of research assumed that verbal reports provided to researchers are the equivalent of actual memories? Spanos (1994) suggested that changes in report in suggestibility research may represent compliance with social demand conditions of the research design rather than actual changes in what is recalled. In what ways were the measures to demonstrate actual changes or creations of memory representations validated and confounding variables (for example, demand characteristics) excluded? Given that being lost while out shopping is apparently a common childhood experience, how is the determination made that the lost-in-the-mall memory is not substantially correct? What supports the claim that "Chris had remembered a traumatic episode that never occurred" (Garry & Loftus, 1994, p. 83). That is, is there any possibility that Chris's family had forgotten an actual event of this type?

4. If the experiment is assumed for heuristic reasons to demonstrate that an older family member can extensively rewrite a younger relative's memory in regard to a trauma at which the older relative was present, why have false memory syndrome proponents presented this research as applying to the dynamics of therapy (for example, Loftus, 1993; Loftus & Ketcham, 1994) but not to the dynamics of families, particularly those in which parents or other relatives may be exerting pressure on an adult to retract reports of delayed recall? Is it possible that older family members can rewrite younger relatives' memories in regard to traumatic events at which they were present? Might this occur in the context of sexual abuse when the repeated suggestion is made by a perpetrator that "nothing happened" and that any subsequent awareness of the abuse constitutes a false memory?

This line of research has been extended by others, and similar research has been carried out in varied designs (for example, "false memories" of words that did not appear in a list of words, suggestions of earaches and trips to the hospital at night, suggestions of rectal enemas).[2] One crucial question is this: Does this research adequately justify the claims that are being made in legal cases and elsewhere? An FMSF (1995b) amicus curiae brief (which includes a list of the forty-seven prominent members of the FMSF Scientific and Professional Advisory Board as an appendix) presented a typical claim: "Memories of truly traumatic events are easily altered and false recollections, though felt to be actual memories of real events, can easily be induced by suggestion" (p. 20).

Loftus (1992) published claims that are even more sweeping: "If handled skillfully, the power of misinformation is so enormous and sufficiently controllable that a colleague and I recently postulated a not-too-distant 'brave new world' in which misinformation researchers would be able to proclaim: 'Give us a dozen healthy memories . . . and our own specified world to handle them in. And we'll guarantee to take any one at random and train it to become any type of memory that we might select . . . regardless of its origin or the brain that holds it.' The implications for the legal field, for advertising, and for clinical settings are far reaching" (p. 123). These expansive claims echo those made by Watson (1939) over a half century ago, when a line of behavioral research led to claims that the power of learning theory was so enormous and sufficiently controllable that psychologists with sufficient resources could take individuals at random and produce any kind of people and behavior they might select. If there was a lesson to be learned from the Watsonian claim, it was modesty. Not only did human beings fail to fall helplessly under the power of conditioning, docile animals often refused to act in accordance with the proclaimed principles of the new science (for example, Breland & Breland, 1961). It was the rush to embrace claims uncritically that went far beyond the data—the failure to question carefully—that caused the Watsonian fall.

Therapists as Perpetrators of False Memory Syndrome

An additional assertion with regard to false memory syndrome has been the claim that significant numbers of therapists engage in behaviors likely to inflict the false memory syndrome iatrogenically. Lindsay and Poole (1995), for example, stated, "In our view there are solid grounds to fear that tens of thousands of people . . . have developed illusory memories or false beliefs about CSA [child sexual abuse] through suggestive memory recovery techniques and ancillary practices in psychotherapy, self-help, or group therapy" (p. 464). In a study to examine clinical practices, Poole, Lindsay, Memon, and Bull (1995) reported data from a study of both U.S. and British clinicians and suggested that their findings indicated that "25 percent of the members of those organizations who conduct psychotherapy with adult female clients believe that recovering memories is an important part of therapy, think they can identify clients with hidden memories during the initial session, and use two or more techniques to help such clients recover suspected memories of CSA" (p. 434; initial findings from Poole et al.'s study were previously presented and discussed in an article by Lindsay & Read, 1994).

Lindsay and Read (1994) "refer to such approaches collectively as 'memory recovery therapies'" (p. 282), "are sharply critical of the memory recovery techniques" (p. 298), and fear "that these powerful techniques are being used in ways that are damaging the lives of many clients and their families" (p. 282).

Others besides the study's authors have cited the results as providing evidence that so-called memory recovery therapies are commonly practiced by psychotherapists and that many therapists are at risk of harming clients by engaging in such behaviors. For example, an FMSF (1995b) amicus curiae brief claimed that "recent surveys of therapists' understanding and practices have shown a number of widely held misconceptions, which if communicated to patients, may increase a client's responsiveness to suggestion (and in turn, [lead] to the development of false memories" (p. 5).

FMSF Scientific and Professional Advisory Board member Dawes (1995) characterized the techniques included in the study as "coercive techniques" (p. 12). Loftus (1995) claimed "that these activities can and do sometimes lead to false memories seems now to be beyond dispute" (p. 24). In an article whose title and text metaphorically refer to therapists using these techniques as "accidental executioners," Loftus, Milo, and Paddock (1995) used Poole et al.'s (1995) data to estimate that as many as 25 percent of clinicians "may be using techniques that are risky if not dangerous" (p. 304). Because they use some techniques included in Poole et al.'s list, specific therapists have been publicly labeled as "dangerous." For example, the *Jerusalem Post* reported opposition to Utrecht University psychology professor Onno van der Hart's plan to lecture in Israel on his treatment of adults who suffered childhood abuse: "Members of the US False Memory Syndrome Foundation and psychologists in various parts of the world charged that van der Hart and his colleagues were 'very dangerous.' His critics charged that van der Hart's techniques represented a 'harmful and unscientific method of pseudotherapy that must be seen as a threat to psychology in Israel. This 'therapy' makes the patient dependent on the therapist by inventing multiple personalities, false memories, and accusations, which have already destroyed tens of thousands of families in the U.S.'" (Siegel-Itzkovich, 1996, p. 7).

Poole et al.'s (1995) study has also been used as the basis for various estimates of the frequency with which illusory memories of abuse may occur. Pendergrast (1995) estimated that "25 percent of doctoral level therapists constitute True Believers" (p. 491; a discussion of True Believers appears later in this chapter) and that "over one million cases of 'recovered memories' each year" (p. 491)—allegedly illusory ones—occur in psychotherapy in the United States. Using similar calculations, FMSF Scientific and Professional Advisory Board member Crews (1995) claimed that "it is hard to form even a rough idea of the number of persuaded clients . . . a conservative guess would be a million persons since 1988 alone" (p. 160). Dawes (1995) estimated a lower bound of 1,475,833 women who, in the last two years, had seen therapists who reported using two or more techniques specified in Poole et al.'s survey to help individuals recover memories. Thus, Dawes concluded that "Wakefield and Underwager are absolutely correct in their assessment that recovered memory therapy is widespread" (p. 12).

Olio (1995a, 1995b, 1996, 1997) suggested, however, that such conclusions might not be valid. She formulated questions about the research design, statistical tests, and inferences that might be useful in evaluating this study, among which are the following four:

1. *Did the survey construction lead to confounded results?* Olio (1996) noted that the critics of recovered memories have repeatedly emphasized the thesis that memory may be particularly susceptible to distorting or confabulating influences when responding to questions (especially related to the past) or giving self-reports. Ironically, this study relies on similar data-gathering procedures in which people are asked numerous questions based on their memory of past complex events. Poole (1996) herself acknowledged that the data "do not

necessarily index what clinicians do in their offices because they are retrospective self-report measures" (p. 1).

The study failed to use free-recall questions. For example, rather than asking, "Do you use any memory-recovery techniques, and if so, what are they?" Poole et al. (1995) used a potentially suggestive technique of the type they criticized therapists for using. Participants were first told that other "therapists use special techniques to help clients remember childhood sexual abuse" (Poole et al., 1995, p. 430) and then were provided a list of techniques to check. Olio (1996) suggested that in light of current theory on memory, recall, and the impact that questioning may exert on responses, the use of these techniques may have unintentionally shaped the findings to confirm the beliefs of false memory syndrome proponents.

2. *Do the measures have face validity?* According to Olio (1996), the conclusions of Poole et al.'s (1995) study are based on the unproven assumption that clinicians with certain (self-reported) beliefs practice differently from clinicians with other beliefs, and that these differences in practice create greater risk for the production of illusory memories. She questioned this assumption that beliefs are reliable predictors of behaviors. The complex chain of assumptions (that is, reported belief, to actual belief, to behavior, to consequences for patients) may be questionable at best. For example, Polusny and Follette (1996) found that despite therapists' beliefs about the prevalence of repressed memories, the majority of therapists holding these beliefs reported that they had not seen any cases of adult clients who entered therapy with no memory of childhood sexual abuse and subsequently recalled abuse during therapy.

Poole et al. (1995), according to Olio (1996), apparently drew inferences about implanting or creating illusory memories of childhood abuse in clients who reported no memories of childhood abuse at the beginning of psychotherapy and who did not, in fact, have an actual history of childhood abuse. Unfortunately, key questions in the survey did not inquire specifically about the use of various therapy techniques with this particular population. The questions used were

Survey 1: "Some therapists use special techniques to help clients remember childhood sexual abuse. Check any technique that you have used with abuse victims in the past two years."

Survey 2: "Check on the left ["tick" for the British survey] any technique that you have used in the past two years to help clients remember childhood sexual abuse" (Poole et al., 1995, p. 430).

The question in Survey 1 specifically asked about techniques used with "abuse victims" and did not inquire how many (if any) of these were clients who denied abuse, but whom the clinician suspected might have had abuse histories. Similarly, the inquiry regarding techniques used to "help clients remember childhood sexual abuse" in Survey 2 did not differentiate between techniques used with clients who reported a history of abuse (both those with continuous or accessible memory and those who recovered memories of abuse prior to psychotherapy) and techniques used with clients who denied such a history.

Olio (1996) suggested that other inconsistencies between the actual survey questions used and the reported conclusions may be important. For example, Poole et al. (1995) claimed that "25 percent . . . believe that recovering memories is an important part of therapy" (p. 434), whereas the actual survey question asked respondents to rate "how important is it 'that a *client who was sexually abused acknowledges or remembers* [italics added] the abuse in order for the therapy to be effective'" (p. 430). Poole et al. (1995) suggested that their survey "indicates that . . . some clinicians believe they can identify clients who were sexually abused as children even when those clients deny abuse histories" (p. 434). However, the survey question (in Survey 2) asked about instances in which the client did not explicitly report any abuse, not about instances in which the client denied abuse histories. Finally, Poole et al.'s (1995) claim that 25 percent "think they can identify clients with hidden memories during the initial session" (p. 434) is based on questions that asked (retrospectively): "Of adult female clients whom you *suspected* [italics added] were sexually abused as children what percentage initially denied any memory of childhood abuse?" (p. 430; Survey 1) and asked whether participants "had ever *suspected* [italics added] that a client had been abused although the client did not explicitly report any abuse" (p. 430; Survey 2). It seems that a clinician's acknowledgment that he or she sometimes had suspected an abuse history significantly differs from a belief that he or she could identify those with hidden abuse memories (see subsequent section "Not Suspecting Child Abuse").

3. *Are the techniques risky?* Poole et al.'s (1995) characterization of potentially risky behaviors practiced by 25 percent of clinicians relied on a "constellation" of three self-report items (discussed previously): two items relating to beliefs and one to practice. Olio (1996) observed, however, that there are no validation studies for this constellation of reported beliefs and practice and therefore no way to determine what is actually being measured by these items, no way to determine what outcome(s) result from this constellation, and no way to know how the results might differ from other psychotherapy practices. According to Olio, the study apparently assumed that some techniques are risky per se, rather than recognizing that virtually all psychotherapy techniques have the potential for damage depending on the manner, context, and timing in which they are used.

Olio (1996) noted that Poole et al. (1995) did not offer any criteria or research to define what might constitute a risky frequency of use for the listed techniques. Despite expressing concerns regarding approaches to therapy "that combine several techniques . . . in a prolonged search for suspected hidden memories" (Lindsay, 1995a, pp. 281–282), in Poole et al.'s data, the criteria for questionable practice is satisfied with the single use of any two techniques (even on a single occasion) during the last two years. Therefore, a therapist who allows one client to keep a journal and bring in family photos as a way of decreasing the anxiety and pain of the remembering process would be counted among those engaging in coercive, risky practices that can create false memories and would be classified as a potentially dangerous recovered-memory therapist.

Olio (1996) argued that, in essence, Poole et al. (1995) created an unvalidated checklist (for risky practices), not dissimilar to the unvalidated checklists of symptoms that Lindsay & Read (1994), among others, correctly criticized some clinicians for using to identify histories of childhood abuse. Responding to Olio's critique, Lindsay (1995b) conceded that he did "agree that there are far too little data to make firm statements about the prevalence of 'risky' memory work" (p. 1).

4. *Did Poole et al. (1995) incorrectly infer causality?* Olio (1996) noted that Poole et al. (1995) claimed "our survey . . . indicates these interventions can have serious implications for clients (for example, lead some clients to terminate relations with their fathers)" (p. 434). This conclusion is based on responses to the following question: "Of the adult female clients who initially denied any memory of sexual

abuse, what percentage came to remember childhood sexual abuse during the course of therapy?" (p. 431). Poole et al. reported that in "Survey 1, we asked respondents to report the percentage of clients, among those who through therapy remembered abuse, who confronted their abuser . . . and who cut off relations with the abuser" (p. 432).

Thus, all abuse reported by therapists as having been recalled during the course of therapy (Poole et al., 1995, p. 431) was claimed by the authors to represent cases of abuse remembered "through" therapy (p. 432). Olio (1996) observed that this is a form of the logical fallacy *post hoc, ergo propter hoc* ("after this, therefore on account of this"). Poole et al. committed this fallacy, according to Olio, with their claim that because therapists reported having used certain techniques and reported that some clients recovered memories during this time span, the techniques must have caused the memories. Furthermore, Poole et al. used this logic to claim that the use of those particular techniques had serious implications; that is, it was the use of those techniques that led clients to terminate relations with their fathers. In both instances, presumed correlation is confused with causation.

Olio (1996) noted that such assumed correlations may be misleading. She used the example of a hypothetical survey in which respondents were asked whether their patients got older during the course of therapy. Even if 100 percent of the therapists reported that their clients became older during therapy, it does not provide evidence that the aging process was attributable to or even differentially associated with therapy. In other words, such data should not be used to prove that therapy leads people to grow older or causes the aging process.

Olio emphasized the importance of placing such data within a 2×2 (whether patients recovered memories by whether therapists used specified interventions) or similar model and of assessing whether randomization and other procedures were adequately considered. Such a statistical model would assess the relationships among (1) patients recovering memories during therapy as reported by therapists using specified interventions, (2) patients not recovering memories during therapy as reported by therapists using specified interventions, (3) patients recovering memories during therapy as reported by therapists not using specified interventions, and (4) patients not recovering memories during therapy as reported by therapists not using specified interventions.

REDEFINING MALPRACTICE
AND THE STANDARD OF CARE

The FMSF and its proponents have published claims not only about scientific findings but also about the nature of malpractice and the standard of care. Pending systematic surveys and other research addressing the issue, it is impossible to know the degree to which such published statements by a prominent organization or professionals may have a chilling effect on the professional services provided by therapists who disagree with these claims. What impact will clinicians' knowledge that prominent expert witnesses may testify that certain services constitute malpractice have on the availability of those kinds of services? As with claims of scientific findings, it is important to respond with neither reflexive acceptance nor rejection but with careful questioning.

Should Therapists Be Required
to Seek External Validation?

One set of claims asserts that without seeking external validation through family members or others, the therapist violates the legal standard of care by providing treatment when recovered memories of abuse are at issue. In its publications, FMSF has highlighted statements about the standard of care by its Scientific and Professional Advisory Board members such as, "To treat for repressed memories without any effort at external validation is malpractice pure and simple" (McHugh, 1993b, p. 1; for an alternate view, see American Psychological Association Task Force on Violence and the Family, 1996, p. 74; Pope & Brown, 1996). FMSF (1992a) also published a statement, adapted from two Scientific and Professional Advisory Board members, of the thirteen steps a therapist needs to take in regard to gathering external validating information when adult patients allege childhood sex abuse. The therapist of a person who has sought treatment for recovered memories of incest must not only contact the parents and seek other sources of validation but must also provide comprehensive information about the patient to clinicians working on behalf of the parents; to refuse to provide such information raises the question of an absence of "good faith" (McHugh, 1993a, p. 3).

Questions that might be useful in evaluating this claim include the following: Do FMSF proponents imply that therapists can accept, without external validation, reports based on memories that have been continuously accessible rather than recovered?; that is, is there no legal mandate to seek external validation when an adult's memories of childhood sex abuse have been continuous? If so, what research findings support this distinction? Do FMSF proponents imply that therapists are legally required to seek external validation only when a patient reports child sex abuse?; that is, is there no legal mandate to seek external validation for all patient reports of violence, abuse, crimes, or other such interactions? If so, what research findings support this distinction?

Are All Recovered Memories False?

Another set of claims holds that all recovered memories are false, and that their presence in the therapeutic situation reflects malpractice and a violation of licensing regulations. Discussing the results of an APA task force study, the APA *Monitor* reported: "'There are some groups that have taken [recovered] memories as prima facie evidence of poor therapeutic practice,' [former APA president Ron] Fox said. 'Some groups have mailed out newsletters instructing people how to make complaints to ethics boards to harass therapists,' he said" (Seppa, 1996, p. 12). Fox noted that some therapists have consequently altered their practice or discontinued providing any services to this population.

Statements by FMSF and some of its proponents have seemed to characterize recovered memories of trauma as objectively false per se. FMSF Scientific and Professional Advisory Board member Harrison Pope and his colleague James Hudson (1995a; see also 1995b) emphasized that "traumatic experiences are memorable" (p. 715), asserted that there has never been a confirmed case of "noncontrived amnesia among neurologically intact individuals over the age of six who experienced events sufficiently traumatic that no one would be expected to simply forget them" (p. 716), and asserted that trauma survivors in scientifically valid studies "unanimously remembered the events" (p. 715).[3] Founding FMSF Scientific and Professional Advisory Board members Hollida Wakefield and Ralph Underwager (1994) wrote, "People who undergo severe trauma remember it" (p. 182).[4] Scientific and Professional Advisory Board member Martin Gardner (1993) asserted that "better-trained, older psychiatrists do not believe that childhood memories of trauma can be repressed for any length of time, except in rare cases of actual brain damage. . . . And there is abundant evidence that totally false memories are easily aroused in the mind of a suggestible patient" (p. 374).

FMSF (1992b) itself published the claim: "Psychiatrists advising the Foundation members seem to be unanimous in the belief that memories of such atrocities cannot be repressed. Horrible incidents of childhood are remembered" (p. 2). According to this reasoning, such amnesia is scientifically impossible because there is no mechanism in the human brain that has the capacity to create or even assist in creating an amnesia for trauma. In an amicus curiae brief argument to the court, FMSF (1997) claimed that no known cognitive mechanism is considered capable of even contributing to an amnesia of a traumatic event: "Although a broad range of mechanisms are known to produce various kinds of memory disturbance and have been examined by memory researchers and theorists, none are, at present, considered capable of contributing to a supposed amnesia for traumatic events" (p. 17). But if they are not actual memories, by what function do recovered memories of abuse arise? Miller (1997) described the growing amount of evidence supporting the claim that recovered memories "are the artifact of the constructive and suggestible nature of our memories (for example, Lindsay & Read, 1994; Loftus, 1993)" (p. 250). Fraser (1997), reviewing work in this area, observed that on the basis of such claims, "many . . . members of the public have been persuaded to believe that all recovered memories are bogus" (p. D14).

POPULATION STUDIES. One question useful in considering claims that horrible incidents of childhood are remembered, that there are no cognitive mechanisms that might enable such amnesia, and that all recovered memories are false is: To what extent have these claims been clearly and convincingly demonstrated by formal population studies or other research in the peer-reviewed scientific literature? A number of studies, for example, have focused on such amnesia among diverse populations (for example, general population, therapy clients, therapists). These population studies, some of them prospective and all of them meeting the criterion of peer-reviewed publication, include Andrews, Morton, Bekerian, Brewin, Davis, & Mollon (1995); Briere & Conte (1993); Burgess, Hartman, & Baker (1995); Cameron (1994); Dalenberg (1996); Elliott (1997); Elliott & Briere, (1995);

Feldman-Summers & Pope (1994); Golding, Sanchez, & Sego (1996); Herman & Schatzow (1987); Hovdestad & Kristiansen (1996); Leavitt (1997); Loftus, Polonsky, & Fullilove (1994); Melchert (1996); Polusny & Follette (1996); Pope & Tabachnick (1995); Roe & Schwartz (1996); Roesler & Wind (1994); van der Kolk & Fisler (1995); Widom & Morris (1997); Widom & Shepard (1996); and Williams (1994). It is important to note, as emphasized throughout this book, that such published studies should prompt deliberation rather than serve as a substitute for it. They themselves must be subjected to active questioning in areas such as assumptions, logic, and methodology.

CASE STUDIES. Another question is useful in considering claims about the impossibility of valid recovered memories: Are such claims consistent with documented case studies? Schooler, Bendiksen, & Ambadar (1997), for example, describe events in the life of Ross Cheit as a case history that seems to provide reasonable corroborative evidence of valid recovered memories of child sex abuse. They report as their source of information a 1993 *U.S. News & World Report* article. They note that the article described "multiple sources of indirect corroboration of the event. Specifically, the author of this article was able to find other individuals who had independently recorded instances of Farmer's sexual improprieties, both before and after Cheit's recovered memory experience" (p. 261). The chapter by Schooler et al. maintains that because people other than Cheit claimed that the alleged abuser (Farmer) had sexually abused other children, the possibility that Cheit also was abused is supported. Thus the evidence that Cheit was abused is not conclusive, but there is evidence that supports the *possibility* that Cheit *may* have been abused. "Although these sources of evidence do not conclusively demonstrate that Cheit himself was the victim of abuse, their implication of Farmer as a sexual abuser clearly supports the possibility that he may have abused Cheit as well" (Schooler et al., 1997, p. 261).

Even this inconclusive evidence, according to Schooler et al., comes from a questionable source whose personal bias may have distorted the reported findings. "It should be noted that the reporter who investigated this case was a friend of Cheit's. While such an affiliation need not invalidate the evidence provided, it is possible that the evidence was not collected in a completely unbiased manner" (p. 261). While questioning the credibility of the *U.S. News & World*

Report reporter, Schooler et al. do not present any facts that would indicate that the evidence in the article was collected or reported using biased methods.

When considering the degree to which such a case study presentation does or does not support the claim that recovered memories are inherently false, the following questions may be useful: What are the primary data on which such a presentation is based? Do they support the conclusion in the Schooler et al. chapter that the evidence is not only indirect (based on allegations by others) but also from a source of questionable credibility? Although the chapter makes no mention of it, the *U.S. News & World Report* article cited as the source for the chapter discusses a taped confession. "For nearly an hour, Cheit held Farmer on the phone, a tape recorder running all the while. Farmer admitted molesting Cheit in his cabin at night" (p. 62). This tape has been the focus of much media attention. For example, among the other reporters who have listened to the tape and reported on its contents, Wagner (1993) published excerpts from the tape and later (1994, p. B7) reported, "At that time, Farmer admitted molesting Cheit, according to the tape." A variety of evidence, including this tape-recorded confession, was reviewed by the court in Cheit's civil suit against Farmer. The outcome was a "judgment from said defendant in the sum of $457,000" (*Cheit* v. *Farmer,* 1994, p. 1). The sponsors of the camp at which Farmer was camp director noted this taped confession in a letter of public apology to Cheit. The public apology expressed to Cheit and his parents that they were "deeply sorry for the harm that came to them while Ross Cheit attended the Chorus' summer camp in 1968 and wishes to assure them that the Chorus is doing everything possible to prevent child molestation at the Chorus and at the summer camp" (San Francisco Boys Chorus, 1994, p. 2). Among other reports of this case are those by MacNeil-Lehrer (1995) and Stanton (1993, 1995).

Behavioral and Pharmacological Therapies and Directing Feelings

Recent claims in the area of recovered memories address the kinds and content of therapy. Loftus (1995), for example, supported the development, evaluation, and use of "behavioral and pharmacological therapies that minimize the possibility of false memories and false diagnoses" and urged therapists to avoid "dwelling on the misery of childhood" (p. 28). Loftus maintained that patients are best served when therapists adhere to the following principles:

> Borrowing from John Gottman's . . . excellent advice on how to make your marriage succeed, patients might be reminded that negative events in their lives do not completely cancel out all the positives (p. 182). Encourage the patient to think about the positive aspects of life—even to look through picture albums from vacations and birthdays. Think of patients as the architects of their thoughts, and guide them to build a few happy rooms. The glass that's half empty is also half full. . . . Campbell (1994) offers similar advice. Therapists, he believes, should encourage their clients to recall some positive things about their families. A competent therapist will help others support and assist the client, and help the client direct feelings of gratitude toward those significant others (Loftus, 1995, p. 28).

Among the questions useful in carefully evaluating these claims are the following:

- Is there research demonstrating that behavioral and pharmacological therapies produce fewer false memories and false diagnoses than other forms of therapy?
- What evidence supports the claim that to be competent a therapist must render help to third parties in their efforts to support and assist a therapy client?
- What evidence supports the claim that to be competent a therapist must help clients to direct feelings of gratitude to third parties?
- What are the possible consequences of helping clients who are incest victims to direct feelings of gratitude to family members and other third parties?

Not Suspecting Child Abuse

Claims that factors such as clothing, attractive appearance, smiling behavior, and chatting provide a reliable basis for concluding that a person has never engaged in child abuse stand in contrast to claims that presenting symptoms must never lead anyone to suspect that a person may have been sexually abused (for documentation and critical review of such claims, see Pope, 1996). For example, Kihl-strom (1995b; see also Olio, 1995c) wrote that "it is not permissible to infer, or frankly even to suspect, a history of abuse in people who present symptoms of abuse." He similarly asserted that "you can never, never, never, never, never, infer a history of sexual abuse from the patient's presenting symptoms. Nevernevernevernevernevernevernevernevernevernevernevernevernevernevernevernevernevernevernevernevernevernevernevernevernevernevernevernevernevernevernevernevernevernevernevernevernevernevernevernevernevernevernevernevernevernevernevernevernevernevernevernevernevernevernevernevernevernevernevernevernevernevernever" (1995a). These claims taken to-gether seem to suggest that although presenting "symptoms of abuse" never justify suspicion that a person was involved in child abuse, pre-senting factors such as clothing and appearance can reliably demon-strate that a person was not involved in child abuse.

In evaluating the effects of prohibiting suspicion of child abuse based on presenting symptoms, it may be useful to ask: How will it affect mandated reporting of suspected child abuse? Reviews of state laws suggest that almost 50 percent use a form of the verb "suspect" (for example, "suspect that a child has been abused") in legislation re-quiring therapists to report suspected child abuse (Kalichman, 1993). Additional states use similar concepts but different wording.

Another question for evaluating this prohibition is this: To what degree, if at all, might therapists refrain from pursuing diagnostic leads based on presenting symptoms because of the threat of malprac-tice suits? Decisions to report suspected child abuse may be covered by at least a qualified immunity but assessment and treatment actions generally are not. Without research data concerning the potential influence of this prohibition, it is impossible to know whether or how this claim affects clinicians' responses to presenting symptoms.

A third question is useful for assessing this claim: To what degree do various arrays of presenting symptoms lead at least some thera-pists to suspect child abuse as one possible event that may be associ-ated with the symptoms and warrant consideration in the assessment process? Approaches to gathering relevant information might take a variety of forms, such as presenting symptom arrays to clinicians and asking whether they might lead to a suspicion of abuse. For example, a cluster of presenting symptoms for a young girl might include panic and avoidant behavior in the presence of her father; nightmares oc-curring every few hours that, according to the patient, involve a shad-owy figure grabbing at her genitals; and refusal to allow a physical examination although she had previously allowed them during med-ical office visits. In regard to such vignettes, clinicians might be asked another question: If suspecting the possibility of child abuse on the basis of such symptoms would subject them to actual or threatened malpractice suits, how, if at all, would such knowledge affect their response to the client and their consideration of whether to file a mandated report of suspected child abuse?

Unacceptable Books and Ideas

In some instances published works condemned by FMSF proponents become targets of legal action. Lawsuits in two California cities blamed a book for leading people to believe false memories of childhood sex abuse ("Author Target of False-Memories Lawsuit," 1994; K. Butler, 1994; Pope, 1995b). A licensing complaint was filed against a therapist asserting "that an article she had written . . . for a journal titled *Medical Aspects of Human Sexuality* could suggest false incest diagnoses" (K. Butler, 1995, p. 28).

Therapists may themselves face formal complaints for using books containing unacceptable ideas. The *Philadelphia Inquirer*, for example, quoted Paul Fink, a past president of the American Psychiatric Association, saying on the topic of therapists who give *The Courage To Heal: A Guide for Women Survivors of Child Sexual Abuse* (Davis & Bass, 1994) and similar books to their patients: "There's a name for this—bibliotherapy. . . . To give a book that espouses a narrow thesis of mental functioning is malpractice" (Sifford, 1992, p. D6).

Careful evaluation of such restrictions on the flow of ideas may include consideration of questions such as the following:

- At what point does a thesis of mental functioning become defined as sufficiently narrow that any book espousing it must be banned from therapy? For example, B. F. Skinner relegated so-called mental functioning to an unobservable epiphenomenon, irrelevant as a variable in the scientific study of human behavior. Would this thesis of mental functioning be considered sufficiently narrow that a behavior therapist's giving one of Skinner's books to a client would be considered malpractice?

- Is it essential to the malpractice claim that the harmful ideas appear in the form of a published book? For example, if instead of giving the book to a patient so that the patient can study and form an opinion about the thesis himself or herself, the therapist were to say to a patient, "There is a book by Bass and Davis that espouses this view of mental functioning," or otherwise discuss the ideas within the book, is that, too, malpractice?

- If it is malpractice for therapists to give such books to their patients, would it also constitute malpractice for supervisors to give such books to their therapy trainees, hospitals and clinics to make such books available in their libraries, professionals leading workshops to use them as texts, or professors to assign them to their students?

- How, if at all, does the prospect of encountering expert testimony that giving a particular sort of book to a patient is per se malpractice influence the behavior of therapists and the range of services, ideas, and choices available to those in need?

Checklists for Assessing Incompetence and Other Forms of Malpractice

Some FMSF proponents have created and endorsed checklists by which patients can supposedly determine whether a therapist is incompetent, is causing harm, or is engaging in other forms of malpractice. For example, an FMSF Scientific and Professional Advisory Board member noted that "whether or not a therapist has a doctoral degree, is irrelevant to his psychotherapeutic competence" (Campbell, 1994, p. 49), and published a forty-item checklist by which patients can supposedly assess a therapist's competence (p. 251). With minor revision, this instrument has been published by others (for example, Wakefield & Underwager, 1994). The number of "yes" responses supposedly indicates the likelihood that the therapist is "incompetent" and that the therapist is causing "much more harm than good." The book, however, provides no references to published research establishing the validity, reliability, sensitivity, or specificity of this instrument. If there is a scientific basis for this instrument, it would be useful for the FMSF Scientific and Professional Advisory Board members endorsing it to provide those research data so that these claims can be carefully evaluated.

CAREFUL EXAMINATION: THE SCIENTIFIC PROCESS

Questioning scientific claims may be difficult if a prestigious group portrays them as the only legitimate scientific view, one that is sufficiently established so as to preclude serious consideration of any alternative views. For example, a prominent regional psychological association invited only certain scientists to discuss the debate about memory and abuse from a scientific perspective. Suggestions that a more balanced program might be achieved by supplementing the members of the FMSF Scientific and Professional Advisory Board who had been invited as speakers with scientists who might present alternatives to the FMSF view were rejected by FMSF as unscientific. The *False Memory Syndrome Newsletter* set forth the rationale for the rejection: "A memory researcher told us that research academics 'don't even know what this memory debate is about. They see the evidence and to them the science of memory is obvious.' He is right. The 'science' of the 'memory' is established. . . . How could a scientific program about memory be 'balanced'? The notion makes no more sense than trying to balance a program in astronomy by including astrologers" ("Social Political Movement," 1996).

As previously noted, the factors that can discourage careful questioning of scientific claims or consideration of alternate views are many. Scientists must be aware of these factors and must carefully and responsibly question claims and consider other explanatory models regardless of the prestige of those who might assert that a particular thesis about memory and abuse is beyond question.

Responsible scientific questioning of specific claims bears at least one similarity to conducting well-designed experimental research. Experimental research must attend not only to variables of primary interest but also to potentially confounding factors. Similarly, careful examination of reported scientific findings and principles must attend not only to central claims but also to potentially confounding factors that may influence the degree to which people are inclined, willing, or free to question or reject certain claims. This section examines such potentially confounding factors and their implications.

Picketing

Picketing therapists is a highly visible tactic. If therapists who disagree with certain claims, voice their disagreement, and behave in ways that are inconsistent with those claims fear that their patients may be forced to cross a picket line in order to obtain their services, it may affect the degree to which they feel free carefully to question and rationally to consider these claims.

As early as 1992 in an FMSF newsletter article titled "What Can Families Do?" the tactic of picketing was discussed (False Memory Syndrome Foundation, 1992c). In his order granting summary judgment in favor of the defendant, trauma therapist Charles Whitfield, M.D., whom Pamela Freyd and Peter Freyd had sued for alleged defamation, U.S. Judge Benson Legg mentioned many aspects of FMSF activities, including picketing. He wrote, "In response, the Freyds mounted a public campaign, challenging the validity of such recovered memories. In 1992, they formed the False Memory Syndrome Foundation (FMSF), aggressively contesting the existence of traumatic amnesia and repressed memories. (Resp. at 12.) Plaintiffs relied on various fora to publicize their foundation and 'to debunk this preposterous theory,' including . . . the picketing of therapists' homes" (*Pamela Freyd et al. v. Charles L. Whitfield,* 1997, pp. 1–2).

FMSF members' picketing of therapists has emerged as a topic at professional conferences and in the literature of this area, sometimes including discussion of the experience of a therapist targeted for picketing (for example, Brown, 1995a; Calof, 1996; Koocher, 1997[5]; see also K. Butler, 1995).

Among questions that might be useful in evaluating the potential consequences and implications of this tactic are the following:

- What is the impact on patients who are forced to cross a picket line to obtain treatment from a provider of a particular form of legal health care service? Will patients choose to cross picket lines, forego treatment altogether, or pursue treatment from someone acceptable to false memory syndrome proponents who establish picket lines?

- Some patients or potential patients may perceive and value a right of privacy and believe it important that no one else know that they seek mental health services. Those wishing to seek treatment for concerns such as sexual abuse from family members, domestic violence, or torture may fear that, should the fact that they are seeking professional help become known, their own lives or the lives of their families might be endangered or that other negative consequences might occur (see, for example, Calof, 1996; J. J. Freyd, 1996; Herman, 1992; Koss et al., 1994; Pope & Brown, 1996; Pope & Garcia-Peltoniemi, 1991; Salter, 1995). How does forcing patients to cross picket lines affect such privacy concerns?

- How do patients (or therapists) evaluate or anticipate what may happen to them should they cross through the picket line (do they believe it possible or likely that they will be followed, their license plate number taken down, their picture taken, and so on)? How do clients form opinions about what the pickets, FMSF, or others may view as justifiable steps to take when targeted services continue despite picketing? K. Butler (1995) quoted the FMSF executive director: "If somebody came into your house and shot your child, it would probably be justifiable homicide if you did something, and that's how these parents feel," says Freyd. "When you get between parents and children, you can expect things to happen" (p. 75).

Describing and Diagnosing Individuals Who Disagree

Diagnosing and otherwise categorizing those who disagree may influence the degree to which people are inclined, willing, and free to question scientific claims. When such diagnoses and categorizations are set forth, it is important to examine the scientific evidence on which they rest, their social or policy consequences, and their potential effects on scientific deliberations. Two founding members of the FMSF Scientific and Professional Advisory Board published an article examining why University of California, Los Angeles, professor Roland Summit and others persist in believing in child abuse phenomena that according to some claims are unscientific and absurd. They concluded that the cause of such beliefs among professionals lay not in the evidence for the hypotheses, or in social or contextual variables, or in differing perspectives, but rather in the relational dysfunctions or psychopathology of those who believe these ideas. Underwager and Wakefield (1991) wrote, "The answer to the question why do some professionals believe and not others is in the internal variables of the personalities of the believers. It ranges from factors that may make a person difficult to relate to but remaining functional to serious psychopathology" (p. 190).

PARANOID. Those disagreeing may be characterized more specifically as manifesting paranoid beliefs or responses. FMSF Scientific and Professional Advisory Board member Richard Ofshe wrote, "These responses signal the collective paranoia of a social movement turning inward" (Ofshe & Watters, 1993, p. 16). Another FMSF Scientific and Professional Advisory Board member explained, in an APA divisional presidential address, that the belief of "abuse-believers" frequently "takes on a paranoid cast" (Spence, 1993; see also Wakefield & Underwager, 1994, pp. 41–43).

CULT AND SECT. *The Washington Post* quoted the FMSF executive director as characterizing those who work to open up the topic of sex abuse to public awareness as cult-like. "'I can understand,' says Freyd, 'people who are trying to open up the area of sexual abuse being infuriated by us. They feel we aren't helping their work. But they are a little like a cult'" (Sherrill, 1995, p. Fl). Pendergrast (1995) recommended different terminology. "Some have called the Survivor Movement not only a religion, but a cult. It is all too easy to label any fervent group a 'cult,' with all its negative connotations. I prefer the word 'sect'" (p. 478). This characterization addresses the motivation of certain therapists who disagree: "Most of the therapists appear to be True Believers on a mission. That fits Hassan's general observations: 'They believe that what they are doing is truly beneficial to you. However, they want something more valuable than your money. They want your mind! Of course, they'll take your money, too, eventually.' Similarly, trauma therapy guarantees a protracted period of recovery and, hence, a steady income" (Pendergrast, 1995, p. 479).

TRUE BELIEVERS. One of the most commonly used labels to describe individuals who disagree with the FMSF is *True Believer*. Loftus used the concept of True Believer to support her claim that resistance to her work is based not on evidence, reason, and good faith but on prejudice and fear (for example, "I know the prejudices and fears that lie behind the resistance to my life's work"; Loftus & Ketcham, 1994, p. 4). She split the profession into two groups. Identifying herself as a skeptic, she and her colleague wrote, "On one side are the 'True Believers,' who insist that the mind is capable of repressing memories and who accept without reservation or question the authenticity of recovered memories. On the other side are the 'Skeptics,' who argue that the notion of repression is purely hypothetical and essentially untestable, based as it is on unsubstantiated speculation and anecdotes that are impossible to confirm or deny" (Loftus & Ketcham, 1994, p. 31).

Loftus makes clear her source by quoting from Hoffer's (1951/ 1989) well-known text, *The True Believer*. If the skeptic demands proof, how does the True Believer decide what to believe in? Hoffer

(1951/1989) observed that True Believers shut themselves off from facts, ignoring a doctrine's validity while valuing its ability to insulate them from reality (p. 80). Hoffer (1951/1989) described the True Believer's passionate hatred and fanaticism, noting "the acrid secretion of the frustrated mind, though composed chiefly of fear and ill will, acts yet as a marvelous slime to cement the embittered and disaffected into one compact whole" (p. 124). Among the most prominent professionals who are True Believers, according to the false memory literature, are psychologists Judith Alpert, Laura Brown, and Christine Courtois, three members of the APA working group on recovered memories. Pendergrast (1995) wrote, "The American Psychological Association has created a six-person committee to study the repressed-memory issue. Three of the members are experimental researchers who are skeptical of massive repression, including Elizabeth Loftus. The other three are True Believer therapists" (pp. 503–504; see also Wakefield & Underwager, 1994, p. 349). The term *True Believers* characterizing those who disagree now appears in the peer-reviewed scientific literature, for example, in an article by a member of the FMSF Scientific and Professional Advisory Board (Crews, 1996, p. 66).

USE OF HOLOCAUST IMAGERY. Those who disagree with FMSF have also been compared to Fascists. In her book *Diagnosis for Disaster: The Devastating Truth About False Memory Syndrome and Its Impact on Accusers and Families,* Wassil-Grimm (1995), for example, used the imagery of the Holocaust, explicitly referring to Hitler and the Jews: "Hitler had the Jews; McCarthy had the communists; radical feminists have perpetrators" (p. 91).

The *Oregonian* quoted the FMSF Executive Director Pamela Freyd as describing the behavior of Professor Jennifer Freyd as "Gestapo-like" (Mitchell, 1993, p. L6), a term she had previously used in a journal article (Doe, 1991, p. 155) later reprinted as a book chapter (Doe, 1994, p. 29).[6] Another use of imagery related to the Holocaust, used on this occasion to compare an FMSF Scientific and Professional Advisory Board member to those who risked their lives to save Jews from the Nazis, appeared in the *Boston Globe:* "'I feel like Oskar Schindler,' Loftus muses, referring to the German financier who rescued doomed Jews from the Nazis. 'There is this desperate drive to work as fast as I can'" (Kahn, 1994, p. 80).

It is important to examine the use of imagery related to the Holocaust to compare explicitly or implicitly one who disagrees to Hitler, the Gestapo, and Nazis, or to portray an FMSF proponent as engaged in a desperate rescue. Among questions to be addressed in careful examination of this use are the following: Do such statements reflect on the motivation, character, and decency of those who disagree with FMSF claims? Do such statements promote a climate of hate and hostility toward those who fail to accept FMSF claims? Do such statements have a chilling effect on some who otherwise might voice questions about FMSF claims? How might such statements affect the scientific and popular (for example, media) evaluation of FMSF claims about the difficult and complex issues of remembering child sex abuse?

Obtaining and Revealing Disclosures to Therapists

According to the Portland *Oregonian,* FMSF director Pamela Freyd recommended tactics to learn about someone else's therapy: "Follow your child to the office, hire a private detective, pry the information from other relatives your child may talk to, pose as a patient yourself" (Mitchell, 1993, p. L1; see also False Memory Syndrome Foundation, 1992c, p. 4; Loftus, 1993, pp. 529–530). Finding out and revealing what people have said to their therapists has placed communications to therapists about alleged child abuse in a new context. In *The Myth of Repressed Memory: False Memories and Allegations of Sexual Abuse,* Loftus and Ketcham (1994) reprinted quotes from a *Playboy: Entertainment for Men* article (Nathan, 1992) that were apparently verbatim statements by women who were meeting with therapists as part of a four-day "retreat for survivors of sexual abuse, physical abuse, emotional abuse and neglect" (p. 202). The *Playboy: Entertainment for Men* article's author was an investigative journalist who had attended the retreat for survivors and therapists. Among the questions that may be useful in evaluating the potential impact of such efforts to reveal disclosures about alleged abuse to therapists are the following:

- Does knowing about such published accounts affect the decisions of those who view themselves as having experienced sexual abuse, physical abuse, emotional abuse, and neglect about whether to seek services in group settings?
- Do the accounts of people's disclosures to therapists accord them basic respect and dignity? For example, *The Myth of Repressed Memory: False Memories and Allegations of Sexual Abuse*

used characterizations such as the following to describe women talking with therapists about abuse: "Soon it was time to plunge into the gory details. A veritable competition . . . began as one woman after another related her grisly stories, progressively upping the ante of horror" (Loftus & Ketcham, 1994, p. 203). FMSF has helped popularize what appears to be ridicule of those who claim to be abuse survivors through publication of articles such as "Whining About Abuse Is an Epidemic" (Nethaway, 1993, p. 6). Research could be useful in exploring whether the manner in which disclosures to therapists about alleged abuse are characterized in books, newsletters, and other works by FMSF proponents has any influence on the willingness of those who view themselves (accurately or inaccurately) as survivors of various forms of abuse to seek professional help.

- Do those who make such disclosures to therapists have concerns about the uses to which their statements may be put? Would they fear that their statements might be used in legal actions to deprive them of their civil rights; that is, that their statements would be construed as evidence of false memory syndrome, rendering them unable to make their own decisions? In *Legal Aspects of False Memory Syndrome,* for example, FMSF (1992b) informed parents that they "may take the legal position that the accusing child is incompetent and seek guardianship proceedings" (p. 3).

- Do these data-gathering activities and publications impose specific informed-consent duties on therapists? Do patients have a right to know that other patients, clerical or support staff, shelter volunteers, or others present may actually be detectives, reporters, and so forth, and that what they say in the presence of these other people may be published or put to use in other ways? Are patients who believe that they are talking to therapists or other helpers aware that in certain circumstances they may find their words quoted, even with a pseudonym? Pseudonyms may not prevent recognition of a specific individual (see, for example, Pope, 1995b). Is it possible that the information gathered may be used in a way patients would not have chosen or given consent for? If informed consent and informed refusal are fundamental rights of those seeking health care services, and if the consent process involves telling potential patients about factors that might reasonably affect their decision to consent to or refuse treatment (Caudill & Pope, 1995; Pope & Brown, 1996; Chapter Eight of this book), it is difficult to imagine any legitimate justification for withholding information about such possibilities from those who will be most affected. This is an important question of professional responsibility and public policy and deserves careful and comprehensive discussion.

CONCLUSION

Claims about a new diagnostic category (false memory syndrome) constituting an epidemic, the ease with which extensive autobiographical memories about trauma can be implanted, and the large number of therapists engaging in behaviors supposedly proven by research to cause false memories of trauma in their patients deserve careful consideration.

It is important to examine carefully the evidence and logic of the claims and to ask, what if these claims are valid? The profound implications for individual lives, public policy, the standard of care, clinical work, and education and training have been compellingly set forth in books by Crews (1995), Dawes (1994), Goldstein & Farmer (1993, 1994), Loftus & Ketcham (1994), Ofshe & Watters (1994), Wakefield & Underwager (1994), and Wassil-Grimm (1995).

An open, fair, and independent analysis must also allow for the possibility that the evidence and logic do not convincingly establish the validity of some or perhaps any such claims. Psychologists must be prepared to examine the profound implications for individual lives, public policy, the standard of care, clinical work, and education and training if these widely accepted and institutionalized claims are invalid. What if, for example, tens of thousands of individuals have been wrongly diagnosed with a label lacking adequate scientific validation?

It is equally important to examine the process by which these claims are evaluated and institutionalized, including tactics used to promote them. Psychologists must be as attentive to factors that, however unintentionally, may confound the process of consideration and discussion as they are to factors that may confound an individual experiment. If disagreement with certain claims is determined to reflect impaired functioning or serious psychopathology, the scientific process may be subverted. If those who question, doubt, or disagree are authoritatively characterized by professionals as hate-filled True

Believers, paranoid cultists, or Hitler-like zealots, the process of free and independent analysis of FMSF claims may be affected. If patients currently seeking legal health care services from those who question or disagree with FMSF are forced to cross picket lines to obtain those services, if the privacy of their therapy is invaded, or if they are diagnosed without their participation as suffering a false memory syndrome, their freedom of choice may be affected.

Claims grounded most firmly in the scientific tradition are those emerging from hypotheses that are falsifiable. Therapists bear an essential responsibility to examine primary data, research methodology, assumptions, and inferences. Science works best when claims and hypotheses can be continually questioned. That which tends to disallow doubt and to discredit anyone who disagrees is unlikely to foster clinical practices based on scientific principles. Each scientific claim should prevail or fall on its research validation and logic. Therapists must continually struggle to evaluate claims about research, theory, ethics, law, and practice, and to try to determine the implications of this daunting array of information, opinion, and argument for each unique client as the therapy evolves.

Notes

1. Legal determinations that allegations of sexual abuse are false because the witness suffers from false memory syndrome generally require expert testimony. The appellate ruling in *State* v. *Warnberg* (1994), for example, described a set of facts in which "sexual assault occurred when Warnberg pulled the car to the side of the road to allow the complainant to be sick, at which time she claimed he approached her from behind, undid her bra, and fondled her breasts while she was vomiting. . . . Warnberg sought to introduce evidence of a sexual assault against the complainant thirteen years prior to the alleged assault. He argued that that evidence was relevant to his contention that the complainant's accusation was the result of a psychologically displaced or repressed memory or 'false memory syndrome.' The trial court rejected Warnberg's proposed evidence on the ground that it could not determine from Warnberg' s offer of proof that such a syndrome existed. Warnberg argues that the trial court should have granted his motion for a continuance to allow him to produce an expert who could testify to the validity of the false memory syndrome. A concept such as false memory syndrome . . . requires an expert witness to testify to its existence."

2. For discussions of this and related lines of research from diverse perspectives, see Bowman & Mertz (1996b); Brewin, Andrews, & Gotlib (1993); D. Brown (1995a, 1995b); J. J. Freyd & Gleaves (1996); Hyman, Husband, & Billings (1995); Koss, Tromp, & Tharan (1995); Loftus & Pickrell (1995); Pezdek et al. (1996, 1997); Roediger & McDermott (1995); Westen (1996); Whitfield (1995); and Zaragoza & Koshmider (1989).

3. H. G. Pope & Hudson (1995a) did not claim that child sexual abuse per se is never forgotten. They asserted that children may actually undergo what a majority of adults would identify as sexual abuse "but the experience may not seem particularly traumatic or strikingly memorable to the child" (p. 716). Their general argument rests on premises such as the absence of proof is equivalent to proof of absence. They asserted that questioning such premises does not reflect sound reasoning: "It might be argued that absence of proof is not proof of absence; the lack of evidence for repression does not refute its existence. But this argument is flawed" (p. 718).

4. Underwager is no longer listed as a member of the FMSF Scientific and Professional Advisory Board.

5. An audiotape of this APA symposium—which includes presentations by Laura Brown, David Calof, Ross Cheit, Jennifer Freyd, Jennifer Hoult, and Anna Salter—is available from the Sidron Foundation at (410) 825-8888.

6. In late February 1992, when she wrote that she was 'going to serve as Executive Director of the FMS Foundation," Pamela Freyd confirmed in the *False Memory Syndrome Newsletter* that "You already know me as Jane Doe" (P. Freyd, 1992, p. 1).

CHAPTER SEVEN

Beginnings and Endings, Absences and Accessibility

A fundamental responsibility of the psychotherapist is to clarify the boundaries of the relationship. Two of the most important boundaries are the beginning and ending of the therapy. The individual seeking help needs to know whether he or she is a client and whether he or she can reasonably expect that a particular clinician will act to fulfill the responsibilities of the role of therapist.

Information about the beginning and ending of therapy, as well as about the availability of services during therapy, is important if the client's decisions about whether to consent to treatment are to be truly informed. Chapter Eight provides a more detailed discussion of the ethical requirement to obtain informed consent from the client to participate in psychotherapy and related procedures.

CLARIFICATION

Therapists must be alert to possible complications and confusions. An individual may call for an initial appointment. The therapist may assume that the session is one of initial evaluation regarding possible courses of action (for example, if therapy makes sense for the individual, or what modality of therapy, under what conditions, implemented by what clinician seems most promising). The individual, however, may assume that the clinician, by virtue of accepting that request for an initial appointment, has become his or her therapist. Similarly, several months into treatment a client may become enraged at the therapist but be unable to express that anger directly. The client may leave suddenly halfway through a session and miss the regular appointment time for the next five weeks, during which the client fails to return any of the therapist's phone calls. Is that client still a client or has a de facto termination occurred?

Acting to prevent unnecessary misunderstandings regarding the beginning and ending of therapy is part of a clinician's more general ethical responsibility to make clear the availability of and access to therapeutic resources. One of the more immediate aspects of this responsibility is for both therapist and client to understand clearly when and under what circumstances the therapist will be available for sessions or for phone communication, and what resources will be available for the client when the therapist is not available.

Clarification is important for a variety of reasons. First, it forces the therapist to consider carefully this client's needs for phone access during the course of therapy. For example, is this an impulsive, depressed client with few friends who might need phone contact with the therapist or some other professional in the middle of the night to avert a suicide? Clarification enables the therapist to plan for such contingencies.

Second, by leading the therapist to specify backup availability—for example, what the client can do if unable to reach the therapist by phone in an emergency—the efforts to clarify availability enable the therapist to prepare for therapeutic needs that are difficult or impossible to anticipate. For example, a client with moderate coping resources may attend appointments regularly over the course of a year or two, never contacting the therapist between sessions. During a period when the therapist is seriously ill and unavailable for any professional activities, however, the client may receive numerous shocks, such as the loss of a job or the death of a child, that may activate self-defeating or self-destructive behaviors that had not emerged during treatment. The client may become acutely suicidal and need prompt access to therapeutic resources. Careful planning by the therapist may meet such needs that are virtually impossible to anticipate with a specific client.

Third, explicit clarification of the client's access to the therapist or to other therapeutic resources encourages the therapist to think carefully about the effects that the therapist's availability and unavailability are likely to have upon the client and upon the course of treatment. For example, some clients are likely to experience overwhelming feelings of sadness, anger, or abandonment when the therapist goes on vacation. Other clients may find the clear boundaries that the therapist has established so uncomfortable and infuriating that they are constantly "testing" both the therapist and the boundaries. Such clients may frequently show up at the therapist's office at the wrong time for their appointment, may leave urgently cryptic messages ("Am quitting therapy; no hope; life too painful; can't go on") on the therapist's answering machine without leaving a number where they can be reached, and may persistently try to discover the therapist's home address and home phone (if the therapist customarily keeps these private).

Fourth, when therapist and client work together to develop a plan for emergencies during which the therapist might not be immediately available, the process can help the patient to acknowledge realistically his or her dependence and needs for help and to assume—to the extent that he or she is able—realistic responsibility for self-care during crises. For example, the therapist may ask the client to locate the nearest hospital providing twenty-four-hour services and to develop ways of reaching the hospital in an emergency. As the client assumes responsibility for this phase of crisis planning, he or she increases the sense of self-efficacy and self-reliance (within a realistic context), becomes less inclined to view therapy as a passive process (in which the therapist does all the "work"), and may feel less panicky and helpless when facing an impending crisis or the therapist's future absences. In this sense, planning becomes an empowering process for the patient.

Fifth, the process of clarification encourages the therapist to consider carefully his or her own needs for time off, for time away from the immediate responsibilities of work. Such planning helps ensure that the therapist does not become overwhelmed by the demands of work and does not experience burnout. The drawing of such boundaries also encourages the therapist to attend explicitly to other sources of meaning, joy, fulfillment, and support so that he or she does not begin looking to clients to fill personal needs. This is a crucial aspect of the therapist maintaining "emotional competence" (see Chapter Five).

What follow are some of the major areas of accessibility that the therapist needs to clarify in a manner consistent with his or her own needs and style of practice and with the clinical needs of each client. Some clinicians hold to exact time boundaries. With virtually no exceptions, they begin and end the session "on the dot." Even if the client has just experienced a painful breakthrough and is in obvious distress, the therapy session is not extended. In some situations, ending promptly is a practical necessity: The therapist may have another client scheduled to begin a session immediately. In other situations, observing strict time boundaries is required by the theoretical orientation: Running over the time boundary might be considered by the therapist to constitute a breaking of the "frame" of therapy or represent the therapist and client colluding in acting out.

Therapists must consider carefully the approach to time boundaries of the session and adopt one that best fits their own theoretical orientation and personal needs. The effects of the policy upon individual clients need to be considered, and the client should understand the policy.

THERAPIST AVAILABILITY BETWEEN SESSIONS

When and under what conditions can the client normally speak with the therapist between sessions? Some therapists receive nonemergency calls from clients during reasonable hours (for example, 9:00 A.M. to 9:00 P.M.) of weekdays when they are not otherwise engaged. A very few therapists take nonemergency calls when they are conducting psychotherapy. We recommend against this practice, which seems disrespectful of the client who is in session and seems to have numerous potentially harmful effects upon the course of therapy of the client whose session is interrupted by nonemergency calls (or who is aware that any session might be interrupted at any time by such calls to the therapist).

The therapist needs to be clear about the times between sessions when he or she can be contacted on a nonemergency basis. For example, are weekend calls or calls on holidays such as Labor Day, Memorial Day, or Martin Luther King Day acceptable?

An extremely important point to clarify is whether the therapist will speak with the client more than briefly by phone when there is no emergency. Some clients may wish to use phone calls to address the unresolved issues from the last therapy session, to share a dream while it is still "fresh," or to talk over how to handle a situation at work. Some therapists may see such ad hoc phone sessions as therapeutically useful for some clients. The sessions may, for example, help particularly fragile and needy clients, who might otherwise require day treatment or periodic hospitalizations, to function under the constraints of once or twice weekly outpatient therapy. They may help some clients to learn how to use and generalize the adaptive skills they are acquiring in office sessions; the phone sessions serve as a bridge between office therapy sessions and independent functioning by the client.

Some therapists, however, believe that such phone sessions during which therapy is conducted are—except under rare emergency conditions—countertherapeutic. For example, such therapists might view extended phone contacts between sessions as similar in nature and effect to going beyond the temporal boundary at the end of a session.

Again, whether the therapist uses an approach that includes therapy sessions conducted by phone on an ad hoc basis or prohibits them is less important than (1) that the therapist think through the issues carefully in terms of consistency with the theoretical orientation, (2) that the therapist consider carefully the implications of the policy for the individual client, (3) that the therapist consider his or her own abilities and resources, and (4) that both therapist and client clearly understand what the ground rules are.

VACATIONS AND OTHER ANTICIPATED ABSENCES

As mentioned earlier, and as readily recognized by almost anyone who has been a therapy client, extended and sometimes even very brief interruptions in the schedule of appointments can evoke deep and sometimes puzzling or even overwhelming reactions in a client. What is important is that the therapist give the client adequate notice of the anticipated absence. If the therapist tends to take a two-week vacation at the same time each year, there may be no reason for the therapist to omit this information from the customary orientation provided to a new client. If the therapist finds that he or she will be taking a six-week sea cruise during the coming year, the therapist should consider carefully whether there is any compelling clinical reason to withhold this information from the client as soon as the therapist decides to take the cruise. Prompt notification of anticipated absences of the therapist minimizes the likelihood that the client will experience a psychologically paralyzing traumatic shock, gives the client maximal time to mobilize the resources to cope with the therapist's absence in a way that promotes independence and growth, and enables the client to become aware of reactions and to work with them during the sessions before and after the absence.

SERIOUS ILLNESS AND OTHER UNANTICIPATED ABSENCES

Both therapists and clients tend to find comforting the fantasy that the therapist is essentially invulnerable. Therapists may enjoy the feeling of strength and of being a perfect caregiver that such a fantasy, which sometimes remains out of the therapist's awareness, provides. Clients may soothe themselves (and avoid confronting some personal issues) with the fantasy that they are being cared for by an omnipotent, immortal parental figure.

As distressing as it may be to acknowledge, however, especially on the day-to-day basis of the practice of psychotherapy, therapists may experience strokes, heart attacks, or other serious medical conditions with sudden onset. They may suffer from Alzheimer's disease, AIDS, or cancer. They may, while driving with caution, be involved in a car wreck. They may come down with a case of food poisoning. They may take a hard fall, leaving them in a coma. They may be stabbed, shot, or beaten during the commission of a crime. They may be called away suddenly to cope with a family emergency. Or, relatively less pernicious, they may come down with a bad case of the flu, confining them to bed for a week or two. These scenarios are not simply the common fantasies of patients experiencing deep negative transference. They represent the possibilities in store for any human, including therapists.

Just as the breadwinners of a family try to take such contingencies into account in planning for their family's welfare, responsible therapists need to take into account these distressing possibilities and to develop reasonable procedures so that the unanticipated absence (whether temporary or permanent) of the therapist will not unduly undermine the client's welfare. Each therapist will create his or her own way of approaching this issue. The approach must be suited to the personal and professional resources of the therapist, the nature and style of the practice, the theoretical orientation and treatment modality, and, of course, the specific needs of individual clients. Among the questions to which therapists must develop practical answers are these:

• If the therapist is incapacitated, who will notify the clients? Will there be clear procedures for informing clients in advance of their next appointment? There should be a clear list—easily accessible to whoever is responsible for notifying the clients—indicating scheduled appointments and phone numbers or addresses for contacting clients. It may be impractical to go through all client files in an effort to figure out who is a current client, when their next appointment is, and what their current phone and address are. The pocket or briefcase schedule books that many therapists keep with them may be difficult (or impossible) for a colleague to locate during a crisis, and many such books would require deciphering skills beyond the abilities of all but the most advanced cryptographers. Providing adequate arrangements for unanticipated absences during which the therapist is incapacitated is a particularly difficult challenge for solo private practitioners who employ no support staff. The method developed for notifying clients must take into account the client's legal and ethical right to confidentiality.

• Is there an individual whom clients, subsequent treating therapists, and others can easily contact to ask about the condition and course of recovery of the temporarily incapacitated therapist?

• If the therapist is unable to attend to any professional responsibilities, how are the therapist's records handled? Who, if anyone, gains legitimate access to the records? Who, if anyone, has proper authority to act on behalf of the therapist and send copies of the records to subsequent treating therapists or to others whom the client authorizes to receive the records? The records of treatment-to-date may gain exceptional importance because clients may be at increased risk for crisis if their therapist has suddenly become unavailable.

STEPS FOR FOSTERING AVAILABILITY OF HELP IN A CRISIS

Once the client clearly understands how he or she can contact the therapist by phone between regularly scheduled appointments, the therapist and client can discuss appropriate arrangements for situations in which this phone system is inadequate. The client, for example, may experience an unanticipated crisis and be unable to reach the therapist promptly by phone because the therapist's line is busy for an extended time, the therapist's answering service mishandles the client's call, the therapist is in session with another client who is in crisis, or any number of other typical or once-in-a-lifetime delays, glitches, or human errors. For the five reasons cited at the beginning of this chapter, planning for such "unanticipated" breakdowns in communication can enable access to prompt clinical services in time of crisis and can foster more careful therapeutic planning.

If the client's need for help is urgent and if the therapist is unavailable, is there a colleague who is providing coverage for the therapist? Some organizational settings such as HMOs or community mental health centers may, as a matter of policy and procedure, assign clinicians to serve "on call" rotations so that there is always someone available to provide coverage in a crisis when a patient's therapist is unavailable. However, many therapists, particularly those in solo independent practice, may need to design and implement their own plans to ensure coverage in an emergency should they be unavailable.

The decision of whether to arrange for coverage for a specific client is complex. Perhaps the first question that must be addressed is what sorts of information will the covering clinician be provided about the client? Will the coverage provider receive a complete review and periodic update of the client's clinical status, treatment plan, and therapeutic progress? Will the coverage provider have access to the client's chart? Will the coverage provider keep a separate set of notes regarding information supplied by the primary therapist? To what extent will the coverage provider need to secure independent informed consent for treatment by the client? The more foreseeable or the greater the risk that the client will experience a serious crisis demanding prompt intervention, the more compelling the reason for the primary therapist to brief the coverage provider in a careful, thorough manner.

Once the therapist has determined what degree of coverage seems necessary or appropriate for a specific client, a second question to consider is how would introducing the possibility of or actually implementing such coverage affect the client's status or treatment dynamics? Some clients might feel greatly reassured to know that the therapist is taking his or her responsibilities seriously and is carefully thinking through various possible, even if unlikely, treatment needs. Other clients may become alarmed and feel as though the therapist were predicting that a crisis would occur. Still other clients may stall in their progress; the strict privacy and confidentiality of therapy is essential for them, and the knowledge that the therapist would be sharing the contents of sessions with the coverage provider would inhibit the client's ability to explore certain issues or feelings. In many cases, discussion between the therapist and client of the question of whether specific coverage will be provided is useful therapeutically.

If it is decided that specific coverage will be provided, there is a third question for the therapist to consider: What will best ensure the client's right to adequate informed consent for sharing information with the coverage provider and otherwise making arrangements for the coverage?

A fourth question involves the selection of a clinician to provide the coverage. The primary therapist may incur legal (that is, malpractice) liability for negligence in selecting the coverage. If, for example, the clinician providing the coverage mishandles a crisis situation or otherwise harms the client through inappropriate acts or failures to act, the primary therapist may be held accountable for failure to screen and select an appropriate clinician. The ethical and clinical issues, however, are much more subtle. It is important to select a clinician who is well trained to provide the type of care that the client may need. The primary therapist may be tempted to select a clinician solely (and perhaps inappropriately) upon grounds of expedience. The primary therapist may know that the clinician is really not a very good clinician and is perhaps less than scrupulous in his or her professional attitudes and actions. Furthermore, the primary therapist may be aware that the clinician does not tend to work effectively with the general client population that the therapist treats. Nevertheless, the therapist may push such uncomfortable knowledge out of awareness because this particular clinician is handy, and it might take considerable effort to locate an appropriate and trustworthy coverage provider. As in so many other situations discussed in this book, the Golden Rule seems salient. If we were the patient, or if it were our parent, partner, or child who desperately needed help in a crisis when the primary therapist was unavailable, if the careful handling of the crisis were potentially a matter of life and death, what level of care would we believe adequate in selecting a clinician to provide the coverage? If, for example, our parent became suddenly despondent, received a totally inadequate response from the clinician providing the coverage, and committed suicide, would convenience seem sufficient rationale for the primary therapist's selection of that clinician to provide the coverage?

If (for clinical or other compelling reasons) no clinician has been identified to provide coverage or if the identified clinician is for some reason unavailable, to whom does the client in crisis turn when the primary therapist is unavailable? It may be useful for the client to locate a hospital that provides emergency mental health services. There are at least five crucial aspects of accessibility of such services. First, is the facility reasonably nearby? Second, are the services available on a twenty-four-hour basis? (That is, if the crisis occurs in the middle of the night, on a weekend, or on a holiday, will the client find help available?) Third, can the client afford to use the facility? Some facilities charge exceptionally high prices and may offer services only to those who can provide proof of ability to pay—for example, an insurance policy currently in effect. Fourth, does the client know where the facility is located and what its phone number is? Especially during a crisis, even basic information (such as the name of a hospital) may be hard to remember. In some instances, when both the therapist and client believe that there is a high risk for a crisis, it may be useful for the client to write down the name of the hospital, the address, and the phone number to carry with him or her and to leave by the phone at home. Sometimes close friends or family play a vital role in supporting a client in times of crisis. If the circumstances are appropriate, the client may also wish to give this information to a close friend or relative. Fifth, both the therapist and client need to have justifiable confidence that the facility provides adequate care. Substandard care may aggravate a crisis; in certain instances, no care from certain facilities may be better than an inappropriate response.

If the primary therapist, secondary coverage, and designated facility are all unavailable—for whatever reason—in time of crisis, is there an appropriate hot line or other twenty-four-hour phone service that can provide at least an immediate first-aid response to the crisis and attempt to help the client locate a currently available source of professional help? Some locales have twenty-four-hour suicide hot lines. There may be a twenty-four-hour crisis line providing help for individuals with certain kinds of problems. At a minimum, such a phone service may help a client to survive a crisis. For some clients (for example, those who cannot afford a phone at their residence), identifying locations of phones that will be accessible in times of crisis will be an important part of the planning.

If all the previously mentioned resources are inaccessible to the client, the client may nevertheless be able to dial 911, the operator, or a similar general call for emergency response. The client may then be guided to sources of help or, if appropriate, an ambulance or other emergency response may be dispatched.

Whenever a therapist is assessing a client's resources for coping with a crisis that threatens to endanger or overwhelm the client, it is important to evaluate not only the professional resources but also the client's social resources. Individual friends and family members may play key roles in helping a client avert or survive a crisis (though a friend or family member can also initiate, intensify, or prolong a crisis). In some instances, nonprofessional groups, such as Alcoholics Anonymous, may provide virtually twenty-four-hour access to support. The presence of such social supports gains in relative importance when the client's access to professional help tends to be difficult. For example, some clients cannot gain easy access to a phone (especially those who cannot afford a phone, particularly if they are experiencing a crisis in the middle of the night). For many clients, the awareness of such social supports helps them to feel less isolated and thus less vulnerable to becoming overwhelmed by a crisis.

It is worth noting that sometimes therapy begins with the patient in crisis, and that the patient's access to a team of clinicians or caregivers may be useful. The *American Psychologist* presented the following case study illustrating a situation in which the immediate creation of a crisis team proved helpful when a person without funds or coverage needed help.

> In an instance in which a woman required daily sessions during a critical time in her life, colleagues accepted [the therapist's] request that they serve pro bono as an interdisciplinary team, offering detailed daily consultation to him and providing periodic psychological assessment and clinical interviews for the woman. Her meetings with diverse professionals let her know that many people cared about her. These colleagues mobilized to help a battered woman, a victim of multiple sexual assault, now penniless and homeless, living in her car and hiding from a stalker. She and [the therapist] began meeting daily (later gradually reduced to weekly) for crisis intervention. They agreed that the first priority was her safety. [The therapist] gave her the number

of an old college friend in another state. The friend immediately wired her $500 for food and housing and an airline ticket with an open date for use any time she felt in danger from the stalker. The friend asked her not to repay this loan directly to him but rather to give the money to someone else for whom it would make a difference as it did for her now. Within a year, the woman had taken legal action against the stalker and recovered enough to support herself ["Biography," 1995, p. 242].

ENDINGS

An easily overlooked responsibility in regard to ending the therapeutic relationship is the therapist's responsibility to terminate the relationship under certain conditions. Standard 4.09b of the APA's (1992) "Ethical Principles of Psychologists and Code of Conduct" clarifies responsibilities to end the therapeutic relationship when appropriate: "Psychologists terminate a professional relationship when it becomes reasonably clear that the patient or client no longer needs the service, is not benefiting, or is being harmed by continued service."

Therapists also have a duty to *refrain* from terminating a therapeutic relationship under certain conditions. The APA's "Ethical Principles of Psychologists and Code of Conduct" (1992) addresses the ethical responsibility to not abandon clients in standard 4.09a, Terminating the Professional Relationship: "Psychologists do not abandon patients or clients" (see also standard 1.25e, under Fees and Financial Arrangements). Some insurance coverage or managed care plans can create stark challenges. For example, an insurance company may refuse to approve continuing services for a patient, despite the therapist's professional judgment that terminating services would be harmful for the patient, perhaps even resulting in the patient's suicide. A managed care company may provide only four to six sessions annually for any patient, with exceptions provided only for "medical necessity," which might be defined as imminent risk of suicide or homicide. Some patients may suffer from conditions or crises that cannot be adequately addressed in four to six sessions but who do not meet the relevant criteria of medical necessity. For some such patients, interruption of their treatment, even though in accordance with a managed care company's policies and procedures, may constitute abandonment.

When approaching termination, therapists must—if they are able—adequately address the questions that tend to be an inherent part of termination. The American Psychological Association's "Ethical Principles of Psychologists and Code of Conduct" (1992, p. 1606) standard 4.09c states the responsibilities of a therapist to engage in a termination process, "Prior to termination for whatever reason, except where precluded by the patient's or client's conduct, the psychologist discusses the patient's or client's views and needs, provides appropriate pre-termination counseling, suggests alternative service providers as appropriate, and takes other reasonable steps to facilitate transfer of responsibility to another provider if the patient or client needs one immediately."

CONCLUSION

Awareness—particularly a careful, imaginative awareness—plays a fundamental role in ensuring that clients have adequate access to the help they need, particularly in times of crisis when the therapist is not immediately available. In hospital and similar organizational settings, the apparent abundance of staff may lead to a diffusion of responsibility in which no one is actually available to help a patient in crisis. Levenson & Pope (1981), for example, present a case study in which a psychology intern was assigned responsibility to contact promptly a suicidal individual who had been referred to the outpatient unit by the crisis service and to arrange for conducting an intake assessment. The intern, however, was absent from the staff meeting at which the assignment was made. His supervisor, also absent from the meeting, had sent him to attend a two-day training session at another institution. During the next few days, the individual committed suicide.

The hospital's thanatology committee concluded that the crisis service had handled the situation appropriately in referring to the outpatient unit. The outpatient unit itself was not involved in the postmortem investigation because, according to the hospital's procedures, outpatient cases are not opened until the potential patient is contacted by the outpatient unit for an intake screening. The article's authors interviewed the intern, who was struggling with his reactions to these events. Among his conclusions was that he had "at some level internalized the organizational view that no one is really responsible" (p. 485).

Imagination is useful in creating an awareness of the types of crises the client might experience and what difficulties he or she might experience in trying to gain timely access to needed resources. The scenarios for discussion presented at the end of this chapter provide examples.

Thinking things through on a "worst possible case" basis can help the therapist anticipate the ways in which Murphy's Law can make itself felt in human endeavors. No therapist is infallible. The most careful and confident assessment of a patient's potential for crisis can go awry for any number of reasons. But the therapist should take into account his or her own fallibility and plan for the unexpected.

Similarly, imaginative approaches can create accessibility to needed resources. For example, a therapist was treating an extremely isolated, anxious, and troubled young woman pro bono because of the client's lack of money. From time to time the client became overwhelmed by anxiety and was acutely suicidal. Yet she had no practical access to hospitalization because of her own financial status and the absence in the community of sufficient beds for those who lacked adequate funds or insurance coverage. In similar cases, the therapist had encouraged clients to make arrangements to have a trusted friend come by to stay with the client during periods of extreme dysfunction and suicidal risk. This client was so socially isolated, however, that she had no friends, and the therapist was unable to locate an individual— from local church and synagogue groups or from hospital volunteer organizations—who could stay with the client in times of crisis. Determined to come up with some arrangement that would help ensure the client's safety and welfare should the client experience a crisis and the therapist be unavailable, the therapist and client finally hit upon the possibility of the client going to the local hospital's waiting room. (The waiting room adjacent to the emergency room was open round-the-clock.) The therapist contacted hospital personnel to make sure that they would nave no objection to her patient showing up at odd hours to sit for indefinite periods of time in the waiting room.

The arrangement worked well during the remaining course of therapy. According to the client, simply knowing that there was some place for her to go frequently helped her to avoid becoming completely overwhelmed by external events or by her own feelings. On those occasions when she did feel herself to be in crisis and at risk for taking her own life, she found that going to the hospital waiting room seemed helpful; it made her feel more active and aware that she was doing something for herself. Being out of her rather depressing and claustrophobic apartment, sitting in a "clean, well-lighted place," and being around other people (who, because they were strangers, would be unlikely to make, in her words, "demands" on her) were all factors that helped her feel better. Knowing that there were health care professionals nearby (even though she had no contact with them) who could intervene should her impulses to take her own life become too much for her, and aware that she was carrying out a "treatment plan" that she and her therapist had developed together helped her to feel more calm, less isolated, and comforted in her time of crisis. The waiting-room strategy enabled this highly suicidal client to be treated safely, even though hospitalization was unfeasible, during the initial period of therapy when outpatient treatment alone seemed, in the judgment of both the therapist and an independent consultant, inadequate and when the client could not afford additional resources. It made imaginative use of resources that were readily available in the community and were accessible to the client.

Understanding the degree to which individual clinicians and mental health organizations will be accessible and will make help available is a crucial aspect of the patient's informed consent, the focus of the following chapter.

SCENARIOS FOR DISCUSSION

You are late for the airport, in danger of missing your plane (during a holiday season when it would be very hard to get space on a later flight) when you receive an emergency call from a local hospital. One of your therapy patients has tried to commit suicide and has been hospitalized. The patient is desperate to talk with you in person immediately, refusing to talk over the phone, about having just discovered a horrifying secret. You have no idea what the "secret" is.

1. How do you feel?
2. Are there any feelings about the patient, the emergency room staff person who called you, or the situation that are particularly difficult to acknowledge?
3. What are your immediate options?

4. What do you think you would do?

5. To what extent, if at all, do any concerns about a malpractice suit influence your judgment?

—∽—

A new client begins the first session by saying, "I need therapy because I lost my job, and my partner, with whom I lived for three years, left me for someone else. I don't know whether to kill myself, kill my boss, kill everyone else, or just try to hang on since now I'm all my little baby has left."

1. How do you feel?

2. Assuming that you cannot rule out that the person's threats are serious, what steps do you take in clarifying access to you and others before the patient leaves this first appointment?

3. What concerns, if any, do you have about this person's access to prompt and adequate help?

4. Is there anything you wish you would have told the person about availability, etc., *before* the person made the statements above?

—∽—

You work for a large managed care company, providing individual and family therapy full time. You meet with your manager late Friday afternoon and are told that the company has been taken over by a new owner who is merging several companies. There are now too many therapists and it is with the greatest regret that your manager tells you that reorganization has led to your no longer being retained by the company. This is your last day. Your patients are being re-assigned. You will be allowed to return to your office only with a security guard, will be able to stay only thirty minutes to clean out your desk, and you will not be allowed to copy any phone numbers or other information or to take any charts with you.

1. How do you feel?

2. What are your options?

3. What are your responsibilities?

4. What steps do you think you would take?

5. Would you make any effort to contact the patients you had been seeing? If so, how? And what would you tell them?

———

A former client, whom you had seen in therapy for three years, called in crisis. She said that she had started psychotherapy with someone else, given a change of jobs and a new insurance plan. You were not listed on the managed care provider list. But she cannot reach that new therapist during her crisis. Besides, she feels more comfortable with you.

1. What do you feel?

2. Do you have any legal or ethical obligations to this former client and, if so, what are they?

3. If you agree to talk with this client on the phone for a while, or meet with her for one or more crisis sessions, what legal, ethical, or clinical responsibilities, if any, do you have in regard to coordinating your work with her current managed care therapist?

4. Do you chart this phone call?

5. Do you have a clear policy regarding contacts with former clients? If so, are clients made aware of this policy prior to termination?

CHAPTER EIGHT

Informed Consent and Informed Refusal

Nothing blocks a patient's access to help with such cruel efficiency as a bungled attempt at informed consent. We may have struggled successfully with the challenges outlined in the previous chapter. The doors to our offices and clinics are open wide. The resources are all in place. But not even the most persistent patients can make their way past our intimidating forms (which clerks may shove at patients when they first arrive), our set speeches full of non-informative information, and our nervous attempts to meet externally imposed legalistic requirements. A first step in remedying the situation is to recognize that informed consent is not a static ritual but a useful process.

THE PROCESS OF INFORMED CONSENT

The process of informed consent provides both the patient and therapist with an opportunity to make sure that they adequately understand their shared venture. It is a process of communication and clarification. Does the therapist possess at least a sufficient initial understanding of why the patient is seeking help? Does the therapist know what the patient expects, or hopes, or fears from the assessment and therapy? Does the patient adequately understand the approach the clinician will be using to assess and address the problem? Does the patient know the common effects of using such an approach and alternative approaches to his or her problem?

Informed consent also involves making decisions. The patient must decide whether to undertake this course of assessment and treatment, whether to begin immediately or to delay, and whether to try an alternative approach or an alternative therapist. The therapist must decide whether the patient is competent to exercise informed consent (very young children may not be capable of providing fully informed consent but may be capable of giving or withholding assent) and whether the situation may justify an intervention in the absence of fully informed consent (the patient is threatening to kill his or her partner and is, in the therapist's judgment, likely to do so). The therapist must also consider whether a fully competent patient has been provided the relevant information with which to make a decision and sufficiently understands that information and whether the patient is providing consent on an adequately voluntary basis.

Finally, informed consent tends to be a recurrent process. The patient may consent to an initial psychological, neuropsychological, and medical assessment as well as to a course of individual psychotherapy based upon an initial, very provisional treatment plan. Several months into treatment, the treatment plan may be significantly altered on the basis of the results of the assessments, the patient's diverse reactions to various components of the treatment plan, and the patient's changing needs. As the treatment plan undergoes significant evolution, the patient must adequately understand these changes and voluntarily agree to them.

THE BASIS OF INFORMED CONSENT

Informed consent is an attempt to ensure that the trust required of the patient is truly justified, that the power of the therapist is not abused intentionally or inadvertently, and that the caring of the therapist is expressed in ways that the patient clearly understands and desires. Case law has provided a clear analysis of the basis and workings of informed consent. Much of this case law has concerned medical practice, but the relevance (not always complete) of the principles to clinical assessment and psychotherapy can be inferred.

Historically, the health care professions took a fairly arrogant and authoritarian position in regard to what the patient needed. Informed consent is a principle absent from the Hippocratic Oath. It was simply assumed that the doctor knew what was best. The patient obviously did not have sufficient training and knowledge, let alone objectivity, to determine what procedures were indicated.

A landmark in the shift away from this authoritarian approach appeared in a New York case. In 1914, Judge Benjamin Cordozo, who later became a justice of the U.S. Supreme Court, wrote that "every human being of adult years and sound mind has a right to determine what shall be done with his own body" (*Schloendorf* v. *Society of New York Hospital,* 1914, p. 93). It was not so much that this case changed the customary procedures by which doctors went about their work, it was more that Judge Cordozo articulated clearly the principle that it was the patient, rather than the doctor, who had the right to decide whether to undertake a specific treatment approach. The implications of this principle lay dormant for decades.

A second landmark appeared in 1960, in the Kansas case of *Natanson* v. *Kline.* The court reaffirmed the Cordozo principle: "Anglo-American law starts with the premise of thorough-going self-determination. It follows that each man is considered to be master of his own body" (p. 1104). The court stated that to make this determination, the patient obviously needed the relevant information. But what information was relevant was left entirely to the community of doctors to decide: "The duty . . . to disclose . . . is limited to those disclosures which a reasonable . . . practitioner would make under the same or similar circumstances. . . . So long as the disclosure is sufficient to assure an informed consent, the physician's choice of plausible courses should not be called into question if it appears, all circumstances considered, that the physician was motivated only by the patient's best therapeutic interests and he proceeded as competent medical men would have done in a similar situation" (1960, p. 1106). This case exemplifies the "community standard" rule: Informed consent procedures must adhere only to what the general community of doctors customarily do.

In 1972, with decisions handed down by the federal district court in Washington, D.C., and the California Supreme Court, the full implications of Judge Cordozo's principle were realized. The reasoning began with the reaffirmation of *Schloendorf* v. *Society of New York Hospital* (1914) and an emphasis that the patient must have relevant information that only the doctor can provide: "The root premise is the concept, fundamental in American jurisprudence, that '[e]very human being of adult years and sound mind has a right to determine what shall be done with his own body.' True consent to what happens to one's self is the informed exercise of a choice, and that entails an opportunity to evaluate knowledgeably the options available and the risks attendant upon each. The average patient has little or no understanding of the medical arts, and ordinarily has only his physician to whom he can look for enlightenment with which to reach an intelligent decision. From these almost axiomatic considerations springs the need, and in turn the requirement, of a reasonable divulgence by physician to patient to make such a decision possible" (*Canterbury* v. *Spence*, 1972, p. 780).

It is thus the patient, and not the doctor, who must make the final decision, and this decision, to be meaningful, must be based on an adequate range of information to be provided by the doctor: "[I]t is the prerogative of the patient, not the physician, to determine for himself the direction in which he believes his interests lie. To enable the patient to chart his course knowledgeably, reasonable familiarity with the therapeutic alternatives and their hazards becomes essential" (*Cobbs* v. *Grant*, 1972, p. 514).

This line of reasoning emphasized the exceptional trust and dependence inherent in health care, differentiating them from the milder versions of trust and dependence—often dealt with using a caveat emptor principle—characteristic of less intense, less intimate transactions in the marketplace: "A reasonable revelation in these aspects is not only a necessity but, as we see it, is as much a matter of the physician's duty. It is a duty to warn of the dangers lurking in the proposed treatment, and that is surely a facet of due care. It is, too, a duty to impart information which the patient has every right to expect. The patient's reliance upon the physician is a trust of the kind which traditionally has exacted obligations beyond those associated with arms-length transactions. His dependence upon the physician for information affecting his well-being, in terms of contemplated treatment, is well-nigh abject" (*Canterbury* v. *Spence*, 1972, p. 782).

This landmark case law specifically rejected the idea that doctors, through their "community standards," could determine what degree of information the patient should or should not have. It was not up to doctors, individually or collectively, to decide what rights a patient should have in regard to informed consent or to determine those rights indirectly by establishing "customary" standards regarding what information was and was not to be provided. Patients were held to have a right to make an informed decision and the courts were to guarantee that they had the relevant information for making the decision. The court observed, "We do not agree that the patient's cause of action is dependent upon the existence and nonperformance of a relevant professional tradition. . . . Respect for the patient's right of self-determination on particular therapy demands a standard set by law for physicians rather than one which physicians may or may not impose upon themselves" (*Canterbury* v. *Spence,* 1972, pp. 783–784).

The case law clearly states the need for doctors to provide adequate relevant information regardless of whether the patient actively asked the "right" questions in each area. Thus doctors were prevented from withholding or neglecting to provide relevant information because a patient did not inquire. The doctors were seen as having an affirmative duty to make an adequately full disclosure:

> We discard the thought that the patient should ask for information before the physician is required to disclose. Caveat emptor is not the norm for the consumer of medical services. Duty to disclose is more than a call to speak merely on the patient's request, or merely to answer the patient's questions: it is a duty to volunteer, if necessary, the information the patient needs for intelligent decision. The patient may be ignorant, confused, overawed by the physician or frightened by the hospital, or even ashamed to inquire. . . . Perhaps relatively few patients could in any event identify the relevant questions in the absence of prior explanation by the physician. Physicians and hospitals have patients of widely divergent socioeconomic backgrounds, and a rule which presumes a degree of sophistication which many members of society lack is likely to breed gross inequalities [*Canterbury* v. *Spence,* 1972, p. 783].

Realizing that some patients would certainly choose not to undertake specific assessment or treatment procedures, the courts emphasized that understanding what might happen as a result of *not* getting adequate assessment or treatment was as relevant to making an informed decision as understanding the assessment and treatment procedures themselves. Thus the California Supreme Court, in 1980, not only reaffirmed the principles previously set forth in *Canterbury* v.

Spence and *Cobbs* v. *Grant* but also affirmed that patients have a right to informed refusal of treatment as well as a right to informed consent to treatment: "The rule applies whether the procedure involves treatment or a diagnostic test. . . . If a patient indicates that he or she is going to *decline* a risk-free test or treatment, then the doctor has the additional duty of advising of all the material risks of which a reasonable person would want to be informed before deciding not to undergo the procedure. On the other hand, if the recommended test or treatment is itself risky, then the physician should always explain the potential consequences of declining to follow the recommended course of action" (*Truman* v. *Thomas,* 1980, p. 312).

Recognizing that some doctors might be intimidated by the daunting thought of presenting to patients essentially all they had learned during their training and that patients might be ill-suited recipients of jargon-filled lectures, the court emphasized that the patient needed only the relevant information to make an informed decision but needed it in clear, straightforward language: "The patient's interest in information does not extend to a lengthy polysyllabic discourse on all possible complications. A mini-course in medical science is not required" (*Cobbs* v. *Grant,* 1972, p. 515).

In summary, the courts, in the 1970s, tended to shift the locus of decision making clearly to the patient and the responsibility for ensuring that the decision was based upon adequate, relevant information clearly to the doctor. The California Supreme Court attempted to articulate the basis of this concept of informed consent:

We employ several postulates. The first is that patients are generally persons unlearned in the medical sciences and therefore, except in rare cases, courts may safely assume the knowledge of patient and physician are not in parity. The second is that a person of adult years and in sound mind has the right, in the exercise of control over his own body, to determine whether or not to submit to lawful medical treatment. The third is that the patient's consent to treatment, to be effective, must be an informed consent. And the fourth is that the patient, being unlearned in medical sciences, has an abject dependence upon and trust in his physician for the information upon which he relies during the decisional process, thus raising an obligation in the physician that transcends arm-length transactions. From the foregoing axiomatic ingredients emerges a necessity, and a resultant requirement, for divulgence by the physician to his patient of all information relevant to a meaningful decisional process [*Cobbs v. Grant*, 1972, p. 513].

These principles have begun to pass from case law into legislation. Indiana's House Enrolled Act of 1984, for example, stated, "All patients or clients are entitled to be informed of the nature of treatment or habilitation program proposed, the known effects of receiving and of not receiving such treatment or habilitation, and alternative treatment or habilitation programs, if any. An adult voluntary patient or client, if not adjudicated incompetent, is entitled to refuse to submit to treatment or to a habilitation program and is entitled to be informed of this right" (section F).

These principles are also reflected in the American Psychological Association's "Ethical Principles of Psychologists and Code of Conduct" (1992). For example, standard 4.01 requires that psychologists discuss with clients or patients, as "early as is feasible in the therapeutic relationship" (p. 1605), issues such as the nature and course of therapy, fees, and confidentiality, as well as whether the therapists work is supervised, including name of the supervisor, and that psychologists make efforts to answer questions, avoid misunderstandings about therapy, and provide oral and/or written information in language that is understandable to the client. Standard 4.02 requires that psychologists obtain informed consent to therapy and related procedures; the standard acknowledges that the content for informed consent will vary depending on several circumstances, but that informed consent generally implies that the person has the capacity to consent, has been informed of "significant information" (p. 1605) concerning the procedure, has freely expressed consent, and that consent has been appropriately documented. Standard 4.02 addresses the issue of "substitute consent" for those legally incapable of giving informed consent.

ADEQUATE INFORMATION

The information provided during the consent process will differ according to the professional service (for example, assessment, therapy) and other factors. However, any consent process can be evaluated in terms of whether it adequately addresses the following questions. This list may be useful in planning and in concurrent review of consent procedures in any setting.

• Does the client understand who is providing the service, and the clinician's qualifications (for example, license status)? If more than one person is involved (for example, a therapist and clinical supervisor—see Chapter Fifteen), does the client understand the nature and implications of this arrangement?

• Does the client understand the reason for the initial session? Although in many instances clients will have scheduled an initial appointment on their own initiative and for relatively clear reasons, in other instances they may have been referred by others (for example, an internist, a court) and not clearly understand the reason for the session.

• Does the client understand the nature, extent, and possible consequences of the services the clinician is offering? Does the client understand the degree to which there may be alternatives to the services provided by the clinician?

• Does the client understand actual or potential limitations to the services (for example, a managed care plan's limitation of eight therapy sessions; an insurance policy's limitation of coverage to a specific dollar amount) or to the clinician (for example, the therapist is an intern whose rotation will conclude in three months, after which he or she will no longer be available to the client)? Does the client understand how services may be terminated?

• Does the client understand fee policies and procedures, including information about missed or canceled appointments?

• Does the client understand policies and procedures concerning access to the clinician, to those providing coverage for the clinician, and to emergency services? For example, under what conditions, if any, will a therapist (or someone providing coverage) be available by phone between sessions during business hours, at night, or on weekends? Does the client understand limits to confidentiality in situations involving partner, family, or group psychotherapy? For a discussion of these issues, see Chapter Seven.

• Does the client understand exceptions to confidentiality, privilege, or privacy? For example, does the client understand the conditions, if any, under which the clinician might disclose information about the client to an insurance company, the police, or the courts? Does the person understand under what conditions other people in the setting (for example, clerical workers, clinical supervisors or consultants, administrative supervisors or other administrative staff, quality control personnel, utilization review committees, auditors, researchers) may learn about the client and the services provided to the client, whether through discussion (for example, case conferences, supervision, consultation) or writings (for example, clinical chart notes, treatment summaries, administrative records). For a discussion of these issues and exceptions, see Chapter Thirteen.

Appendix D presents a sample informed consent form, in this case for a somewhat complex situation: conducting a forensic assessment.

CONSIDERATIONS IN FULFILLING INFORMED CONSENT RESPONSIBILITIES

An unvarying and inflexible method does not exist for legitimately ensuring a client's informed consent. No method can relieve us of a thoughtful response to the particulars before us. All of us have developed unique and personal styles as therapists or counselors. Each of our clients is unique.

Informed consent is a recurrent process, not a static set of pro forma gestures, that develops out of the relationship between clinician and client. It must fit the situation and the setting. It must respond not only to the explicit standards of the clinician's professional associations, such as the American Psychological Association, but also to the relevant state and federal laws and to the evolving case law. It must be sensitive to the client's ability to understand (is the client a young child, developmentally disabled, suffering from severe thought disorder?), the relevant information, and the client's situation (is the client in the midst of a crisis, referred for mandatory treatment by the courts, being held against his or her will in a mental hospital?). Human sensitivity and professional judgment are required.

As we attempt to create and sustain the process of informed consent, several considerations, noted in the remainder of this chapter, are useful.

Failing to Provide Informed Consent

In considering how we are to meet the client's right to informed consent, we must remain aware that that right is violated, perhaps frequently. We can take those instances to justify our own decisions not to accord clients informed consent, or we can use those instances as an opportunity to consider the matter from the client's perspective.

How would we feel if we were the clients who had been kept in the dark, who had not been given the chance to make a decision on an informed basis?

One of the most egregious examples of the withholding of informed consent involved the provision of free medical care to hundreds of U.S. citizens (J. H. Jones, 1981; see also Rivers, Schuman, Simpson & Olansky, 1953; U.S. Public Health Service, 1973). The program began in 1932 and continued to 1972. If all we were told was that the government (through what eventually became the U.S. Public Health Service) was giving us comprehensive medical care, how would we likely feel? Grateful? Relieved that we would be spared financial burdens? Excited that we would have access to state-of-the-science medical interventions provided by the federal government? Who among us would turn down this rare opportunity?

What the participants of the Tuskegee syphilis study were not told is that they were being used to research the effects of syphilis when it goes untreated. Treatment for syphilis was in fact withheld from all the individuals. Research procedures were presented as treatment; for example, painful spinal taps were described to the subjects as a special medical treatment. Although Public Health Service officials denied that there were any racist aspects to this research, admission to the program was limited to male African Americans.

More recent examples are numerous. Hospitals, for example, may perform AIDS tests on virtually all patients without patients' knowledge or permission, sometimes in direct violation of state law (Pope & Morin, 1990). As another example, Stevens (1990) described a testing center that administered the Stanford-Binet Intelligence Scale so that students could be placed in the appropriate classes at school. The information schools received contradicted that given to the child's parents. In one case, for example, the report sent to the school "recommended that David be placed in a class for average students"; the report sent to the parents recommended that "David should be placed in a class for superior students" (p. 15). Here is how the testing center explained the policy: "The [report] we send to the school is accurate. The report for the parents is more soothing and positive" (p. 15).

How would we feel if we relied on the government and health care professions to provide us with free medical care when in fact they were observing the untreated consequences of a painful, virulent, usually fatal disease? How would we feel if we went to a hospital for help and were given an AIDS test without our knowledge or permission? How would we feel if we were given completely inaccurate information about the results of an intelligence assessment because someone else thought it would be "more soothing"?

Benefits of Informed Consent

Approaching the issue of informed consent, we may, as clinicians, fear that providing adequate information to clients and explicitly obtaining their consent will somehow derail therapy and may, in fact, have detrimental consequences for our clients. The research has not supported these fears. The process of informed consent tends to be beneficial. A variety of studies have indicated that the use of informed consent procedures makes it more likely that clients will become less anxious, follow the treatment plan, recover more quickly, and be more alert to unintended negative consequences of the treatment (Handler, 1990).

The Limits of Consent

Informed consent is not a strategy to insulate a clinician from responsibility when performing unethical or illegal acts.

> At least one case has suggested that there are limits to what a patient can validly consent to. In that case, several adults were treated with a form of psychotherapy that involved physically beating them. The defendants argued they could not be sued because the plaintiffs had consented to the treatment; however, the Court of Appeals refused to accept the consents as a defense. This decision implies that a patient's consent will not be deemed valid if acts consented to would otherwise be illegal or contrary to public policy (such as a sexual relationship between therapist and patient). An earlier case held that whether touching is therapeutic or nontherapeutic goes to the essence of the act and may vitiate a consent [Caudill & Pope, 1995, pp. 553–554].

Consent for Families and Other Multiple Clients

Individual psychotherapy is, of course, only one model for providing services. Sometimes clinicians will provide therapy to couples, families, or groups. Therapists must ensure that adequate informed consent and informed refusal are provided for each person, and that the consent addresses issues specific to therapy when more than one client is involved. For example, what are the limits of confidentiality and privilege for material disclosed by *one* of the clients? Will the therapist hold confidential from one family member material disclosed by another family member? If one client receiving couple therapy waives privilege, does the privilege still apply to the other member of the couple? What special issues of confidentiality and privilege arise when family therapy includes minors?

Unequal Opportunity for Informed Consent

It is crucial that we do not accord unequal opportunities to our clients for informed consent based upon prejudice and stereotypes (see Chapter Twelve). Research suggests that this unfortunately happens, at least occasionally, thus depriving some clients of their right to informed consent. For example, in an examination of informed consent practices, Benson (1984) found that whether important information was disclosed by a sample of physicians was systematically related to factors such as the patient's race and socioeconomic status.

Cognitive Processes

Clinicians must maintain a current knowledge of the evolving research and theory regarding the cognitive processes by which people arrive at decisions (see, for example, Bell, Raiffa & Tversky, 1989; Evans, 1989; Goldstein & Hogarth, 1997; Goleman, 1985; Janis, 1982; Kahneman, Slovic & Tversky, 1982; Langer, 1989; Pope, Butcher & Seelen, 1993; Rachim, 1989; Schick, 1997; Wang, 1993). This research and theory can help clinicians understand the factors that influence clients who are choosing whether to participate in assessment or treatment procedures.

At a Harvard University hospital, Barbara McNeil and her colleagues (1982) presented individuals with two options, based upon actuarial data concerning patients suffering from lung cancer. The actuarial data indicated whether patients had chosen a surgical or a radiological treatment for their cancer and what the outcome had been. Of those who chose surgery, 10 percent died during the operation itself, an additional 22 percent died within the first year after the surgery, and another 34 percent died within five years. Of those who chose radiation therapy, none died during the radiation treatments,

23 percent died within the first year, and an additional 55 percent died by the end of five years.

If you were given those actuarial data, which intervention would you choose? When these data were presented, 42 percent of the participants in the study indicated that they would choose radiation. Note that the data were presented in terms of mortality—the percentages of patients who died. When the same actuarial information was presented in terms of percentages of patients who survived at each stage—for radiation, 100 percent survived the treatment, 73 percent survived the first year, and 22 percent survived five years—only 25 percent chose radiation. The change from a mortality to a survivability presentation caused a change in the way individuals cognitively processed the information and arrived at a decision.

Because our interventions may have profound effects for our clients, and the decisions they may make regarding whether to begin therapy and what sort of therapeutic approaches to try are significant, we have an important ethical responsibility to attend carefully to the form in which we present information relevant to those decisions.

Problems with Forms

Many of us may be so eager to begin doing therapy that we do not feel inclined to make the effort to talk with our clients about the issues and information relevant to informed consent. We attempt to push all the responsibility off onto a set form, and we try to let the form do all the work. Those of us who work within clinics or hospitals may not even handle such forms. The client who shows up for an initial appointment may be handed an imposing-looking form by the receptionist, asked to read it, sign it, and return it before seeing the therapist. The form itself may have been crafted by the clinic or hospital's attorney and may not even have been reviewed by a clinician. The wording may be in intimidating legalese and bureaucratic jargon. Such forms may be intended more to protect the organization against lawsuits than to enable the client to understand the options and to make reasonable decisions.

Providing information in written form can be vital in ensuring that clients have the information they need. But the form cannot be a substitute for an adequate process of informed consent. At a minimum, the clinician must discuss the information with the client and arrive at a professional judgment that the client has adequate understanding of the relevant information.

Clinicians using consent forms must ensure that their clients have the requisite reading skills. Illiteracy is a major problem in the United States; clinicians cannot simply assume that all of their clients can read. Moreover, some clients may not be well versed in English, perhaps having only rudimentary skills in spoken English as a second or third language.

Not only must the client be able to read but the form itself also must be readable. Grundner (1980, p. 900) noted that great effort has been made to ensure that "consent forms have valid content, but little effort has been made to ensure that the average person can read and understand them." He obtained five forms and analyzed them with two standardized readability tests. He found that "the readability of all five was approximately equivalent to that of material intended for upper division undergraduates or graduate students. Four of the five forms were written at the level of a scientific journal, and the fifth at the level of a specialized academic magazine" (p. 900).

Reading a form does not ensure that the client understands the material or can remember it even a short time later. Robinson & Merav (1976) re-interviewed twenty patients four to six months after they had read and signed a form for informed consent and had undergone treatment. They found that all patients showed poor recall regarding all aspects of the information covered by the form, including the diagnosis, potential complications, and alternate methods of management. Cassileth, Zupkis, Sutton-Smith, & March (1980) found that only one day after reading and signing a form for informed consent, only 60 percent of the patients understood the purpose and nature of the procedures. A perfunctory indication from clients that they understand can be unreliable (Irwin et al., 1985). The clinician bears the responsibility for ensuring that the client actually understands the information. Determining the client's ability to understand as well as the degree to which he or she actually does understand relevant information is part of the larger task of assessment, the subject of the next chapter.

SCENARIOS FOR DISCUSSION

You work full time for an HMO that requires the clinician to obtain written informed consent from all patients before providing psychotherapy. One of the HMO physicians refers a patient to you for psychotherapy. When the patient shows up for the initial session, you discover that the patient has recently been permanently blinded by an explosion and wants help in making the transition to living without reliance on this particular sense.

1. How do you feel?

2. What are the initial consent issues that you consider?

3. In what ways, if at all, should the consent process explicitly address therapeutic approaches specifically developed for those without sight?

4. If you were not fluent in Braille, the HMO provided no consent forms in Braille, and no HMO employee could write in Braille, how would you approach the HMO's requirement that written consent be obtained before clinical services were provided?

5. If the patient asked whether any of the interventions you planned to use had been validated as effective for those without sight, how would you respond?

6. If the patient asked whether your graduate training and supervised experience included adequate work with sightless patients so that you were competent to provide services to this population, how would you respond?

—⌇—

You work for a managed care facility that allows no more than eight sessions of outpatient psychotherapy in any given year. A new patient tells you during the first session that surprising and intrusive memories have started to occur about the patient's experiencing incest when a child. The patient thinks that the parent who perpetrated the incest may now be sexually abusing several grandchildren.

1. How do you feel?

2. What are the informed consent and informed refusal issues, if any, that you consider during this initial session regarding a formal assessment of this patient?

3. What are the informed consent and informed refusal issues, if any, that you consider during this initial session regarding potential clinical interventions for this patient?

—⌇—

You have just begun working as a counselor at a university counseling center. At your first meeting with the counseling center director, you ask whether they have consent forms. The director replies, "I'm so glad you brought that up. We've been leaving that up to individual counselors but we need one that everyone can use. I've been looking at your c.v. and I think you're the perfect person to design the form. Please have it on my desk by next Thursday."

1. How do you feel?
2. Assuming that there is no way you can get out of this task, what process would you use for designing the form?
3. What issues or elements are you sure the informed consent form should address?

―᷾ᨓ᷾―

You have agreed to provide psychotherapy to an adolescent who had gotten in trouble for drinking. The parents have agreed to allow the sessions to be confidential, given your ethical responsibilities. However, they now request to see the records because they have reason to believe that their adolescent is smoking pot.

1. How do you feel?
2. What are the legal and ethical factors you consider?
3. What do you think you might say to the parents?
4. What do you think you might say to your client?
5. To what extent does your form for informed consent adequately address the issues that this scenario raises?

―᷾ᨓ᷾―

You are a provider of services for a managed care company. Utilization reviews are required before additional sessions are provided. You realize, during the review, that although you believe sexual orientation to be a critical issue and focus for your gay client, you did not inform your client that the information would be revealed to the reviewer.

1. How do you feel?
2. What consent issues does this situation involve?

3. What possible approaches do you consider in deciding how to handle this situation?

4. What information concerning utilization review, peer review, and similar review processes should an adequate form for informed consent and informed refusal contain?

CHAPTER NINE

Assessment, Testing, and Diagnosis

D iagnosis, testing, and assessment can greatly affect our clients. Improper diagnoses can deprive clients of appropriate and effective treatment. Jobs and promotions may be unavailable, freedom from prisons or locked wards may be denied, and custody hearings may be lost, all on the basis of a test report.

Those of us who practice within institutional settings may face externally imposed limitations on the time and other resources we can devote to assessment. Those of us who practice independently rather than within institutional settings, however, may face challenges in consistently performing evaluations that are ethical, accurate, useful, and consistent with the latest advances in research and theory. We tend to lack the "ready-made" professional support, educational resources, and peer review characteristic of many clinics and hospitals, with their in-service training programs, grand rounds, case conferences, and program evaluation. We may need to be more active in updating, improving, and monitoring our evaluation services.

The following considerations are useful in identifying ethical pitfalls and in helping to ensure that diagnosis, testing, and assessment are as valid and useful as possible for both clinician and client.

AWARENESS OF STANDARDS
AND GUIDELINES

The American Psychological Association publishes several documents relevant to testing, assessment, and diagnosis (see Chapter Two). Reviewing them on a periodic basis can help ensure that work in this area meets the highest standards. The most relevant documents include *Standards for Educational and Psychological Testing* [1985, revision in progress; co-authored with the American Educational Research Association (AERA) and the National Council on Measurement in Education (NCME)] and the "Ethical Principles of Psychologists and Code of Conduct" (APA, 1992). Ethical standard 2 of the ethics code is entitled "Evaluation, Assessment, or Intervention" and has ten specific enforceable rules of conduct. The *Casebook on Ethical Principles of Psychologists* (APA, 1987a) presents vignettes illustrating common violations of principle 8.

STAYING WITHIN AREAS
OF COMPETENCE

A psychology degree from a particular program, a specific internship experience, and a license to practice psychology do not, in and of themselves, qualify a professional to administer, score, interpret, or otherwise use psychological tests (see Chapter Five).

Hall and Hare-Mustin (1983, p. 718) reported an APA ethics case in which "one psychologist charged another with incompetence, especially in testing. . . . CSPEC (Committee on Scientific and Professional Ethics and Conduct) [Authors' note: CSPEC was the former name of the APA Ethics Committee] reviewed the report of the state committee, which had carried out the investigation, and found that the person had no training or education in principles of psychological testing but was routinely engaged in evaluations of children in child custody battles. The committee found violation of principle 2a, competence in testing, and stipulated that the member should work under the supervision of a clinical psychologist for one year. To conduct psychological testing, one must have competence in psychological testing. This competence cannot merely be asserted, but must be shown to have developed through formal education, training, and experience (see Chapter Five). This point is relevant to the process of diagnosis, evaluation, and assessment more generally, even if testing were not involved. For example, when the diagnosis is based upon interview and observation, training and supervised experience in those assessment methods are necessary.

UNDERSTANDING MEASUREMENT, VALIDATION, AND RESEARCH

Being able to document substantial course work, supervised training, and extensive experience in a given area of testing such as neuropsychological assessment of geriatric populations, intelligence testing of young children, or personality testing of adults helps a professional to establish competence in that area of testing in an ethics committee hearing, licensing hearing, or malpractice suit. But beyond this evidence of competence, one must also be able to demonstrate understanding of measurement, validation, and research.

Sanders and Keith-Spiegel (1980) described an APA ethics case in which a psychologist evaluated a person via a Minnesota Multiphasic Personality Inventory (MMPI), among other resources. The person who was evaluated felt that the test report, particularly the part based upon the MMPI results, was inaccurate. All materials, including the test report and raw data, were eventually submitted to the APA Ethics Committee, which in turn submitted the materials for evaluation to two independent diplomates with expertise in testing.

The committee concluded that the psychologist did not demonstrate an adequate understanding of measurement, validation, and inference in his report: "The only test used by the complainee that has any established validity in identifying personality disorders is the MMPI, and none of the conclusions allegedly based on the MMPI are accurate. We suspect that the complainee's conclusions are based upon knowledge of a previous psychotic episode and information from the psychiatric consultant, whose conclusions seem to have been accepted uncritically. The complainee's report is a thoroughly unprofessional performance, in our opinion. Most graduate students would do much better" (Sanders & Keith-Spiegel, 1980, p. 1098).

Principle 2.02, "Competence and Appropriate Use of Assessments and Intervention" of the "Ethical Principles of Psychologists and Code of Conduct" (APA, 1992, p. 1603) summarizes this requirement: "A) psychologists who develop, administer, score, interpret or use psychological assessment techniques, interviews, tests or instruments do so in a manner and for purposes that are appropriate in light of the research on or evidence of the usefulness and proper application of the techniques; B) psychologists refrain from misuse of assessment techniques, interventions, results and interpretations and take reasonable steps to prevent others from misusing the information these techniques provide."

ENSURING THAT THE CLIENT UNDERSTANDS AND CONSENTS TO TESTING

Ensuring that a client fully understands the nature, purposes, and techniques of a given instrument helps fulfill the client's right to give or withhold informed consent to any phase of assessment or treatment (see Chapter Eight). Determining that the client understands the testing is different from just providing information aloud or in written form. Some clients may be anxious, distracted, preoccupied, or so eager to please the clinician that they nod their heads as though to acknowledge that they understand an explanation when, in fact, they have understood none or little of the information. Some clients are unfamiliar with technical terms and concepts that the clinician tends to take for granted. Often this lack of communication is worsened by the clinician's eagerness to proceed with the testing and the client's fear of appearing ignorant.

It is the clinician's responsibility to make the necessary effort to provide a fully understandable explanation and to form a professional opinion regarding whether a client understands and consents. Ethical standard 2.09, "Explaining Assessment Results," of the "Ethical Principles of Psychologists and Code of Conduct" (APA, 1992, p. 1604) defines this professional responsibility as follows: "Unless the nature of the relationship is clearly explained to the person being assessed in advance and precludes provision of an explanation of results (such as in some organizational consulting, pre-employment or security screenings, and forensic evaluations), psychologists ensure that an explanation of the results is provided using language that is reasonably understandable to the person assessed or to another legally authorized person on behalf of the client, regardless of whether the scoring and interpretation are done by the psychologist, by assistants, or by automated or other outside services, psychologists take reasonable steps to ensure that appropriate explanations of results are given."

To be adequately informed, the consent must be given or withheld in light of adequate knowledge about who will or may receive the results (see Chapter Thirteen). Although these issues concern the variety of people who may eventually receive copies of the report and the associated raw data once the assessment has been completed, they must be addressed with the client *before* starting the assessment, so that the client's decision to give or withhold consent is adequately informed. The following section discusses clarifying these issues.

CLARIFYING ACCESS TO THE TEST REPORT AND RAW DATA

Psychologists function within a complex framework of legal and ethical standards regarding the discretionary and mandatory release of test information. The Privacy Act of 1974, the California "truth in testing" statute, and *Detroit Edison Company* v. *National Labor Relations Board* are examples of federal and state legislation and case law that make test information more accessible to consumers.

The APA's Committee on Psychological Tests and Assessment (1996) issued a statement addressing the concerns of psychologists who develop, validate, and use tests in a variety of settings regarding the issue of disclosure of test data. The statement addresses various dilemmas regarding disclosure of test data, which may include an individual's test results, raw test data, records, written or computer-generated reports, and test scores and materials, including those materials considered secure by the test developer or publisher. The "Statement on the Disclosure of Test Data" provides helpful discussion of ethical aspects of situations such as releasing test data with or without the consent of the test taker, releasing data while maintaining test security, releasing data only to qualified persons, protecting copyright interests when releasing data, conforming to federal and state statutes and rules, regulations, and court precedents, releasing test data to third-party payers, and releasing test data when the organization is the client.

The following fictional vignette illustrates the complex judgments psychologists may have to make regarding responsibilities to withhold or disclose assessment information:

A seventeen-year-old boy comes to your office and asks for a comprehensive psychological evaluation. He has been experiencing some headaches, anxiety, and depression. A high-school dropout, he has been married for a year and has a one-year-old baby, but has left his wife and child and returned to live with his parents. He works full time as an auto mechanic and has insurance that covers the testing procedures. You complete the testing. During the following year you receive requests for information about the testing from

- The boy's physician, an internist
- The boy's parents, who are concerned about his depression
- The boy's employer, in connection with a worker's compensation claim filed by the boy
- The attorney for the insurance company that is contesting the worker's compensation claim
- The attorney for the boy's wife, who is suing for divorce and for custody of the baby
- The boy's attorney, who is considering suing you for malpractice because he does not like the results of the tests

Each of the requests asks for the full formal report, the original test data, and copies of each of the tests you administered (for example, instructions and all items for the MMPI-II).

To which of these people are you ethically or legally obligated to supply all information requested, partial information, a summary of the report, or no information at all? For which requests is having the boy's written informed consent for release of information relevant?

There is no set of answers to these complex questions that would be generally applicable for all or even most readers. Each state has its own evolving legislation and case law that address, sometimes in an incomplete or confusing manner, clinician responsibilities. Such questions can, however, provide a basis for discussion in ethics courses, in clinical supervision and consultation, in staff meetings, or in workshops; answers can be sought that are relevant for a specific state. Practitioners may want to consider working through their state associations to develop clear guidelines to the current legal requirements. If the legal requirements in this or any other area of practice seem unethical, unreasonable, unclear, or potentially damaging to clients, practitioners may want to propose and support remedial legislation.

FOLLOWING STANDARD PROCEDURES FOR ADMINISTERING TESTS

When we are reciting the instructions to the Wechsler Intelligence Scale for Children-Revised (WISC-R) or the Halstead Category Test for the 500th time, we may experience the urge to break the monotony, to get creative, to let our originality show through. And, particularly when we are in a hurry, we may want to abbreviate the instructions. After all, the client will catch on as the subtest progresses.

The assumption underlying standardized tests is that the test-taking situation and procedures are as similar as possible for everyone. When one departs from the procedures on which the norms are based, the standardized norms lose their direct applicability and the "standard" inferences drawn from those norms become questionable. Standard 6.2 of the *Standards for Educational and Psychological Testing* (APA, 1985, p. 41) states: "When a test user makes a substantial change in test format, mode of administration, instructions, language, or content, the user should revalidate the use of the test for the changed conditions or have a rationale supporting the claim that additional validation is not necessary or possible."

The Committee on Professional Standards of the APA (1984) published a finding that allowing a client to take home a test such as the MMPI departs from the "standard procedure." The "Casebook for Providers of Psychological Services" (Committee on Professional Standards, 1984) describes a case in which a psychologist permitted his client to take home the MMPI to complete. When the complaint was filed with APA, the Committee on Professional Standards stated that whenever a psychologist "does not have direct, first-hand information as to the condition under which the test is taken, he or she is forced (in the above instance, unnecessarily) to assume that the test responses were not distorted by the general situation in which the test was taken (for example, whether the client consulted others about test responses). Indeed the psychologist could have no assurance that this test was in fact completed by the client. In the instance where the test might be introduced as data in a court proceeding it would be summarily dismissed as hearsay evidence" (p. 664).

AWARENESS OF BASIC ASSUMPTIONS

Our most fundamental assumptions or theoretical frameworks can significantly affect our assessments. Langer & Abelson's (1974) classic study, "A Patient by Any Other Name . . . ," for example, illustrates one way in which behavior therapists and psychoanalytically oriented therapists can differ when viewing the same individual: "Clinicians representing two different schools of thought, behavioral and analytic, viewed a single videotaped interview between a man who had recently applied for a new job and one of the authors. Half of each group was told that the interviewee was a 'job applicant,' while the remaining half was told that he was a 'patient.' At the end of the videotape, all clinicians were asked to complete a questionnaire evaluating the interviewee. The interviewee was described as fairly well adjusted by the behavioral therapists regardless of the label supplied. This was not the case, however, for the more traditional therapists. When the interviewee was labeled 'patient,' he was described as significantly more disturbed than he was when he was labeled 'job applicant'" (p. 4).

The point here is not whether either of these two orientations is more valid, reliable, respectable, empirically based, or useful, but rather to illustrate the obvious: Various basic theoretical orientations can lead to very different assessments. Psychologists conducting assessments and assigning diagnoses need to be continually aware of their own theoretical orientation and how this orientation is likely to affect the evaluation. Langer and Abelson (1974, p. 9) state clearly: "Despite the questionable light in which the analytic therapist group was cast in the present study, one strongly suspects that conditions might be arranged wherein the behavior therapists would fall into some kind of error, as much as the traditionalists. No single type of orientation toward clinical training is likely to avoid all types of biases or blind spots."

AWARENESS OF PERSONAL FACTORS LEADING TO MISUSING DIAGNOSIS

In addition to a lack of awareness of our basic assumptions and our assumptions in specialty areas, insufficient attention to our own personal reactions and dynamics may tend to make us vulnerable to faulty evaluations. Reiser & Levenson's (1984) excellent article "Abuses of the Borderline Diagnosis" focuses on six ways in which the diagnosis of borderline personality disorder is commonly abused "to express countertransference hate, mask imprecise thinking, excuse treatment failures, justify the therapist's acting out, defend against sexual clinical material, and avoid pharmacologic and medical treatment interventions" (p. 1528). Openness to such issues within ourselves and frequent consultations with colleagues can help prevent abuses of this kind and help ensure that our assessments meet the highest ethical standards.

AWARENESS OF FINANCIAL FACTORS LEADING TO MISUSING DIAGNOSIS

Third-party reimbursement has become so prevalent that most psychologists have become acutely aware of which diagnostic categories are "covered" and which are not. Insurance companies, HMOs, and a wide variety of managed care organizations may authorize services only for a very restricted range of diagnoses. For example, the personality or character disorders are rarely covered. Unfortunately, the temptation to substitute a fraudulent but "covered" diagnosis for an honest but unreimbursable one can influence even senior and well-respected practitioners, as shown in a national study (Pope & Bajt, 1988). Kovacs (1987), in his strongly worded article on insurance billing, issues a stern warning that those "who are naive about insurance billing or who play a little fast and loose with carriers are beginning to play Russian Roulette. The carriers are now prepared to spend the necessary funds for investigators and for lawyers which will be required to sue in civil court and/or to bring criminal charges against colleagues who do not understand their ethical and legal responsibility in completing claim forms on behalf of their patients" (p. 24).

The article "Advice on Ethics of Billing Clients" (1987) in the *APA Monitor* lists among "billing practices that should be avoided": "Changing the diagnosis to fit reimbursement criteria" (p. 42; see also Ethics Committee of the American Psychological Association, 1988b; standards 1.25, "Fees and Financial Arrangements," 1.26, "Accuracy in Reports to Payors and Funding Sources," and 1.27, "Referrals and Fees" in the APA ethics code, 1992).

In addition, many organized systems of care, such as managed care, have reduced reimbursement for assessment to one hour. Often, a full evaluation to determine accurate diagnoses requires several hours of testing and report preparation. Either the provider of services must provide rationale for further reimbursement or provide pro bono services.

ACKNOWLEDGING THE
LOW BASE RATE PHENOMENON

When a particular diagnostic category or an attribute being assessed rarely occurs in the population, ignoring this fact can lead to significant error in conducting evaluations. Even when the psychological tests are accurate, the statistical properties of a phenomenon with a low base rate can cause problems. Perhaps the most frequently cited example concerns assessing individuals for the potential for lethal violence: "Assume that one person out of a thousand will kill. Assume also that an exceptionally accurate test is created which differentiates with 95 percent effectiveness those who will kill from those who will not. If 100,000 people were tested, out of the 100 who would kill, 95 would be isolated. Unfortunately, out of the 99,900 who would not kill, 4,995 people would also be isolated as potential killers" (Livermore, Malmquist & Meehl, 1968, p. 84).

AWARENESS OF FORENSIC ISSUES

Our society has become more litigious, and we tend to find ourselves, as psychologists, appearing in court more frequently or preparing documents that will become part of legal proceedings. Forensic settings set forth specific demands, and practitioners need to become aware of them. For example, financial factors (see previous section "Awareness of Financial Factors Leading to Misusing Diagnosis") can, under certain circumstances, create a bias—or at least the appearance of bias—in carrying out and reporting assessments. For this reason, forensic texts mandate that no psychologist accept a contingency fee. Blau (1984, p. 336) wrote: "The psychologist should never accept a fee contingent upon the outcome of a case." Shapiro (1990, p. 230) stated: "The expert witness should never, under any circumstances, accept a referral on a contingent fee basis." Only about 15 percent of the respondents in a national survey reported engaging in this practice (Pope, Tabachnick, & Keith-Spiegel, 1987), and about the same percentage (14 percent) believe it to be good practice or good under most circumstances (Pope, Tabachnick, & Keith-Spiegel, 1988).

Another potentially troublesome area in forensic practice involves conducting child custody assessments. Shapiro (1990, p. 99) for example, states that "under no circumstances should a report on child custody be rendered to the court, based on the evaluation of only one party to the conflict." "Guidelines for Child Custody Evaluations in Divorce Proceedings" (APA, 1994) provides guidance for psychologists in this area. According to this document, the best interest of the child is the primary purpose of the evaluation and is considered paramount.

The current APA (1992) ethics code offers guidance specifically on forensic issues; section 7 includes six standards. In addition, frequent consultation with those who are well trained and experienced in forensic practice, particularly those who are Fellows of APA Division 41 and who hold a forensic diplomate, can be useful in becoming aware of and avoiding the pitfalls of conducting and reporting assessments in the forensic arena.

ATTENTION TO POTENTIAL MEDICAL CAUSES

Particularly when a constellation of symptoms fits a well-known psychological diagnosis, it is tempting to ignore possible medical causes for a distress or disability (such as pain, weight loss, or bleeding from bodily orifices). A comprehensive evaluation, however, needs to rule out (or identify) possible medical causes. Rick Imbert, president of the American Professional Agency, stresses that "if there is any indication of a physical problem, then have a full medical screening; for example, symptoms which appear to be part of a schizophrenic process can actually be caused by a brain tumor" (personal communication, April 18, 1988).

AWARENESS OF PRIOR RECORDS AND HISTORY

Prior records of assessment and treatment can be an invaluable resource as part of a comprehensive psychological evaluation. The courts have held that neglecting to make any effort to recognize, obtain, and use this resource violates, in some instances, the standard of care. In the federal case of *Jablonski* v. *United States* (1983), for example, the U.S. Ninth Circuit Court of Appeals upheld a "district court judge's findings of malpractice . . . for failure to obtain the past medical records."

Regardless of whether prior records exist or are obtainable, obtaining an adequate history can be crucial to an adequate assessment.

Psychologist Laura Brown (1994), for instance, discussed the pioneering work of independent practitioner Lynne Rosewater and George Washington University professor Mary Anne Dutton in demonstrating how overlooked history could lead to misdiagnosis when relying on standardized tests.

> Their work has involved collecting data on large numbers of battered women and identifying common patterns of response on the testing. In effect, they have noted that the standard mainstream texts and computerized scoring systems for the MMPI do not take into account the possibility that the person taking the test is a woman who currently is, or recently has been, beaten by her spouse or partner. . . .
>
> As Rosewater first pointed out, without the context, specifically the identification of the presence of violence, battered women look like schizophrenics or borderline personalities on the MMPI. With the context of violence explicitly framing the interpretation of the test findings, however, it is possible to note that the sort of distress indicated on the testing is a reasonable response to events in the test-taker's life. That is to say, when a woman's partner is beating her, it makes sense that she is depressed, confused, scattered, and feeling overwhelmed. It is not necessarily the case that this state of response to life-threatening violence is either usual for the woman in question or a sign of psychopathology [L. S. Brown, 1994, p. 187].

INDICATING ALL RESERVATIONS ABOUT RELIABILITY AND VALIDITY

If any circumstances might have affected the results of psychological testing, such as dim lighting, frequent interruptions, a noisy environment, or medication, or if there is doubt that the person being tested shares all relevant characteristics with the reference groups on which the norms are based, these factors must be taken into account when interpreting test data and must be included in the formal report. Ethical standard 2.05, "Interpreting Assessment Results" (APA, 1992, p. 1603), states: "When interpreting assessment results, including automated interpretations, psychologists take into account the various test factors and characteristics of the person being assessed that might affect psychologists' judgments or reduce the accuracy of their interpretations. They indicate any significant reservations they have about the accuracy or limitations of their interpretations."

One implication of this responsibility is that psychologists must remain alert to the diverse array of factors that may affect validity and reliability. For example, psychologists have a responsibility to understand the issues related to test bias and unfairness in testing. A test user evaluates the validity of an intended interpretation and use of test scores by relying on all the available evidence relevant to the technical quality of testing system, including evidence of careful test construction, adequate score reliability, appropriate test administration and scoring, accurate score scaling, equating, and standard setting, and careful attention to fairness for all examinees (APA, AERA, NCME, 1985, revision in progress).

In addition, psychologists who test individuals whose first language is not English face a challenge to determine whether the testing in English is appropriate. Often, referral of the client to a mental health professional who is competent in the client's language may be important. If translation is necessary, psychologists do not retain the services of translators or paraprofessionals, who may have a dual role with the client, to avoid jeopardizing the validity of evaluation or the effectiveness of intervention. Various other issues of validity of particular tests with a client whose language or culture is different are addressed is the new draft of the test standards (APA, AERA, NCME, 1985, revision in progress).

The APA's "Ethical Principles of Psychologists and Code of Conduct" (1992, p. 1603) standard 2.04c, "Use of Assessment in General and with Special Populations," states: "Psychologists attempt to identify situations in which particular interventions or assessment techniques or norms may not be applicable or may require adjustment in administration or interpretation because of factors such as individuals' gender, age, race, ethnicity, national origin, religion, sexual orientation, disability, language, or socioeconomic status."

PROVIDING ADEQUATE FEEDBACK

Feedback is a dynamic, interactive process in which the results and implications of testing or other forms of assessment are shared with the person who is being assessed (Pope, 1992). Many factors can block this process. First, HMOs and other managed care organizations can inflict harsh, sometimes unrealistic demands on a clinician's time. The rationing of time may allow too little opportunity to sit down with a client to discuss an assessment and attend carefully to the client's questions and concerns. Similarly, federal, state, and private mental health insurance may disallow coverage for all but the most minimal feedback session. For example, there may be a standard, fixed payment for administrating a specific psychological test; the payment may barely (sometimes inadequately) cover the time necessary to administer the test and prepare a brief write-up of the results. The clinician may have to donate pro bono the time required to provide adequate feedback.

Second, advertisements and marketing literature may promote individual tests, versions of tests, or test batteries by stressing how little time they take. One continually reads of quick, brief, short, and abbreviated tests. Such promotion may unintentionally nurture the notion that a complex assessment can be carried out in just a few minutes with no real demands on the clinician's time, skills, judgment, or even attention. This "rush to judgment" may encourage clinicians to match their quick, brief, short, and abbreviated testing with quick, brief, short, and abbreviated feedback.

Third, on a personal level, therapists and counselors may be uncomfortable discussing assessment results with a client. Some may be reluctant to be the bearer of what they fear the client will receive as "bad news." Others may be uncomfortable trying to translate for the client the technical jargon that clogs so many test interpretation texts, computer interpretation printouts, volumes on diagnosis, and so forth. Still others may be uneasy facing a client's expectations of clear results with test results that may necessarily leave many important questions unanswered.

These and other factors may encourage clinicians to forget that feedback is a dynamic, interactive process that is an aspect of the larger process of assessment, and that the assessment often continues during what is called the *feedback session* or *phase*. Consequently, feedback may come to be viewed as simply a pro forma, static method of closure or an obligatory technicality in which the "results" are dumped in the client's lap (or referral source, etc.); this view of feedback seems so aversive and unproductive that some clinicians may decide—wrongly—to withhold feedback altogether. No rote, by-the-numbers approach to feedback can legitimately replace a thoughtful discussion with the client of what the results are, what they mean, and what they do not mean.

SCENARIOS FOR DISCUSSION

You are attending your first rounds at the community mental health center where you began working last week. Your supervisor discusses a recent intake who will be assigned to you for therapy. The supervisor, who assessed the new patient using the MMPI-II and a clinical interview, says that the assessment shows that the patient's claims about being raped are clearly false. The treatment plan, which you will be implementing, will be to help the new patient realize that this confabulation is not real.

1. How do you feel?

2. What options do you have?

3. What would you like to say?

4. What do you think that you would say?

You work for an HMO. A new patient shows up at your office for an initial session. The person says: "I have felt so incredibly edgy all week. I don't know what's wrong with me. But I feel like I want to smash someone in the mouth, like I want to get my gun and blow someone's brains out. I don't even know who, but it's like something's building up and it just won't be stopped."

1. How do you feel?

2. When the person stopped talking, what would be the first things you'd say?

3. How do you go about creating an assessment plan in this situation? What phases of the assessment would you make sure to complete before the person left your office, and how would you go about completing them? What phases of the assessment would you schedule for later? Who else, if anyone, would you involve in the assessment?

You are responsible for all intakes on Mondays, Wednesdays, and Fridays. After discussing recent intakes with you, your supervisor tells you: "From now on, I want to obtain standardized testing data on all intakes. I want you to administer the _____ to all intakes. I think we need to base our decisions on test data." You believe that the _____ is not a useful test and that it lacks adequate validity and reliability for clinical work. You diplomatically say that you aren't sure about giving the _____, but your supervisor says, "I can understand that. No method is endorsed by everyone. But I'm responsible for intakes and I'll take responsibility for this. All you need to do is administer, score, and interpret them."

1. How do you feel?

2. What would you like to say?

3. What do you think you'd end up saying?

4. What are your options?

5. What would you do?

—⁓—

A parent schedules an appointment with you. The parent shows up with a child, and says, "The people at school say that my Jesse here cheats at school. Can you talk with Jesse and give some tests to find out if that's true?"

1. How do you feel?

2. What are your options?

3. What ethical concerns do you have? How would you address them?

—⁓—

A former client, whom you liked very much, calls and reports that she and her spouse are now getting divorced. The client asks to return for an evaluation, as requested by her attorney, regarding a child custody dispute. She expresses her assumption that you will testify in court on her behalf.

1. How do you feel?

2. What are your options?

3. What issues do you consider?

4. How do you think you would respond?

—⁓—

An attorney calls to ask you to provide a basic evaluation for a client who will be deported unless proof can be provided that the attorney's client is under severe duress as a refugee. The hearing is in one week and the attorney says that no other resources for obtaining an evaluation are available, and that there are waiting lists at the clinics providing such evaluations. The hearing judge has refused to grant an extension. The client does not speak English but has a family member who can interpret. You do not speak the client's language. You have attended multicultural diversity workshops and classes.

1. How do you feel?

2. What issues do you consider in deciding whether to schedule the assessment?

3. What assessment approaches, including any standardized tests, would you consider in planning such an evaluation?

4. Assume that you had agreed to conduct the assessment. When you began, you found that the family member had minimal skills in speaking English. What would you do?

CHAPTER TEN

Sexual Relationships with Clients

One of the oldest ethical mandates in the health care professions is the prohibition against engaging in sexual involvement with a patient. Brodsky (1989) notes that this rule is in fact older than the 2,500-year-old Hippocratic Oath; it was mentioned in the even more ancient code of the Nigerian healing arts.

The modern codes of clinical ethics contained no explicit mention of this topic until research began revealing that substantial numbers of therapists were violating the prohibition. Although the codes had not highlighted this particular form of patient exploitation by name, therapist-patient sex was in violation of various sections of the codes prior to the 1970s. Hare-Mustin (1974), a former chair of the American Psychological Association's Ethics Committee, for example, noted that the 1963 "Ethical Standards of Psychologists" of the American Psychological Association contained standards that would prohibit therapist-patient sexual involvement. She stated that in light of "a review of principles relating to competency, community standards and the client relationship that genital contact with patients is ethically unacceptable" (p. 310). Similarly, UCLA Professor Jean Holroyd, senior author of the first national study of therapist-patient sex, explained that the 1977 code did not represent a change in the standards regarding sexual activities with patients.

ADMINISTRATIVE LAW JUDGE: Was it [the 1977 ethics code] a codification of what was already the standard of practice?

HOLROYD: Yes, it was making it very explicit in the ethics code.

ADMINISTRATIVE LAW JUDGE: What I am asking is whether or not the standard of practice prior to the inclusion of that specific section in the [1977] ethics code, whether or not that changed the standard of practice.

HOLROYD: No, it did not change the standard of practice. The standard of practice always precluded a sexual relationship between therapist and patient.

ADMINISTRATIVE LAW JUDGE: Even though it was not expressed in the ethics codes?

HOLROYD: From the beginning of the term psychotherapy with Sigmund Freud, he was very clear to prohibit it in his early publications [*In the Matter of the Accusation Against: Myron E. Howland,* 1980, pp. 49–50].

The long history of prohibition against therapist-patient sexual involvement has been recognized by the courts. In the mid-1970s, New York Supreme Court Presiding Justice Markowitz recognized evidence that from the time of Freud to the present, the health care professions had agreed that therapist-patient sex harms patients: "Thus from [Freud] to the modern practitioner we have common agreement of the harmful effects of sensual intimacies between patient and therapist" (*Roy v. Hartogs,* 1976, p. 590).

That this prohibition has remained constant over so long a time and throughout so many diverse cultures reflects to some extent the recognition that such intimacies place the patient at risk for exceptional harm.

Until relatively recently, our understanding of therapist-client sexual involvement was based mainly upon theory, common sense, and individual case studies. Only in the past quarter century has a considerable body of diverse systematic investigations informed our understanding with empirical data. Some of the findings will be summarized in this chapter. (For more detailed presentations of this research, see Gabbard, 1989, and Pope, 1993, 1994.)

HOW CLIENTS CAN BE INJURED

Beginning with Masters & Johnson (1966, 1970, 1975), a number of investigators have examined how therapist-client sexual involvement affects clients (Bouhoutsos, Holroyd, Lerman, Forer, & Greenberg, 1983; L. S. Brown, 1988; S. E. Butler & Zelen, 1977; Feldman-Summers & G. Jones, 1984; Herman, Gartrell, Olarte, Feldstein, & Localio, 1987; Pope & Vetter, 1991; Sonne, Meyer, Borys, & Marshall, 1985; Vinson, 1987). Approaches to learning about effects have included studies of clients who have returned to therapy with a subsequent therapist as well as those who undertook no further therapy after their sexual involvement with a therapist. The consequences for clients who have been sexually involved with a psychotherapist have been compared to those for matched groups of therapy clients who have not been sexually involved with a therapist and of patients who have been sexually involved with a (nontherapist) physician. Subsequent treating therapists (of those clients who undertook a subsequent therapy), independent clinicians, and the clients themselves have evaluated the effects. Standardized psychological assessment instruments have supplemented clinical interview and behavioral observation. These diverse approaches to systematic study have supplemented individual patients' firsthand accounts (Bates & Brodsky, 1989; Freeman & Roy, 1976; Noel & Watterson, 1992; Plaisil, 1985; Walker & Young, 1986).

The consequences for the clients seem to cluster into ten very general categories: ambivalence, guilt, emptiness and isolation, sexual confusion, impaired ability to trust, confused roles and boundaries, emotional lability, suppressed rage, increased suicidal risk, and cognitive dysfunction (frequently in the areas of concentration and memory and often involving flashbacks, intrusive thoughts, unbidden images, and nightmares) (Pope, 1988b; 1994).

Patterns of Perpetrators and Victims

Despite the prohibition and the harm that can occur to sexually abused clients, a significant number of therapists report on anonymous surveys that they have become sexually involved with at least one client. Table 10.1 presents the eight national self-report surveys that have been published in peer-reviewed scientific journals.

When the data from these eight national studies are pooled, there are 5,148 participants providing anonymous self-reports. Each of three professions (psychiatry, psychology, and social work) is represented by at least two studies conducted in different years.

According to these pooled data, about 4.4 percent of the therapists reported becoming sexually involved with a client. The gender differences are significant: 6.8 percent of the male therapists and 1.6 percent of the female therapists reported engaging in sex with a client.

Data from these studies as well as others (for example, reports by therapists working with patients who have been sexually involved with a prior therapist) suggest that therapist-patient sex is consistent with other forms of abuse such as rape and incest: the perpetrators are overwhelmingly (though not exclusively) male and the victims are overwhelmingly (though not exclusively) female (Pope, 1990c). For example, Bouhoutsos, Holroyd, Lerman, Forer, & Greenberg (1983) reported a study in which 92 percent of the cases of therapist-patient sex involved a male therapist and female patient. Gartrell, Herman, Olarte, Feldstein, & Localio (1986), who reported the first national self-report study of sexual involvement between psychiatrists and their patients, found that 88 percent of the "contacts for which both the psychiatrist's and the patient's gender were specified occurred between male psychiatrists and female patients" (Gartrell et al., 1986, p. 1128).

Data based on therapists' reports of engaging in sex with patients or on therapists' work with patients who have been sexually exploited by a prior therapist has been supplemented with national survey data from patients who have been sexually involved with a therapist. In one study, about 2.19 percent of the men and about 4.58 percent of the women reported having become sexually involved with their own therapists (Pope & Feldman-Summers, 1992).

Yet another source of data (supplementing those provided through reports by subsequent therapists, therapists' anonymous self-reports, and patients' anonymous self-reports) is consistent with the significant gender differences. Data obtained from licensing disciplinary actions suggest that about 86 percent of the therapist-patient cases are those in which the therapist is male and the patient is female (Pope, 1993).

This significant gender difference has long been a focus of scholarship in the area of therapist-patient sex but is still not well understood. Holroyd & Brodsky's (1977) report of the first national study of

Study	Publica-tion date	Discipline	Sample size	Return rate	Percentage reporting sex with clients	
					Male	Female
Holroyd & Brodsky[a]	1977	psychologists	1,000	70%	12.1%	2.6%
K. S. Pope, Levenson, & Schover	1979	psychologists	1,000	48%	12.0%	3.0%
K. S. Pope, Keith-Spiegel, & Tabachnick	1986	psychologists	1,000	58.5%	9.4%	2.5%
Gartrell, Herman, Olarte, Feldstein, & Localio[b]	1986	psychiatrists	5,574	26%	7.1%	3.1%
K. S. Pope, Tabachnick, & Keith-Spiegel[c]	1987	psychologists	1,000	46%	3.6%	0.4%
Akamatsu[d]	1988	psychologists	1,000	39.5%	3.5%	2.3%
Borys & Pope[e]	1989	psychiatrists, psychologists and social workers	4,800	56.5%	0.9%	0.2%
Bernsen, Tabachnick, & Pope	1994	social workers	1,000	45.3%	3.6%	0.5%

Table 10.1.   Self-Report Studies of Sex with Clients
Using National Samples of Therapists.

Source: Adapted from Pope, 1994. Copyright © 1994 by the American Psychological Association. Adapted with permission.

Note: This table presents only national surveys that have been published in peer-reviewed scientific and professional journals. Exceptional caution is warranted in comparing the data from these various surveys. For example, the frequently cited percentages of 12.1 and 2.6, reported by Holroyd & Brodsky (1977), exclude same-sex involvements. Moreover, when surveys included separate items to assess post-termination sexual involvement, these data are reported in footnotes to this table. Finally, some published articles did not provide sufficiently detailed data for this table (for example, aggregate percentages); the investigators supplied the data needed for the table.

[a]Although the gender percentages presented in the table for the other studies represent responses to one basic survey item in each survey, the percentages presented for Holroyd & Brodsky's study span several items. The study's senior author confirmed through personal communication that the study's findings were that 12.1 percent of the male and 2.6 percent of the female participants reported having engaged in erotic contact (whether or not it included intercourse) with at least one opposite-sex patient; that about 4 percent of the male and 1 percent of the female participants reported engaging in erotic contact with at least one same-sex patient; and that, in response to a separate survey item, 7.2 percent of the male and 0.6 percent of the female psychologists reported that they had "had intercourse with a patient within three months after terminating therapy" (p. 846; see also Pope, Sonne, & Holroyd, 1993).

[b]"Respondents were asked to specify the number of male and female patients with whom they

Table 10.1. (*continued*)

had been sexually involved" (p. 1127); they were also asked "to restrict their answers to adult patients" (p. 1127).

[c] The survey also included a question about "becoming sexually involved with a former client" (p. 996). Gender percentages about sex with current or former clients did not appear in the article but were provided by an author. Fourteen percent of the male and 8 percent of the female respondents reported sex with a former client.

[d] The original article also noted that 14.2 percent of male and 4.7 percent of female psychologists reported that they had "been involved in an intimate relationship with a former client" (p. 454).

[e] This survey was sent to 1,600 psychiatrists, 1,600 psychologists, and 1,600 social workers. In addition to the data reported in the table, the original article also asked whether respondents had "engaged in sexual activity with a client after termination" (p. 288). Six percent of the male and 2 percent of the female therapists reported engaging in this activity.

> therapist-patient sex concluded with a statement of major issues that had yet to be resolved. "[T]hree professional issues remain to be addressed: (a) that male therapists are most often involved, (b) that female patients are most often the objects, and (c) that therapists who disregard the sexual boundary once are likely to repeat" (p. 849). Holroyd suggested that the significant gender differences reflected sex role stereotyping and bias: "Sexual contact between therapist and patient is perhaps the quintessence of sex-biased therapeutic practice" (Holroyd, 1983, p. 285). Holroyd & Brodsky's (1977) landmark research was followed by a second national study focusing on not only therapist-patient but also professor-student sexual relationships (Pope, Levenson, & Schover, 1979).

>> When sexual contact occurs in the context of psychology training or psychotherapy, the predominant pattern is quite clear and simple: An older higher status man becomes sexually active with a younger, subordinate woman. In each of the higher status professional roles (teacher, supervisor, administrator, therapist), a much higher percentage of men than women engage in sex with those students or clients for whom they have assumed professional responsibility. In the lower status role of student, a far greater proportion of women than men are sexually active with their teachers, administrators, and clinical supervisors [Pope, Levenson, & Schover, 1979, p. 687; see also Pope, 1989b].

> Although statistical analyses of the eight studies in Table 10.1 reveal significant gender effects and also significant effects related to the

year of the study (that is, the pooled data suggest that each year there are about 10 percent fewer self-reports of therapist-patient sex than the year before), there is no significant effect due to profession. According to these pooled data, psychologists, psychiatrists, and social workers report engaging in sex with their patients at about the same rates. Apparent differences are actually due to differing years in which the studies were conducted (that is, there was a confounding correlation between the professions and the years they were studied). The statistical analysis tested the predictive power of each variable (i.e., profession and year) once the variance accounted for by the other variable had been subtracted. Year had significantly more predictive power once effects due to profession had been accounted for than the predictive power of profession once effects due to year had been accounted for. Once year of study is taken into account, significant differences between professions disappear.

Bates & Brodsky (1989) examined the various risk factors that have been hypothesized, at one time or another, to make certain clients more vulnerable to sexual exploitation by a therapist. Their analysis led them not to the personal history or characteristics of the client but rather to prior behavior of the therapist: The most effective predictor of whether a client will become sexually involved with a therapist is whether that therapist has previously engaged in sex with a client (Bates & Brodsky, 1989). With access to a considerable set of historical and actuarial data, the APA Insurance Trust (1990, p. 3) revealed that "the recidivism rate for sexual misconduct is substantial." Holroyd & Brodsky's (1977) landmark survey found that 80 percent of the therapists who reported engaging in therapist-patient sexual intimacies indicated that they became involved with more than one patient. The California Department of Consumer Affairs (1990; see also 1997) published its findings in a document that was sent to all licensed therapists and counselors in California and that must, according to California law, be provided by a therapist to any patient who reports having been sexually involved with a prior therapist. This document notes that "80 percent of the sexually exploiting therapists have exploited more than one client. In other words, if a therapist is sexually exploiting a client, chances are he or she has done so before" (p. 14).

Table 10.2 presents additional information, based on a national survey, of 958 patients who had been sexually involved with a therapist. In this study, 80 percent of the patients who had begun sexual intimacies with a therapist *only after termination of the therapy* were found to have been harmed.

Characteristic	N	Percent
Patient was a minor at the time of the involvement	47	5
Patient married the therapist	37	3
Patient had experienced incest or other child sex abuse	309	32
Patient has experienced rape prior to sexual involvement with therapist	92	10
Patient required hospitalization considered to be at least partially a result of the sexual involvement	105	11
Patient attempted suicide	134	14
Patient committed suicide	7	1
Patient achieved complete recovery from any harmful effects of sexual involvement	143	17[a]
Patient seen pro bono or for reduced fee	187	20
Patient filed formal (for example, licensing, malpractice) complaint	112	12

Table 10.2. Characteristics of 958 Patients Who Had Been Sexually Involved with a Therapist.

[a] 17 percent of the 866 patients who experienced harm.

Source: Adapted from Pope & Vetter, 1991, p. 431. Copyright © 1991 by Division of Psychotherapy (22) of the American Psychological Association. Reprinted with permission.

Five percent of the patients described in Table 10.2 were minors at the time that they were sexually involved with a therapist. This finding underscores an important aspect of therapist-patient sex: Although much of the literature on this topic seems to assume that the patient is an adult, this is not always the case. In a national study focusing exclusively on minor patients who were sexually involved with a therapist, most (56 percent) were female (Bajt & Pope, 1989). The average age of these girls who were sexually involved with a therapist was thirteen, and the range was from seventeen down to three. The average age of the male minor patients was twelve, ranging from sixteen down to seven.

Common Scenarios

It is useful for therapists to be aware of the common scenarios in which therapists sexually exploit their patients. Pope & Bouhoutsos (1986, p. 4) presented ten of the most common scenarios as follows:

- *Role trading:* Therapist becomes the "patient" and the wants and needs of the therapist become the focus.
- *Sex therapy:* Therapist fraudulently presents therapist-patient sex as valid treatment for sexual or related difficulties.
- *As if. . . :* Therapist treats positive transference as if it were not the result of the therapeutic situation.
- *Svengali:* Therapist creates and exploits an exaggerated dependence on the part of the patient.
- *Drugs:* Therapist uses cocaine, alcohol, or other drugs as part of the seduction.
- *Rape:* Therapist uses physical force, threats, and/or intimidation.
- *True love:* Therapist uses rationalizations that attempt to discount the clinical/professional nature of the professional relationship and its duties (see also Twemlow & Gabbard, 1989).
- *It just got out of hand:* Therapist fails to treat the emotional closeness that develops in therapy with sufficient attention, care, and respect.
- *Time out:* Therapist fails to acknowledge and take account of the fact that the therapeutic relationship does not cease to exist between scheduled sessions or outside the therapist's office.
- *Hold me:* Therapist exploits patient's desire for nonerotic physical contact and possible confusion between erotic and nonerotic contact.

It is important to emphasize, however, that these are only general descriptions of some of the most common patterns, and many instances of therapist-patient sexual involvement will not fall into these ten.

Why Do Therapists Refrain?

Although our seeming insights into our own motives as therapists may be questionable at best, it is worth asking: Why do the overwhelming majority of therapists avoid sexually exploiting patients? Table 10.3 presents the answers to this question as provided by therapists in two national studies: one of psychologists, the other of social workers.

Reason	Social workers[a]	Psychologists[b]
Unethical	210	289
Countertherapeutic/exploitative	130	251
Unprofessional practice	80	134
Against therapist's personal values	119	133
Therapist already in a committed relationship	33	67
Feared censure/loss of reputation	7	48
Damaging to therapist	39	43
Disrupts handling transference/ countertransference	10	28
Fear of retaliation by client	2	19
Attraction too weak/short-lived	16	18
Illegal	14	13
Self-control	8	8
Common sense	7	8
Miscellaneous	13	32

Table 10.3.   Reasons Therapists Offer for Refraining from Sexual Involvement with Clients.

Sources: [a] Social work data are from Bernsen et al. (1994); [b] Psychology data are from Pope et al. (1986). Copyright © 1986, 1994 by the American Psychological Association. Adapted with permission.

CONFRONTING DAILY ISSUES

The issue of therapist-client sexual involvement focuses many of the major themes of this book. The great vulnerability of the client highlights the power of the therapist and the trust that must characterize the client's relationship with the therapist. The therapist's caring may be crucial in protecting against the temptation to exploit the client.

The issue of therapist-client sexual involvement also illustrates ethics as more than the following of a list of "do's and don't's," as discussed in Chapter Four. There is, of course, a clear prohibition: Avoid any sexual intimacies with clients. No cause, situation, or condition could ever legitimize such intimacies with any client (see, for example, Gabbard & Pope, 1989; Pope, Sonne & Holroyd, 1993; Pope, 1994). The prohibition stands as a fundamental ethical mandate no matter what the rationalizations. Taking this prohibition seriously and adhering to it without exception, however, mark the initial rather than the final steps in meeting our ethical responsibilities in this area. Several associated issues that we must confront and struggle with follow.

Physical Contact with Clients

The very topic of therapist-client sexual involvement as well as concern that we may be subject to an ethics complaint or malpractice suit may make many of us very nervous. We may go to great lengths to ensure that we maintain physical distance from our clients and under no circumstances touch them for fear that this might be misconstrued. A similar phenomenon seems to be occurring in regard to increasing public acknowledgment of child sexual abuse: Adults may be reluctant to hold children and to engage in nonsexual touch that is a normal part of life.

Is there any evidence that nonsexual touching of patients is actually associated with therapist-client sexual involvement? Holroyd & Brodsky (1980) examined this question and found no indications that physical contact with patients made sexual contact more likely. They *did* find evidence that differential touching of male and female clients (that is, touching clients of one gender significantly more than clients of the other gender) was associated with sexual involvement: "Erotic contact not leading to intercourse is associated with older, more experienced therapists who do not otherwise typically touch their patients at a rate different from other therapists (except when mutually initiated). Sexual intercourse with patients is associated with the touching of opposite-sex patients but not same-sex patients. It is the differential application of touching—rather than touching per se—that is related to intercourse" (p. 810).

If the therapist is personally comfortable engaging in physical contact with a patient, maintains a theoretical orientation for which therapist-client contact is not antithetical, and has competence (education, training, and supervised experience) in the use of touch, then the decision of whether or not to make physical contact with a particular client must be based on a careful evaluation of the clinical needs of the client at that moment. When solidly based upon clinical needs and a clinical rationale, touch can be exceptionally caring, comforting, reassuring, or healing. When not justified by clinical need and therapeutic rationale, nonsexual touch can also be experienced as intrusive, frightening, or demeaning. The decision must always be made carefully and in full awareness of the power of the therapist and the trust (and vulnerability) of the client.

Our responsibility to be sensitive to the issues of nonsexual touch and to explore them carefully extends to other therapeutic issues conceptually related to the issue of therapist-client sexual involvement. Our unresolved concerns with therapist-client sexual involvement may prompt us to respond to the prospect of nonsexual touching either phobically (avoiding in an exaggerated manner any contact or even physical closeness with a client) or counterphobically (engaging in apparently nonsexual touching such as handshakes and hugs as though to demonstrate that we are very comfortable with physical intimacy and experience no sexual impulses). These unresolved concerns can also elicit phobic or counterphobic behavior in other areas, such as the clinician's initiating or focusing on sexual issues to an extent that is not based on the client's clinical needs. To respond ethically, authentically, and therapeutically to such issues, we must come to terms with our own unresolved feelings of sexual attraction to our clients.

Sexual Attraction to Patients

Sexual attraction to patients seems to be a prevalent experience that evokes negative reactions. National survey research suggests that over four out of five psychologists (87 percent) and social workers (81 percent) report experiencing sexual attraction to at least one client (Pope et al., 1986; Bernsen et al., 1994). As Table 10.4 illustrates, therapists identify many aspects of patients that, according to the therapists, are the source or focus of the attraction. Yet simply experiencing the attraction (without necessarily even feeling tempted to act on it) causes most of the therapists who report such attraction (63 percent of the psychologists; 51 percent of the social workers) to feel guilty, anxious, or confused about the attraction.

That sexual attraction causes such discomfort among so many psychologists and social workers may be a significant reason that graduate training programs and internships tend to neglect training in this area. Only 9 percent (of psychologists) or 10 percent (of social workers) in these national studies reported that their formal training on the topic in graduate school and internships had been adequate. A majority of psychologists and social workers reported receiving *no* training about attraction.

This discomfort may also be a significant reason the scientific and professional books seem to neglect this topic.

In light of the multitude of books in the areas of human sexuality, sexual dynamics, sex therapies, unethical therapist-patient sexual

Characteristic	Social workers[a]	Psychologists[b]
Physical attractiveness	175	296
Positive mental/cognitive traits or abilities	84	124
Sexual	40	88
Vulnerabilities	52	85
Positive overall character/personality	58	84
Kind	6	66
Fills therapist's needs	8	46
Successful	6	33
"Good patient"	21	31
Client's attraction	3	30
Independence	5	23
Other specific personality characteristics	27	14
Resemblance to someone in therapist's life	14	12
Availability (client unattached)	0	9
Pathological characteristics	13	8
Long-term client	7	7
Sociability (sociable, extroverted, etc.)	0	6
Miscellaneous	23	15
Same interests/philosophy/background to therapist	10	0

Table 10.4.   Characteristics of Clients to Whom Psychotherapists Are Attracted.

Sources: [a] Social Work data are from Bernsen et al. (1994); [b] Psychology data are from Pope et al. (1986). Copyright © 1986, 1994 by the American Psychological Association. Adapted with permission.

contact, management of the therapist's or patient's sexual behaviors, and so on, it is curious that sexual attraction to patients per se has not served as the primary focus of a wide range of texts. The professor, supervisor, or librarian seeking books that turn their *primary* attention to exploring the therapist's *feelings* in this regard would be hard pressed to assemble a selection from which to choose an appropriate course text. If someone unfamiliar with psychotherapy were to judge the prevalence and significance of therapists' sexual feelings on the basis of the books that focus exclusively on that topic, he or she might conclude that the phenomenon is neither wide-spread nor important [Pope, Sonne, & Holroyd, 1993, p. 23].

These and similar factors may form a vicious circle: Discomfort with sexual attraction may have fostered an absence of relevant textbooks and graduate training; in turn, an absence of relevant text books and programs providing training in this area may sustain or intensify discomfort with the topic (Pope et al., 1993). The avoidance of the topic may produce a real impact. Koocher wrote, "How can the extant population of psychotherapists be expected to adequately address [these issues] if we pay so little attention to training in these matters?" (1994, p. viii).

These studies reveal significant gender effects in reported rates of experiencing sexual attraction to a patient. About 95 percent of the male psychologists and 92 percent of the male social workers compared with 76 percent of the female psychologists and 70 percent of the female social workers reported experiencing sexual attraction to a patient. The research suggests that just as male therapists are significantly more likely to become sexually involved with their patients, male therapists are also more likely to experience sexual attraction to their patients.

These national surveys suggest that a sizable minority of therapists carry with them—in the physical absence of the client—sexualized images of the client, and that a significantly greater percentage of male than of female therapists experience such cognitions. About 27 percent of male psychologists and 30 percent of male social workers, compared with 14 percent of female psychologists and 13 percent of female social workers, reported engaging in sexual fantasies about a patient while engaging in sexual activity with another person (that is, not the patient). National survey research has found that 46 percent of psychologists reported engaging in sexual fantasizing (regardless of the occasion) about a patient on a rare basis and that an additional 26 percent reported more frequent fantasies of this kind (Pope et al., 1987), and 6 percent have reported telling sexual fantasies to their patients (Pope & Tabachnick, 1993). Such data may be helpful in understanding not only how therapists experience and respond to sexual feelings but also how therapists and patients represent (for example, remember, anticipate, think about, fantasize about) each other when they are apart and how this affects therapeutic process and outcome (see, for example, Geller, Cooley, & Hartley, 1981–1982; Orlinsky & Geller, 1993; Pope & Brown, 1996; Pope & Singer, 1978a, 1978b). For any of us who experience sexual attraction to a client, it is important to recognize that the research suggests that this is a common experience. To feel attraction to a client is *not* unethical; to acknowledge and address the attraction promptly, carefully, and adequately is an important ethical responsibility. For some of us, consultation with respected colleagues will be useful. For others, obtaining formal supervision for our work with that client may be necessary. For still others, entering or reentering psychotherapy can be helpful.

When the Therapist Is Unsure What to Do

This section of this chapter addresses the question: What can the therapist do when the therapist doesn't know what to do? The book *Sexual Feelings in Psychotherapy* (Pope et al., 1993) suggests a ten-step approach to such daunting situations, which are summarized here. A repeated theme of that book is that therapists lack easy, one-size-fits-all "answers" to what sexual feelings about patients mean or their implications for the therapy. Different theoretical orientations provide different, sometimes opposing ways of approaching such questions. Each person and situation is unique. Therapists must explore and achieve a working understanding of their own unfolding, evolving feelings, and the ways in which these feelings may play a helpful role in deciding what to say or do next. "Cookbook" approaches can block rather than foster this process.

The approach outlined here places fundamental trust in the individual therapist, adequately trained and consulting with others, to draw his or her own conclusions. Almost without exception, therapists learn at the outset the fundamental resources for helping themselves explore problematic situations. Depending on the situation, they may introspect, study the available research and clinical literature, consult, seek supervision, and/or begin or resume personal therapy. But sometimes, even after the most sustained exploration, the course is not clear. The therapist's best understanding of the situation suggests a course of action that seems productive yet questionable and perhaps potentially harmful. To refrain from a contemplated action may cut the therapist off from legitimately helpful spontaneity, creativity, intuition, and ability to respond effectively to the patient's needs. Engaging in the contemplated action, however, may lead to disaster. When reaching such an impasse, therapists may find it useful to consider the potential intervention in light of the following ten considerations:

1. *The fundamental prohibition.* Is the contemplated action consistent with the fundamental prohibition against therapist-patient sexual intimacy? Therapists must never violate this special trust. If the

considered course of action includes any form of sexual involvement with a patient, it must be rejected.

2. *The slippery slope.* The second consideration may demand deeper self-knowledge and self-exploration. Is the contemplated course of action likely to lead to or create a risk for sexual involvement with the patient? The contemplated action may seem unrelated to any question of sexual exploitation of a patient. Yet depending on the personality, strengths, and weaknesses of the therapist, the considered action may constitute a subtle first step on a slippery slope. In most cases, the therapist alone can honestly address this consideration.

3. *Consistency of communication.* The third consideration invites the clinician to review the course of therapy from the start to the present: Has the therapist consistently and unambiguously communicated to the patient that sexual intimacies cannot and will not occur, and is the contemplated action consistent with that communication? Does the contemplated action needlessly cloud the clarity of that communication? The human therapist may be intensely tempted to act in ways that stir the patient's sexual interest or respond in a self-gratifying way to the patient's sexuality. Does the contemplated action represent, however subtly, a turning away from the legitimate goals of therapy?

4. *Clarification.* The fourth consideration invites therapists to ask whether the contemplated action would be better postponed until sexual and related issues have been clarified. Assume, for example, that a therapist's theoretical orientation does not preclude physical contact with patients and that a patient has asked that each session conclude with a reassuring hug between therapist and patient. Such ritualized hugs could raise complex questions about their meaning for the patient, about their impact on the relationship, and about how they might influence the course and effectiveness of therapy. It may be important to clarify such issues with the patient before making a decision to conclude each session with a hug.

5. *The patient's welfare.* The fifth consideration is one of the most fundamental touchstones of all therapy: Is the contemplated action consistent with the patient's welfare? The therapist's feelings may become so intensely powerful that they may create a context in which the patient's clinical needs may blur or fade out altogether. The patient may express wants or feelings with great force. The legal context—with the litigiousness that seems so prevalent in current

society—may threaten the therapist in a way that makes it difficult to keep a clear focus on the patient's welfare. Despite such competing factors and complexities, it is crucial to assess the degree to which any contemplated action supports, is consistent with, is irrelevant to, or is contrary to the patient's welfare.

6. *Consent.* The sixth consideration is yet another fundamental touchstone of therapy: Is the contemplated action consistent with the basic informed consent of the patient?

7. *Adopting the patient's view.* The seventh consideration urges the therapist to empathize imaginatively with the patient: How is the patient likely to understand and respond to the contemplated action?

> Therapy is one of many endeavors in which exclusive attention to theory, intention, and technique may distract from other sources of information, ideas, and guidance. Therapists-in-training may cling to theory, intention, and technique as a way of coping with the anxieties and overwhelming responsibilities of the therapeutic venture. Seasoned therapists may rely almost exclusively on theory, intention, and technique out of learned reflex, habit, and the sheer weariness that approaches burn-out. There is always risk that the therapist will fall back on repetitive and reflexive responses that verge on stereotype. Without much thought or feeling, the anxious or tired therapist may, if analytically minded, answer a patient's question by asking why the patient asked the question; if holding a client-centered orientation, may simply reflect or restate what the client has just said; if gestalt-trained, may ask the client to say something to an empty chair; and so on.
>
> One way to help avoid responses that are driven more by anxiety, fatigue, or other similar factors is to consider carefully how the therapist would think, feel, and react if he or she were the patient. Regardless of the theoretical soundness, intended outcome, or technical sophistication of a contemplated intervention, how will it likely be experienced and understood by the patient? Can the therapist anticipate at all what the patient might feel and think? The therapist's attempts to try out, in his or her imagination, the contemplated action and to view it from the perspective of the patient may help prevent, correct, or at least identify possible sources of misunderstanding, miscommunication, and failures of empathy [Pope, Sonne, & Holroyd, 1993, pp. 185–186].

8. *Competence*. The eighth consideration is one of competence: Is the therapist competent to carry out the contemplated intervention? Ensuring that a therapist's education, training, and supervised experienced is adequate and appropriate for his or her work is a fundamental responsibility.

9. *Uncharacteristic behaviors*. The ninth consideration involves becoming alert to unusual actions: Does the contemplated action fall substantially outside the range of the therapist's usual behaviors? That an action is unusual does not, of course, mean that something is necessarily wrong with it. Creative therapists will occasionally try creative interventions, and it is unlikely that even the most conservative and tradition-bound therapist conducts therapy the same way all the time. However, possible actions that are considerably outside the therapist's general approaches probably warrant special consideration.

10. *Consultation*. The tenth consideration concerns secrecy: Is there a compelling reason for not discussing the contemplated action with a colleague, consultant, or supervisor? Therapists' reluctance to disclose an action to others is a "red flag" to a possibly inappropriate action. Therapists may consider any possible action in light of the following question: If they took this action, would they have any reluctance for all of their professional colleagues to know that they had taken it? If the response is "yes," the reasons for the reluctance warrant examination. If the response is "no," it is worth considering whether one has adequately taken advantage of the opportunities to discuss the matter with a trusted colleague. If discussion with a colleague has not helped to clarify the issues, consultation with additional professionals, each of whom may provide different perspectives and suggestions, may be useful.

WORKING WITH PATIENTS WHO HAVE BEEN SEXUALLY INVOLVED WITH A THERAPIST

It is not unlikely that any therapist, counselor, or trainee reading this book will encounter clients who have been sexually victimized by a prior therapist. A national study of 1,320 psychologists found that 50 percent reported working with at least one client who, in the therapist's professional opinion, had been a victim of therapist-client

1. *Disbelief and denial.* The tendency to reject reflexively—without adequate data-gathering—allegations about therapist-patient sex (because, for example, the activities described seem per se outlandish and improbable)

2. *Minimization of harm.* The tendency to assume reflexively—without adequate data-gathering—that harm did not occur, or that, if it did, the consequences were minimally, if at all, harmful

3. *Making the patient fit the textbook.* The tendency to assume reflexively—without adequate data-gathering and examination—that the patient *must* inevitably fit a particular schema

4. *Blaming the victim.* The tendency to attempt to make the patient responsible for enforcing the therapist's professional responsibility to refrain from engaging in sex with a patient and holding the patient responsible for the therapist's offense

5. *Sexual reaction to the victim.* The clinician's sexual attraction to or feelings about the patient; such feelings are normal but must not become a source of distortion in the assessment process

6. *Discomfort at the lack of privacy.* The clinician's (and sometimes patient's) emotional response to the possibility that under certain conditions (for example, malpractice, licensing, or similar formal actions against the offending therapist; a formal review of assessment and other services by the insurance company providing coverage for the services), the raw data and the results of the assessment may not remain private

7. *Difficulty "keeping the secret."* The clinician's possible discomfort (and other emotional reactions) when he or she has knowledge that an offender continues to practice and to victimize other patients but cannot, in light of confidentiality and/or other constraints, take steps to intervene

8. *Intrusive advocacy.* The tendency to want to guide, direct, or determine a patient's decisions about what steps to take or what steps not to take in regard to a perpetrator

9. *Vicarious helplessness.* The clinician's discomfort when a patient who has filed a formal complaint seems to encounter unjustifiable obstacles, indifference, lack of fair hearing, and other responses that seem to ignore or trivialize the complaint and fail to protect the public from offenders

10. *Discomfort with strong feelings.* The clinician's discomfort when experiencing strong feelings (for example, rage, neediness, or ambivalence) expressed by the patient and focused on the clinician

---

Table 10.5. Common Clinician Reactions to Victims of Therapist-Patient Sexual Involvement.

Source: Adapted from Pope, Sonne, & Holroyd, 1993, pp. 241–261. Copyright © 1993 by the American Psychological Association. Adapted with permission.

sexual intimacies (Pope & Vetter, 1991). Only 4 percent reported working with at least one client who, in the therapist's opinion, had made false allegations about sex with a prior therapist.

It is crucial that clinicians working with such clients be genuinely knowledgeable about this area (see Chapter Five). Clients who have been sexually exploited tend to be exceptionally vulnerable to revictimization when their clinical needs are not recognized. Special methods and considerations for providing therapeutic services to victims of therapist-patient sexual intimacies have been developed and continue to evolve (Pope, 1994). One of the first steps toward gaining competence in this area is recognition of the diverse and sometimes extremely intense reactions that encountering a patient who reports sexual involvement with a former therapist can evoke in the subsequent therapist. Table 10.5 identifies some of the most common reactions.

Awareness of these reactions can prevent them from blocking the therapist from rendering effective services to the patient. The therapist can be alert for such reactions, and sort through them should they occur. In some instances, the therapist may seek consultation to help gain perspective and understanding.

REPORTING

As previously noted, research suggests that most therapists encounter at least one patient who has reportedly engaged in sex with a prior therapist. Unless there is legislation to the contrary (that is, legislation that permits or mandates reporting such matters without the patient's informed consent), the therapist will likely be obligated to keep the patient's communication confidential unless the patient provides informed consent for a waiver of confidentiality. Some states, however, have enacted reporting statutes which authorize or require mental health professionals to file formal reports when their patients disclose sexual involvement with a prior therapist [for example Minn. Stat., 147.111 (1995); Tex. Civ. Prac. and Rem. Code Ann., 81.001 (1) et seq. (1996); Wis. Stat., 940.22 (1)(i) et seq. (1994); see Pope, 1994]. California does not require reporting but does mandate that subsequent therapists provide the pamphlet *Professional Therapy Never Includes Sex* (California Department of Consumer Affairs, 1997; see also Caudill & Pope, 1995) to patients who report sexual involvement with a prior therapist and to discuss the pamphlet with them.

ETHICAL ASPECTS OF REHABILITATION

Unfortunately, therapists and counselors may act in ways that discount the harm done by perpetrators of therapist-patient sex, that obscure the responsibilities of perpetrators, and that enable perpetrators to continue victimizing clients—sometimes after a period of suspension (Bates & Brodsky, 1989; Gabbard, 1989). The rehabilitation methods by which perpetrators are returned to practice focus many of this book's themes and pose difficult ethical dilemmas. Pope (1990c, 1990d, 1994) reviewed some of the crucial but difficult ethical questions facing therapists and counselors considering rehabilitation efforts; they are summarized below.

Competence

Does the clinician who is implementing the rehabilitation plan possess demonstrable competence (see Chapter Five) in the areas of rehabilitation and of therapist-patient sexual intimacies? Has the rehabilitation method the clinician uses been adequately validated through independent studies? (See the section "Approaches, Strategies, and Techniques" in Chapter Five.) Obviously, if the clinician were claiming an effective "cure" for pedophilia, kleptomania, dyslexia, panic attacks, or a related disorder, that clinician would need to present the scientific evidence for the intervention's effectiveness. Ethical standards for claims *based on evidence* in this area—particularly given the risks for abuse to which future patients may be exposed—should not be waived. Such evidence must meet the customary requirement of publication in peer-reviewed scientific or professional journals. As Pope (1990d, p. 482) noted, "Research results that survive and benefit from this painstaking process of systematic review created to help ensure the scientific integrity, merit, and trustworthiness of new findings may be less likely (than data communicated *solely* through press conferences, popular lectures, books, workshops, and television appearances) to contribute to what Tavris (1987) terms 'social-science fiction.'" We have been unable to locate any independently conducted, replicated research published in peer-reviewed scientific or professional journals that supports the effectiveness of rehabilitation efforts in this area.

Informed Consent

Whether the rehabilitation technique is viewed as an intervention of proven effectiveness (through independently conducted research trials) or an experimental research trial for a promising approach, have those who are put at risk for harm been adequately informed and been given the option of not assuming the risk, should the rehabilitation fail to be 100 percent effective? (See the section "Failing to Provide Informed Consent" in Chapter Eight.)

Assessment

Do the research trials investigating the potential effectiveness of the rehabilitation method meet at least minimal professional standards (see Chapter Nine)? For example, is the research conducted independently? (We are rarely disinterested judges of the profundity, effectiveness, and near-perfection of our own work.)

A more complex requirement concerns whether the base rate of discovery of abuse is adequately taken into account in conducting and reporting the results of experimental trials of rehabilitation efforts. Perpetrators may continue to engage in sexual intimacies with clients during (or after) rehabilitation efforts, even when they are supervised (see, for example, Bates & Brodsky, 1989). The abuse may only come to light if the client reports it. Yet the base rate of such reports by clients is quite low. Surveys of victims suggest that only about 5 percent report the behavior to a licensing board (see, for example Pope & Vetter, 1991). The percentage appears to be significantly lower when the number of instances of abuse estimated from anonymous surveys of clinicians (who report instances in which they have engaged in abuse) are compared with complaints filed with licensing boards, ethics committees, and the civil and criminal courts. Using the higher 5 percent reporting estimate, assume that you conduct research in which a licensing board refers ten offenders to you for rehabilitation. You work with the offenders for several years and are convinced that you have completely rehabilitated all ten. You assure the licensing board of your complete confidence that none of the ten will pose any risk to future clients. But also assume that your rehabilitation effort fails miserably: All ten offenders will engage in sex with a future client. What are the probabilities that *any* of the ten future abuse victims will file a complaint? If each client has only a 5 percent probability of reporting the abuse, there is a 59.9 percent probability that *none* of the ten will file a complaint. Thus there is close to a 60 percent chance that these research trials, even if independently evaluated, will appear to validate your approach as 100 percent effective, when in fact it was 100 percent ineffective. If ignored in conducting and reporting research, the low base rate can make a worthless intervention appear completely reliable.

A set of questions for forensic assessment of rehabilitation in this area is provided in Pope, Butcher, & Seelen (1993, Chapter 9; see also Pope, 1994).

Power and Trust

The ethics of psychotherapy and counseling are inherently related to power and trust (see Chapter Three). How are these factors relevant to the dilemmas of rehabilitation?

If a judge were convicted of abusing the power and trust inherent in the position of judgeship by allowing bribes to determine the outcome of cases, numerous sanctions, both criminal and civil, might follow. However, even after the judge "paid the debt" due society by the abuse of power and trust, the judge would not be allowed to resume the bench, regardless of any "rehabilitation."

Similarly, if a preschool director were discovered to have sexually abused the students, he or she would probably face both civil and criminal penalties. The director might undergo extensive rehabilitation efforts to help reduce the risk that he or she would engage in further abuse of children. However, regardless of the effectiveness of the rehabilitation efforts, the state would not issue the individual a new license to found and direct another preschool.

Neither of these two offenders would necessarily be precluded from practicing their professions. The former judge and preschool director, once rehabilitated, might conduct research, consult, publish, lecture, or pursue other careers within the legal and educational fields. However, serving as judge or as preschool director are positions that involve such trust—by both society and the individuals subject to their immediate power—that the violation of such an important and clearly understood prohibition against abuse of trust (and power) precludes the opportunity to hold such special positions within the fields of law and education.

The helping professions must consider the ethical, practical, and policy implications of allowing and enabling offenders to resume the positions of special trust that they abused. Do psychotherapy and counseling involve or require a comparable degree of inviolable trust, from individual clients and from the society more generally, and ethical integrity as the positions of judge and preschool director within the legal and educational fields?

HIRING, SCREENING, AND SUPERVISING

Those who work within health maintenance organizations (HMOs), hospitals, and other structures hiring clinicians have a responsibility to attend carefully to the risks that staff may sexually exploit clients. Carefully structured and adequately comprehensive forms and procedures (verifying education, supervision, licensure, employment, history of licensing or ethics complaints, etc.) for screening potential personnel, for establishing and monitoring policies prohibiting sex with clients, and so on, have long been advocated as important in minimizing the risk that organizational personnel will sexually exploit clients (see, for example, Pope & Bouhoutsos, 1986; Pope, 1994). More recently, however, the usefulness of such forms and procedures that operationally define screening procedures and policy implementation has been recognized as an important component of malpractice risk management not only in hospitals but also in clinics, group practices, and similar settings. As defense attorney Brandt Caudill (1993) stated, "Given the current state of the law, it seems clear that psychologists must assume that they may be sued if a partner, employee, or supervisee engages in a sexual relationship with a patient, because it appears that the courts are moving to the position that a sexual relationship between a therapist and a patient is a recognizable risk of employment which would be within the scope of the employer-employee relationship" (p. 17). It may be very difficult for employers and those with administrative or clinical supervisory responsibilities to argue successfully that the sexual relationship involving a supervisee or employee was not within the scope of employment. As one court held: "We believe that the nature of the work performed by a psychotherapist is substantially different than that of a day-care teacher as in *Randi F.* or a security guard as in *Webb* or a medical doctor as in *Hoover* so that a psychotherapist who engages in sexual relations with a patient could not be said, as a matter of law, to have acted outside the scope of his employment" (*St. Paul Fire & Marine Insurance Company* v. *Downs,* 1993, p. 344).

Illinois is an example of a state that enacted legislation making an employer liable when it knows or should reasonably know that a psychotherapist-employee engaged in sexual contact with a patient (*Ill.Rev.Stat.*1991, chap. 70, par. 803).

Here are some steps that have previously been suggested as useful in addressing these issues when screening job applicants (Pope & Bouhoutsos, 1986; Pope, 1994):

- Discuss with the applicant any formal or informal training experiences in areas such as identifying and addressing both the clinician's and the client's sexual feelings. Are there classroom teachers, practicum supervisors, or previous employers who have provided such training and who could be contacted to obtain information?

- Use an employment application form that traces back in sufficient detail from the present to college graduation. Ensure that there are no gaps in education or employment that are not clearly explained in writing.

- Provide a form for release of information that will enable the prospective employer to check with each setting of previous training, employment, or experience.

- Check with supervisors at any institutions at which the applicant obtained graduate training.

- Verify that the applicant was awarded all degrees claimed on the application form.

- Verify that any internships, practica, or post-docs were successfully completed. Check with a supervisor at each site.

- Check for information with each state that has issued the applicant a clinical license. Verify that no license has been revoked or subject to disciplinary procedures in which the applicant was found to have engaged in prohibited activities.

- Obtain a copy of all significant certifications.

- Obtain a copy of the applicant's resume or curriculum vitae. Ensure that it is consistent with the responses to the application form described in item 2 above.

- Ensure that the applicant fully understands the explicit policies of the HMO, hospital, etc., in regard to prohibited activities with clients and that he or she signs an agreement to that effect.

Therapists violate their patients' trust not only when they enter into sexual relationships with patients but also when they establish other, distinct, additional relationships that place the patient at risk for harm. Chapter Eleven focuses on these nonsexual dual relationships.

SCENARIOS FOR DISCUSSION

As noted, Chapters Seven through Fifteen of this book end with scenarios, each accompanied with a set of questions for discussion. This approach had been used in *Sexual Feelings in Psychotherapy: Explorations for Therapists and Therapists-in-Training* (Pope et al., 1993). Although we have created original vignettes for the other chapters in this book, the following scenarios and questions come from *Sexual Feelings in Psychotherapy*.

—◆—

It has been an extremely demanding week, and you're looking forward to going to the new movie with your life partner. The theater is packed but you find two seats on the aisle not too close to the screen. You feel great to have left work behind you at the office and to be with your lover for an evening on the town. As the lights go down, you lean over to give your partner a passionate kiss. For some reason, while kissing, you open your eyes and notice that, sitting in the seat on the other side of your partner and watching you, is a therapy patient who has, just that afternoon, revealed an intense sexual attraction to you.

Questions

What feelings does this scenario evoke in you?

If you were the therapist, what, if anything, would you say to the patient at the time of this event? What would you say during the next therapy session?

How would the patient's presence affect your subsequent behavior at the theater?

How might this event affect the therapy and your relationship with the patient?

What, if anything, would you say to your partner—either at the theater or later—about what had happened? Are there any circumstances under which you would phone the patient before the next scheduled appointment to discuss the matter?

Imagine that during a subsequent therapy session the patient begins asking about whom you were with at the theater. How would you feel? What would you say?

What if the patient were a business client of your partner (or knew your partner in another context) and they begin talking before the movie begins. What feelings would this discovery evoke in you? What would you consider in deciding how to handle this matter?

To what extent do you believe that therapists should be free to "be themselves?" To what extent should they behave in public as though a patient might be observing them?

—⁓—

During your first session with a new patient, he tells you that he has always been concerned that his penis was too small. Suddenly, he pulls down his pants and asks you if you think it is too small. [Consider the same scenario with a new patient who is concerned about the size of her breasts.]

Questions

What are you feeling? What are you thinking? What are your fantasies about this scenario?

What would you, as therapist, want to do first? Why? What do you think you would do first? Why?

What difference would it make if this were a patient whom you had been treating for a year rather than a new patient?

How, if at all, would your feelings and actions be different according to whether treatment were conducted on an inpatient or an outpatient basis?

How, if at all, would your feelings and actions differ according to the gender of the patient?

Imagine that the male and female patients in the scenario are fifteen years old. What feelings does the scenario evoke in you? What do you do? What fantasies occur to you about what might happen after the event described in the scenario?

———

Your patient describes to you her troubled marriage. Her husband used to get mad and hit her—"not too hard," she says—but he's pretty much gotten over that. Their sex life is not good. Her husband enjoys anal intercourse, but she finds it frightening and painful. She tells you that she'd like to explore her resistance to this form of sexual behavior in her therapy. Her goal is to become comfortable engaging in the behavior so that she can please her husband, enjoy sex with him, and have a happy marriage.

Questions

What are you feeling when the patient says that her husband "used to get mad and hit her?" What are you thinking?

What are you feeling when she says that she finds anal intercourse frightening and painful? What are you thinking?

What do you feel when she describes her goals in therapy? What are you thinking?

In what ways do you believe that your feelings may influence how you proceed with this patient?

———

The therapy group you are leading is into its eighth month of weekly meetings. One of the members of the group begins sobbing, describes terrible feelings of depression, and ends by pleading, "I need someone to hold me!"

Bob, another member of the group, spontaneously jumps up and goes over to the other member, who stands up. As they embrace, it becomes obvious that Bob is getting an erection. He continues the hugging, which the other group member seems to find comforting, and seems to be stimulating himself by rubbing up against the other person.

Questions

When you imagine this scenario, what do you feel?

Would you, as therapist, call attention to what is happening? If so, how?

If you were the therapist, could you imagine that such an event might make you feel aroused? frightened? upset? angry? confused?

Do any of the following considerations change the feelings that this scenario evokes in you?

- Whether your supervisor is watching this scene through a one-way mirror
- Whether Bob and the client are the same gender
- Whether Bob is suffering from schizophrenia
- Whether Bob is a pedophile
- Whether the client receiving the hug seems to be aroused
- Whether Bob had been sexually abused during childhood
- Whether this is an inpatient group
- Whether all members of this group are suffering from terminal illnesses
- Whether the client receiving the hug had been sexually abused during childhood
- Whether the client receiving the hug has sued a prior therapist for malpractice in regard to sexual issues

———

You are working in a busy mental health center in which the doors to the consulting rooms, while offering some privacy, are not completely sound-proofed. As long as therapist and client are talking at a normal level, nothing can be heard from outside the door. But words spoken loudly can be heard and understood in the reception area.

A patient, Sal, sits in silence during the first five minutes of the session, finally saying, "It's been hard to concentrate today. I keep hearing these sounds, like they're ringing in my ear, and they're frightening to me. I want to tell you what they're like, but I'm afraid to."

After offering considerable reassurance that describing the sounds would be OK and that you and Sal can work together to try to understand what is causing the sounds, what they mean, and what you might do about them, you notice that Sal seems to be gathering the courage to reveal them to you.

Finally, Sal leans back in the chair and imitates the sounds. They build quickly to a very high pitch and loud volume. They sound exactly like someone becoming more and more sexually aroused and then experiencing an intense orgasm.

You are reasonably certain that these sounds have been heard by the receptionist, some of your colleagues, the patients sitting in the waiting room, and a site visitor from the Joint Commission for the Accreditation of Hospitals who is deciding whether the hospital in which your clinic is based should have its accreditation renewed.

Questions

What feelings does this scenario evoke in you?

As you imagined the scene, was the client male (for example, Salvador) or female (for example, Sally)? Does the client's gender make any difference in the way you feel?

If Sal began to make the sounds again, would you make any effort to interrupt or to ask the client to be a little quieter? Why?

If none of the people who might have heard the sounds mentioned this event to you, would you make any effort to explain what had happened?

Imagine that just as Sal finishes making these sounds, someone knocks loudly on the door and asks, "What's going on in there?" What do you say or do?

Would your feelings or behavior be any different if the sounds were of a person being beaten rather than having an orgasm?

How would you describe this session in your chart notes?

If you were being supervised, would you feel at all apprehensive about discussing this session with your supervisor?

What approach do you usually take toward your clients making loud noises that might be heard outside the consulting room?

CHAPTER ELEVEN

Nonsexual Multiple Relationships

I n his discussion of dual relationships, Gabbard (1994) quotes Sullivan on the difficulties of maintaining clear and ethical boundaries. "Harry Stack Sullivan . . . once observed that psychotherapy is a unique profession in that it requires therapists to set aside their own needs in the service of addressing the patient's needs. He further noted that this demand is an extraordinary challenge for most people, and he concluded that few persons are really suited for the psychotherapeutic role. Because the needs of the psychotherapist often get in the way of the therapy, the mental health professions have established guidelines, often referred to as *boundaries,* that are designed to minimize the opportunity for therapists to use their patients for their own gratification" (p. 283).

Dual relationships are relatively easy to define; they are much more difficult for many of us to recognize in our practice. A dual relationship in psychotherapy occurs when the therapist is in another, significantly different relationship with one of his or her patients. Most commonly, the second role is social, financial, or professional.

In some cases, one relationship follows the other. The mere fact that the two roles are apparently sequential rather than clearly concurrent does not, in and of itself, mean that the two relationships do not constitute a dual relationship. Most of the important relationships in our lives have at least some sort of carry-over. Thus a therapist would avoid treating her ex-husband even though they were divorced and the marriage was clearly over.

In part it may be the relative simplicity and abstraction of the definition that lulls many of us into ignoring the diverse ways, many of them exceptionally subtle, that dual relationships occur in psychotherapy, sometimes with potentially devastating results. Specific examples, more than abstract definitions, may provide us with a useful awareness of how these entanglements occur. The following three fictional scenarios, dismayingly typical of actual practice, illustrate nonsexual dual relationships. (As mentioned previously, the vignettes are not based on actual cases or individuals.)

HELPING AS A FRIEND

Rosa, an attorney, is going through one of the worst times in her life. For several weeks, she had been experiencing mild abdominal discomfort and had dismissed it as a muscle strained while jogging or nervousness about the case she was preparing to argue in her first appearance before the state supreme court. The pains become worse and she manages to drive herself to the emergency room. A rather brusque medical resident informs her that he has located a large lump on her ovary. He advises her to make an appointment to undergo extensive tests to determine the nature of the lump, which may be cancerous. Rosa is terrified. The tests are scheduled for two days from now. She has to cope not only with the pain but also with the uncertainty of what the physicians will discover. She goes immediately to the house of her best friend, June, a psychotherapist. June suggests showing Rosa some self-hypnotic and imagery techniques that might help her cope with her pain and anxiety. As June leads her through the exercises, Rosa begins to feel relieved and comforted. However, when she tries to use the techniques by herself, she experiences no effects at all. June agrees to lead her through the hypnotic and imagery exercises two or three times a day until the medical crisis is resolved. During the fourth meeting, spontaneous images that are quite troubling begin occurring. Rosa starts talking about them and feels they are related to things that happened to her as a little child. She discusses them in detail with June, and by the end of the sixth session, June recognizes that an intense transference has developed. She encourages Rosa to consult another therapist but Rosa refuses, saying that there is no one else she could trust with these matters and that terminating the sessions would make her feel so betrayed and abandoned that she fears she would take her own life.

THE OPPORTUNITY

Bill has just opened a private practice office and has exactly two patients. One of them, Mr. Lightfoot, is an extremely successful investment analyst who is grateful to Bill for all the benefits he is getting from psychotherapy. The worst of Mr. Lightfoot's depression seems to be in remission, and he is now focusing on his relationships to those whose financial matters he handles. Bill, who genuinely likes Mr. Lightfoot, finds himself especially attentive when his patient talks about new investment opportunities. Unexpectedly, Mr. Lightfoot says that Bill might make a great deal of money if he invests in a certain project that is now being planned. The more Bill thinks about it, the more this seems like a terrific opportunity. It will help Mr. Lightfoot's sense of self-esteem because he will be in the position of helping Bill rather than always receiving help from him. It will not cost Mr. Lightfoot anything. Finally, it may allow Bill to survive in private practice and thus enable him to continue to help others. (Bill's overhead was greater than expected, the anticipated referrals were just not materializing, and he was down to his last $10,000 in savings, which would not last long given his office rent and other expenses.) He decides to give his savings to Mr. Lightfoot to invest for him.

EMPLOYEE BENEFITS

Dr. Ali is a successful psychotherapist who now owns and manages his own mental health clinic. Lately, he has noticed that his normally outstanding secretary, Mr. Miller, has been making numerous mistakes, some of them resulting in considerable financial losses for the clinic. Dr. Ali's customary toleration, encouragement, and nonjudgmental pointing out of the errors have not improved his secretary's performance. He decides that a serious and frank discussion of the situation is necessary. When he begins talking with his secretary about the deteriorating performance, Mr. Miller begins telling him about some personal and financial stresses that he has been encountering that make it difficult for him to attend to his work. Dr. Ali is aware that his secretary cannot afford therapy and that the chances of hiring a new secretary with anywhere near Mr. Miller's previous level of skills is at best a long shot. Even if a good secretary could be found in what is a cutthroat job market, there would be a long period of orientation and training during which Dr. Ali anticipates he would continue to lose revenue. He decides that the only course of action that makes sense, and that creatively solves all problems, is for Dr. Ali to take on Mr. Miller as a patient for two or three hours each week until Mr. Miller has a chance to work through his problems. Mr. Miller could continue to work as secretary and would not be charged for the therapy sessions. Dr. Ali would provide them without charge as part of a creative and generous "employee benefit."

PROBLEMS WITH
DUAL RELATIONSHIPS

As these fictional scenarios illustrate and as the clinical and research literature have discussed, dual relationships can jeopardize professional judgment, clients' welfare, and the process of therapy itself (see, for example, Borys & Pope, 1989; Ethics Committee of the American Psychological Association, 1988b; Pope, 1988a; Sonne, 1994). Some of the major difficulties with dual relationships follow.

First, the dual relationship can erode and distort the professional nature of the therapeutic relationship, which is secured within a reliable set of boundaries upon which both therapist and patient can depend. When the therapist is also the patient's lover, landlord, best friend, or employer, the crucial professional nature of the therapeutic relationship is compromised. Note that terming the therapeutic relationship "professional" in no way implies that it is or needs to be cold, distant, unfeeling, uncaring, or otherwise stereotypical of the worst professionals.

Second, dual relationships can create conflicts of interest and thus compromise the disinterest (*not* lack of interest) necessary for sound professional judgment. The therapist as professional professes to place the interests of the patient foremost (except in those rare instances in which to do so would place third parties at unacceptable risk for harm). But if the therapist allows another relationship to occur, the therapist creates a second set of interests to which he or she will be subject. Thus the therapist who is treating a friend may be reluctant to allow the patient to explore options that may upset the therapist's social network; additionally, the patient may be afraid to explore such options. The therapist who is treating a patient in exchange for some services may find himself or herself manipulating or otherwise influencing the patient to provide better services or might become so critical of the patient's seemingly poor services that the therapeutic process becomes destructive for the patient. In dual relationships, the therapist is engaged in meeting his or her own needs (for example, sexual or social).

Third, dual relationships can affect the cognitive processes that research has shown to play a role in the beneficial effects of therapy and that help the patient to maintain the benefits of therapy after termination (see Gabbard & Pope, 1989).

Fourth, because of the therapist-patient relationship, the patient cannot enter into a business or other secondary relationship with the therapist on equal footing (see Pope, 1988a). One aspect of the power differential is as follows. When we believe we have been wronged by, say, our plumber or next-door neighbor, we can attempt various methods to resolve the difficulty and, if those methods are unsuccessful, we can take the matter to court. But the patient who feels seriously wronged in a business, financial, or social transaction with his or her therapist faces troubling obstacles in seeking legal redress. The therapist can use the secrets and intensely private material about the patient that the therapist became aware of during the psychotherapy in planning the most effective defense. Further, therapists may use a variety of false diagnostic labels by which to discredit the patient, a practice that is unfortunately common (Pope, 1988a).

Fifth, if it became acceptable practice for therapists to engage in dual financial, social, and professional relationships with their patients, whether prior or subsequent to termination, the nature of psychotherapy would be drastically changed. Psychotherapists could begin using their practices to screen their patients for each patient's likelihood of meeting—either during therapy or some time after termination—the therapists' social, sexual, financial, or professional needs or desires. The lonely therapist could look for patients with whom he or she might like to socialize after termination. The therapist who wanted a second (or subsequent) career in the film industry could keep an eye out for a famous but troubled screenwriter with whom the therapist could collaborate on scripts, either as part of the process of therapy or after waiting a suitable time after termination of therapy. Therapists could use their practices as a dating service, looking for prospective dates or mates (the therapist being in an exceptionally good position to learn about the prospect before actually asking them out after termination). If dual relationships were acceptable, patients also would learn that therapists were available for extratherapeutic possibilities (perhaps after termination) and could alter their behavior accordingly.

Sixth, both during the course of therapy and at any time after, the therapist may be invited or compelled (through subpoena or court order) to offer testimony regarding the patient's diagnosis, treatment, or prognosis. Such testimony may be crucial to the patient in personal injury suits, custody hearings, criminal trials, and other judicial proceedings. If the therapist was also the business partner, live-in lover, or "we frequently share vacations together" type of friend, the objectivity, reliability, and integrity of the testimony as well as the information and documents reflecting the therapy (such as chart notes and insurance form diagnoses) become suspect.

Seventh, Pipes (1997), in discussing post-termination nonsexual dual relationships, notes the formal complaints that may arise.

> Finally, from a more pragmatic perspective, there are often legal reasons for avoiding post-therapy nonsexual relationships. Because state boards vary in their interpretation of ethical standards, and because legal statutes vary from state to state, it is clear that the safest approach to post-therapy relationships is to use caution and discretion when contemplating entering one. Following a survey of state association ethics committees and state licensing boards, Gottlieb et al. (1988) noted: "One psychologist was considered in violation for an affair that began 4 years after termination. It is now quite clear that SBs [state boards] are deciding that a psychologist may be held liable for his or her actions long after terminating a therapeutic relationship and that in such matters the therapeutic relationship may be assumed to never end" (p. 461). Despite the external constraints imposed on the behavior of psychologists by legal and regulatory bodies such as state boards, and whatever the view of the APA Ethics Committee, it is the responsibility of each psychologist to consider carefully what duty is owed former clients and what behaviors on the part of the psychologist adequately (and preferably, best) represent ethical obligations to former clients [p. 35].

EXPLICIT STANDARDS AND MECHANISMS OF ACCOUNTABILITY

Dual relationships form the major basis of licensing disciplinary actions, financial losses in malpractice suits involving psychologists, and ethics complaints against psychologists (see Chapter Two). Vested with statutory authority to protect consumers from harm or abuse by therapists, licensing boards originally addressed dual relationships by focusing mainly on allegations of sexual dual relationships (for example, *Colorado State Board of Medical Examiners* v. *Weiler,* 1965; *Cooper* v. *Board of Medical Examiners,* 1975; *Morra* v. *State Board of Examiners of Psychologists,* 1973; see also Chapter Ten). In the past two decades, however, state licensing boards have addressed more vigorously—in words and actions—the issue of nonsexual dual relationships, particularly bartering of professional services. For example, the California licensing boards distributed to all licensed therapists in the state a pamphlet emphasizing that "hiring a client to do work for the therapist, or bartering goods or services to pay for therapy" constituted "inappropriate behavior and misuse of power" (California Department of Consumer Affairs, 1990, p. 3). The APA ethics code states that "psychologists ordinarily refrain from accepting goods, services, or other nonmonetary remuneration from patients or clients in return for psychological services because such arrangements create inherent potential for conflicts, exploitation, and distortion of the professional relationship. A psychologist may participate in bartering *only* [only is underlined in original] if (1) it is not clinically contraindicated, *and* [and is underlined in the original] (2) the relationship is not exploitative (see also standards 1.17, "Multiple Relationships," and 1.25, "Fees and Financial Arrangements" (APA, 1992, p. 1602; see also Ethics Committee of the APA, 1988b; Sonne, 1994). Similarly, some licensing boards have imposed periods of suspension and additional terms following investigations of allegations concerning nonsexual dual relationships. Licensing boards' attention to such cases may parallel the APA's highlighting of nonsexual dual relationship ethics cases (1987a, pp. 79–85), the formal resolutions of which were intended by the association (p. vii) to serve as precedents for national, state, and local ethics committees of psychologists (see also Ethics Committee of the APA, 1988b).

A REVIEW OF RESEARCH

There has been considerable research regarding sexual dual relationships (see Chapter Ten). Research concerning the prevalence of nonsexual dual relationships, however, has been relatively rare. Tallman (1981) conducted perhaps the earliest study on nonsexual dual relationships. Of the thirty-eight psychotherapists participating, about 33 percent indicated that they had formed social relationships with at least some of their patients. An intriguing aspect of the findings was that, although only half of the participants were male, *all* of the therapists who developed these social relationships with patients were male. This significant gender difference is remarkably consistent not only in terms of both sexual and nonsexual dual relationships in psychotherapy but also in terms of dual relationships involving teaching and supervision.

Borys & Pope (1989, p. 290) summarize the research that has accumulated over the past dozen or fifty years: "First, the significant difference (i.e., a greater proportion of male than of female psychologists) that characterizes sexualized dual relationships conducted by both therapists and educators (teachers, clinical supervisors, and administrators) also characterizes nonsexual dual relationships conducted by therapists in the areas of social/financial involvements and dual professional roles. Male respondents tended to rate social/ financial involvements and dual professional roles as more ethical and reported engaging in these involvements with more clients than did female respondents. Second, the data suggest that male therapists tend to engage in nonsexual dual relationships more with female clients than with male clients. . . . Third, these trends hold for psychologists, psychiatrists, and clinical social workers." Note that these statistical analyses take into account the fact that most therapists are male and most patients are female.

Pope, Tabachnick, & Keith-Spiegel (1987) included several items regarding nonsexual dual relationships—"accepting services from a client in lieu of fee," "providing therapy to one of your friends," "going into business with a former client"—in their survey of the ethical beliefs and practices of 1,000 clinical psychologists (return rate = 46 percent). Their findings were consistent with a larger scale multidisciplinary study focusing on dual relationships reported in the next paragraph.

A survey of 1,600 psychiatrists, 1,600 psychologists, and 1,600 social workers (with a 49 percent return rate) examined beliefs and behaviors regarding a range of dual relationships in the light of factors such as therapist gender, profession (psychiatrist, psychologist, social worker), therapist age, experience, marital status, region of residence, client gender, practice setting (such as solo or group private practice and outpatient clinics), practice locale (size of the community), and theoretical orientation (Borys & Pope, 1989). The survey's findings included these three points:

1. There was no significant difference among the professions in terms of sexual intimacies with clients before or after termination (see Chapter Ten) or in terms of nonsexual dual professional

roles, social involvements, or financial involvements with patients.

2. The percentage of therapists who rated each dual relationship behavior as ethical under most or all conditions was invariably less than the percentage of therapists viewing it as never ethical or ethical under only some or rare conditions.

3. Psychiatrists tend, as a whole, to view such relationships as less ethical than do psychologists or social workers.

In a separate analysis of these data, Borys (1988, p. 181) found that "there was a clear relationship between sexual and nonsexual dual role behaviors" (see also Ethics Committee of the American Psychological Association, 1988b). She used a systems perspective to explore this association between nonsexual and sexual dual relationships: "As with familial incest, sexual involvement between therapist and client may be the culmination of a more general breakdown in roles and relationship boundaries which begin on a nonsexual level. This link was predicted by the systems perspective, which views disparate roles and behaviors within a relational system as interrelated. Changes in one arena are expected to affect those in other realms of behavior. The results of the current study suggest that the role boundaries and norms in the therapeutic relationship, just as those in the family, serve a protective function that serves to prevent exploitation" (p. 182).

Baer & Murdock (1995) conducted a national survey with a slightly-modified version of the Therapeutic Practices Survey (TPS) reported by Borys & Pope (1989). Their findings suggested "that overall, therapists thought that nonerotic dual-relationship behaviors were ethical in only limited circumstances at best. . . . Therapists judged social and/or financial involvements with their clients as the least ethical of the three classes of nonerotic dual relationships. . . . That psychologists appear clear about the importance of meeting their own social and financial needs (other than payment for therapy) through people who are not their clients is important and can be viewed as promising" (p. 143).

These studies of nonsexual dual relationships in psychotherapy provide some initial empirical data upon which to develop an understanding of the phenomenon and provide some intriguing hypotheses. What is striking, however, is the scarcity of such studies. We need critical self-study, including the systematic collection of data, regarding the occurrence and effects of dual relationships.

STRATEGIES OF TOLERATION AND JUSTIFICATION

If both sexual and nonsexual dual relationships have historically been viewed by the mental health professions as harmful, what strategies enable us to tolerate or justify them? Any answer, at least at this stage, can only be speculative, but such speculation may help generate research hypotheses and prompt more thoughtful consideration of any temptations we may feel to engage in harmful dual relationships with our patients. Perhaps part of the answer lies in the consistent research finding that for not only sexual but also nonsexual dual relationships in therapy (as well as for dual relationships in teaching, supervision, and administration), the perpetrators are overwhelmingly (but not exclusively) male and the victims are overwhelmingly (but not exclusively) female. Reflecting the larger society, the mental health professions unfortunately seem exceptionally resourceful in finding ways to deny, justify, trivialize, and discount forms of serious harm for which the perpetrators are mostly men and the victims are mostly women (Pope, 1990c, 1994; Walker & Young, 1986). Perhaps another part of the answer lies in some of the strategies outlined below.

Selective Inattention

One of the most prevalent ways in which dual relationships—and many other forms of unethical behavior—are made tolerable is through selective inattention. The therapist blocks out sustained, useful awareness of the duality of relationships by splitting the two relationships and refusing to acknowledge that both relationships involve the same patient and have implications for the patient and the patient's treatment.

Selective inattention is a more advanced version of carelessness or negligence, and all of us who have maintained a clinical practice have probably engaged in it in one form or another. For example, we may have been treating a patient and have found ourselves becoming terribly drowsy or bored during a session. Such feelings may have important implications for the treatment of that patient and may represent an evolving countertransference reaction. However, attending to such feelings may make us uncomfortable and we may choose to treat them carelessly, trying to ease or shove them out of our awareness and to split off any remaining awareness we have of those feelings from our considerations about this particular patient and the treatment. As another example, we may work in a hospital and find ourselves talking with other treatment and clerical staff about patients over lunch in the hospital cafeteria. At the end of the day, were anyone to ask us, we would deny having breached any patient's confidentiality, having blocked off awareness that chatting about patients in an informal public setting, such as a hospital cafeteria, violates our responsibilities to safeguard the privacy of our patients and their treatment.

One indication that selective inattention may have played a role in the development of a dual relationship is the lack of any mention of a second relationship in the treatment notes. Thus anyone reviewing the patient's chart would be completely unaware that the therapist has formed a business partnership with the patient, has borrowed next month's rent from the patient, or has moved into the same house with the patient. The chart contains no mention of the duality of the relationship, no consideration of how the two relationships may be interacting, and no discussion of how the dual relationship may affect the patient's clinical status, prognosis, treatment plan, or response to the treatment plan. The form for informed consent to treatment will also lack any information regarding how the dual relationship may affect the treatment.

Selective inattention may foster dual relationships in another manner. Often the colleagues of a therapist who is entering a dual relationship may choose to screen out and remain selectively inattentive to evidence that the therapist is engaging in activities that put the patient at risk for harm. Again, such selective inattention regarding some of our closest colleagues is common to virtually all of us who practice as clinicians. At times, we may not want to risk losing a friendship; we fear that the warmth of our relationship with a colleague who is engaging in a harmful dual relationship with a patient might disappear, perhaps permanently. At times, we may fear the anger or the power of our colleague. Perhaps she is our employer or supervisor; perhaps he is a valuable source of referrals. At times, we may not want to rock the boat and upset the tranquility of a formal organization, such as a clinic, or an informal network of colleagues. And at times, we may experience the "glass house" phenomenon: We may avoid raising ethical issues with others because we are afraid that they will begin raising them with us. Thus we may enter into a tacit pact with our colleagues: Everyone will ignore everyone else's ethical violations. In such situations, selective inattention becomes an important aspect of the interpersonal or social ecology. When selective inattention becomes the norm, any attempt to overcome the splitting off of awareness must overcome the tendency of the interpersonal or social system to maintain homeostasis. The accumulated resistance to acknowledging the duality of the treatment relationship becomes quite powerful.

Benefits

A second way in which dual relationships are sometimes justified is that they are beneficial for the patient. When the initial malpractice suits alleging sexual dual relationships were tried, defendants frequently stressed that the sexual relationship was an important component of the treatment plan. The addition of the sexual relationship was said to provide the patient with a more nurturing, less coldly professional relationship; a more complete sense of acceptance; a way for the patient to experience and work through "overt transference"; and a safe "bridge" between the therapeutic and nontherapeutic environment (that is, the patient could "try out" on the therapist what the patient had discovered about sex and intimacy during the early stages of therapy so that the patient could be sure of making it work "in real life"). The sexual relationship was also claimed to help the patient develop—under the watchful eye of the therapist—a healthier view of his or her own sexuality and a more varied and complete array of sexual responses; to provide sexually corrective experiences that would help the patient recover from dysfunction caused by prior sexual trauma; and to give the opportunity to overcome a disabling "mind-body" split in which the patient's reactions were overly intellectualized.

One difficulty the proponents of this view experienced was that mention of the dual relationship—supposedly a key component of the treatment plan—was often absent from any part of the chart notes or informed consent procedures. Therapists had difficulty explaining why, if they had carefully considered how a dual relationship was the treatment of choice and had implemented it carefully, they had neglected to obtain the patient's informed consent for the procedure and why they failed to note the consideration or use of the treatment strategy in the chart notes.

A second problem faced by those who sought to justify their behavior to the civil courts, licensing boards, and ethics committees was their difficulty finding substantial research evidence that implementing dual-relationship treatment was a safe and effective way to produce positive therapeutic change. Such research was exceedingly rare. Perhaps the most frequently cited exception was the study of 1,500 cases of therapist-patient sexual intimacy, each supposedly benefiting the patient, reported by McCartney (1966). McCartney maintained that engaging in sexual dual relationships must be done in an exceptionally careful manner with scrupulous attention to all ethical aspects, an approach that is still frequently echoed today by those who would defend sexual or nonsexual dual relationships. The therapist, for example, must be certain that he or she is free from any self-serving or self-interested motives. In all cases the patient's welfare must be protected. McCartney's approach and the conclusions he drew from the 1,500 patients, however, were not persuasive to most therapists, or to most courts, licensing boards, or ethics committees.

Some therapists acknowledged that there was virtually no research evidence or other systematic data supporting the hypothesis that dual relationships are a safe and effective method to produce therapeutic change. They maintained that their implementation of the dual relationship was on a trial basis, as part of a research or quasi-research effort to obtain just such evidence. However, it was often difficult for these therapists to establish that they had provided adequate procedural safeguards (such as informed consent) to the patients on whom this experimental method was being tested (see Levine, 1988; Pope, 1990b, 1990c, 1990d, 1994).

Prevalence

Therapists may attempt to justify engaging in dual relationships with their patients by asserting that many other therapists engage in the practice. In some instances, this assertion is carelessly made and seems little more than the frequent claim of those in the public eye who cannot find other means to justify less-than-savory behavior: "Everybody does it!" But in other cases, it is a carefully crafted and articulated attempt to establish the legitimacy and acceptability of a behavior because at least a "sizable minority" of the professional community engage in it. Such a defense is often effective in malpractice trials. The professional does not need to establish that the method he or she used is generally accepted by peers but only to show that a sizable or "respectable" minority endorse the procedure. This approach was used in some of the early malpractice trials in which therapists who acknowledged engaging in sexual dual relationships with their patients emphasized that the early surveys of therapist-patient sexual involvement (for example, Holroyd & Brodsky, 1977) indicated that around 10 percent of male therapists reported engaging in sexual relationships with their patients. This 10 percent figure, according to the defense, represented a sizable minority of the professional community who accepted and endorsed, via their own behavior with patients, the legitimacy of therapist-patient sexual relations.

The reflexive acceptance of the "prevalence" argument may have encouraged or facilitated both sexual and nonsexual dual relationships. But the argument itself does not seem to address the issue of whether dual relationships are indeed a safe and effective way to produce beneficial change in the patient. Various behaviors that may be unethical, illegal, or clinically contraindicated may unfortunately be practiced, from time to time, by a sizable minority and sometimes even a majority of the professional community. National surveys of therapists have indicated, for example, that over 20 percent of the participants have rendered clinical services for which they (by their own judgment) were clearly incompetent, over 20 percent intentionally breached their patient's legal right to confidentiality, a majority performed clinical work when they were so distressed that they were unable to function effectively, and a majority breached their patient's legal right to confidentiality through negligence (Pope & Bajt, 1988; Pope, Tabachnick & Keith-Spiegel, 1987). The fact that a substantial number of professionals engage in a practice does not, in and of itself, indicate whether the practice is ethical, legal, safe, or effective.

Tradition

Some dual relationships are created through an exchange of services. For example, the therapist provides psychotherapy to the patient; in exchange, the patient does typing and filing for the therapist, creates a painting to decorate the therapist's waiting room, or provides child care for the therapist's sons and daughters. Therapists who develop this kind of dual relationship with their patients often assume that the practice is ethical and not harmful because bartering has a rich historical tradition.

The problem for this justification is that the tradition of service bartering in early American life and culture did not include psychotherapy. Attempts to assert that psychotherapy is functionally equivalent to those services that have traditionally been the subject of bartering ignore the context. Nearly any practice such as bartering may be not only sensible and safe but also socially beneficial in certain forms of exchange and may indicate no harm or risks in the abstract. In virtually all cases, however, the context is crucial. Thus the tradition of giving gifts may be a wonderful one; giving an expensive gift to a judge who is trying a case in which one is a principle participant is frowned upon. The tradition of passionate sexual relationships may be treasured by many; such relationships, when they involve therapist and patient, can be disastrous. The professional or psychotherapeutic context cannot be ignored.

Client Autonomy

Sexual and nonsexual dual relationships are often rationalized by reflexively asserting the concept of "client autonomy." This concept becomes a cloak for unethical behavior; it appears to refer to a client's right that is so fundamental, absolute, and unquestionable that no other consideration could possibly intervene.

The basic premise is that if the client desires a sexual or nonsexual dual relationship with a therapist, whether before or after termination, the therapist has no right—let alone responsibility—to refuse because to do so would interfere with the client's autonomy. Thus ethical, professional, and similar prohibitions against harmful behaviors must be set aside, according to this argument, if they threaten the fundamental value of client autonomy.

Such arguments tend to appear merely as assertions, rather than in the context of coherent ethical and clinical theory. But perhaps most striking is their proponents' failure to apply the concept to other areas of practice. For example, for a nonmedical therapist (one neither trained nor licensed to prescribe medication) to provide drugs to a client would put that client at risk. Yet what if a client begged his or her nonmedical therapist to personally provide drugs? An ethical therapist would respectfully but firmly decline, explaining the reasons for declining and exploring options such as referral to a physician. An ethical nonmedical therapist would *not* invoke the concept of the client's inviolable autonomy as a rationalization to provide the client with drugs. As another example, if a client or former client wanted to take up residence in the therapist's waiting room, the therapist would not agree to such an arrangement to avoid interfering with the client's autonomy.

Proponents' inconsistent use of the concept of client autonomy (or other superficial rationalizations such as "right to assemble") reveals the degree to which the actual meaning of this concept has been taken out of concept and misused in service of the therapist's desire to engage in sex (or in some other dual relationship) with someone to whom he or she has agreed to provide professional services.

Necessity

Dual relationships may be accepted with virtually no ethical or clinical scrutiny when they are asserted to be "necessary." The therapist claims that there was no alternative but to engage in a dual relationship. The therapist using this justification refuses to accept any responsibility for entering a dual relationship; the therapist must simply accept what is determined by forces beyond his or her control. Thus dual relationships may be termed "inevitable" or "unavoidable."

Yet the "my hands were tied" approach may represent a combination of a failure to explore and create alternative approaches that meet the highest clinical, legal, and ethical standards and an unsubtle attempt to evade responsibility. Careful, determined, imaginative attempts to meet the needs of patients without resorting to sexual or nonsexual dual relationships can overcome the rationalization of necessity. Michael Enright, for example, discussed the dilemma of therapists in a very small town in which the hospital administration called for a periodic review of all current patients (personal communication, May 13, 1989). The therapists at the hospital were to conduct this review. The problem it presented is obvious: Although they had scrupulously avoided treating patients with whom they had other ongoing (social or business) relationships, the therapists would, by conducting this periodic review of all cases, become aware of diagnostic and treatment issues as well as other "private" information about their friends and business associates. Enright pointed out that among a whole tangle of ethical and clinical issues is that of informed consent: The patients did not understand that their social and business associates would be reviewing their course of treatment, nor had they consented to such a review. Examination of these issues led to the idea that a clinician from a different community could be brought in on a regular basis both to review current cases and to ensure that all patients adequately understood and consented to the review process.

CONCLUSION

The harm and exploitation that can result from both sexual and nonsexual dual relationships is perpetrated overwhelmingly by male professionals on an overwhelmingly female patient population, a pattern that may have played a role in our difficulty addressing this issue vigorously and effectively. The initial research has led to specific recommendations for education and training (Borys & Pope, 1989), but much remains to be done. The vulnerability of individuals who are seeking help from a therapist and the harm that is done both to the welfare of the patient and to the integrity of the profession when the role of therapist is abused makes it extremely hard to justify further neglect of the issue in our research, writings, and professional efforts to ensure the highest level of ethical and clinical practice.

It is crucial to clarify our relationship to each patient and to avoid sexual and nonsexual dual relationships which prevent that clarity and place the patient at great risk for harm. Achieving that clarity is impossible without adequate awareness and appreciation of cultural, contextual, and individual differences—the subject of the next chapter.

SCENARIOS FOR DISCUSSION

You decide to teach a course in basic psychopathology as part of the local community college's associate of arts degree program. You show up on the first day of class and see that there are ten students who have signed up. Two of them are current psychotherapy clients in your practice.

1. How do you feel?
2. Does their presence change how you teach your first class session?
3. What options do you have for addressing this issue?

4. What do you think you would do?

5. How, if at all, would you address this issue in the chart notes for these two clients?

———∿∿∿———

You live in a very small community. You are the only psychotherapist providing services through the local managed care plan. One day one of your closest friends, someone you have known for several decades, shows up at your office, seeking therapy.

1. How do you feel?

2. Do you share any of your feelings or concerns with the client during this session? If so, what do you say?

3. Assume that you do not believe that you can serve as therapist in light of your close friendship with this person. However, the patient points out that not only are you the only one designated to provide therapy under the managed care plan, but that since you are also virtually the only one anywhere near this small community who matches the client in terms of characteristics that the patient feels are important (that is, the patient believes that only someone who matches the patient's gender, race, and sexual orientation will understand the issues and be able to help), the patient can't really get help from anyone but you. How do you address this? What are your options? What steps would you take?

———∿∿∿———

You've been suffering some financial losses and are close to bankruptcy. You will probably lose everything if you are unable to sell your house. You have been trying to sell your house for close to two years and have not received a serious offer. You hold yet another open house. The only person to show up is one of your psychotherapy clients who says, "This is a great house! I'd love to buy it. And although I'd be buying it anyway, its nice that it'll end up helping you."

1. How do you feel?

2. What do you think you would say?

3. What options do you consider?

4. What do you think you'd end up doing?

———

A couple, who are your close friends, are aware that you will probably be spending Thanksgiving alone. They invite you to share Thanksgiving day with them, preparing the meal during the morning, feasting at lunch, going for a leisurely walk in the woods during the afternoon, then returning for a light dinner. You show up to discover that they have, without letting you know, invited another "unattached" person who is presumably your blind date for the day. That person is currently a client to whom you've been providing psychotherapy for two years.

1. How do you feel?

2. What are your options?

3. What do you think you would do?

4. How, if at all, would your feelings, options, or probable-course change if the person was a former client?

5. What if, rather than your client, the person was your therapy supervisor?

6. What if the person was your own therapist?

———

During a session a client mentions that, because of her job, she receives many free tickets to concerts, plays, and other events. She loves giving them to her various doctors because she greatly appreciates their hard work and because it costs her nothing. She tells you that she has already mailed to you the day before a pair of tickets to an upcoming concert because you had happened to mention that you are a fan of the performer, who has never held a concert in your part of the country before. You have tried to find tickets to take your daughter, who very much wants to attend, but tickets were immediately sold out and no source seems to have them available at any price.

1. What do you feel?

2. What issues do you consider?

3. Is there any more information that you would want before deciding what to do? If so, what information would you seek?

4. Under what conditions, if any, would you accept the tickets?

5. After the session is over, how, if at all, would you describe this situation in your chart notes?

—⁓—

You are very involved in your community; you've been appointed to a new board, which is engaged in the kind of activism you value. You attend your first board meeting to discover that one of your new clients is also on the board. Your client comes over at a break to tell you how pleased she is that you share similar values and will be working together.

1. How do you feel?

2. What feelings do you imagine that your client might be experiencing?

3. What issues do you consider?

4. What do you think you would say to your client?

5. Would you remain on the board or not? What reasoning leads you to this decision?

6. How, if at all, would you chart this interaction?

CHAPTER TWELVE

Cultural, Contextual, and Individual Differences

Our society's cultural diversity and broad range of social classes have important ethical implications for counselors and psychotherapists. Differences in cultural background or social class between clinician and client can create needless barriers to the delivery of effective services by the ethically unaware, unprepared, or careless clinician.

One of the major responsibilities is twofold. On the one hand, the clinician must become adequately knowledgeable and respectful of the client's relevant cultural or socioeconomic contexts. Therapists who ignore cultural values, attitudes, and behaviors different from their own deprive themselves of crucial information and may tend to impose their own worldview and assumptions upon clients in an exceptionally fallacious and destructive manner. On the other hand, the clinician must avoid making simplistic, unfounded assumptions on the basis of cultural or socioeconomic contexts. Knowledge about cultural and socioeconomic contexts becomes the basis for informed inquiry rather than the illusion of uniform group characteristics with which to stereotype the client. Neither variation between groups nor within groups can be discounted or ignored.

Some readers may object to the apparent restriction of this two-fold ethical responsibility to clinical situations in which the clinician and client are of different cultural or socioeconomic backgrounds. They might argue that the need to understand any client's background or context and to avoid assuming that the individual can somehow be "summarized" by certain group characteristics are essential ethical responsibilities in any clinical endeavor. They would be emphasizing an important point. As Pedersen, Draguns, Lonner, & Trimble (1989, p. 1) emphasize in *Counseling Across Cultures:* "Multicultural counseling is not an exotic topic that applies to remote regions, but is the heart and core of good counseling with any client."

Our training, however, often fails to teach us how to apply the basic principles of counseling beyond the values and ethos of the majority culture. Greene (1997), for example, notes some of the ways in which the empirical literature does not take adequate account of cultural and other differences.

A preponderance of the empirical research on or with lesbians and gay men has been conducted with overwhelmingly white, middle-class respondents. . . . Similarly, research on members of ethnic minority groups rarely acknowledges differences in sexual orientation among group members. Hence there has been little exploration of the complex interaction between sexual orientation and ethnic identity development, nor have the realistic social tasks and stressors that are a component of gay and lesbian identity formation in conjunction with ethnic identity formation been taken into account. Discussion of the vicissitudes of racism and ethnic identity in intra- and interracial couples of the same gender and their effects on these couples' relationships has also been neglected in the narrow focus on heterosexual relationships found in the literature on ethnic minority clients. There has been an equally narrow focus on predominantly white couples in the gay and lesbian literature [pp. 216–217].

Yet even within such a complex framework of cultural and other forms of difference, it may be deceptively tempting to view each person as a fixed set of descriptors.

Although identity is a fluid concept in psychological and sociological terms, we tend to speak of identities in fixed terms. In particular, those aspects of identity that characterize observable physical characteristics, such as race or gender, are perceived as unchanging ascribed identities. Examples of these would include identifications such as *Chinese woman,* or *Korean American woman,* or even broader terms such as *woman of color,* which are ways of grouping together individuals who are not of the hegemonic "white" race in the United States. We base these constructions of identity upon physical appearance and an individual's declaration of identity. However, even these seemingly clear distinctions are not definitive. For example, I, as a woman of Asian racial background, may declare myself a woman of color because I see myself as belonging to a group of ethnic/racial minorities. However, my (biological) sister could insist that she is not a woman of color because she does not feel an affiliation with our group goals, even though she is a person of Chinese ancestry. Does her nonaffiliation take her out of the group of people of color? Or does she remain in regardless of her own self-identification because of her obvious physical characteristics? Generally, in the context of identities based upon racial and physical characteristics, ascribed identities will, rightly or wrongly, continue to be attributed to individuals by others. It is left up to individuals themselves to assert their identities and demonstrate to others that they are or are *not* what they might appear to be upon first notice [Chan, 1997, pp. 240–241; see also Wyatt, 1997].

In our society, furthermore, culture, race, ethnicity, socioeconomic status, and related factors of "difference" are frequently emotion-laden concepts that may inhibit, distort, or diminish rather than enrich the caring and trust necessary to an effective therapeutic process (see Chapter Three). Similarly, the differential power between therapist and client (see Chapter Three) may lose its enabling, healing, or therapeutic potential and become instead a reflection of the power differential that is frequently perceived between the rich and the poor, between the racial majority and minorities, and between other social, economic, or political groupings. For such reasons, a chapter focusing on issues of cultural, socioeconomic, and similar differences seems useful and warranted, even though it will address some of the same topic areas—competence and assessment, for example—explored in other chapters. The purpose is not only to identify some of the barriers to fulfilling our ethical responsibilities in regard to these forms of "difference" (and by implication or analogy, to other forms of difference) but also to note effective approaches to transcending these barriers.

OVERCOMING BARRIERS
TO ETHICAL SERVICES

The following steps exemplify approaches that can be effective in transcending barriers to ethical services.

Acknowledging Socioeconomic Differences

One of the initial steps in an ethical approach to the issue of difference is simply an awareness of the great socioeconomic differences that exist in our society. It is exceptionally easy for us to create a cognitive map of the world in which over 90 percent of the area is represented by our own immediate environment. We lose active awareness that many people live in significantly different contexts. We minimize the differences and forget the contrasts and their implications. One vivid example of the extreme conditions in which some U.S. citizens live was provided by the epidemiological study of New York published in the *New England Journal of Medicine* (McCord & Freeman, 1990). The analysis showed that fifty-four of the 353 health areas in New York had at least double the anticipated mortality rate for individuals under sixty-five years old. With only one exception, all of these fifty-four areas were predominantly African-American or Hispanic. "Survival analysis showed that black men in Harlem were less likely to reach the age of 65 than men in Bangladesh" (p. 173). The authors pointed out that their findings were similar to those for natural disaster areas.

What does it mean to us as therapists and counselors that fellow citizens live in such conditions? At a minimum, it requires that we acknowledge the reality of such conditions and that we inform ourselves adequately when we provide professional services to those from such lethal conditions or from other distinct contexts that differ from our own.

But such conditions also confront us with inescapable ethical questions regarding the degree to which we as individuals and as a profession view ourselves as responsible in some part for addressing these conditions, regardless of whether circumstances bring clients from those conditions to our offices. Goodyear & Sinnett (1984), for example, are among those who argue that counselors and therapists have an ethical responsibility to work to protect client populations against harm imposed by oppressive systems. Such work might include advocating against agency policies that have a deleterious effect on ethnic minority clients or developing preventive and developmental interventions as strategies to enhance the quality of life for ethnic minorities (Casas & Vasquez, 1989).

Remaining Alert to Possible Bias in Interpreting Research

A second step in an ethical approach to the issue of difference is to remain alert to the tendency for group differences to form a basis for stereotyping, bias, and discrimination, whether based on factors of race, culture, gender, sexual orientation, religions, physical disability, geography, or socioeconomics. The extent to which our vulnerability to such prejudice can shape our interpretation of "scientific" research is illustrated by a carefully planned study by Bache (1894). Conducting his research (in collaboration with Professor Lightner Witmer) at the University of Pennsylvania by using a finely calibrated, state-of-the-art magnetoelectric apparatus, Bache was concerned with both gender-based and racially based differences in reaction time, or "automatic movements."

Bache was convinced that men would have faster reaction times than women and that this would prove the intellectual (and perhaps overall) superiority of men. Moreover, Bache was convinced that the "Caucasian Race" would manifest faster reaction times than both the "Indian Race" and the "African Race."

The first set of experiments focused on differences between men and women. The men had faster reaction times than the women, leading Bache to conclude that men were intellectually superior: "The reaction time of women, as settled by the same indisputable method, was . . . determined as less than that of men, and this result, it will be observed, is in strict accordance with the fact that the brain development of men, as compared with that of women, is greater, even when taking into account the relatively greater weight of normal individuals of the male sex as compared with that of normal individuals of the opposite one" (p. 482).

When he conducted the research into racial differences, he was surprised. "The first thing that strikes one, upon examination of the tables, is the relative slowness of the Whites, as compared with the Indians and Africans" (p. 484). These results led Bache to conclude that the whites were intellectually superior to the Indians and Africans! Despite his prior analysis of male-female differences (in which faster reaction times indicated intellectual superiority), Bache reasoned that the white "intellectuality [had] been gained at the expense of his automatic capacity" (p. 480). Thus, the advancement of the intellect had caused, "through the law of compensation" (p. 480), a slowing down of reflexes.

In other words, doing well on a test that had been set forth as positively correlated with intelligence (based on purported faster reaction times for men in comparison with women) was interpreted as proof of inferior intellect: "That the negro is, in the truest sense, a race inferior to that of the white can be proved by many facts, and among these by the quickness of his automatic movements as compared with those of the white" (p. 481). Reviews of more recent research and assessment strategies indicate that such bias has been, unfortunately, a continuing problem (see, for example, Block & Dworkin, 1976; Cole & Bruner, 1972; Geller, 1988; J. T. Gibbs & Huang, 1989; Gossett, 1963; Gould, 1981; Guthrie, 1998; E. E. Jones & Korchin, 1982; J. M. Jones, 1990a, 1990b; J. M. Jones & Block, 1984; Murphy, 1976; Ridley, 1989; Scarr & Weinberg, 1976; W. Stanton, 1960; Thomas & Sillen, 1972).

The empirical literature suggests that just as racial or gender bias can influence interpretation of research findings, such biases may also be manifested in work with patients. Garb's (1997) review of the research, for example, found that

> misdiagnoses of schizophrenia occur more often for Black and Hispanic patients than for White patients when the patients have psychotic affective disorders. Another well-replicated finding is that diagnoses of antisocial personality disorder are more likely to be made for males than females while diagnoses of histrionic personality disorder are more likely to be made for females than males, even when males and females are described by the same case histories. Another important finding is that referrals for psychotherapy were more often made for middle-class clients than for lower-class clients. Also, when both middle-class and lower-class clients were referred for psychotherapy, middle-class clients were more often recommended for insight-oriented psychotherapy and lower-class clients were more often recommended for supportive psychotherapy. As another example of bias, antipsychotic medications were more often prescribed for Black patients than for other patients even when the Black patients were not more psychotic, and affective symptoms in severely mentally ill patients were more often under-treated when patients were Black or Hispanic compared to when they were White.

Potential Problems with Assessment Instruments

A third useful step in confronting ethically the issue of difference is to remain alert to the possibility that standardized tests and other assessment instruments may manifest bias. LaFromboise & Foster (1989), for example, discuss the case of *Larry P.* v. *Riles* in which the intelligence testing that led to the placement of an African-American student into a special education class was unlawful because of the bias of the tests used. They describe two instruments that were specifically developed to avoid racial or cultural bias in assessment of abilities: the Adaptive Behavior Scale (American Association on Mental Deficiency, 1974) and the System of Multicultural Pluralistic Assessment (Mercer, 1979).

An example of a standardized personality test that has been called into question in regard to potential bias is the original Minnesota Multiphasic Personality Inventory (MMPI; not the revised MMPI-II). African Americans, Native Americans, Hispanics, and Asian Americans were among the groups omitted from the sample from which the original MMPI norms were developed. What implications does this exclusion have for the ethical use of the test? Faschingbauer (1979, p. 385) vividly described his reservations: "The original Minnesota group seems to be an inappropriate reference group for the 1980s. The median individual in that group had an eighth-grade education, was married, lived in a small town or on a farm, and was employed as a lower level clerk or skilled tradesman. None was under sixteen or over sixty-five years of age, and all were white. As a clinician I find it difficult to justify comparing anyone to such a dated group. When the person is fourteen years old, Chicano, and lives in Houston's poor fifth ward, use of original norms seems sinful."

A former president of the APA Division of the Society for Personality Assessment, Erdberg (1988) reported that in one research study, a single item from the original MMPI discriminated perfectly on the basis of race, that is to say, it differentiated all African-American test takers from all Caucasian test takers in this rural community.

POTENTIAL PROBLEMS IN THE CLINICAL RELATIONSHIP

Whether we are conducting an assessment or are conducting therapy or counseling, our interaction with the client is obviously of great significance. J. M. Jones (1990b) reviewed a variety of research studies demonstrating the degree to which factors such as race could, if not addressed carefully, undermine the process. For example, failing to take such factors into account can contribute to a high premature dropout rate for minorities seeking mental health services.

One set of studies conducted by Word, Zanna, & Cooper (1974; reviewed by J. M. Jones, 1990b) demonstrates the degree to which subtle, unintentional discrimination by the individual conducting the assessment can lead to impaired performance by the person being assessed. In the first part of the study, white interviewers asked questions of both white and African-American individuals. There were significant differences in interviewer behavior. Those conducting the assessment spent more time with the white interviewees, looked directly at white interviewees a greater portion of the time, maintained less physical distance from white interviewees, and made fewer speech errors with white interviewees.

For the second part of the study, white interviewers were trained to become aware of and to use both styles of interview. They were then asked to interview a number of white people. With half of the white interviewees, the interviewer conducted the interview in a style consistent for white interviewees (for example, a longer interview at less distance). With the other half of the white interviewees, the interviewer followed a style consistent for black interviewees (shorter interview, more distance). The latter interviewees performed much less well on a series of objective measures during the assessment interview. Thus even if the tests or assessment instruments themselves are relatively free of bias, the behavior of the interviewer can influence those who are being assessed in a discriminatory way that impairs performance.

Understanding the Context

Addressing the issue of difference involves more than acknowledging important differences and avoiding prejudice and stereotyping; it involves an active appreciation of the context in which clients live and understand their lives. Westermeyer (1987, pp. 471–472) provides an example of this appreciation.

A forty-eight-year-old ethnic Chinese woman had been receiving antipsychotic and antidepressant medication for psychotic depression. On this regimen, the patient had lost even more weight and more hope and had become more immobilized. A critical element in this diagnosis of psychosis was the woman's belief that her deceased mother, who had been appearing in her dreams, had traveled from the place of the dead to induce the patient's own death and to bring her to the next world. We interpreted this symptom not as a delusional belief but as a culturally consistent belief in a depressed woman who had recently begun to see her deceased mother in her dreams (a common harbinger of death in the dreams of some Asian patients). This patient responded well after the antipsychotic medication was discontinued, the antidepressant medication was reduced in dosage, and weekly psychotherapy was instituted.

Similarly, the research of Amaro, Russo, & Johnson (1987) demonstrates the importance of an attentive and informed appreciation of different contexts. In comparing sources of strength and stress for Hispanic and Anglo female professionals, they found similar family and work characteristics to be associated with positive mental health. Income was the most consistently related demographic factor across all measures of psychological well-being. In addition, however, Hispanic women's psychological well-being was related to the experience of discrimination, which was reported by more than 82 percent of the sample. Those of us who are not subject to discrimination in our day-to-day lives may find it easy to misinterpret and mistreat the distress and dysfunction that can result from prejudice.

In some cases, cultural and other forms of difference are relevant to therapists and counselors assessing their fundamental competence to render services.

When approached by people in need, therapists need to evaluate whether the anticipated issues fall within their realm of competence or expertise. To use an extreme example, an Anglo therapist who speaks only English and has never learned about or conducted clinical work with abuse victims should evaluate carefully whether he or she is the best person to work with a Hispanic patient who speaks very little English and who has recently recovered memories of childhood sexual abuse. Even when therapist and client speak the same basic language, it can be important to attend carefully to possible regional cultural or language differences that could lead to potentially problematic confusions of meaning. In one instance, a woman born in Puerto Rico walked into her office and found someone rifling through her purse. The potential thief ran off in the midst of an emotional confrontation, although no one was touched. Later, the woman described this event in Spanish to a social worker who had been born in Cuba. She used the word *asalto* to mean a "confrontation." The social worker, however, understood this term to refer to a physical assault . . . because the term was used differently in Cuban Spanish than in Puerto Rican Spanish [Pope & Brown, 1996, pp. 179–180].

Creativity

A final step to be mentioned in this discussion of differences involves a creative and thorough approach to human diversity. In a series of studies at Harvard University, Langer, Bashner, & Chanowitz (1985) asked children to consider individuals who were different from the mainstream in that they were physically challenged. In one study, the experimental group of children were asked to think of as many ways as possible that a disabled person might meet a particular challenge whereas the control group children were simply asked whether the disabled person could meet the challenge. For example, children were shown a picture of a woman in a wheelchair and were asked either *how* the woman could drive a car or *whether* the woman could drive a car. In another study, children in the experimental group were asked to give numerous reasons not only why a handicapped individual—a blind person, for example—might be bad at a particular profession but also why he or she might be good at it.

In these and other studies, Langer (1989) found that creativity in responding to forms of human difference can indeed be taught and that it can lead to more realistic, less prejudiced reactions to individuals who differ in some way from the mainstream. The research showed "that children can be taught that handicaps are function-specific and not person-specific.

Those given training in making mindful distinctions learned to be discriminating without prejudice. This group was also less likely than the control group to avoid a handicapped person. In essence, the children were taught that attributes are relative and not absolute, that whether or not something is a disability depends on context" (pp. 169–170).

Whether we practice in private offices, HMOs, hospitals, clinics, community mental health centers, university settings, or elsewhere, we must remain alert and creative in regard to the contexts in which we work and the characteristics of those who need our help. Is our setting responsive to the needs of those who use wheelchairs, those for whom English is a new language, those who use American Sign Language to communicate, or those who are blind? For whom is our setting open, inviting, accessible, and genuinely helpful? Who is shut out or discouraged from approaching? To what degree do we acknowledge or assume responsibility for the nature of the settings in which we practice?

SCENARIOS FOR DISCUSSION

You are conducting an intake examination at an HMO. The patient's first words to you are: "I'm having some problems with my sexual identity but I think I can only work with someone who understands where I'm coming from, who has faced these same issues, and who knows what it's like. What's your sexual orientation?"

1. How do you feel?
2. What goals would you have in mind in responding to the patient?
3. Under what conditions, if any, would you disclose your sexual identity to the patient?
4. To what extent has your training included research and theory relevant to sexual identity?

—⁄⁄⁄—

You are a Latino therapist who speaks Spanish moderately. Your policy is to try to refer all those who speak only Spanish to fluent Spanish speakers, but you will see Spanish speakers who also speak English, if they wish. A South American client, who speaks fluent English and Spanish sees you because you are the only Latino available on her HMO list. At the first session, she insists that you should be ashamed for not speaking better Spanish, and that you therefore have no culture.

1. How do you feel?
2. What are your thoughts and feelings about this client?
3. How would you respond to this client?

4. Under what conditions would you continue to see or decline to see this client?

—◠◠—

You have been leading a therapy group at a large mental health facility. As one of the sessions begins, a group member interrupts you and says, "I want to ask you about something. Have you noticed how none of the doctors here are black or Hispanic but almost all the cleaning crew are? Why do you work in a system like that? Don't you think that has any effects on us patients?"

1. How do you feel?
2. What are the possible replies you consider?
3. What do you think you would say?
4. What effects, if any, might such a system have on patients?

—◠◠—

You are working with a patient who is of a different race and sexual orientation from you and your supervisor. One day, the patient is fifteen minutes late for a session and you spend some of the session discussing the reasons for the patient's not being on time. When you bring up the topic to your supervisor, the response is: "Oh, that lateness doesn't mean anything psychological. That's just the way those people are."

1. How do you feel?
2. What possible responses to your supervisor's comments do you consider?
3. What do you think that you'd actually say to your supervisor?
4. When you imagined this scenario, what race and sexual orientation did you imagine the patient was? Why?

—◠◠—

A married couple come to you for counseling. Both believe that men are the natural leaders in a marriage and that a woman's rightful place is to be obedient to her husband. However, they often have what they describe as "slips" when he seems to look to her for guidance or when she finds it hard to accept his decisions. They are seeking marital counseling to help them eliminate these "slips."

1. How do you feel?

2. What are your thoughts and feelings about the wife?

3. What are your thoughts and feelings about the husband?

4. What are your thoughts and feelings about the marital relationship that they value and have chosen for themselves?

5. How do you think you would respond?

—⁓—

You are a therapist at an agency with a policy that says that if a client misses two appointments without calling, the therapy automatically terminates. A client who is a single mother, uses public transportation, has no phone, and is often distressed by a baby sitter who does not show up, does not show up for her appointment for the second time. Your supervisor insists that you terminate by letter, given the long waiting list of potential clients.

1. What feelings do you experience?

2. What are your assumptions about the client's not showing up? In what way, if any, might her diagnosis be relevant?

3. What do you think and feel about the relevance of the policy for clients such as this one?

4. What are your options in responding to your supervisor? To the agency policy? To the client?

CHAPTER THIRTEEN

Maintaining and Waiving Confidentiality

thics complaints, malpractice suits, and licensing disciplinary actions make clear the difficulties most of us encounter in addressing issues of confidentiality (see Chapter Two). A review of four years of annual reports by the APA Ethics Committee indicated that violation of general standard 5, "Privacy and Confidentiality," which applies to the professional and scientific activities of all psychologists who are members of APA (APA, 1992), was the fifth most frequent allegation resulting in opened cases (American Psychological Association, Ethics Committee, 1994, 1995, 1996, 1997). An examination of malpractice suits closed during the 1976–1991 period found that breach of confidentiality accounted for 7 percent of the total claims against psychologists covered under the APA's professional liability policy (personal correspondence, APAIT Central Office, October 7, 1997). Finally, confidentiality was one of ten violations most frequently serving as a basis for disciplinary actions taken against psychologists by state licensing boards (personal correspondence, ASPPB Central Office, September 29, 1997).

Frequencies of formal complaints or disciplinary actions may significantly underestimate the scope of the problem. Over half (61.9

percent) of the psychologists responding in one national study reported *unintentionally* violating their patients' confidences (Pope, Tabachnick, & Keith-Spiegel, 1987). Another national study found that the most frequently reported *intentional* violation of the law or ethical standards by senior, prominent psychologists involved confidentiality (Pope & Bajt, 1988). In 21 percent of the cases, psychologists violated confidentiality in transgression of law. In another 21 percent of the cases, psychologists refused to breach confidentiality to make legally required reports of child abuse.

Therapists may have experienced and been affected by violations of confidentiality when they themselves were patients. In one national survey, about 10 percent of the therapists who had been in therapy reported that their own therapist had violated their rights to confidentiality (Pope & Tabachnick, 1994).

Because each state differs from the others in terms of applicable legislation, case law, and administrative licensing regulations, there is considerable variation in how the distinct (but interrelated) issues of privacy, confidentiality, and privilege as well as mandatory or discretionary reporting authorizations are defined.

This chapter will highlight some major aspects of clinical work in which therapists and counselors frequently run afoul of ethical or legal standards.

ORGANIZED SYSTEMS OF CARE

One of the most easily overlooked aspects of confidentiality is the degree to which confidential information circulates within health maintenance organizations and other managed care facilities. Many patients feel betrayed when records of their psychotherapy sessions become part of their general medical or health record in an HMO, and may in turn find their way into the hands of third parties. One woman was shocked to find her treatment mentioned on the employee relations bulletin board where she worked. Management and the union, eager to cut both sick leave and the costs for their health care plan, had decided to post all utilizations of the health care plan by the employees. Under the terms of the contract that had been negotiated by labor and management, the date and reason for each utilization was provided by the health care organization to officials for both union and management.

To some extent, questions about confidentiality within managed care organizations have become more complex because these organizations tend to seek more information traditionally regarded as private in order to monitor the allocation of resources and compliance with eligibility criteria.

> Managed care companies generally ask for much more information than third parties have traditionally requested from clinicians. The ethical explanations given for such requests generally have fallen into two categories. One is based on the known history of some clinicians to distort information on forms. . . . Then managed care companies began to discover that some clinicians charged for sessions not provided or approved. A more general reason applicable to all clinicians is to make sure that the intended treatment meets criteria of medical necessity as designated in the third-party benefits. In addition to treatment plans, managed care companies will often ask for copies of any notes kept on patients; they sometimes do on-site reviews of charts in hospitals, and on occasion they even talk directly to the patient to try to verify information [Moffic, 1997, p. 97].

The council of the National Academies of Practice (including dentistry, medicine, nursing, optometry, osteopathic medicine, podiatric medicine, psychology, social work, and veterinary medicine) has adopted "Ethical Guidelines for Professional Care in a Managed Care Environment" (see Appendix C). Confidentiality is one of five guidelines listed as a primary concern. Whereas the National Academies of Practice acknowledges that utilization and quality assurance reviews are appropriate functions in a health care system, they indicate the importance of safeguards to protect the privacy and confidentiality of patient data and the practitioner's clinical materials, and of obtaining client consent. They state "the rationale for this position is founded on the patient's autonomous right to control sensitive personal information. It is further based upon an historical recognition in the Oath of Hippocrates and corroborated throughout the centuries, of the enduring value of preserving confidentiality in order to enhance mutual trust and respect in the patient-provider relationship" (p. 5).

In some cases, health care organizations may not adequately monitor who attends case conferences, and discussions of a patient's condition may be overheard inadvertently by an inappropriate audience.

Who participates in treatment planning, implementation, and review may be a particularly problematic issue in small towns. In one instance, the chief health care administrator proposed a periodic case review of current patients to be conducted by staff psychologists. In this town of fewer than 10,000 people, the psychologists would have known many of the patients in a variety of other (that is, social and business) roles. The patients had not given informed consent for this review.

This confidentiality issue is not easily addressed. One solution would have been for the administrator to agree to hire a psychologist from another community who did not know the population served by the hospital to visit the hospital once a month to review the cases, and to ensure that patients understood the review process.

In still other instances, health care organizations may not provide adequate security for patients' charts and other documents. Too often charts with patient names clearly visible to passersby may be left unattended in public or inadequately secured areas. One prominent teaching facility with an APA-approved internship stacked records in an unlocked public hallway for several weeks so they could be conveniently accessible during a remodeling program. Psychologists have an obligation to ensure that patients are accorded due privacy and confidentiality and that they adequately understand who will have access to information about their treatment.

WRITTEN CONSENT

Perhaps one of the most frequent errors that psychologists make regarding consent for releasing confidential information is to fail to obtain informed consent *in writing*. The "General Guidelines for Providers of Psychological Services" (APA, 1987b) emphasizes that, unless authorized otherwise by law, "Psychologists do not release confidential information, except with the written consent of the user involved, or of his or her legal representative, guardian, or other holder of the privilege on behalf of the user, and only after the user has been assisted to understand the implications of the release" (p. 717).

Obtaining written consent helps promote clarity of communication between therapist and client in situations when misunderstandings can be disastrous. Both need to understand exactly what information is to be sent to a third party. Is the therapist free to discuss any aspect of the client's history, situation, and treatment? Is the therapist authorized to provide a written summary or all clinical files? When, exactly, does the client's authorization end? If the person who is to receive the confidential information contacts the therapist with additional requests for information next month, next year, or several years from now, does the written consent need to be renewed, or does it explicitly cover such future requests?

DIVULGING CONFIDENTIAL INFORMATION ONLY TO THE EXTENT REQUIRED BY LAW

Ethical standard 5.05 ("Disclosures") of the American Psychological Association's (1992) "Ethical Principles of Psychologists and Code of Conduct" mandates that psychologists disclose confidential information without consent of the individual only as mandated by law, or where permitted by law for a valid purpose.

It is thus crucial that therapists remain aware of evolving legislation and case law regarding how much information is to be disclosed in making legally mandated reports. As an example, a psychologist was contacted by a mother who wished to arrange appointments for her daughter and her daughter's stepfather to see the therapist regarding allegations that the stepfather engaged in sexual intimacies with his stepdaughter. The psychologist agreed to meet with him and immediately filed a formal report of suspected child abuse. The next day, a deputy sheriff contacted the psychologist for information. The psychologist furnished information concerning his meeting with the daughter. He would meet with the stepfather later in the day. The deputy called later and asked for information concerning the session with the stepfather and, reading from the Child Abuse Reporting Law, emphasized that the psychologist was obligated to supply additional information, which the psychologist reluctantly provided.

The stepfather claimed in court that the psychologist, after making the initial formal report, should not have disclosed any additional information. The Supreme Court of California agreed with the stepfather: "The psychologist was under no statutory obligation to make a second report concerning the same activity. . . . We have recognized the contemporary value of the psychiatric [sic] profession, and its potential for the relief of emotional disturbances and of the inevitable tensions produced in our modern, complex society. . . . That value is bottomed on a confidential relationship; but the doctor can be of assistance only if the patient may freely relate his thoughts and actions, his fears and fantasies, his strengths and weaknesses, in a completely uninhibited manner" (*People* v. *Stritzinger,* 1983, p. 437).

In some cases, therapists who disclose confidential information *even in court settings* may be subject to suit by the patient. California, for example, has general legislation protecting individuals from lawsuits for any statements made as part of court proceedings. Nevertheless, a district court of appeal ruled that a psychologist "can be sued for disclosing privileged information in a court proceeding when it violates the patient's constitutional right of privacy" (Chiang, 1986, p. 1).

CLIENT COMPREHENSION OF THE LIMITATIONS OF PRIVACY, CONFIDENTIALITY, AND PRIVILEGE

A patient should understand *in advance* the circumstances under which the therapist is required or allowed to communicate information about the patient to third parties. Without such understanding, the patient's consent to treatment is not genuinely informed. The primary philosophical issue underlying the obligation to obtain informed consent involves the principle of *autonomy*. Giving the client an opportunity to make choices regarding limits of confidentiality enhances the client's autonomy.

Psychotherapists are often faced with subpoenas to compel court testimony regarding client records or test data. APA's Committee on Legal Issues (COLI) developed "Strategies for Private Practitioners Coping with Subpoenas or Compelled Testimony for Client Records or Test Data" (APA, 1996) in an attempt to identify ethical responsibilities and legal issues that arise when practitioners are faced with subpoenas or compelled court testimony. COLI acknowledged that the demands of the legal system sometimes conflict with psychologists' ethical obligation to maintain confidentiality of client records as well as to protect the integrity and security of test materials.

The following list of some exceptions to the privilege set forth in the California evidence code illustrates the array of circumstances that may arise under which the therapist may or must divulge confidential information.

• There is no privilege where litigation is pending and the mental or emotional condition of the patient has been tendered as an issue by the patient, a party claiming through the patient, a party claiming as a beneficiary of the patient on a contract to which the patient was a party, or the patient's heirs in an action for the injury or death of the patient.

• There is no privilege if the psychotherapist is appointed by order of the court to examine the patient, except where the psychotherapist is appointed by order of the court upon request of the lawyer for a criminal defendant to assist the lawyer in determining whether the defendant should enter or withdraw a plea based on insanity, or present a defense based on his mental condition.

• There is no privilege if the services of the psychotherapist were sought or obtained to enable or aid someone to plan or commit a crime or a tort, or to escape detection or apprehension after the commission of the crime or tort.

• There is no privilege as to communications relevant to an issue between parties to litigation, all of whose claims derive from a deceased patient, without regard to whether the claims arise technically from a will or whether the patient has died without a will.

• There is no privilege as to communications relevant to an issue of a breach by the therapist or by the patient of a duty arising out of the psychotherapist-patient relationship (such as where the patient alleges that the therapist committed malpractice).

• There is no privilege as to a deed of conveyance, will, or other writing affecting an interest in property, or where there is an issue as to the validity of such an instrument executed by a now-deceased patient.

• There is no privilege for proceedings initiated at the request of a criminal defendant to determine his or her sanity.

• There is no privilege if the psychotherapist has a reasonable belief that the patient is a danger to himself, or to the person or property of another, and the disclosure of the communication is necessary to prevent the threatened danger (in fact, in such circumstances disclosure may be mandated).

• There is no privilege in any action brought by or on behalf of the patient to establish his or her competency.

• There is no privilege as to any information that the psychotherapist or the patient is required to report to a public employee, or information required to be recorded in a public office if the report or record is open for public inspection.

- There is no privilege where the psychologist or psychotherapist is mandated to make a report of child or elder abuse, although this exception is to be read restrictively. However, reports of child abuse and elder abuse are themselves confidential and cannot be disclosed except as specified by statute; thus the exception to the psychotherapist-patient privilege is somewhat offset by the confidentiality accorded the reports.

- There is no privilege where the patient is a child under age sixteen, and the psychotherapist has reasonable cause to believe the patient has been the victim of a crime and believes that disclosure is in the best interest of the child.

Therapists need to clarify what their ethical and legal obligations are to patients in this regard (according to legislation and case law applicable in their state). The clinical implications of withholding this information from patients also need to be considered. As one appeal court judge wrote in consideration of the patient's lack of privilege regarding disclosure of child abuse, "In order to protect a patient's expectation of privacy regarding the seemingly therapeutic and confidential therapy session, however, the therapist should warn the patient of his or her statutory duty to testify against the patient, concerning instances of child abuse" (*People* v. *Younghanz,* 1984, p. 911).

Privacy issues can become much more complicated when the client is a minor. Taylor & Adelman (1995) recommend a statement worded along the following lines:

> Although most of what we talk about is private, there are three kinds or problems you might tell me about that we would have to talk about with other people. If I find out that someone has been seriously hurting or abusing you, I would have to tell the police about it. If you tell me you have made a plan to seriously hurt yourself, I would have to let your parents know. If you tell me you have made a plan to seriously hurt someone else, I would have to warn that person. I would not be able to keep these problems just between you and me because the law says I can't. Do you understand that it's OK to talk about most things here but that these are three things we must talk about with other people? [p. 198]

They recommend that hearing such exceptions may be overwhelming for many minor clients. To soften the impact, Taylor and Adelman recommend adding a statement such as: "Fortunately, most of what we talk over is private. If you want to talk about any of the three problems that must be shared with others, we'll also talk about the best way for us to talk about the problem with others. I want to be sure I'm doing the best I can to help you" (p. 198).

Practitioners must remain informed in regard to the situations that limit confidentiality. For example, the complex responsibilities in the "duty to protect" can be confusing and anxiety-producing. Monahan (1993) identified a series of guidelines for enhancing decision making and reducing therapist exposure to suit, based on his expert witness experience in many cases related to Tarasoff liability. Borum (1996) identified an overview of recent research developments on the risk assessment of violence. Despite our limited ability to assess and predict violence, some research has illustrated some strategies for improving the clinical practice of risk assessment. APA's Committee on Psychological Tests and Assessment (1996) developed a statement regarding the responsibilities of psychologists regarding the disclosure of test data. Continuing education and consultation are additional valuable strategies in remaining informed about the obligation to obtain informed consent and the events and situations that may conflict with our obligations to maintain confidentiality.

INSURANCE FORMS

Clients may not adequately understand the type of information that insurance companies require to authorize coverage and the degree to which information will or will not be sufficiently safeguarded by the insurance company. Keith-Spiegel & Koocher (1985) describe a hypothetical example of a therapist's routine statement to patients regarding insurance coverage: "If you choose to use your coverage, I shall have to file a form with the company telling them when our appointments were and what services I performed (i.e., psychotherapy, consultation, or evaluation). I will also have to formulate a diagnosis and advise the company of that. The company claims to keep this information confidential, although I have no control over the information once it leaves this office. If you have questions about this you may wish to check with the company providing the coverage. You may certainly choose to pay for my services out-of-pocket and avoid the use of insurance altogether, if you wish" (p. 76).

COMMUNICATIONS IN GROUP
OR FAMILY THERAPY

When treatment encompasses more than one individual, as in group and family therapy, therapists must clarify the extent to which state law provides for the privilege and confidentiality of information obtained in the course of treatment and must furthermore clarify in advance with all parties the extent to which information provided to the therapist by one patient may be shared by the therapist with other patients involved in the treatment. For example, if a clinician is providing family therapy, will he or she keep confidential from other family members information conveyed in a phone call from a minor son that he is using drugs, from a minor daughter that she is pregnant, from the father that he is engaging in an extramarital affair and plans to leave his wife, or from the mother that she has secretly withdrawn the family's savings and is using it to gamble? As another example, a counselor may provide services to a couple who subsequently file for divorce; the counselor may be called to testify by an attorney for one of the clients at a custody hearing.

CASE NOTES AND PATIENT FILES

The "Ethical Principles of Psychologists and Code of Conduct" (APA, 1992) provide standards for confidentiality but they do not spell out how confidentiality should be maintained in all settings and situations. What is troubling is that many institutions and individuals fail to guard rigorously the confidentiality of records. In most cases this is unintentional. During a visit to a prestigious university-affiliated teaching hospital, one of the authors noticed, while walking down a public hallway, that the mental health clinic's patient charts were stacked along the walls. The hallway was unattended. The names of the patients were clearly visible, and had the author opened any of the charts, he could have read a wealth of confidential information. When he asked later about charts being left in the hall, he was assured that this was temporary: Due to insufficient funds, additional storage space was not yet available, and this manner of "filing" was most convenient for the business office personnel.

Similarly, some of us may have visited colleagues who leave charts and other patient information lying around on top of their desks. Not only patients' names but also other information may be in full view.

There are at least two important issues here. One is keeping information about clients out of sight of people who are not authorized to see that information. Making sure that documents are inside the chart (or some other protective covering), that the chart folder is closed, and that the client's name does not appear on the outside of the chart (a coding system can provide for convenient filing and retrieval) are useful steps to take when charts are visible in a well-attended area open to the public or other patients. The protection of even the patient's name may seem excessive to some, yet the fact that a person is consulting a mental health professional is a fact worth treating confidentially.

The second important issue concerns the security of charts left in an unattended area. There should be a lock between the charts and anyone not authorized to see those charts. Regarding the security of charts, as in so many aspects of maintaining appropriate confidentiality, the Golden Rule can be a useful guide. What steps would we want a therapist to take if it were our chart, containing our deepest secrets, our personal history, our conflicts, our diagnosis, and our prognosis? What steps would we want our therapist to take to ensure that part or all of this confidential information was not carelessly made available to whoever—other patients, our employer or employees, neighbors, relatives, colleagues—might, for any reason, pass by? How much care would we want our own therapist to use in handling these documents?

DISPOSING OF CHARTS

In reviewing standards applicable to the disposal of treatment records and other documents related to patients, *The Psychologist's Legal Handbook* (Stromberg et al., 1988) notes that "records should not simply be placed in the trash, since methods of trash collection and disposal can be haphazard and can result in confidential papers being seen by passersby. Instead, records should be shredded and destroyed" (p. 403).

The Specialty Guidelines for the Delivery of Services (APA, 1981) specify that, in the absence of contravening federal, state, or administrative statutes or regulations, APA policy is for clinical psychologists to preserve full records at least three years after termination or the last session, and to preserve either full records or an adequate summary for an additional twelve years. Similarly, counseling psychologists are to keep the full record for at least four years after termination or the last session and the full record or summary for an additional three years.

The "Ethical Principles of Psychologists and Code of Conduct" (APA, 1992) addressed the requirement that if confidential information is "to be entered into databases or systems of records available to persons whose access has not been consented to by the recipient, then psychologists use coding or other techniques to avoid the inclusion of personal identifiers" (p. 1607, principle 5.07a). With the increase in use of technology by practitioners, agencies, and institutions, psychologists must be vigilant to protect the confidentiality from persons whose access to the database has not been consented to by the client.

PHONE MESSAGES

Similar precautions need to be taken with phone messages and other written communications to us regarding patients. Written phone messages taken by a clinic's receptionist should not be left where they can be read by unauthorized individuals. Therapists receiving an emergency call during another patient's session must use exceptional care to ensure that neither patient's privacy is violated.

Answering machines create special pitfalls. It is tempting, if our time for lunch is limited, to play back accumulated messages (some from patients) while a colleague or friend is waiting to accompany us to the nearest restaurant. Similarly, if our answering machine is at home, it may take special measures to ensure that family members, friends, and others do not overhear messages as they are recorded or played back. Again, the Golden Rule can provide a useful guide to anticipating potential problems and to recognizing the importance of providing adequate confidentiality.

REFERRAL SOURCES

However grateful we may be to colleagues, friends, and others who refer patients to us, such third parties have no inherent right to learn from us whether a specific individual has scheduled an appointment with us, whether or not the individual kept the initial appointment, or what might have been discussed or decided, unless the patient has provided us with written informed consent to provide that information to the referral source (or to any third party). Unfortunately, therapists may unintentionally violate the confidentiality of their patients by sending referral sources a "thank-you" note mentioning a specific patient.

SOUNDPROOFING

Confidentiality of assessment or therapeutic sessions cannot be maintained if offices are not adequately soundproofed. Some of us may have had the experience of sitting in a colleague's waiting room, in a clinic's reception area, or in corridors connecting suites of therapy offices and being able to hear what the patient and therapist are discussing.

"PUBLIC" CONSULTATION

There are few resources as valuable as consultation to our meeting the highest ethical, legal, and clinical standards. It provides easy access to new information, support, informal "peer review," and a different perspective. In fact, a national study by Pope, Tabachnick, & Keith-Spiegel (1987) found that for psychologists, consultation with colleagues is the most effective source of guidance for practice; participants in the study rated such consultation as more effective than fourteen other possible sources such as graduate programs, internships, state licensing boards, and continuing education programs (see Chapter Five).

Such consultation, however, deserves the same confidentiality as the therapy or other service that is its subject. We lead busy lives and want to make the most of our time. Often the most convenient way to obtain a colleague's advice about the therapy we are conducting is to do so as we are walking through the halls of a clinic, or when we are sitting together at a large table while waiting for the last arrivals so that a meeting can begin, or at a restaurant during a lunch break, or in some other public place. The problem with such "on the run" or ad hoc consultations is that often confidential information is discussed within earshot of people who are not authorized to receive the information. Most of us have probably overheard such consultations in the hallways or elevators of clinics. In some cases we have probably known (socially) the person who was being discussed. In one case (on a crowded elevator), a therapist was consulting a colleague about a particularly "difficult" patient, unaware that the patient was standing only a few feet behind her, listening with intense interest and dismay.

When consulting, taking the time to ensure privacy is an important ethical principle.

GOSSIP

Few people would argue that therapy is easy work. Sometimes it involves considerable stress, and we need to blow off steam. Occasionally this gives rise to the impulse to talk about our work with others—at parties, in the staff lounge, on the racquetball court. At such times, it is easy to let slip the identity of one of our patients or some other bit of confidential information.

Moreover, some of our patients may be famous or may tell us fascinating information. The urge to let others know of such impressive information may be almost overwhelming at times. Many of us may know "through the grapevine" who is in treatment with whom. To the extent that the information nourishing the grapevine is provided by counselors or therapists rather than by the clients, it is a clear ethical breach.

PUBLISHING CASE STUDIES

Extreme care must be taken whenever material concerning patients is published in the form of case studies or is otherwise publicly presented. Merely changing the patient's name and a few other details may not be sufficient (Pope, 1995b). Pope, Simpson, & Weiner (1978), for example, discussed a case in New York in which a therapist was successfully sued for publishing a book in which he described his treatment of a patient. The patient asserted that the therapist had not obtained her consent to write about her treatment and had not adequately disguised the presentation of her history.

APA's (1987a, p. 72) *Casebook on Ethical Principles of Psychologists* presents a situation in which a psychologist wished to write a book about an assessment.

> Psychologist G conducted a professional evaluation of the accused murderer in a sensational and well-publicized case in which six teenage girls, who vanished over a period of eighteen months, were later found stabbed to death in an abandoned waterfront area of the city.

The lurid nature of the crimes attracted nationwide publicity, which only increased as allegations of negligence were pressed against the city administration and the police force. In order to construct a psychological diagnostic profile, Psychologist G spent several days with the accused, conducting interviews and psychometric tests. He presented his findings in court with the full consent of the accused.

Six months later, following the sentencing of the now convicted murderer, Psychologist G determined that he would like to write a book about the murderer and the psychology behind the crimes, which he anticipated would be a lucrative undertaking.

Psychologist G wrote to the Ethics Committee to inquire whether it would be ethical for him to do so. The convicted murderer had refused permission to publish in a book the results of the psychological evaluation, despite the fact that the information was now considered part of the public domain because it had been admitted in court as evidence.

Opinion: The Ethics Committee responded to Psychologist G that to write the proposed book would be a legal but unethical undertaking. The fact that material has entered the public domain or that there may have been an implied waiver of consent does not free the psychologist from the obligation under Principle 5.b of the "Ethical Principles" to obtain prior consent before presenting in a public forum personal information acquired through the course of professional work. In this case, the ethics code sets a higher standard than the law would require. Psychologist G thanked the Committee for its advice and dropped the idea of writing the book.

VIOLATIONS BASED ON COUNTERTRANSFERENCE

No matter how senior our status, how extensive our training, or how naturally skilled any of us may be, all of us are prone to personal factors that may lead us to violate the confidentiality of our patients. James F. Masterson, a prominent therapist who has written extensively concerning borderline personality disorders, showed courage in writing about an instance in which he betrayed a patient's confidence because of a disconcerting event in his own life: "Sometimes countertransference can arise from the most mundane distractions or preoccupations. One morning I was late and dented my car as I parked in the office garage. A bit frazzled from the experience, I rushed into my office and admitted my first patient who asked me how another patient of mine was doing, calling her by name. I was startled because their appointments were at very different times. I wondered if they had met socially, or if he was dating her. Then I realized what had happened. Worried about my dented fender, I had inadvertently picked her file out of the drawer instead of his, and he had read her name on the folder. My distraction represented a countertransferential failure to pay proper attention to my patient. I apologized for taking out the wrong chart and told him I was distracted by the accident" (Masterson, 1989, p.26).

Maintaining Confidentiality with Secured Test Materials

In some instances, psychologists have a responsibility to safeguard the confidentiality of test instruments (as distinct from the data those tests produced). This responsibility is noted in standard 2.10 ("Maintaining Test Security") in the "Ethical Principles of Psychologists and Code of Conduct" (APA, 1992, p. 1604): "Psychologists make reasonable efforts to maintain the integrity and security of tests and other assessment techniques consistent with law, contractual obligations, and in a manner that permits compliance with the requirements of this Ethics Code (see also Standard 1.02, Relationship of Ethics and Law.)"

A creative approach to establishing a framework in which this responsibility may be fulfilled when conducting forensic work was developed by psychologists and attorneys in New Mexico (Pope, Butcher, & Seelen, 1993; Appendix D). The presidents of the state bar and state psychological association developed a formal statement of principles to which their respective associations formally agreed. The *Statement of Principles Relating to the Responsibilities of Attorneys and Psychologists in Their Inter-professional Relations: An Interdisciplinary Agreement Between the New Mexico Bar Association and the New Mexico Psychological Association* (originally drafted by Frank L. Spring, J.D., Ph.D. and William E. Foote, Ph.D.) includes the following section: "Secured instruments, such as Rorschach or TAT cards, testing materials, or other copyrighted materials, should be forwarded only to certified psychologists retained by the requesting attorney" (p. 1).

DECEASED PATIENTS

Many psychologists may assume that the death of a patient marks the end of privacy, confidentiality, and/or privilege. Some states, however, have enacted legislation specifically extending the therapist's responsibility to safeguard information regardless of whether the patient is alive. As with all the issues mentioned in this article, practitioners need to remain aware of the evolving legislation and case law applicable in their state.

EVOLVING TECHNOLOGY

Rapidly evolving technological advances have created new risks for unintentional (and in some cases, intentional) breaches of confidentiality. Elaborate computer networks are now used in some settings to maintain records of assessment, treatment, billing, and other aspects of health care. Gellman & Frawley (1996) note that a secure computer system

1. Does not permit unauthorized users access to information

2. Maintains the continuing integrity of data by preventing alteration or loss, verifies the source of data to assure its authenticity, and retains a record of communications to and from the system

3. Is available to users, and recovers completely, rapidly, and effectively from unanticipated disruptions (disasters) (p. 203)

The APA "Ethical Principles of Psychologists and Code of Conduct" (1992) requires that information stored in databases must be coded in a way that no personal identifying information is revealed.

Any system to which confidential patient information is entrusted must be evaluated on a "worst possible case" basis to discover vulnerabilities to viruses, bugs, dedicated hackers, and careless users.

The practice of faxing or e-mailing confidential material must also be carried out with exceptional care. Confidential or sensitive information should be faxed or e-mailed *only* if both sender and recipient have sufficient reason to be confident that the data will be protected both during transmission and once it arrives. Some state statutes may limit confidential fax and other electronic transmission, and psychologists should be familiar with those statutes.

Cordless phones are a great convenience but by no means provide security of communication. Confidential information should not be discussed over any type of phone whose transmissions may unintentionally be picked up by other receivers.

THE UNAVAILABLE THERAPIST

As fallible mortals doing our best to lead our lives, which are frequently unpredictable, we need to take into account our own vulnerabilities and the vicissitudes of life in making arrangements for our records. We may suddenly be called away to provide virtually round-the-clock care for a friend or family member. We may suffer a stroke or be involved in an automobile accident that incapacitates us for a long time, perhaps indefinitely. Without warning, we may, to grab the nearest euphemism, shuffle off this mortal coil. In such cases, have we made adequate preparations so that the appropriate confidentiality of our records will be maintained? Have we provided such arrangements in a way that permits those with a legitimate need for the records—an interim or subsequent therapist for one of our patients—and the appropriate informed consent to gain access to the records without violating the confidentiality of other patients? (See Chapters Eight and Thirteen.)

Access to patient records can be particularly important for clinicians providing coverage in regard to suicidal clients. Information in the record (describing, for example, prior attempts, treatment dynamics, current medications, and prior strategies to handle suicidal impulses or crises) can enable clinicians to respond more knowledgeably and effectively to suicidal risk, the subject of Chapter Fourteen.

SCENARIOS FOR DISCUSSION

You have been working for two years with a client who has multiple problems and has disclosed extremely sensitive information to you. The insurance company sends you a letter requesting the entire file, including all your chart notes and all raw data from the psychological assessment, in order to determine whether further therapy is warranted and if so, in what form. When you call the insurance company to discuss the matter, the head of claims review (an MBA whose last job was quality control officer in a paper clip company) tells you that they must have all these materials within five business days or else therapy will be discontinued.

1. How do you feel?

2. What options do you consider?

3. If the client refuses to provide consent for you to send the materials, even though it means there are no longer resources to pay for the therapy, and decides to terminate therapy rather than allow the information to go to third parties, what do you do?

―⁂―

You have been working with a fourteen-year-old client for several months. During one session, the client suddenly discloses that they have been having sex with a parent for the past four years. The client, who has been chronically depressed, tells you: "If you tell anyone about this, I will find a way to kill myself." You believe that this is not an idle threat.

1. How do you feel?

2. Under what circumstances, if any, do you believe you might disclose information about the client's claim of having been sexually involved with a parent to any of the following: (a) child protective services or other governmental agency authorized to receive reports of suspected child abuse, (b) your clinical supervisor, (c) any family member, (d) anyone else?

3. What objectives or priorities would shape your interventions?

4. To what extent, if at all, would your own potential legal liability affect your emotional responses to this situation and your course of action?

―⁂―

You are working with a client who enjoys unprotected sex with a variety of partners. Two months ago, the client was diagnosed with HIV. Recent sessions have focused on many topics, one of which is the client's decision not to begin using protection during sex and not to disclose the HIV status to any partners. The client shows no likelihood of changing this decision.

1. How do you feel?

2. Does the client's decision affect your ability to empathize in any way?

3. Under what conditions, if any, would you act against the client's wishes and communicate information about the client's HIV status and sexual activity to third parties? What information would you disclose, to whom would you disclose it, and what are the likely or possible outcomes?

―⁓―

You work for an HMO, spending four hours a day, three days a week providing outpatient therapy at their facility. Four other clinicians provide therapy in the same office. According to HMO policy, all patient charts of all clinicians using that room must remain locked in a single filing cabinet in the corner of the room. Each clinician has a key to the filing cabinet. You become aware that several of your clients have social relationships with the other therapists. You are also aware that their charts contain extremely sensitive information about them. You also notice the names of two of your friends on the charts of the other clinicians. The HMO refuses to change this policy.

1. How do you feel?

2. What courses of action do you consider?

3. Are the clients entitled to know about this arrangement? If so, at what point should they be made aware of it?

4. If you were the client in such a situation, do you believe that you would be entitled to know about this arrangement?

―⁓―

You've reached a therapeutic impasse with a client. For weeks, the therapy has seemed stalled, but you haven't understood what is wrong. During the last few supervision sessions, you've discovered that this client has stirred up some intense emotions in you. You've mentioned to your supervisor some painful events in your own history about which you have felt ashamed and confused. You have yet to discuss these events with anyone else, even your own therapist. One afternoon, you head to the staff lounge but pause just before entering the room. Through the door you hear your supervisor talking with others about the painful events you had discussed in supervision.

1. How do you feel?

2. What do you think you'd do and why: (a) leave immediately, hoping no one saw you, (b) linger at the door, hoping to hear more; (c) enter the room, pretending that you hadn't heard anything; (d) enter the room and indicate that you had heard what they had said; or (e) something else?

3. Under what circumstances, if any, do you believe that clinical supervisors should discuss what their supervisees tell them? In your experience, have these boundaries of confidentiality been explicit and well-understood by supervisees and supervisors? In your experience, have supervisors respected these boundaries?

4. Have the clinical supervisors you've known or known of kept notes or otherwise documented the supervision sessions? What ethical, legal, or other considerations affect the privacy and confidentiality of supervision notes (for example, are they legally privileged communications)?

Responding to Suicidal Risk

Few responsibilities are so heavy and intimidating for therapists as carefully assessing and responding to their clients' suicidal risk. The need for attending to this lethal potential is pressing. Suicide remains among the top ten causes of death in the United States, as high as number two for some groups. The high rate of homicide has seized popular attention and concern, but more people kill themselves than kill others. Even psychotherapists limiting their practice to certain highly defined groups are virtually never free of the responsibility to assess and respond to the risk. For example, younger people have generally been at lower risk for suicide, but over the past quarter century the suicide rate for adolescents has increased two- or threefold. Authorities in the field are almost unanimous in their view that the reported figures vastly understate the problem due to difficulties in reporting procedures.

The evaluation and response to suicidal risk is a source of extraordinary stress for many therapists. This aspect of our work focuses virtually all of the troublesome issues that run through this volume: questions of the therapist's influence, competence, efficacy, fallibility, over- or under-involvement, responsibility, and ability to make life-or-death decisions. Litman's (1965) study of over 200 clinicians soon after their clients had committed suicide found the experience to have had an almost nightmarish quality. Clinicians tended to have intense feelings of grief, loss, and sometimes depression, as anyone—professional or nonprofessional—might at the death of someone they cared about. But they also had feelings associated with their professional role as psychotherapist: guilt, inadequacy, self-blame, and fears of being sued, investigated, or vilified in the media. In a similar study, both the short-term and permanent effects of a client's suicide upon the therapist were so intense that L. S. Goldstein & Buongiorno (1984) recommended providing support groups for surviving therapists.

The solo practitioner may be even more vulnerable than his or her colleagues who practice within the contexts of institutions with their natural support systems. Those who are still in training may constitute one of the most vulnerable groups. Kleespies, Smith, & Becker (1990) found that "trainees with patient suicides reported stress levels equivalent to that found in patient samples with bereavement and higher than that found with professional clinicians who had patient suicides" (p. 257). They recommend that all training programs have a protocol for assisting trainees with client suicide: "There is a need for an immediate, supportive response to the student to prevent traumatization and minimize isolation . . . and . . . for a safe forum that will allow the student to express his or her feelings, will ensure positive learning from the experience, and will help the student to integrate it constructively into future work with high-risk patients" (pp. 262–263).

If the challenges of helping the suicidal client evoke extraordinary feelings of discomfort from many therapists, they also serve as the occasion for therapists to take extraordinary measures to help their clients remain alive. Davison & Neale (1982), for instance, describe the ways in which "the clinician treating a suicidal person must be prepared to devote more energy and time than he or she usually does even to psychotic patients. Late-night phone calls and visits to the patient's home may be frequent."

Bruce Danto, a former director of the Detroit Suicide Prevention Center and former president of the American Association of Suicidology, states: "With these problems, you can't simply sit back in your chair, stroke your beard and say, 'All the work is done right here in my office with my magical ears and tongue.' There has to be a time when you shift gears and become an activist. Support may involve helping a patient get a job, attending a graduation or play, visiting a hospital, even making house calls. I would never send somebody to a therapist who has an unlisted phone number. If therapists feel that being available for phone contact is an imposition, then they're in the wrong field or they're treating the wrong patient. They should treat only well people. Once you decide to help somebody, you have to take responsibility down the line" (Colt, 1983, p. 50).

Norman Farberow, one of the preeminent pioneers in the treatment of the suicidal client, described instances in which the therapist provided very frequent and very long sessions (some lasting all day) to a severely suicidal client as "examples of the extraordinary measures which are sometimes required to enable someone to live. Providing this degree of availability to the client gives the client evidence of caring when that caring is absolutely necessary to convince that client that life is both livable and worth living, and nothing less extreme would be effective in communicating the caring. In such circumstances, all other considerations—dependence, transference, countertransference, and so on—become secondary. The overwhelming priority is to help the client stay alive. The secondary issues—put 'on hold' during the crisis—can be directly and effectively addressed once the client is in less danger" (Farberow, 1985, p. C9).

M. T. Stone (1982) describes a vivid example of the lengths to which a therapist can go to communicate caring in an effective and therapeutic manner to a client in crisis. Suffering from schizophrenia, a young woman who had been hospitalized during a psychotic episode continuously vilified her therapist for "not caring" about her. Without warning, she escaped from the hospital: "The therapist, upon hearing the news, got into her car and canvassed all the bars and social clubs in Greenwich Village which her patient was known to frequent. At about midnight, she found her patient and drove her back to the hospital. From that day forward, the patient grew calmer, less impulsive, and made great progress in treatment. Later, after making substantial recovery, she told her therapist that all the interpretations during the first few weeks in the hospital meant very little to her. But after the 'midnight rescue mission' it was clear, even to her, how concerned and sincere her therapist had been from the beginning" (p. 171).

EVALUATION OF SUICIDAL RISK

Awareness of the following twenty factors may be useful to clinicians evaluating suicidal risk. Four qualifications are particularly important. First, the comments concerning each factor are extremely general, and exceptions are frequent. In many instances, two or more factors may interact. For example, being married and being younger, taken as individual factors, tend to be associated with lower risk for suicide. However, married teenagers show an extremely high suicide rate (Peck & Seiden, 1975). Second, the figures are not static; new research is refining our understanding of the data as well as reflecting apparent changes. The suicide rate for women, for example, has been increasing, bringing it closer to that for men. Third, the list is not comprehensive. Fourth, these factors may be useful as general guidelines but cannot be applied in an unthinking, mechanical, conclusive manner. A given individual may rank in the lowest risk category of each of these factors and nonetheless commit suicide. These factors can legitimately function as aids to, not as substitutes for, a comprehensive, humane, and personal evaluation of suicidal risk. Again it is worth emphasizing a central theme of this volume's approach to ethics: Perhaps the most frequent threat to ethical behavior is the therapist's inattention. Making certain that we consider such factors with each client can help us prevent the ethical lapses that come from neglect.

1. *Direct verbal warning.* A direct statement of intention to commit suicide is one of the most useful single predictors. Take any such statement seriously. Resist the temptation to reflexively dismiss such warnings as "a hysterical bid for attention," "a borderline manipulation," "a clear expression of negative transference," "an attempt to provoke the therapist," or "yet another grab for power in the interpersonal struggle with the therapist."

2. *Plan.* The presence of a plan increases the risk. The more specific, detailed, lethal, and feasible the plan, the greater the risk.

3. *Past attempts.* Most, and perhaps 80 percent of, completed suicides were preceded by a prior attempt. Schneidman (1975) found that the client group with the greatest suicidal rate were those who had entered into treatment with a history of at least one attempt.

4. *Indirect statements and behavioral signs.* People planning to end their lives may communicate their intent indirectly through their

words and actions—for example, talking about "going away," speculating on what death would be like, giving away their most valued possessions, or acquiring lethal instruments.

5. *Depression.*   The suicide rate for those with clinical depression is about twenty times greater than for the general population. Guze & Robins (1970), in a review of seventeen studies concerning death in primary affective disorder, found that 15 percent of the individuals suffering from this disorder killed themselves.

6. *Hopelessness.*   The sense of hopelessness appears to be more closely associated with suicidal intent than any other aspect of depression (Beck, 1990; Beck, Kovaks, & Weissman, 1975; Petrie & Chamberlain, 1983; Wetzel, 1976; however, see also Nimeus, Traskman-Bendz, & Alsen, 1997).

7. *Intoxication.*   Between one-fourth and one-third of all suicides are associated with alcohol as a contributing factor; a much higher percentage may be associated with the presence of alcohol (without clear indication of its contribution to the suicidal process and lethal outcome).

8. *Clinical syndromes.*   As mentioned earlier, people suffering from depression or alcoholism are at much higher risk for suicide. Other clinical syndromes may also be associated with an increased risk. Kramer, Pollack, Redick, & Locke (1972), for example, found that the highest suicide rates exist among clients diagnosed as having primary mood disorders and psychoneuroses, with high rates also among those having organic brain syndrome and schizophrenia. Drake, Gates, Cotton, & Whitaker (1984) discovered that those suffering from schizophrenia who had very high internalized standards were at particularly high risk. In a long-term study, Tsuang (1983) found that the suicide rate among the first-degree relatives of schizophrenic and manic-depressive clients was significantly higher than that for a control group of relatives of surgery patients; furthermore, relatives of clients who had committed suicide showed a higher rate than relatives of clients who did not take their lives. Using meta-analytic techniques, Harris & Barraclough (1997) obtained results suggesting that "virtually all mental disorders have an increased risk of suicide excepting mental retardation and dementia. The suicide risk is highest for functional and lowest for organic disorders" (p. 205).

9. *Sex.*   The suicide rate for men is about three times that for women. For youths, the rate is closer to five to one (see, e.g., Safer,

1997). The rate of suicide attempts for women is about three times that for men.

10. *Age.* The risk for suicide tends to increase over the adult life cycle, with the decade from the mid-fifties to the mid-sixties constituting the age span of highest risk. Attempts by older people are much more likely to be lethal. The ratio of attempts to completed suicides for those up to age sixty-five is about seven to one, but is two to one for those over sixty-five. Suicide risk assessment differs also according to whether the client is an adult or minor. Safer's review of the literature indicated that the "frequent practice of combining adult and adolescent suicide and suicide behavior findings can result in misleading conclusions" (1997, p. 61).

11. *Race.* Generally in the United States, Caucasians tend to have one of the highest suicide rates. J. T. Gibbs (1997) discusses the apparent cultural paradox: "African-American suicide rates have traditionally been lower than White rates despite a legacy of racial discrimination, persistent poverty, social isolation, and lack of community resources" (p. 68). EchoHawk (1997) notes that the suicide rate for Native Americans is "greater than that of any other ethnic group in the U.S., especially in the age range of 15–24 years" (p. 60).

12. *Religion.* The suicide rates among Protestants tend to be higher than those among Jews and Catholics.

13. *Living alone.* The risk of suicide tends to be reduced if someone is not living alone, reduced even more if he or she is living with a spouse, and reduced even further if there are children.

14. *Bereavement.* Brunch, Barraclough, Nelson, & Sainsbury (1971) found that 50 percent of those in their sample who had committed suicide had lost their mothers within the last three years (compared with a 20 percent rate among controls matched for age, sex, marital status, and geographic location). Furthermore, 22 percent of the suicides, compared with only 9 percent of the controls, had experienced the loss of their father within the past five years. Krupnick's (1984) review of studies revealed "a link between childhood bereavement and suicide attempts in adult life," perhaps doubling the risk for depressives who had lost a parent compared to depressives who had not experienced the death of a parent. Klerman & Clayton (1984; see also Beutler, 1985) found that suicide rates are higher among the widowed than the married (especially among elderly men) and that, among women, the suicide rate is not as high for widows as for the divorced or separated.

15. *Unemployment.*   Unemployment tends to increase the risk for suicide.

16. *Health status.*   Illness and somatic complaints are associated with increased suicidal risk, as are disturbances in patterns of sleeping and eating. Clinicians who are helping people with AIDS, for example, need to be sensitive to this risk (Pope & Morin, 1990).

17. *Impulsivity.*   Those with poor impulse control are at increased risk for taking their own lives (Patsiokas, Clum, & Luscumb, 1979).

18. *Rigid thinking.*   Suicidal individuals often display a rigid, all-or-none way of thinking (Neuringer, 1964). A typical statement might be: "If I don't find work within the next week then the only real alternative is suicide."

19. *Stressful events.*   Excessive numbers of undesirable events with negative outcomes have been associated with increased suicidal risk (Cohen-Sandler, Berman & King, 1982; Isherwood, Adam, & Homblow, 1982). Bagley, Bolitho, & Bertrand (1997), in a study of 1,025 adolescent women in Grades 7–12, found that "15 percent of 38 women who experienced frequent, unwanted sexual touching had 'often' made suicidal gestures or attempts in the previous 6 months, compared with 2 percent of 824 women with no experience of sexual assault" (p. 341; see also McCauley, Kern, Kolodner, Dill, et al., 1997). Some types of recent events may place clients at extremely high risk. For example, Ellis, Atkeson, and & Calhoun (1982) found that 52 percent of their sample of multiple-incident victims of sexual assault had attempted suicide.

20. *Release from hospitalization.*   A. T. Beck (1967, p. 57) has noted that "the available figures clearly indicate that the suicidal risk is greatest during weekend leaves from the hospital and shortly after discharge."

SPECIAL CONSIDERATIONS

Coping with the risk that clients may commit suicide creates a special set of responsibilities for the therapist. The themes stressed throughout this book gain exceptional importance and are placed in sharp relief: Failure of the therapist to take necessary steps can literally be fatal for the client. The following steps, which extend or supplement this book's themes, may be helpful in identifying and coping with the chance that a client may be at risk for suicide.

1. *Screen all clients for suicidal risk during initial contact and re-main alert to this issue throughout the therapy.* Even clients who are seriously thinking of taking their own life may not present the classic picture of agitated depression or openly grim determination that is stereotypically (and sometimes falsely) portrayed as characteristic of the suicidal individual. In some cases the suicidal client may seem, during initial sessions, calm, composed, and concerned with a seem-ingly minor presenting problem. Clients who may in fact not be suicidal during initial sessions and who may actually have sought therapy to help them cope with a relatively minor problem may, dur-ing the course of therapy, become suicidal. The increase in suicidal risk may be due to external events, such as the loss of a job or a loved one, or to internal events, such as setting aside psychological defenses or discovering traumatic incidents—for example, incest—that had been repressed. What is crucial is that the therapist must not neglect an adequate assessment of the client's suicidal potential at adequate intervals. In some cases, comprehensive psychological testing or the use of standardized scales developed to evaluate suicidal risk may be useful (see, for example, Beck, Resnick, & Lettieri, 1974; Butcher, Graham, Williams, & Ben-Porath, 1990; Lettieri, 1982; Neuringer, 1974; Schulyer, 1974; Weisman & Worden, 1972). Range & Knott (1997) evaluated twenty suicide assessment instruments for validity and reliability. On the basis of their analysis, they recommended three most highly: Beck's Scale for Suicide Ideation series, Linehan's Reasons for Living Inventory, and Cole's self-administered adapta-tion of Linehan's structured interview called the Suicidal Behaviors Questionnaire.

2. *Work with the suicidal client to arrange an environment that will not offer easy access to the instruments the client might use to commit suicide.* Suicidal clients who have purchased or focused upon a specific gun or other weapon may agree to place the weapon where they will not have access to it until the crisis or period of greatest risk is over. Suicidal clients who are currently taking psychotropic or other medication may be planning an overdose. The use of materials prescribed by and associated with mental health professionals may have great symbolic meaning for the client. Arrange that the client does not have access to sufficient quantities of the medication to carry out a suicidal plan.

3. *Work with the client to create an actively supportive environ-ment.* To what extent can family, friends, and other resources such

as community agencies and group or family therapy help a suicidal person through a crisis?

4. *While not denying or minimizing the client's problems and desire to die, also recognize and work with the client's strengths and (though temporarily faint) desire to live.*

5. *Make every effort to communicate and justify realistic hope.* Discuss practical approaches to the client's problems.

6. *Consider the use of contracts between therapist and client.* Some suicidal clients will welcome such contracts in which the client agrees either to refrain from suicide (at least for a given time—sometimes only until the next session) or to take certain steps such as contacting the therapist before making a suicide attempt. Other clients may initially resist but gradually, grudgingly agree to a contract. Regardless of the client's attitude when the contract is made (and there is, of course, no way to "enforce" such a contract), the contract may give the client a psychological reason to resist an otherwise overwhelming suicidal impulse.

7. *Explore any fantasies the client may have regarding suicide.* Reevaluating unrealistic beliefs about what suicide will and will not accomplish can be an important step for clients attempting to remain alive.

8. *Ensure clear communication and evaluate the probable impact of any interventions.* Ambiguous or confusing messages are unlikely to be helpful and may cause considerable harm. The literature documents the hazards of using techniques such as paradoxical intention with suicidal clients. Even well-meant and apparently clear messages may go awry in the stress of crisis. Beck (1967, p. 53) provides an example: "One woman, who was convinced by her psychotherapist that her children needed her even though she believed herself worthless, decided to kill them as well as herself to 'spare them the agony of growing up without a mother.' She subsequently followed through with her plan."

9. *When considering hospitalization as an option, explore the drawbacks as fully as the benefits—the probable long-term and the immediate effects of this intervention.* Farberow (see Colt, 1983, p. 58) warns: "We tend to think we've solved the problem by getting the person into the hospital, but psychiatric hospitals have a suicide rate more than 35 percent greater than in the community."

10. *Be sensitive to negative reactions to the client's behavior.* Alan Stone, professor of psychiatry and law at Harvard, has been a pioneer

in the acknowledgment of the ways in which some overly fatigued therapists may react with boredom, malice, or even hatred to some suicidal clients. James Chu (quoted by Colt, 1983, p. 56), a psychiatrist in charge of Codman House at McClean Hospital, comments: "When you deal with suicidal people day after day after day, you just get plain tired. You get to the point of feeling, 'All right, get it over with.' The potential for fatigue, boredom, and negative transference is so great that we must remain constantly alert for signs that we are beginning to experience them. Maltsberger and Buie discuss therapists' repression of such feelings. A therapist may glance often at his watch, feel drowsy, or daydream—or rationalize referral, premature termination, or hospitalization just to be rid of the patient. (Many studies have detailed the unintentional abandonment of suicidal patients; in a 1967 review of 32 suicides . . . Bloom found 'each . . . was preceded by rejecting behavior by the therapist.') Sometimes, in frustration, a therapist will issue an ultimatum. Maltsberger recalls one who, treating a chronic wrist-cutter, just couldn't stand it, and finally she said, 'If you don't stop that I'll stop treatment.' The patient did it again. She stopped treatment and the patient killed herself" (Colt, 1983, p. 57).

11. *Perhaps most important, communicate caring.* Therapists differ in how they attempt to express this caring. The ways are influenced by the personality, values, beliefs, needs, resources, and immediate situation of the therapist as well as by the personality, resources, immediate and long-term needs, and situation of the client. A therapist (cited by Colt, 1983, p. 60) recounts an influential event early in her career: "I had a slasher my first year in the hospital. She kept cutting herself to ribbons—with glass, wire, anything she could get her hands on. Nobody could stop her. The nurses were getting very angry. . . . I didn't know what to do, but I was getting very upset. So I went to the director, and in my best Harvard Medical School manner began in a very intellectual way to describe the case. To my horror, I couldn't go on, and I began to weep. I couldn't stop. He said, 'I think if you showed the patient what you showed me, I think she'd know you cared.' So I did. I told her that I cared, and that it was distressing to me. She stopped. It was an important lesson." The home visits, the long and frequent sessions, the therapist's late-night search for a runaway client, and other special measures mentioned earlier are ways some therapists have found useful to communicate this caring, although such approaches obviously would not fit all therapists, all

clients, or all theoretical orientations. One of the most fundamental aspects of this communication of caring is the therapist's willingness to listen, to take seriously what the client has to say. Farberow (1985, p. C9) puts it well: "If the person is really trying to communicate how unhappy he is, or his particular problems, then you can recognize that one of the most important things is to be able to hear his message. You'd want to say, 'Yes, I hear you. Yes, I recognize that this is a really tough situation. I'll be glad to listen. If I can't do anything, then we'll find someone who can.'"

AVOIDABLE PITFALLS: ADVICE FROM EXPERTS

A central theme of this book is that inattention or a lack of awareness is a (if not the) most frequent cause for a therapist's violation of his or her clinical responsibilities and of the client's trust. We asked a number of prominent therapists with expertise in identifying and responding to suicidal risk to discuss factors that contribute to therapists' inattention or lack of awareness when working with potentially suicidal clients. Careful attention to these factors can enable therapists to practice more responsively and responsibly.

Norman Farberow, cofounder and former codirector and chief of research at the Los Angeles Suicide Prevention Center, believes that there are four main problem areas. First, therapists tend to feel uncomfortable with the subject; they find it difficult to explore and investigate suicidal risk: "We don't want to hear about it. We discount it. But any indication of risk or intention must be addressed." Second, we must appreciate that each client is a unique person: "Each person becomes suicidal in his or her own framework. The person's point of view is crucial." Third, we tend to forget the preventive factors: "Clinicians run scared at the thought of suicide. They fail to recognize the true resources." Fourth, we fail to consult: "Outside opinion is invaluable."

Erika Fromm, a diplomate in both clinical psychology and clinical hypnosis, is professor emeritus of psychology at the University of Chicago, clinical editor of *The Journal of Clinical and Experimental Hypnosis,* and recipient of the American Psychological Association Division 39 (Psychoanalysis) 1985 Award for Distinguished Contributions to the Field. She states: "Perhaps it's the countertransference or the highly stressful nature of this work, but some clinicians seem reluctant to provide suicidal patients anything more than minimal reassurance. We need to realize that the people who are about to take their own lives are crying out, are communicating their feelings that no one really cares about them. They are crying, in the only way they know how: 'Show me that you really care!' It is so important for us to communicate that we care about them. When my patients are suicidal, I tell them that I care deeply about them and am fond of them. I do everything I can to let them know this."

Jesse Geller, formerly director of the Yale University Psychological Services Clinic and director of the Psychotherapy Division of the Connecticut Mental Health Center, currently maintains an independent practice. He asserts:

> One of the two main problems in treating suicidal patients is our own anger and defensiveness when confronted by someone who does not respond positively—and perhaps appreciatively—to our therapeutic efforts. It can stir up very primitive and childish feelings in us—we can start to feel vengeful, withholding, and spiteful. The key is to become aware of these potential reactions and not to act them out in our relationship with the patient. The other main problem seems to be more prevalent among beginning therapists. When we are inexperienced, we may be very cowardly regarding the mention of suicide in our initial interviews. We passively wait for the patient to raise the subject and we may unconsciously communicate that the subject is "taboo." If the subject does come up, we avoid using "hot" language such as "murder yourself" or "blow your brains out." Our avoidance of clear and direct communication, our clinging to euphemisms implies to the patient that we are unable to cope with his or her destructive impulses.

Don Hiroto maintains a private practice as a licensed psychologist, is chief of the Depression Research Laboratory at the Brentwood Veterans Administration Medical Center, and is a former president of the Los Angeles Society of Clinical Psychologists. He believes that a major area of difficulty involves alcohol use: "Alcoholics may constitute the highest risk group for violent death. The potential for suicide among alcoholics is extraordinarily high. At least 85 percent of completed suicides show the presence of at least some level of alcohol in their blood. There are two aspects to the problem for the clinician. First, there is the tendency for us to deny or minimize alcohol consumption as an issue when we assess all of our clients. Second, we are not sufficiently alert to the suicidal risk factors which are especially associated with alcoholics: episodic drinking, impulsivity, increased stress in relationships (especially separation), alienation, and the sense of helplessness."

Larke Nahme Huang, a psychologist formerly on the faculty of the University of California, Berkeley, is currently an independent research and clinical consultant in the Washington, D.C., area. She stresses the problems involved in treating people with schizophrenia: "Especially as the treatment becomes a matter of years, there's a tendency to become less sensitive, to forget how painful their life can be. This can lead to problems as the clinician sets ever higher goals as the client continues to improve. A client can experience these goals as insufferable pressure. Frequently the client may make a very serious suicide attempt in an effort to escape the pressure. In working with severely disturbed people, clinicians need to utilize hospitalization, especially in times of crisis. Hospital management issues, power struggles, rivalries between professional disciplines, and so on can aggravate the client's crisis. Don't wait until the last minute, when you're in the midst of a crisis, to learn about these realities and to take steps to prevent them from adding to your client's misery."

The late *Helen Block Lewis* was a diplomate in clinical psychology who maintained a private practice in New York and Connecticut; she also was professor emeritus at Yale University, president of the American Psychological Association Division of Psychoanalysis, and editor of *Psychoanalytic Psychology*. She believed that therapists tend to pay insufficient attention to the shame and guilt their clients experience. For example, clients may experience a sense of shame for needing psychotherapy and for being "needy" in regard to the therapist. The shame often leads to rage, which in turn leads to guilt because the client is not sure if the rage is justified. According to Lewis, the resultant "shame/rage" or "humiliated fury" can be a major factor in client suicides: "Clients may experience this progression of shame-rage-guilt in many aspects of their lives. It is important for the therapist to help the client understand the sequence not only as it might be related to a current incident 'out there' but also as it occurs in the session. Furthermore, it is helpful for clients who are in a frenzied suicidal state to understand that the experience of shame and guilt may represent their attempt to maintain attachments to important people in their lives. Understanding these sequences is important not only for the client but also for the therapist. It is essential that we maintain good feelings for our clients. Sometimes this is difficult when the client is furious, suicidal, and acting out. Our understanding that such feelings and behaviors by a client represent desperate attempts to maintain a connection can help us as therapists to function effectively and remain in touch with our genuine caring for the client."

Ricardo F. Munoz is professor of psychology at the University of California, San Francisco; principal investigator on the National Institutes of Health–funded Depression Prevention Research Project involving English, Spanish, and Chinese-speaking populations; and coauthor of *Control Your Depression.*

First, clinicians often fail to identify what suicidal clients have that they care about, that they are responsible for, that they can live for. Include animals, campaigns, projects, religious values. Second, inexperienced liberal therapists in particular may fall into the trap of attempting to work out their philosophy regarding the right to die and the rationality or reasonableness of suicide while they are working with a client who is at critical risk. These issues demand careful consideration, but postponing them till the heat of crisis benefits no one. In the same way that we try to convince clients that the darkest hour of a severe depressive episode is not a good time to decide whether to live or die, clinicians must accept that while attempting to keep a seriously suicidal person alive is not a good time to decide complex philosophical questions. Third, don't overestimate your ability to speak someone else's language. Recently, a Spanish-speaking woman, suicidal, came to the emergency room talking of pills. The physician, who spoke limited Spanish, obtained what he thought was her promise not to attempt suicide and sent her back to her halfway house. It was later discovered that she'd been saying that she'd already taken a lethal dose of pills and was trying to get help.

Michael Peck, a diplomate in clinical psychology, maintains a private practice and was a consultant to the Los Angeles Suicide Prevention Center. He observes, "Many therapists fail to consult. Call an experienced clinician or an organization like the L.A. Suicide Prevention Center. Review the situation and get an outside opinion. Therapists may also let a client's improvement (for example, returning to school or work) lull them to sleep. Don't assume that if the mood is brighter, then the suicidal risk is gone." He stresses the importance of keeping adequate notes, including at least the symptoms, the clinician's response, and consultations and inquiries. "There are special issues in treating adolescents," Peck adds. "When they're under sixteen, keep the parents informed. If they are seventeen (when the client, rather than the parents, possesses the privilege) or older but still living with the parents, tell the client that you will breach confidentiality only to save his or her life. In almost every case, the family's cooperation in treatment is of great importance."

Hans Strupp, a diplomate in clinical psychology, is distinguished professor of psychology and director of clinical training at Vanderbilt University. He believes that one of the greatest pitfalls is the failure to assess suicidal potential comprehensively during initial sessions. Another frequent error, he says, is that there too often is a failure to have in place a network of services appropriate for suicidal clients in crisis: "Whether it is an individual private practitioner, a training program run by a university . . . , a small . . . clinic, or [therapists] associated in group practice—there needs to be close and effective collaboration with other mental health professions . . . and with facilities equipped to deal with suicidal emergencies. I'm not talking about pro forma arrangements but a genuine and effective working relationship. In all cases involving suicidal risk, there should be frequent consultation and ready access to appropriate hospitals."

SCENARIOS FOR DISCUSSION

You've been working with a moderately depressed client for 4 months. You feel that you have a good rapport but the treatment plan doesn't seem to be doing much good. Between sessions you check your answering machine and find this message from the client: "I want to thank you for trying to help me, but now I realize that nothing will do me any good. I won't be seeing you or anyone else ever again. I've left home and won't be returning. I didn't leave any notes because there really isn't anything to say. Thank you again for trying to help. Goodbye." Your next client is scheduled to see you in two minutes and you have clients for the next four hours.

1. What feelings do you experience?

2. What do you want to do?

3. What are your options?

4. What do you think you would do?

5. If there are things that you want to do but don't do, why do you reject these options?

6. What do you believe that your ethical and legal obligations are? Are there any contradictions between your legal responsibilities and constraints and what you believe is ethical?

7. To what extent do you believe that your education and training have prepared you to deal with this situation?

―――ᴧᴧ―――

You have been working with a client within a managed care framework. You believe that the client's reports of mild suicidal ideation are potentially very serious. The case reviewer decides that in the absence of evidence that the client is at serious risk, the case should be terminated and no additional sessions should be approved.

1. How do you feel?

2. What are your options?

3. What do you believe your legal obligations to the client are?

4. What do you believe your ethical responsibilities to the client are?

5. What would you do?

―――ᴧᴧ―――

You have been providing family therapy to a mother and father and their three adolescents for four sessions. After the fourth session, you find that one of the adolescents has left a note on your desk. Here is what the note says: "My father has molested me for the last two years. He has threatened to kill my mother and me if anyone else finds out. I could not take it if you told anyone else. If you do, I will find a way to kill myself." Your clinical judgment, based on what you've learned during the course of the four sessions, is that the adolescent is extremely likely to commit suicide under those circumstances.

1. How do you feel?

2. More specifically, what are your feelings about the client who left you the note? What are your feelings about the father? What are

your feelings about the mother? What are your feelings about the other two adolescents?

3. What do you believe that your legal obligations are?

4. What do you believe that your ethical responsibilities are?

5. What, if any, conflicts do you experience? How do you go about considering and deciding what to do about these conflicts?

6. What do you believe that you would do?

———

A client you've been seeing in outpatient therapy for two years doesn't show up for an appointment. The client has been depressed and has recently experienced some personal and occupational disappointments but the risk of suicide as you've assessed it has remained at a very low level. You call the client at home to see whether they've forgotten the appointment or if there's been a mix-up in scheduling. You reach a family member who tells you that the client has committed suicide.

1. What do you feel?

2. Are there any feelings that are difficult to identify or put into words?

3. What options do you consider?

4. Do you tell the family member that you were the person's therapist? Why or why not? What, if anything, do you volunteer to tell the family?

5. Do you attend the funeral? Why or why not? Do you send flowers? Why or why not?

6. If a family member says that the suicide must have been your fault, what do you feel? What would you do?

7. Do you tell any of your friends or colleagues? Why? What concerns, if any, do you have?

8. Do your case notes and documentation show your failure to assess accurately the client's suicidal risk? Why or why not? Do you have any concerns about your documentation?

———

You've been discussing a new HMO patient, whom you've seen for three outpatient sessions, with both your clinical supervisor and the chief of outpatient services. The chief of services strongly believes that the client is at substantial risk for suicide but the clinical supervisor believes just as strongly that there is no real risk. You are caught in the middle, trying to create a treatment plan that makes sense in light of the conflicting views of the two people to whom you report. One morning you arrive at work and are informed that your clinical supervisor has committed suicide.

1. What do you feel?
2. Are there any feelings that are particularly difficult to identify, acknowledge, or articulate?
3. How, if at all, do you believe that this might influence your work with any of your patients?
4. Assume that at the first session you obtained the client's written informed consent for the work to be discussed with this particular clinical supervisor who has been counter-signing the client's chart notes. What, if anything, do you tell the client about the supervisor's suicide or the fact that the clinical work will now be discussed with a new supervisor?
5. To what extent has your graduate training and internship addressed issues of clinician's own suicidal ideation, impulses, or behaviors?

CHAPTER FIFTEEN

The Supervisory Relationship

T his closing chapter addresses supervision not only because it is a key task for many clinicians but also because supervision brings into focus so many of the themes running through this book. All of us began our clinical careers as supervisees. It is not difficult for us to think of the important ways, some of them perhaps unintentional, in which our supervisors influenced our development. The supervisory relationship involves considerable power, trust, and caring, although these factors manifest themselves in forms different from those in the therapeutic or counseling relationship.

CLEAR TASKS, ROLES, AND RESPONSIBILITIES

Because supervision involves a minimum of three people—client, supervisee, and supervisor—relationships and agendas can easily become confused, sometimes with severely detrimental effects. The supervisor has an ethical obligation to ensure that the tasks, roles, and responsibilities are clear. The supervisor, for example, must ensure that the supervisee is neither encouraged nor allowed to become the supervisor's therapy patient. Some forms of supervision may share common aspects with some forms of therapy. Sometimes supervisees, in the course of supervision, become aware of personal concerns, psychological problems, or behavioral difficulties that might benefit from therapy. If the supervisee decides to seek therapy for these matters, he or she should consult a separate therapist (one with whom the supervisee has no dual relationship).

Although the supervisor has responsibilities both for the care of the client and for the professional growth of the supervisee, the client's welfare must be primary. The supervisor must ensure that no aspect of the training process unduly jeopardizes the client. Supervision frequently occurs within a hospital or clinic, and the therapist-trainees may have predetermined internships or rotations (for example, six months or an academic calendar year). Such time sequences and boundaries must be taken into account when considering the client's welfare (Pope, 1990a). Some clients may be severely damaged if they experience frequent terminations and transfers. Virtually any client will suffer if not informed in advance of the foreseeable end of his or her therapist's period of availability and if such issues are not addressed adequately both in the therapy and in the supervision.

If a therapist-trainee leaves a setting because he or she has become licensed and is ready to practice independently, numerous issues are likely to arise regarding whether the clients are to remain at the training setting (to be assigned to another therapist-trainee) or will follow their original therapist to his or her new practice setting. When such issues are not comprehensively and definitively addressed *at the beginning of training,* problems are likely to arise and the clients may suffer (see, for example, scenario 5 in Chapter One). Occasionally such problems become the basis of lawsuits and ethics complaints (Pope, 1990a).

The supervisor is ultimately responsible—both ethically and legally—for the clinical services that the individuals functioning under his or her supervision provide. Any conflicts between a supervisor and supervisee regarding the best course of treatment must be promptly, honestly, and comprehensively addressed. Both individuals may avoid addressing such conflicts because they are ill at ease with conflict itself or authority issues. If conflicts between a supervisor and supervisee are not adequately addressed, it is almost certain that both the supervision and the therapy will suffer. Such conflicts are often acted out or otherwise recreated in the relationship between a supervisee and client. Similarly, the dynamics of the relationship between a supervisee and client are often recreated, acted out, or symbolically represented in the supervisor-supervisee relationship. Such phenomena are like countertransference; they are a customary and normal part of the supervisory process. They are not a sign that the therapy is terribly misguided, that the supervisee needs to withdraw from graduate training and seek a line of work that does not involve being around other people, or that the supervisor is an ogre suffering from delusions of adequacy. What they do signal is that important dynamics of the supervisor-supervisee-client triad need to be fully considered, frankly discussed, and sensitively addressed. Porter and Vasquez (1997), for example, discuss principles of supervision within a feminist framework. They describe a process of achieving ethical, collaborative, and mutual goals in supervision, which includes analysis of power dynamics in relationship, facilitation of openness and authenticity, promotion of life-long learning, and attention to developmental shifts in the supervisory process.

COMPETENCE

As a complex and significant professional activity, supervision requires the same demonstrable competence that clinical assessment, therapy, and counseling require. "It is vital that the supervisor be well trained, knowledgeable, and skilled in the practice of clinical supervision" (Stoltenberg & Delworth, 1987, p. 175). It would be no more ethical to "improvise" supervision if one lacked education, training, and supervised experience than if one were to improvise group therapy, systematic desensitization, or administration of a Hallstead-Reitan Neuropsychological Test Battery without adequate preparation. As with other aspects of professional work, supervisory knowledge must be continually updated so that the supervision is informed by the evolving research and theory.

In addition to maintaining competence in supervision, the supervising therapist must be competent in the approaches used to assess and treat the client and must ensure that the supervisee is at least minimally competent to provide services to the client. One of the greatest temptations for some supervisors is to form a relationship with a promising supervisee who has had course work in clinical techniques for which the supervisor may have only superficial or outdated knowledge. Such supervisors may, if they are not scrupulously careful, find themselves supervising interventions in which they themselves have no demonstrable competence. Thus a supervisor whose practice is exclusively psychoanalytic and who has not been trained in cognitive-behavioral techniques may find himself or herself supervising a student employing covert conditioning with a client; a supervisor whose training and practice are exclusively in child psychology may unwittingly become supervisor to interventions with older adults; an existential-humanistic counselor who does not use standardized tests may find himself or herself trying to help a supervisee interpret an MMPI-II profile.

ASSESSMENT AND EVALUATION

The supervisor must assess continually not only the appropriateness and adequacy of the clinical services provided to the client but also the professional development of the supervisee. Some supervisors may be uncomfortable with this significant responsibility.

Supervisees may also be uncomfortable being evaluated, an issue that needs to be addressed in the supervision. In graduate training programs, internships, arrangements in which supervised hours are being accumulated as a prerequisite to licensure, and many institutional settings, the supervisor's assessment of the supervisee's strengths, weaknesses, and progress must be reported to third parties. These reports may profoundly influence the supervisee's opportunities for continuing in the training program or for future employment.

Supervisors must clearly, frankly, and promptly communicate *to the supervisee* his or her assessment of strengths, weaknesses, and development. Koocher & Keith-Spiegel (1998) point out that lack of timely feedback is the most common basis of ethics complaints regarding supervision.

In some cases, the supervisor may determine that the supervisee is unable, either temporarily or more permanently, to conduct clinical work. The supervisor must conscientiously seek to determine why the supervisee is experiencing difficulties. Some supervisees may be experiencing intense personal stress due to overwork, personal loss, or environmental stress. Others may find that doing therapy or counseling has brought to the surface personal conflicts or developmental issues that have not been adequately acknowledged and worked through. Others may experience acute symptoms such as thought disorders, depression, or anxiety to such a degree that they are unable to function effectively. And still others may seem to suffer from relatively long-term developmental or personality disorders.

The supervisor's responsibility is clear and unavoidable in such circumstances. The APA's policy for training programs more generally is also relevant for individual supervisors. The Committee on Accreditation for the American Psychological Association (1989) has stated that all programs "have special responsibility to assess continually the progress of each student" and that "students who exhibit continued serious difficulties and do not function effectively in academic and/or interpersonal situations should be counseled early, made aware of career alternatives, and, if necessary, dropped from the program" (p. B10).

While supervisors must, when circumstances warrant, ensure that unsuitable and unqualified individuals do not become therapists or counselors—a responsibility we owe to future clients who might be harmed by incompetent or unscrupulous practice—we must also do so in a way that is not unnecessarily hurtful for the supervisee.

INFORMED CONSENT

Supervisors have an ethical responsibility to accord appropriate informed consent to both supervisee and client. Supervisees have a right to know how they will be evaluated—what sorts of information the supervisor will use for forming an opinion and what criteria will be used for evaluating that information. They must understand clearly what is expected of them, and what resources are available to them. They need to know to what degree or under what conditions what they reveal to the supervisor will be kept confidential. For example, supervisees may disclose in the course of supervision that they are in therapy, that they are members of a twelve-step program, or that they were abused as children. They must understand clearly whether such information will be shared with third parties.

Clients whose therapists are being supervised also have an ethical right to informed consent to the supervisory arrangements. The first step, of course, is simply to ensure that they know that the clinical services they are receiving are being formally supervised. On January 30, 1984, the APA's Committee on Scientific and Professional Ethics and Conduct (currently termed the Ethics Committee) issued a formal statement regarding ethical standards applicable to supervision. The committee emphasized "that during the onset of a professional relationship with a client, a client should be informed of the psychologist's intended use of supervisors/consultants, and the general nature of the information regarding the case which will be disclosed to the supervisor/consultant. This permits the client to make an informed decision regarding the psychological services with an understanding of the limits of confidentiality attendant to the relationship. Failure to inform the client of such limits violates the patient's confidentiality when the psychologist, without the patient's awareness, discusses the patient/client and his/her diagnosis and treatment or consultation with a supervisor/consultant. The Committee feels that during the onset of a professional relationship with a client/patient, the client/patient should be clearly informed of the limits of confidentiality in that relationship."

In some cases, state laws or regulations may specify the obligation of supervisees to disclose their status. Section 1396.4 of California's Rules of Professional Conduct (Title 16) states: "A psychological assistant shall at all times and under all circumstances identify himself or herself to patients or clients as a psychological assistant to his or her employer or responsible supervisor when engaged in any psychological activity in connection with that employment."

APA's (1992) "Ethical Principles and Code of Conduct," standard 4.01 ("Structuring the Relationship"), include the following requirements: "b) When the psychologist's work with clients or patients will be supervised, the above discussion includes that fact, and the name of the supervisor, when the supervisor has legal responsibility for the case. c) When the therapist is a student intern, the client or patient is informed of that fact."

Both supervisor and supervisee have an ethical responsibility to ensure that the client is accurately informed and clearly understands the qualifications and credentials that the supervisee possesses (Pope, 1990a). Clinicians may engage in extensive rationalizations regarding fraudulently presenting supervisees as possessing a level of training that they have not achieved. For example, in many hospital settings, psychological interns may be presented to patients as "Dr. _____ " even though they have not yet received a doctorate. Clients have a fundamental right to know whether their therapist possesses a doctorate and whether he or she is licensed to practice independently.

SEXUAL ISSUES

Sexual attraction to clients is a common occurrence for psychotherapists (see Chapter Ten). Supervisors have an important ethical responsibility to ensure that the supervisory relationship provides a safe and supportive opportunity to learn to recognize and handle such feelings appropriately. Most training programs spend little or no time addressing the prohibition against sexual contact with clients, yet it is the most commonly violated of the ethical principles. Training strategies for preventing therapist-client sexual contact include promotion of knowledge, activities that promote self-awareness, and provision of a climate that enhances the development of moral values and behavior (Pope, 1994; Pope, Sonne, & Holroyd, 1993; Vasquez, 1988, 1992).

Supervisors also have an important ethical responsibility to ensure that a sexual relationship between supervisor and supervisee does not occur. The APA, for example, on the basis of its "Ethical Principles of Psychologists and Code of Conduct" (1992) currently prohibits sexualized dual relationships between clinical supervisors and supervisees. Ethical standard 1.19b states that "psychologists do not engage in sexual relationships with students or supervisees in training over whom the psychologist has evaluative or direct authority, because such relationships are so likely to impair judgment or be exploitative."

A variety of anonymous surveys have attempted to gather information about such intimacies (Glaser & Thorpe, 1986; Harding, Shearn, & Kitchener, 1989; Pope, Levenson, & Schover, 1979; W. L. Robinson & Reid, 1985). The evidence strongly suggests that female trainees, much more than male trainees, are involved in such intimacies, even when data are adjusted for the relative numbers of male and female supervisors and of male and female supervisees. One study found that one out of every four women who had received her doctorate in psychology within the past six years had engaged in sexual intimacies with at least one of her psychology educators (Pope, Levenson, & Schover, 1979; see also Pope, 1989b). Glaser & Thorpe (1986) found that in most cases (62 percent), the intimacy occurred either before or during the student's working relationship with the educator.

Supervisors bear the responsibility not only of seeing that such intimacies do not occur but also of ensuring that sexual issues arising in the therapy are addressed frankly, sensitively, and respectfully: "Students need to feel that discussion of their sexual feelings will not be taken as seductive or provocative or as inviting or legitimizing a sexualized relationship with their educators. . . . Educators must display the same frankness, honesty, and integrity regarding sexual attraction that they expect their students to emulate. Psychologists need to acknowledge that they may feel sexual attraction to their students as well as their clients. They need to establish with clarity and maintain with consistency unambiguous ethical and professional standards regarding appropriate and inappropriate handling of these feelings" (Pope, Keith-Spiegel, & Tabachnick, 1986, p. 157).

BEGINNINGS AND ENDINGS, ABSENCE AND AVAILABILITY

From the beginning of supervision, the supervisee must clearly understand to what degree and under what circumstances the supervisor will be available. If the client has an emergency, does the supervisee know how to reach the supervisor promptly? Will the supervisor be available for phone supervision between the scheduled sessions? Can the supervisor be reached during late-night hours, on weekends, or on holidays? Are there adequate preparations for supervisor absences—both planned and unanticipated? If the supervisor is unavailable during a crisis, does the supervisee have several options for securing necessary help?

As discussed earlier in this chapter, issues regarding the beginning and ending of the supervisory process must be adequately addressed. The termination is likely to elicit from us a variety of feelings. Both supervisor and supervisee may feel tempted to collude in avoiding issues related to the termination of patients. They may also find it easy to avoid issues related to the termination of supervision. If the process has not gone as well as expected, both supervisor and supervisee may feel frustration, regret, anger, and relief at the prospect that it is all— *finally—over.* Open and honest discussion of how the problems arose and why they were not resolved more effectively may be difficult. If the process has gone well, both may feel joy, pride, and exhilaration, but they may also experience a sense of loss and sorrow that the frequent meetings and shared, intense, productive work are ending.

Such responses should not be denied or neglected. An important aspect of the supervisory process—an aspect that is especially prominent during termination—involves supervisor and supervisee honestly confronting their reactions to each other and to their collaborative work together. What has each gained from the other? In what ways has each surprised, disappointed, angered, or hurt the other? In what ways has the relationship been characterized by interest, attentiveness, support, and creativity? In what ways has it been characterized by dishonesty, betrayal, and stubbornness? How has their relationship been influenced by the setting in which they work? How have power, trust, and caring manifested themselves in the relationship between supervisor and supervisee and during supervision?

The integrity of the supervisory process depends on the degree to which we acknowledge and confront such issues. We begin our clinical work as supervisees and, unless we are exceptionally afraid or uncaring, our growth and development as therapists and counselors continues during our career. If we do not continue in supervision, we must find alternate ways to nurture this process.

We have chosen work that is done in the context of and frequently focuses on intense and intimate relationships with other people. It is work involving great influence but also great vulnerability. Whether our relationships with our clients and supervisees are helpful or hurtful depends to a great extent upon fulfilling our ethical responsibilities in regard to power, trust, and caring.

SCENARIOS FOR DISCUSSION

You are conducting family therapy with a family of five. The mother, age thirty-one, is Caucasian. The mother's partner, age fifty-four, is Hispanic. The three children are pre-teens. You discuss with your supervisor the tensions that the family are experiencing and your beliefs about the causes of those tensions. Your supervisor says: "I think maybe you're seeing it that way because you are [your own race or ethnicity]."

1. How do you feel?

2. What do you think you might say to your supervisor?

3. What would you like to say to your supervisor?

4. Would your supervisor's race or ethnicity make any difference in how you feel or how you react to this situation? If so, what difference would it make and why?

5. Did you imagine the mother's partner as male or female? What do you believe influenced whether you imagined the person as a man or a woman?

———

You have just completed an intake session with a person who is extremely fearful, hears voices, and seems to have a thought disorder. Your provisional diagnosis is some form of schizophrenia, although there are other possibilities you plan to explore during the next session. You meet with your supervisor, review your notes for the intake, state your opinion that the difficulty probably involves a schizophrenic process, and list the questions that you plan to address in your next session. Your supervisor's first comment is: "Boy, those schizos really are interesting, aren't they!"

1. How do you feel?
2. What responses do you consider giving to this comment?
3. How do you think you actually would respond to this comment?
4. If this supervisor had a reputation as extremely thin-skinned and averse to criticism, and if this supervisor were also someone with considerable power over your training, how, if at all, might this affect your decision about responding?

———

You are a supervisor who has had a very challenging supervisee. The supervisee has, for example, made demeaning and passive-aggressive comments to patients and often jokes about them in a cruel and disrespectful way. You have attempted to provide feedback throughout supervision, and have documented these attempts and their (lack of) effect. The supervisee schedules an additional session with you and says: "I've been looking at my evaluation forms and I think you've been very unfair with me. I've talked to some other people and they agree with me. It is important that you change some of these ratings so that they reflect a fair and unbiased evaluation. If you don't, it will continue to hurt my career and I think I have a legal right to a fair evaluation that does not defame me."

1. How do you feel?

2. How, if at all, would your feelings differ depending on the supervisee's gender, race, age, or other demographics?

3. What are your options for responding?

4. How would you like to respond? How do you think you would respond? If there is any difference between your answers to these 2 questions, what causes the difference?

5. How, if at all, would the way you responded be affected by the supervisee's gender, race, age, or other demographics?

———

You have been working with a client who is in desperate need of treatment for multiple serious problems. Without treatment, the client, who is a single parent, is likely to decompensate and perhaps place the children at risk. Suicide is a possibility. Unfortunately, the client does not qualify for therapy in light of their current symptoms and the terms of their insurance coverage. Your supervisor and you discuss all the alternatives, none of which seem acceptable. Finally, your supervisor says, "Look, the only way to get this client the help that is absolutely necessary is to come up with a diagnosis that will meet the terms of the insurance coverage." The supervisor then suggests a diagnosis that, while it will ensure coverage, clearly does not fit the client in any way.

1. How do you feel? Are there any feelings that are difficult to acknowledge, disclose, or consider?

2. Aside from your feelings, what thoughts do you have about your supervisor's suggestion?

3. What courses of action do you consider in light of your supervisor's suggestion? What are your feelings in regard to each one?

4. What do you think you would end up doing?

5. How, if at all, would your chart notes be affected by your supervisor's suggestion?

———

You are working with a client who describes graphic sexual fantasies that make you somewhat uncomfortable. At your next supervision session, you tell the supervisor about the counseling session and also about your discomfort with the fantasies. Your supervisor says, "So you are uncomfortable with that kind of sexual fantasizing. What kind of sexual fantasies are you comfortable with?"

1. How do you feel?
2. What would you like to say to your supervisor?
3. What do you think you would end up saying to your supervisor?
4. If there is any difference between your answers to questions 2 and 3 above, why is there a difference?
5. Does the gender, sexual orientation, age, or race of your supervisor make any difference in terms of the feelings you experience or the responses you would make or would like to make?

You and your supervisor have had substantial disagreements about clients' diagnoses and treatment planning. You discuss your differences extensively but neither convinces the other. During one supervision session, your supervisor says, "I've been concerned about the difficulties you seem to have in conceptualizing these cases and in formulating effective treatment plans. I believe that there are some personal factors interfering with your clinical judgment. I've discussed these issues with the director of clinical training and senior staff and we think that you need to enter psychotherapy to address these problems."

1. How do you feel? Are there any feelings that are particularly hard to acknowledge, disclose, or discuss?
2. What are the possible ways you might respond to the supervisor's comments?
3. How would you like to respond to the comments?
4. How do you think you would end up responding to the comments?
5. If there is any difference between your response to questions 3 and 4 above, what is the difference and what is the reason for the difference?

6. If you were the supervisor and you believed that the supervisee was experiencing personal problems that interfered with clinical judgment, how would you address it? What feelings would you experience as you addressed this situation? How, if at all, would your feelings affect your ability to address this situation effectively and humanely?

7. If you ever experienced problems that interfered with your clinical judgment or competence and you were unaware of the situation, how would you like others to respond? What would you find helpful and what would you find hurtful?

Ethical Principles of Psychologists and Code of Conduct

CONTENTS
INTRODUCTION
PREAMBLE
GENERAL PRINCIPLES

ETHICAL STANDARDS
1.   General Standards

2. Evaluation, Assessment, or Intervention

3. Advertising and Other Public Statements

4. Therapy

5.   Privacy and Confidentiality

6.   Teaching, Training Supervision, Research, and Publishing

INTRODUCTION

The American Psychological Association's (APA's) Ethical Principles of Psychologists and Code of Conduct (hereinafter referred to as the Ethics Code) consists of an Introduction, a Preamble, six General

Principles (A–F), and specific Ethical Standards. The Introduction discusses the intent, organization, procedural considerations, and scope of application of the Ethics Code. The Preamble and General Principles are *aspirational* goals to guide psychologists toward the highest ideals of psychology. Although the Preamble and General Principles are not themselves enforceable rules, they should be considered by psychologists in arriving at an ethical course of action and may be considered by ethics bodies in interpreting the Ethical Standards. The Ethical Standards set forth *enforceable* rules for conduct as psychologists. Most of the Ethical Standards are written broadly, in order to apply to psychologists in varied roles, although the application of an Ethical Standard may vary depending on the context. The Ethical Standards are not exhaustive. The fact that a given conduct is not specifically addressed by the Ethics Code does not mean that it is necessarily either ethical or unethical.

Membership in the APA commits members to adhere to the APA Ethics Code and to the rules and procedures used to implement it. Psychologists and students, whether or not they are APA members, should be aware that the Ethics Code may be applied to them by state psychology boards, courts, or other public bodies.

This Ethics Code applies only to psychologists' work-related activities, that is, activities that are part of the psychologists' scientific and professional functions or that are psychological in nature. It includes the clinical or counseling practice of psychology, research, teaching, supervision of trainees, development of assessment instruments, conducting assessments, educational counseling, organizational consulting, social intervention, administration, and other activities as well. These work-related activities can be distinguished from the purely private conduct of a psychologist, which ordinarily is not within the purview of the Ethics Code.

The Ethics Code is intended to provide standards of professional conduct that can be applied by the APA and by other bodies that choose to adopt them. Whether or not a psychologist has violated the Ethics Code does not by itself determine whether he or she is legally liable in a court action, whether a contract is enforceable, or whether other legal consequences occur. These results are based on legal rather than ethical rules. However, compliance with or violation of the Ethics Code may be admissible as evidence in some legal proceedings, depending on the circumstances.

In the process of making decisions regarding their professional behavior, psychologists must consider this Ethics Code, in addition to applicable laws and psychology board regulations. If the Ethics Code establishes a higher standard of conduct than is required by law, psychologists must meet the higher ethical standard. If the Ethics Code standard appears to conflict with the requirements of law, then psychologists make known their commitment to the Ethics Code and take steps to resolve the conflict in a responsible manner. If neither law nor the Ethics Code resolves an issue, psychologists should consider other professional materials [1] and the dictates of their own conscience, as well as seek consultation with others within the field when this is practical.

The procedures for filing, investigating, and resolving complaints of unethical conduct are described in the current Rules and Procedures of the APA Ethics Committee. The actions that APA may take for violations of the Ethics Code include actions such as reprimand, censure, termination of APA membership, and referral of the matter to other bodies. Complainants who seek remedies such as monetary damages in alleging ethical violations by a psychologist must resort to private negotiation, administrative bodies, or the courts. Actions that violate the Ethics Code may lead to the imposition of sanctions on a psychologist by bodies other than APA, including state psychological associations, other professional groups, psychology boards, other state or federal agencies, and payors for health services. In addition to actions for violation of the Ethics Code, the APA Bylaws provide that APA may take action against a member after his or her conviction of a felony, expulsion or suspension from an affiliated state psychological association, or suspension or loss of licensure.

PREAMBLE

Psychologists work to develop a valid and reliable body of scientific knowledge based on research. They may apply that knowledge to human behavior in a variety of contexts. In doing so, they perform many roles, such as researcher, educator, diagnostician, therapist, supervisor, consultant, administrator, social interventionist, and expert witness. Their goal is to broaden knowledge of behavior and, where appropriate, to apply it pragmatically to improve the condition of both the individual and society. Psychologists respect the central importance of freedom of inquiry and expression in research, teaching, and publication. They also strive to help the public in developing informed judgments and choices concerning human behavior. This Ethics Code provides a common set of values upon which psychologists build their professional and scientific work.

This Code is intended to provide both the general principles and the decision rules to cover most situations encountered by psychologists. It has as its primary goal the welfare and protection of the individuals and groups with whom psychologists work. It is the individual responsibility of each psychologist to aspire to the highest possible standards of conduct. Psychologists respect and protect human and civil rights, and do not knowingly participate in or condone unfair discriminatory practices.

The development of a dynamic set of ethical standards for a psychologist's work-related conduct requires a personal commitment to a lifelong effort to act ethically; to encourage ethical behavior by students, supervisees, employees, and colleagues, as appropriate; and to consult with others, as needed, concerning ethical problems. Each psychologist supplements, but does not violate, the Ethics Code's values and rules on the basis of guidance drawn from personal values, culture, and experience.

GENERAL PRINCIPLES
Principle A: Competence

Psychologists strive to maintain high standards of competence in their work. They recognize the boundaries of their particular competencies and the limitations of their expertise. They provide only those services and use only those techniques for which they are qualified by education, training, or experience. Psychologists are cognizant of the fact that the competencies required in serving, teaching, and/or studying groups of people vary with the distinctive characteristics of those groups. In those areas in which recognized professional standards do not yet exist, psychologists exercise careful judgment and take appropriate precautions to protect the welfare of those with whom they work. They maintain knowledge of relevant scientific and professional information related to the services they render, and they recognize the need for ongoing education. Psychologists make appropriate use of scientific, professional, technical, and administrative resources.

Principle B: Integrity

Psychologists seek to promote integrity in the science, teaching, and practice of psychology. In these activities psychologists are honest, fair, and respectful of others. In describing or reporting their qualifications, services, products, fees, research, or teaching, they do not make statements that are false, misleading, or deceptive. Psychologists strive to be aware of their own belief systems, values, needs, and limitations and the effect of these on their work. To the extent feasible, they attempt to clarify for relevant parties the roles they are performing and to function appropriately in accordance with those roles. Psychologists avoid improper and potentially harmful dual relationships.

Principle C: Professional and Scientific Responsibility

Psychologists uphold professional standards of conduct, clarify their professional roles and obligations, accept appropriate responsibility for their behavior, and adapt their methods to the needs of different populations. Psychologists consult with, refer to, or cooperate with other professionals and institutions to the extent needed to serve the best interests of their patients, clients, or other recipients of their services. Psychologists' moral standards and conduct are personal matters to the same degree as is true for any other person, except as psychologists' conduct may compromise their professional responsibilities or reduce the public's trust in psychology and psychologists. Psychologists are concerned about the ethical compliance of their colleagues' scientific and professional conduct. When appropriate, they consult with colleagues in order to prevent or avoid unethical conduct.

Principle D: Respect for People's Rights and Dignity

Psychologists accord appropriate respect to the fundamental rights, dignity, and worth of all people. They respect the rights of individuals to privacy, confidentiality, self-determination, and autonomy, mindful that legal and other obligations may lead to inconsistency and conflict with the exercise of these rights. Psychologists are aware of cultural, individual, and role differences, including those due to age, gender, race, ethnicity, national origin, religion, sexual orientation, disability, language, and socioeconomic status. Psychologists try to eliminate the effect on their work of biases based on those factors, and they do not knowingly participate in or condone unfair discriminatory practices.

Principle E: Concern for Others' Welfare

Psychologists seek to contribute to the welfare of those with whom they interact professionally. In their professional actions, psychologists weigh the welfare and rights of their patients or clients, students, supervisees, human research participants, and other affected persons, and the welfare of animal subjects of research. When conflicts occur among psychologists' obligations or concerns, they attempt to resolve these conflicts and to perform their roles in a responsible fashion that avoids or minimizes harm. Psychologists are sensitive to real and ascribed differences in power between themselves and others, and they do not exploit or mislead other people during or after professional relationships.

Principle F: Social Responsibility

Psychologists are aware of their professional and scientific responsibilities to the community and the society in which they work and live. They apply and make public their knowledge of psychology in order to contribute to human welfare. Psychologists are concerned about and work to mitigate the causes of human suffering. When undertaking research, they strive to advance human welfare and the science of psychology. Psychologists try to avoid misuse of their work. Psychologists comply with the law and encourage the development of law and social policy that serve the interests of their patients and clients and the public. They are encouraged to contribute a portion of their professional time for little or no personal advantage.

ETHICAL STANDARDS
1.   General Standards

These General Standards are potentially applicable to the professional and scientific activities of all psychologists.

1.01 Applicability of the Ethics Code

The activity of a psychologist subject to the Ethics Code may be reviewed under these Ethical Standards only if the activity is part of his or her work-related functions or the activity is psychological in nature. Personal activities having no connection to or effect on psychological roles are not subject to the Ethics Code.

1.02 Relationship of Ethics and Law

If psychologists' ethical responsibilities conflict with law, psychologists make known their commitment to the Ethics Code and take steps to resolve the conflict in a responsible manner.

1.03 Professional and Scientific Relationship

Psychologists provide diagnostic, therapeutic, teaching, research, supervisory, consultative, or other psychological services only in the context of a defined professional or scientific relationship or role. (See also Standards 2.01, Evaluation, Diagnosis, and Interventions in Professional Context, and 7.02, Forensic Assessments.)

1.04 Boundaries of Competence

(a) Psychologists provide services, teach, and conduct research only within the boundaries of their competence, based on their education, training, supervised experience, or appropriate professional experience.

(b) Psychologists provide services, teach, or conduct research in new areas or involving new techniques only after first undertaking appropriate study, training, supervision, and/or consultation from persons who are competent in those areas or techniques.

(c) In those emerging areas in which generally recognized standards for preparatory training do not yet exist, psychologists nevertheless take reasonable steps to ensure the competence of their work and to protect patients, clients, students, research participants, and others from harm.

1.05 Maintaining Expertise

Psychologists who engage in assessment, therapy, teaching, research, organizational consulting, or other professional activities maintain a reasonable level of awareness of current scientific and professional information in their fields of activity, and undertake ongoing efforts to maintain competence in the skills they use.

1.06 Basis for Scientific and Professional Judgments

Psychologists rely on scientifically and professionally derived knowledge when making scientific or professional judgments or when engaging in scholarly or professional endeavors.

1.07 Describing the Nature and Results of Psychological Services

(a) When psychologists provide assessment, evaluation, treatment, counseling, supervision, teaching, consultation, research, or other psychological services to an individual, a group, or an organization, they provide, using language that is reasonably understandable to the recipient of those services, appropriate information beforehand about the nature of such services and appropriate information later about results and conclusions. (See also Standard 2.09, Explaining Assessment Results.)

(b) If psychologists will be precluded by law or by organizational roles from providing such information to particular individuals or groups, they so inform those individuals or groups at the outset of the service.

1.08 Human Differences

Where differences of age, gender, race, ethnicity, national origin, religion, sexual orientation, disability, language, or socioeconomic status significantly affect psychologists' work concerning particular individuals or groups, psychologists obtain the training, experience, consultation, or supervision necessary to ensure the competence of their services, or they make appropriate referrals.

1.09 Respecting Others

In their work-related activities, psychologists respect the rights of others to hold values, attitudes, and opinions that differ from their own.

1.10 Nondiscrimination

In their work-related activities, psychologists do not engage in unfair discrimination based on age, gender, race, ethnicity, national origin, religion, sexual orientation, disability, socioeconomic status, or any basis proscribed by law.

1.11 Sexual Harassment

(a) Psychologists do not engage in sexual harassment. Sexual harassment is sexual solicitation, physical advances, or verbal or nonverbal conduct that is sexual in nature, that occurs in connection with the psychologist's activities or roles as a psychologist, and that either: (1) is unwelcome, is offensive, or creates a hostile workplace environment, and the psychologist knows or is told this; or (2) is sufficiently severe or intense to be abusive to a reasonable person in the context. Sexual harassment can consist of a single intense or severe act or of multiple persistent or pervasive acts.

(b) Psychologists accord sexual-harassment complainants and respondents dignity and respect. Psychologists do not participate in denying a person academic admittance or advancement, employment, tenure, or promotion, based solely upon their having made, or their being the subject of, sexual-harassment charges. This does not preclude taking action based upon the outcome of such proceedings or consideration of other appropriate information.

1.12 Other Harassment

Psychologists do not knowingly engage in behavior that is harassing or demeaning to persons with whom they interact in their work based on factors such as those persons' age, gender, race, ethnicity, national origin, religion, sexual orientation, disability, language, or socioeconomic status.

1.13 Personal Problems and Conflicts

(a) Psychologists recognize that their personal problems and conflicts may interfere with their effectiveness. Accordingly, they refrain from undertaking an activity when they know or should know that their personal problems are likely to lead to harm to a patient, client, colleague, student, research participant, or other person to whom they may owe a professional or scientific obligation.

(b) In addition, psychologists have an obligation to be alert to signs of, and to obtain assistance for, their personal problems at an early stage, in order to prevent significantly impaired performance.

(c) When psychologists become aware of personal problems that may interfere with their performing work-related duties adequately, they take appropriate measures, such as obtaining professional consultation or assistance, and determine whether they should limit, suspend, or terminate their work-related duties.

1.14 Avoiding Harm

Psychologists take reasonable steps to avoid harming their patients or clients, research participants, students, and others with whom they work, and to minimize harm where it is foreseeable and unavoidable.

1.15 Misuse of Psychologists' Influence

Because psychologists' scientific and professional judgments and actions may affect the lives of others, they are alert to and guard against personal, financial, social, organizational, or political factors that might lead to misuse of their influence.

1.16 Misuse of Psychologists' Work

(a) Psychologists do not participate in activities in which it appears likely that their skills or data will be misused by others, unless corrective mechanisms are available. (See also Standard 7.04, Truthfulness and Candor.)

(b) If psychologists learn of misuse or misrepresentation of their work, they take reasonable steps to correct or minimize the misuse or misrepresentation.

1.17 Multiple Relationships

(a) In many communities and situations, it may not be feasible or reasonable for psychologists to avoid social or other nonprofessional contacts with persons such as patients, clients, students, supervisees, or research participants. Psychologists must always be sensitive to the potential harmful effects of other contacts on their work and on those persons with whom they deal. A psychologist refrains from entering into or promising another personal, scientific, professional, financial, or other relationship with such persons if it appears likely that such a relationship reasonably might impair the psychologist's objectivity or otherwise interfere with the psychologist's effectively performing his or her functions as a psychologist, or might harm or exploit the other party.

(b) Likewise, whenever feasible, a psychologist refrains from taking on professional or scientific obligations when preexisting relationships would create a risk of such harm.

(c) If a psychologist finds that, due to unforeseen factors, a potentially harmful multiple relationship has arisen, the psychologist attempts to resolve it with due regard for the best interests of the affected person and maximal compliance with the Ethics Code.

1.18 Barter (With Patients or Clients)

Psychologists ordinarily refrain from accepting goods, services, or other nonmonetary remuneration from patients or clients in return for psychological services because such arrangements create inherent potential for conflicts, exploitation, and distortion of the professional relationship. A psychologist may participate in bartering *only* if (1) it is not clinically contraindicated, *and* (2) the relationship is not exploitative. (See also Standards 1.17, Multiple Relationships, and 1.25, Fees and Financial Arrangements.)

1.19 Exploitative Relationships

(a) Psychologists do not exploit persons over whom they have supervisory, evaluative, or other authority such as students, supervisees, employees, research participants, and clients or patients. (See also Standards 4.05–4.07 regarding sexual involvement with clients or patients.)

(b) Psychologists do not engage in sexual relationships with students or supervisees in training over whom the psychologist has evaluative or direct authority, because such relationships are so likely to impair judgment or be exploitative.

1.20 Consultations and Referrals

(a) Psychologists arrange for appropriate consultations and referrals based principally on the best interests of their patients or clients, with appropriate consent, and subject to other relevant considerations, including applicable law and contractual obligations. (See also Standards 5.01, Discussing the Limits of Confidentiality, and 5.06, Consultations.)

(b) When indicated and professionally appropriate, psychologists cooperate with other professionals in order to serve their patients or clients effectively and appropriately.

(c) Psychologists' referral practices are consistent with law.

1.21 Third-Party Requests for Services

(a) When a psychologist agrees to provide services to a person or entity at the request of a third party, the psychologist clarifies to the extent feasible, at the outset of the service, the nature of the relationship with each party. This clarification includes the role of the psychologist (such as therapist, organizational consultant, diagnostician, or expert witness), the probable uses of the services provided or the information obtained, and the fact that there may be limits to confidentiality.

(b) If there is a foreseeable risk of the psychologist's being called upon to perform conflicting roles because of the involvement of a third party, the psychologist clarifies the nature and direction of his or her responsibilities, keeps all parties appropriately informed as matters develop, and resolves the situation in accordance with this Ethics Code.

1.22 Delegation to and Supervision of Subordinates

(a) Psychologists delegate to their employees, supervisees, and research assistants only those responsibilities that such persons can reasonably be expected to perform competently, on the basis of their education, training, or experience, either independently or with the level of supervision being provided.

(b) Psychologists provide proper training and supervision to their employees or supervisees and take reasonable steps to see that such persons perform services responsibly, competently, and ethically.

(c) If institutional policies, procedures, or practices prevent fulfillment of this obligation, psychologists attempt to modify their role or to correct the situation to the extent feasible.

1.23 Documentation of Professional and Scientific Work

(a) Psychologists appropriately document their professional and scientific work in order to facilitate provision of services later by them or by other professionals, to ensure accountability, and to meet other requirements of institutions or the law.

(b) When psychologists have reason to believe that records of their professional services will be used in legal proceedings involving recipients of or participants in their work, they have a responsibility to create and maintain documentation in the kind of detail and quality that would be consistent with reasonable scrutiny in an adjudicative forum. (See also Standard 7.01, Professionalism, under Forensic Activities.)

1.24 Records and Data

Psychologists create, maintain, disseminate, store, retain, and dispose of records and data relating to their research, practice, and other work in accordance with law and in a manner that permits compliance with the requirements of this Ethics Code. (See also Standard 5.04, Maintenance of Records.)

1.25 Fees and Financial Arrangements

(a) As early as is feasible in a professional or scientific relationship, the psychologist and the patient, client, or other appropriate recipient of psychological services reach an agreement specifying the compensation and the billing arrangements.

(b) Psychologists do not exploit recipients of services or payors with respect to fees.

(c) Psychologists' fee practices are consistent with law.

(d) Psychologists do not misrepresent their fees.

(e) If limitations to services can be anticipated because of limitations in financing, this is discussed with the patient, client, or other appropriate recipient of services as early as is feasible. (See also Standard 4.08, Interruption of Services.)

(f) If the patient, client, or other recipient of services does not pay for services as agreed, and if the psychologist wishes to use collection agencies or legal measures to collect the fees, the psychologist first informs the person that such measures will be taken and provides that person an opportunity to make prompt payment. (See also Standard 5.11, Withholding Records for Nonpayment.)

1.26 Accuracy in Reports to Payors and Funding Sources

In their reports to payors for services or sources of research funding, psychologists accurately state the nature of the research or service provided, the fees or charges, and where applicable, the identity of the provider, the findings, and the diagnosis. (See also Standard 5.05, Disclosures.)

1.27 Referrals and Fees

When a psychologist pays, receives payment from, or divides fees with another professional other than in an employer-employee relationship, the payment to each is based on the services (clinical, consultative, administrative, or other) provided and is not based on the referral itself.

2.   Evaluation, Assessment, or Intervention

2.01 Evaluation, Diagnosis, and Interventions in Professional Context

(a) Psychologists perform evaluations, diagnostic services, or interventions only within the context of a defined professional relationship. (See also Standard 1.03, Professional and Scientific Relationship.)

(b) Psychologists' assessments, recommendations, reports, and psychological diagnostic or evaluative statements are based on information and techniques (including personal interviews of the individual when appropriate) sufficient to provide appropriate substantiation for their findings. (See also Standard 7.02, Forensic Assessments.)

2.02 Competence and Appropriate Use of Assessments and Interventions

(a) Psychologists who develop, administer, score, interpret, or use psychological assessment techniques, interviews, tests, or instruments do so in a manner and for purposes that are appropriate in light of the research on or evidence of the usefulness and proper application of the techniques.

(b) Psychologists refrain from misuse of assessment techniques, interventions, results, and interpretations and take reasonable steps to prevent others from misusing the information these techniques provide. This includes refraining from releasing raw test results or raw data to persons, other than to patients or clients as appropriate, who are not qualified to use such information. (See also Standards 1.02, Relationship of Ethics and Law, and 1.04, Boundaries of Competence.)

2.03 Test Construction

Psychologists who develop and conduct research with tests and other assessment techniques use scientific procedures and current professional knowledge for test design, standardization, validation, reduction or elimination of bias, and recommendations for use.

2.04 Use of Assessment in General and With Special Populations

(a) Psychologists who perform interventions or administer, score, interpret, or use assessment techniques are familiar with the reliability, validation, and related standardization or outcome studies of, and proper applications and uses of, the techniques they use.

(b) Psychologists recognize limits to the certainty with which diagnoses, judgments, or predictions can be made about individuals.

(c) Psychologists attempt to identify situations in which particular interventions or assessment techniques or norms may not be applicable or may require adjustment in administration or interpretation because of factors such as individuals' gender, age, race, ethnicity, national origin, religion, sexual orientation, disability, language, or socioeconomic status.

2.05 Interpreting Assessment Results

When interpreting assessment results, including automated interpretations, psychologists take into account the various test factors and characteristics of the person being assessed that might affect psychologists' judgments or reduce the accuracy of their interpretations. They indicate any significant reservations they have about the accuracy or limitations of their interpretations.

2.06 Unqualified Persons

Psychologists do not promote the use of psychological assessment techniques by unqualified persons. (See also Standard 1.22, Delegation to and Supervision of Subordinates.)

2.07 Obsolete Tests and Outdated Test Results

(a) Psychologists do not base their assessment or intervention decisions or recommendations on data or test results that are outdated for the current purpose.

(b) Similarly, psychologists do not base such decisions or recommendations on tests and measures that are obsolete and not useful for the current purpose.

2.08 Test Scoring and Interpretation Services

(a) Psychologists who offer assessment or scoring procedures to other professionals accurately describe the purpose, norms, validity, reliability, and applications of the procedures and any special qualifications applicable to their use.

(b) Psychologists select scoring and interpretation services (including automated services) on the basis of evidence of the validity of the program and procedures as well as on other appropriate considerations.

(c) Psychologists retain appropriate responsibility for the appropriate application, interpretation, and use of assessment instruments, whether they score and interpret such tests themselves or use automated or other services.

2.09 Explaining Assessment Results

Unless the nature of the relationship is clearly explained to the person being assessed in advance and precludes provision of an explanation of results (such as in some organizational consulting, preemployment or security screenings, and forensic evaluations), psychologists ensure that an explanation of the results is provided using language that is reasonably understandable to the person assessed or to another legally authorized person on behalf of the client. Regardless of whether the scoring and interpretation are done by the psychologist, by assistants, or by automated or other outside services, psychologists take reasonable steps to ensure that appropriate explanations of results are given.

2.10 Maintaining Test Security

Psychologists make reasonable efforts to maintain the integrity and security of tests and other assessment techniques consistent with law, contractual obligations, and in a manner that permits compliance with the requirements of this Ethics Code. (See also Standard 1.02, Relationship of Ethics and Law.)

3. Advertising and Other Public Statements

3.01 Definition of Public Statements

Psychologists comply with this Ethics Code in public statements relating to their professional services, products, or publications or to the field of psychology. Public statements include but are not limited to paid or unpaid advertising, brochures, printed matter, directory listings, personal resumes or curricula vitae, interviews or comments for use in media, statements in legal proceedings, lectures and public oral presentations, and published materials.

3.02 Statements by Others

(a) Psychologists who engage others to create or place public statements that promote their professional practice, products, or activities retain professional responsibility for such statements.

(b) In addition, psychologists make reasonable efforts to prevent others whom they do not control (such as employers, publishers, sponsors, organizational clients, and representatives of the print or broadcast media) from making deceptive statements concerning psychologists' practice or professional or scientific activities.

(c) If psychologists learn of deceptive statements about their work made by others, psychologists make reasonable efforts to correct such statements.

(d) Psychologists do not compensate employees of press, radio, television, or other communication media in return for publicity in a news item.

(e) A paid advertisement relating to the psychologist's activities must be identified as such, unless it is already apparent from the context.

3.03 Avoidance of False or Deceptive Statements

(a) Psychologists do not make public statements that are false, deceptive, misleading, or fraudulent, either because of what they state, convey, or suggest or because of what they omit, concerning their research, practice, or other work activities or those of persons or organizations with which they are affiliated. As examples (and not in limitation) of this standard, psychologists do not make false or deceptive statements concerning (1) their training, experience, or competence; (2) their academic degrees; (3) their credentials; (4) their institutional or association affiliations; (5) their services; (6) the scientific or clinical basis for, or results or degree or success of, their services; (7) their fees; or (8) their publications or research findings. (See also Standards 6.15, Deception in Research, and 6.18, Providing Participants With Information About the Study.)

(b) Psychologists claim as credentials for their psychological work, only degrees that (1) were earned from a regionally accredited educational institution or (2) were the basis for psychology licensure by the state in which they practice.

3.04 Media Presentations

When psychologists provide advice or comment by means of public lectures, demonstrations, radio or television programs, prerecorded tapes, printed articles, mailed material, or other media, they take reasonable precautions to ensure that (1) the statements are based on appropriate psychological literature and practice, (2) the statements are otherwise consistent with this Ethics Code, and (3) the recipients of the information are not encouraged to infer that a relationship has been established with them personally.

3.05 Testimonials

Psychologists do not solicit testimonials from current psychotherapy clients or patients or other persons who because of their particular circumstances are vulnerable to undue influence.

3.06 In-Person Solicitation

Psychologists do not engage, directly or through agents, in uninvited in-person solicitation of business from actual or potential psychotherapy patients or clients or other persons who because of their particular circumstances are vulnerable to undue influence. However, this does not preclude attempting to implement appropriate collateral contacts with significant others for the purpose of benefiting an already engaged therapy patient.

4.   Therapy

4.01 Structuring the Relationship

(a) Psychologists discuss with clients or patients as early as is feasible in the therapeutic relationship appropriate issues, such as the nature and anticipated course of therapy, fees, and confidentiality. (See also Standards 1.25, Fees and Financial Arrangements, and 5.01, Discussing the Limits of Confidentiality.)

(b) When the psychologist's work with clients or patients will be supervised, the above discussion includes that fact, and the name of the supervisor, when the supervisor has legal responsibility for the case.

(c) When the therapist is a student intern, the client or patient is informed of that fact.

(d) Psychologists make reasonable efforts to answer patients' questions and to avoid apparent misunderstandings about therapy. Whenever possible, psychologists provide oral and/or written information, using language that is reasonably understandable to the patient or client.

4.02 Informed Consent to Therapy

(a) Psychologists obtain appropriate informed consent to therapy or related procedures, using language that is reasonably understandable to participants. The content of informed consent will vary depending on many circumstances; however, informed consent generally implies that the person (1) has the capacity to consent, (2) has been informed of significant information concerning the procedure, (3) has freely and without undue influence expressed consent, and (4) consent has been appropriately documented.

(b) When persons are legally incapable of giving informed consent, psychologists obtain informed permission from a legally authorized person, if such substitute consent is permitted by law.

(c) In addition, psychologists (1) inform those persons who are legally incapable of giving informed consent about the proposed interventions in a manner commensurate with the persons' psychological capacities, (2) seek their assent to those interventions, and (3) consider such persons' preferences and best interests.

4.03 Couple and Family Relationships

(a) When a psychologist agrees to provide services to several persons who have a relationship (such as husband and wife or parents and children), the psychologist attempts to clarify at the outset (1) which of the individuals are patients or clients and (2) the relationship the psychologist will have with each person. This clarification includes the role of the psychologist and the probable uses of the services provided or the information obtained. (See also Standard 5.01, Discussing the Limits of Confidentiality.)

(b) As soon as it becomes apparent that the psychologist may be called on to perform potentially conflicting roles (such as marital counselor to husband and wife, and then witness for one party in a divorce proceeding), the psychologist attempts to clarify and adjust, or withdraw from, roles appropriately. (See also Standard 7.03, Clarification of Role, under Forensic Activities.)

4.04 Providing Mental Health Services to Those Served by Others

In deciding whether to offer or provide services to those already receiving mental health services elsewhere, psychologists carefully consider the treatment issues and the potential patient's or client's welfare. The psychologist discusses these issues with the patient or client, or another legally authorized person on behalf of the client, in order to minimize the risk of confusion and conflict, consults with the other service providers when appropriate, and proceeds with caution and sensitivity to the therapeutic issues.

4.05 Sexual Intimacies With Current Patients or Clients

Psychologists do not engage in sexual intimacies with current patients or clients.

4.06 Therapy With Former Sexual Partners

Psychologists do not accept as therapy patients or clients persons with whom they have engaged in sexual intimacies.

4.07 Sexual Intimacies with Former Therapy Patients

(a) Psychologists do not engage in sexual intimacies with a former therapy patient or client for at least two years after cessation or termination of professional services.

(b) Because sexual intimacies with a former therapy patient or client are so frequently harmful to the patient or client, and because such intimacies undermine public confidence in the psychology profession and thereby deter the public's use of needed services, psychologists do not engage in sexual intimacies with former therapy patients and clients even after a two-year interval except in the most unusual circumstances. The psychologist who engages in such activity after the two years following cessation or termination of treatment bears the burden of demonstrating that there has been no exploitation, in light of all relevant factors, including (1) the amount of time that has passed since therapy terminated, (2) the nature and duration of the therapy, (3) the circumstances of termination, (4) the patient's or client's personal history, (5) the patient's or client's current mental status, (6) the likelihood of adverse impact on the patient or client and others, and (7) any statements or actions made by the therapist during the course of therapy suggesting or inviting the possibility of a posttermination sexual or romantic relationship with the patient or client. (See also Standard 1.17, Multiple Relationships.)

4.08 Interruption of Services

(a) Psychologists make reasonable efforts to plan for facilitating care in the event that psychological services are interrupted by factors such as the psychologist's illness, death, unavailability, or relocation or by the client's relocation or financial limitations. (See also Standard 5.09, Preserving Records and Data.)

(b) When entering into employment or contractual relationships, psychologists provide for orderly and appropriate resolution of responsibility for patient or client care in the event that the employment or contractual relationship ends, with paramount consideration given to the welfare of the patient or client.

4.09 Terminating the Professional Relationship

(a) Psychologists do not abandon patients or clients. (See also Standard 1.25e, under Fees and Financial Arrangements.)

(b) Psychologists terminate a professional relationship when it becomes reasonably clear that the patient or client no longer needs the service, is not benefiting, or is being harmed by continued service.

(c) Prior to termination for whatever reason, except where precluded by the patient's or client's conduct, the psychologist discusses the patient's or client's views and needs, provides appropriate pre-termination counseling, suggests alternative service providers as appropriate, and takes other reasonable steps to facilitate transfer of responsibility to another provider if the patient or client needs one immediately.

5. Privacy and Confidentiality

These Standards are potentially applicable to the professional and scientific activities of all psychologists.

5.01 Discussing the Limits of Confidentiality

(a) Psychologists discuss with persons and organizations with whom they establish a scientific or professional relationship (including, to the extent feasible, minors and their legal representatives) (1) the relevant limitations on confidentiality, including limitations where applicable in group, marital, and family therapy or in organizational consulting, and (2) the foreseeable uses of the information generated through their services.

(b) Unless it is not feasible or is contraindicated, the discussion of confidentiality occurs at the outset of the relationship and thereafter as new circumstances may warrant.

(c) Permission for electronic recording of interviews is secured from clients and patients.

5.02 Maintaining Confidentiality

Psychologists have a primary obligation and take reasonable precautions to respect the confidentiality rights of those with whom they work or consult, recognizing that confidentiality may be established by law, institutional rules, or professional or scientific relationships. (See also Standard 6.26, Professional Reviewers.)

5.03 Minimizing Intrusions on Privacy

(a) In order to minimize intrusions on privacy, psychologists include in written and oral reports, consultations, and the like, only information germane to the purpose for which the communication is made.

(b) Psychologists discuss confidential information obtained in clinical or consulting relationships, or evaluative data concerning patients, individual or organizational clients, students, research participants, supervisees, and employees, only for appropriate scientific or professional purposes and only with persons clearly concerned with such matters.

5.04 Maintenance of Records

Psychologists maintain appropriate confidentiality in creating, storing, accessing, transferring, and disposing of records under their control, whether these are written, automated, or in any other medium. Psychologists maintain and dispose of records in accordance with law and in a manner that permits compliance with the requirements of this Ethics Code.

5.05 Disclosures

(a) Psychologists disclose confidential information without the consent of the individual only as mandated by law, or where permitted by law for a valid purpose, such as (1) to provide needed professional services to the patient or the individual or organizational client, (2) to obtain appropriate professional consultations, (3) to protect the patient or client or others from harm, or (4) to obtain payment for services, in which instance disclosure is limited to the minimum that is necessary to achieve the purpose.

(b) Psychologists also may disclose confidential information with the appropriate consent of the patient or the individual or organizational client (or of another legally authorized person on behalf of the patient or client), unless prohibited by law.

5.06 Consultations

When consulting with colleagues, (1) psychologists do not share confidential information that reasonably could lead to the identification of a patient, client, research participant, or other person or organization with whom they have a confidential relationship unless they have obtained the prior consent of the person or organization or the disclosure cannot be avoided, and (2) they share information only to the extent necessary to achieve the purposes of the consultation. (See also Standard 5.02, Maintaining Confidentiality.)

5.07 Confidential Information in Databases

(a) If confidential information concerning recipients of psychological services is to be entered into databases or systems of records available to persons whose access has not been consented to by the recipient, then psychologists use coding or other techniques to avoid the inclusion of personal identifiers.

(b) If a research protocol approved by an institutional review board or similar body requires the inclusion of personal identifiers, such identifiers are deleted before the information is made accessible to persons other than those of whom the subject was advised.

(c) If such deletion is not feasible, then before psychologists transfer such data to others or review such data collected by others, they take reasonable steps to determine that appropriate consent of personally identifiable individuals has been obtained.

5.08 Use of Confidential Information for Didactic or Other Purposes

(a) Psychologists do not disclose in their writings, lectures, or other public media, confidential, personally identifiable information concerning their patients, individual or organizational clients, students, research participants, or other recipients of their services that they obtained during the course of their work, unless the person or organization has consented in writing or unless there is other ethical or legal authorization for doing so.

(b) Ordinarily, in such scientific and professional presentations, psychologists disguise confidential information concerning such persons or organizations so that they are not individually identifiable to others and so that discussions do not cause harm to subjects who might identify themselves.

5.09 Preserving Records and Data

A psychologist makes plans in advance so that confidentiality of records and data is protected in the event of the psychologist's death, incapacity, or withdrawal from the position or practice.

5.10 Ownership of Records and Data

Recognizing that ownership of records and data is governed by legal principles, psychologists take reasonable and lawful steps so that records and data remain available to the extent needed to serve the best interests of patients, individual or organizational clients, research participants, or appropriate others.

5.11 Withholding Records for Nonpayment

Psychologists may not withhold records under their control that are requested and imminently needed for a patient's or client's treatment solely because payment has not been received, except as otherwise provided by law.

6. Teaching, Training Supervision, Research, and Publishing

6.01 Design of Education and Training Programs

Psychologists who are responsible for education and training programs seek to ensure that the programs are competently designed, provide the proper experiences, and meet the requirements for licensure, certification, or other goals for which claims are made by the program.

6.02 Descriptions of Education and Training Programs

(a) Psychologists responsible for education and training programs seek to ensure that there is a current and accurate description of the program content, training goals and objectives, and requirements that must be met for satisfactory completion of the program. This information must be made readily available to all interested parties.

(b) Psychologists seek to ensure that statements concerning their course outlines are accurate and not misleading, particularly regarding the subject matter to be covered, bases for evaluating progress, and the nature of course experiences. (See also Standard 3.03, Avoidance of False or Deceptive Statements.)

(c) To the degree to which they exercise control, psychologists responsible for announcements, catalogs, brochures, or advertisements describing workshops, seminars, or other non-degree-granting educational programs ensure that they accurately describe the audience for which the program is intended, the educational objectives, the presenters, and the fees involved.

6.03 Accuracy and Objectivity in Teaching

(a) When engaged in teaching or training, psychologists present psychological information accurately and with a reasonable degree of objectivity.

(b) When engaged in teaching or training, psychologists recognize the power they hold over students or supervisees and therefore make reasonable efforts to avoid engaging in conduct that is personally demeaning to students or supervisees. (See also Standards 1.09, Respecting Others, and 1.12, Other Harassment.)

6.04 Limitation on Teaching

Psychologists do not teach the use of techniques or procedures that require specialized training, licensure, or expertise, including but not limited to hypnosis, biofeedback, and projective techniques, to individuals who lack the prerequisite training, legal scope of practice, or expertise.

6.05 Assessing Student and Supervisee Performance

(a) In academic and supervisory relationships, psychologists establish an appropriate process for providing feedback to students and supervisees.

(b) Psychologists evaluate students and supervisees on the basis of their actual performance on relevant and established program requirements.

6.06 Planning Research

(a) Psychologists design, conduct, and report research in accordance with recognized standards of scientific competence and ethical research.

(b) Psychologists plan their research so as to minimize the possibility that results will be misleading.

(c) In planning research, psychologists consider its ethical acceptability under the Ethics Code. If an ethical issue is unclear, psychologists seek to resolve the issue through consultation with institutional review boards, animal care and use committees, peer consultations, or other proper mechanisms.

(d) Psychologists take reasonable steps to implement appropriate protections for the rights and welfare of human participants, other persons affected by the research, and the welfare of animal subjects.

6.07 Responsibility

(a) Psychologists conduct research competently and with due concern for the dignity and welfare of the participants.

(b) Psychologists are responsible for the ethical conduct of research conducted by them or by others under their supervision or control.

(c) Researchers and assistants are permitted to perform only those tasks for which they are appropriately trained and prepared.

(d) As part of the process of development and implementation of research projects, psychologists consult those with expertise concerning any special population under investigation or most likely to be affected.

6.08 Compliance With Law and Standards

Psychologists plan and conduct research in a manner consistent with federal and state law and regulations, as well as professional standards governing the conduct of research, and particularly those standards governing research with human participants and animal subjects.

6.09 Institutional Approval

Psychologists obtain from host institutions or organizations appropriate approval prior to conducting research, and they provide accurate information about their research proposals. They conduct the research in accordance with the approved research protocol.

6.10 Research Responsibilities

Prior to conducting research (except research involving only anonymous surveys, naturalistic observations, or similar research), psychologists enter into an agreement with participants that clarifies the nature of the research and the responsibilities of each party.

6.11 Informed Consent to Research

(a) Psychologists use language that is reasonably understandable to research participants in obtaining their appropriate informed consent (except as provided in Standard 6.12, Dispensing With Informed Consent). Such informed consent is appropriately documented.

(b) Using language that is reasonably understandable to participants, psychologists inform participants of the nature of the research;

they inform participants that they are free to participate or to decline to participate or to withdraw from the research; they explain the foreseeable consequences of declining or withdrawing; they inform participants of significant factors that may be expected to influence their willingness to participate (such as risks, discomfort, adverse effects, or limitations on confidentiality, except as provided in Standard 6.15, Deception in Research); and they explain other aspects about which the prospective participants inquire.

(c) When psychologists conduct research with individuals such as students or subordinates, psychologists take special care to protect the prospective participants from adverse consequences of declining or withdrawing from participation.

(d) When research participation is a course requirement or opportunity for extra credit, the prospective participant is given the choice of equitable alternative activities.

(e) For persons who are legally incapable of giving informed consent, psychologists nevertheless (1) provide an appropriate explanation, (2) obtain the participant's assent, and (3) obtain appropriate permission from a legally authorized person, if such substitute consent is permitted by law.

6.12 Dispensing With Informed Consent

Before determining that planned research (such as research involving only anonymous questionnaires, naturalistic observations, or certain kinds of archival research) does not require the informed consent of research participants, psychologists consider applicable regulations and institutional review board requirements, and they consult with colleagues as appropriate.

6.13 Informed Consent in Research Filming or Recording

Psychologists obtain informed consent from research participants prior to filming or recording them in any form, unless the research involves simply naturalistic observations in public places and it is not anticipated that the recording will be used in a manner that could cause personal identification or harm.

6.14 Offering Inducements for Research Participants

(a) In offering professional services as an inducement to obtain research participants, psychologists make clear the nature of the services, as well as the risks, obligations, and limitations. [See also Standard 1.18, Barter (With Patients or Clients).]

(b) Psychologists do not offer excessive or inappropriate financial or other inducements to obtain research participants, particularly when it might tend to coerce participation.

6.15 Deception in Research

(a) Psychologists do not conduct a study involving deception unless they have determined that the use of deceptive techniques is justified by the study's prospective scientific, educational, or applied value and that equally effective alternative procedures that do not use deception are not feasible.

(b) Psychologists never deceive research participants about significant aspects that would affect their willingness to participate, such as physical risks, discomfort, or unpleasant emotional experiences.

(c) Any other deception that is an integral feature of the design and conduct of an experiment must be explained to participants as early as is feasible, preferably at the conclusion of their participation, but no later than at the conclusion of the research. (See also Standard 6.18, Providing Participants With Information About the Study.)

6.16 Sharing and Utilizing Data

Psychologists inform research participants of their anticipated sharing or further use of personally identifiable research data and of the possibility of unanticipated future uses.

6.17 Minimizing Invasiveness

In conducting research, psychologists interfere with the participants or milieu from which data are collected only in a manner that is warranted by an appropriate research design and that is consistent with psychologists' roles as scientific investigators.

6.18 Providing Participants With Information About the Study

(a) Psychologists provide a prompt opportunity for participants to obtain appropriate information about the nature, results, and conclusions of the research, and psychologists attempt to correct any misconceptions that participants may have.

(b) If scientific or humane values justify delaying or withholding this information, psychologists take reasonable measures to reduce the risk of harm.

6.19 Honoring Commitments

Psychologists take reasonable measures to honor all commitments they have made to research participants.

6.20 Care and Use of Animals in Research

(a) Psychologists who conduct research involving animals treat them humanely.

(b) Psychologists acquire, care for, use, and dispose of animals in compliance with current federal, state, and local laws and regulations, and with professional standards.

(c) Psychologists trained in research methods and experienced in the care of laboratory animals supervise all procedures involving animals and are responsible for ensuring appropriate consideration of their comfort, health, and humane treatment.

(d) Psychologists ensure that all individuals using animals under their supervision have received instruction in research methods and in the care, maintenance, and handling of the species being used, to the extent appropriate to their role.

(e) Responsibilities and activities of individuals assisting in a research project are consistent with their respective competencies.

(f) Psychologists make reasonable efforts to minimize the discomfort, infection, illness, and pain of animal subjects.

(g) A procedure subjecting animals to pain, stress, or privation is used only when an alternative procedure is unavailable and the goal is justified by its prospective scientific, educational, or applied value.

(h) Surgical procedures are performed under appropriate anesthesia; techniques to avoid infection and minimize pain are followed during and after surgery.

(i) When it is appropriate that the animal's life be terminated, it is done rapidly, with an effort to minimize pain, and in accordance with accepted procedures.

6.21 Reporting of Results

(a) Psychologists do not fabricate data or falsify results in their publications.

(b) If psychologists discover significant errors in their published data, they take reasonable steps to correct such errors in a correction, retraction, erratum, or other appropriate publication means.

6.22 Plagiarism

Psychologists do not present substantial portions of elements of another's work or data as their own, even if the other work or data source is cited occasionally.

6.23 Publication Credit

(a) Psychologists take responsibility and credit, including authorship credit, only for work they have actually performed or to which they have contributed.

(b) Principal authorship and other publication credits accurately reflect the relative scientific or professional contributions of the individuals involved, regardless of their relative status. Mere possession of an institutional position, such as Department Chair, does not justify authorship credit. Minor contributions to the research or to the writing for publications are appropriately acknowledged, such as in footnotes or in an introductory statement.

(c) A student is usually listed as principal author on any multiple-authored article that is substantially based on the student's dissertation or thesis.

6.24 Duplicate Publication of Data

Psychologists do not publish, as original data, data that have been previously published. This does not preclude republishing data when they are accompanied by proper acknowledgment.

6.25 Sharing Data

After research results are published, psychologists do not withhold the data on which their conclusions are based from other competent professionals who seek to verify the substantive claims through re-analysis and who intend to use such data only for that purpose, provided that the confidentiality of the participants can be protected and unless legal rights concerning proprietary data preclude their release.

6.26 Professional Reviewers

Psychologists who review material submitted for publication, grant, or other research proposal review respect the confidentiality of and the proprietary rights in such information of those who submitted it.

7.   Forensic Activities

7.01 Professionalism

Psychologists who perform forensic functions, such as assessments, interviews, consultations, reports, or expert testimony, must comply with all other provisions of this Ethics Code to the extent that they apply to such activities. In addition, psychologists base their forensic work on appropriate knowledge of and competence in the areas underlying such work, including specialized knowledge concerning special populations. (See also Standards 1.06, Basis for Scientific and Professional Judgments; 1.08, Human Differences; 1.15, Misuse of Psychologists' Influence; and 1.23, Documentation of Professional and Scientific Work.)

7.02 Forensic Assessments

(a) Psychologists' forensic assessments, recommendations, and reports are based on information and techniques (including personal interviews of the individual, when appropriate) sufficient to provide appropriate substantiation for their findings. (See also Standards 1.03, Professional and Scientific Relationship; 1.23, Documentation of Professional and Scientific Work; 2.01, Evaluation, Diagnosis, and Interventions in Professional Context; and 2.05, Interpreting Assessment Results.)

(b) Except as noted in (c), below, psychologists provide written or oral forensic reports or testimony of the psychological characteristics of an individual only after they have conducted an examination of the individual adequate to support their statements or conclusions.

(c) When, despite reasonable efforts, such an examination is not feasible, psychologists clarify the impact of their limited information on the reliability and validity of their reports and testimony, and they appropriately limit the nature and extent of their conclusions or recommendations.

7.03 Clarification of Role

In most circumstances, psychologists avoid performing multiple and potentially conflicting roles in forensic matters. When psychologists may be called on to serve in more than one role in a legal proceeding—for example, as consultant or expert for one party or for the court and as a fact witness—they clarify role expectations and the extent of confidentiality in advance to the extent feasible, and thereafter as changes occur, in order to avoid compromising their professional judgment and objectivity and in order to avoid misleading others regarding their role.

7.04 Truthfulness and Candor

(a) In forensic testimony and reports, psychologists testify truthfully, honestly, and candidly and, consistent with applicable legal procedures, describe fairly the bases for their testimony and conclusions.

(b) Whenever necessary to avoid misleading, psychologists acknowledge the limits of their data or conclusions.

7.05 Prior Relationships

A prior professional relationship with a party does not preclude psychologists from testifying as fact witnesses or from testifying to their services to the extent permitted by applicable law. Psychologists appropriately take into account ways in which the prior relationship might affect their professional objectivity or opinions and disclose the potential conflict to the relevant parties.

7.06 Compliance With Law and Rules

In performing forensic roles, psychologists are reasonably familiar with the rules governing their roles. Psychologists are aware of the occasionally competing demands placed upon them by these principles and the requirements of the court system, and attempt to resolve these conflicts by making known their commitment to this Ethics Code and taking steps to resolve the conflict in a responsible manner. (See also Standard 1.02, Relationship of Ethics and Law.)

8.   Resolving Ethical Issues

8.01 Familiarity With Ethics Code

Psychologists have an obligation to be familiar with this Ethics Code, other applicable ethics codes, and their application to psychologists' work. Lack of awareness or misunderstanding of an ethical standard is not itself a defense to a charge of unethical conduct.

8.02 Confronting Ethical Issues

When a psychologist is uncertain whether a particular situation or course of action would violate this Ethics Code, the psychologist ordinarily consults with other psychologists knowledgeable about ethical issues, with state or national psychology ethics committees, or with other appropriate authorities in order to choose a proper response.

8.03 Conflicts Between Ethics and Organizational Demands

If the demands of an organization with which psychologists are affiliated conflict with this Ethics Code, psychologists clarify the nature of the conflict, make known their commitment to the Ethics Code, and to the extent feasible, seek to resolve the conflict in a way that permits the fullest adherence to the Ethics Code.

8.04 Informal Resolution of Ethical Violations

When psychologists believe that there may have been an ethical violation by another psychologist, they attempt to resolve the issue by bringing it to the attention of that individual if an informal resolution appears appropriate and the intervention does not violate any confidentiality rights that may be involved.

8.05 Reporting Ethical Violations

If an apparent ethical violation is not appropriate for informal resolution under Standard 8.04 or is not resolved properly in that fashion, psychologists take further action appropriate to the situation, unless such action conflicts with confidentiality rights in ways that cannot be resolved. Such action might include referral to state or national committees on professional ethics or to state licensing boards.

8.06 Cooperating With Ethics Committees

Psychologists cooperate in ethics investigations, proceedings, and resulting requirements of the APA or any affiliated state psychological association to which they belong. In doing so, they make reasonable efforts to resolve any issues as to confidentiality. Failure to cooperate is itself an ethics violation.

8.07 Improper Complaints

Psychologists do not file or encourage the filing of ethics complaints that are frivolous and are intended to harm the respondent rather than to protect the public.

Footnote #1

[1]Professional materials that are most helpful in this regard are guidelines and standards that have been adopted or endorsed by professional psychological organizations. Such guidelines and standards, whether adopted by the American Psychological Association (APA) or its Divisions, are not enforceable as such by this Ethics Code, but are of educative value to psychologists, courts, and professional bodies. Such materials include, but are not limited to, the APA's *General Guidelines for Providers of Psychological Services* (1987), *Specialty Guidelines for the Delivery of Services by Clinical Psychologists, Counseling Psychologists, Industrial/Organizational Psychologists, and School Psychologists* (1981), *Guidelines for Computer Based Tests and Interpretations* (1987), *Standards for Educational and Psychological Testing* (1985), *Ethical Principles in the Conduct of Research With Human Participants* (1982), *Guidelines for Ethical Conduct in the Care and Use of Animals* (1986), *Guidelines for Providers of Psychological Services to Ethnic, Linguistic, and Culturally Diverse Populations* (1990), and *Publication Manual of the American Psychological Association* (3rd ed., 1983). Materials not adopted by APA as a whole include the APA Division 41 (Forensic Psychology)/American Psychology-Law Society's *Specialty Guidelines for Forensic Psychologists* (1991).

This version of the APA Ethics Code was adopted by the American Psychological Association's Council of Representatives during its meeting, August 13 and 16, 1992, and is effective beginning December 1, 1992. Inquiries concerning the substance or interpretation of the APA Ethics Code should be addressed to the Director, Office of Ethics, American Psychological Association, 750 First Street, NE, Washington, DC 20002-4242.

This Code will be used to adjudicate complaints brought concerning alleged conduct occurring on or after the effective date. Complaints regarding conduct occurring prior to the effective date will be adjudicated on the basis of the version of the Code that was in effect at the time the conduct occurred, except that no provisions repealed in June 1989 will be enforced even if an earlier version contains the provision. The Ethics Code will undergo continuing review and study for future revisions; comments on the Code may be sent to the above address.

The APA has previously published its Ethical Standards as follows:

American Psychological Association. (1953). *Ethical standards of psychologists.* Washington, DC: Author.

American Psychological Association. (1958). Standards of ethical behavior for psychologists. *American Psychologist, 13,* 268–271.

American Psychological Association. (1963). Ethical standards of psychologists. *American Psychologist, 18,* 56–60.

American Psychological Association. (1968). Ethical standards of psychologists. *American Psychologist, 23,* 357–361.

American Psychological Association. (1977, March). Ethical standards of psychologists. *APA Monitor,* pp. 22–23.

American Psychological Association. (1979). *Ethical standards of psychologists.* Washington, DC: Author.

American Psychological Association. (1981). Ethical principles of psychologists. *American Psychologist, 36,* 633–638.

American Psychological Association. (1990). Ethical principles of psychologists (amended June 2, 1989). *American Psychologist, 45,* 390–395.

Request copies of the APA's Ethical Principles of Psychologists and Code of Conduct from the APA Order Department, 750 First Street, NE, Washington, DC 20002-4242, or phone (202) 336-5510.

Patients' Mental Health Rights

The following "Bill of Rights" was developed by several participating groups, including American Association for Marriage and Family Therapy, American Counseling Association, the American Family Therapy Academy, American Nurses Association, American Psychiatric Association, American Psychiatric Nurses Association, American Psychological Association, Clinical Social Work Federation, and National Association of Social Workers.

Note: The material in Appendix B is copyright © 1997 by the American Psychological Association. Reprinted with permission.

YOUR MENTAL HEALTH RIGHTS
Right to Know
Benefits

Individuals have the right to be provided information from the purchasing entity (such as the employer or union or public purchaser) and the insurance/third party payor describing the nature and extent of their mental health and substance abuse treatment benefits. This information should include details on procedures to obtain access to services, on utilization management procedures, and on appeal rights. The information should be presented clearly in writing with language that the individual can understand.

Professional Expertise

Individuals have the right to receive full information from the potential treating professional about that professional's knowledge, skills, preparation, experience, and credentials. Individuals have the right to be informed about the options available for treatment interventions and the effectiveness of the recommended treatment.

Contractual Limitations

Individuals have the right to be informed by the treating professional of any arrangements, restrictions, and/or covenants established between the third party payor and the treating professional that could interfere with or influence treatment recommendations. Individuals have the right to be informed of the nature of information that may be disclosed for the purposes of paying benefits.

Appeals and Grievances

Individuals have the right to receive information about the methods they can use to submit complaints or grievances regarding provision of care by the treating professional to that profession's regulatory board and to the professional association. Individuals have the right to be provided information about the procedures they can use to appeal benefit utilization decisions to the third party payor systems, to the employer or purchasing entity, and to external regulatory entities.

Confidentiality

Individuals have the right to be guaranteed the protection of the confidentiality of their relationship with their mental health and substance abuse professional, except when laws or ethics dictate otherwise. Any disclosure to another party will be time-limited and made with the full written, informed consent of the individuals.

Individuals shall not be required to disclose confidential, privileged or other information other than diagnosis, prognosis, type of treatment, time and length of treatment, and cost.

Entities receiving information for the purposes of benefits determination, public agencies receiving information for health care planning, or any other organization with a legitimate right to information will maintain clinical information in confidence with the same rigor and be subject to the same penalties for violation as is the direct provider of care.

Information technology will be used for transmission, storage or data management *only* with methodologies that remove individual identifying information and assure the protection of the individual's privacy. Information should not be transferred, sold, or otherwise utilized.

Choice

Individuals have the right to choose any duly licensed/certified professional for mental health and substance abuse services. Individuals have the right to receive full information regarding the education and training of professionals, treatment options (including risks and benefits), and cost implications to make an informed choice regarding the selection of care deemed appropriate by individual and professional.

Determination of Treatment

Recommendations regarding mental health and substance abuse treatment shall be made only by a duly licensed/certified professional in conjunction with the individual and his or her family as appropriate. Treatment decisions should not be made by third party payers. The individual has the right to make final decisions regarding treatment.

Parity

Individuals have the right to receive benefits for mental health and substance abuse treatment on the same basis as they do for any other illnesses, with the same provisions, co-payments, lifetime benefits, and catastrophic coverage in both insurance and self-funded, self-insured health plans.

Nondiscrimination

Individuals who use mental health and substance abuse benefits shall not be penalized when seeking other health insurance or disability, life, or any other insurance benefit.

Benefit of Usage

The individual is entitled to the entire scope of the benefits within the benefit plan that will address his or her clinical needs.

Benefit Design

Whenever both federal and state law and/or regulations are applicable, the professional and all payors shall use whichever affords the individual the greatest level of protection and access.

Treatment Review

To assure that treatment review processes are fair and valid, individuals have the right to be guaranteed that any review of their mental health and substance abuse treatment shall involve a professional having the training, credentials, and licensure required to provide the treatment in the jurisdiction in which it will be provided. The reviewer should have no financial interest in the decision and is subject to the section on confidentiality.

Accountability

Treating professionals may be held accountable and liable to individuals for any injury caused by gross incompetence or negligence on the part of the professional. The treating professional has the obligation to advocate for and document necessity of care and to advise the individual of options if payment authorization is denied. Payors and other third parties may be held accountable and liable to individuals for any injury caused by gross incompetence or negligence or by their clinically unjustified decisions.

Ethical Guidelines for Professional Care in a Managed Care Environment

The following [g]uidelines were published by the National Academies of Practice (NAP), an interdisciplinary association of professionals including Dentistry, Medicine, Nursing, Optometry, Osteopathic Medicine, Podiatric Medicine, Psychology, Social Work, and Veterinary Medicine. Each academy was represented on the team which developed the guidelines, including Alden N. Haffner, O.D., Ph.D., (Chair), Daniel M. Laskin, D.D.S., M.S., Tracy Gordy, M.D., Roberta Conti, Ph.D., R.N., Stephen Urban, D.O., Larry Harkless, D.P.M., Norma Simon, Ed.D., Jean L. Athey, M.A., Ph.D., David Phillips, DSW, and Alex Ardans, D.V.M. The guidelines were approved by mail ballot of the Council of the National Academies of Practice and affirmed by President Ron Fair, O.D., on 2 June 1997. They were distributed to the membership on August 14, 1997.

Note: These guidelines are from National Academies of Practice (1997). *Ethical guidelines for professional care in a managed care environment.* Washington, DC: Author. Reprinted with permission.

NATIONAL ACADEMIES OF PRACTICE, AN INTERDISCIPLINARY ASSOCIATION OF PROFESSIONALS: ETHICAL GUIDE-LINES FOR PROFESSIONAL CARE IN A MANAGED CARE ENVIRONMENT

Preamble

Ethical guidelines of the National Academies of Practice regarding professional care and services are founded on an ideology of patient advocacy. Moreover, preserving the patient's welfare must be the principal objective in resolving ethical dilemmas or challenges that arise from patient care delivery systems. Many health care professionals recognize that managed care was created with the intent to offer an excellent opportunity to advance quality standards of practice and care while reducing unnecessary and wasteful health care. A further purpose was to achieve a more balanced and socially responsive approach to the achievement of desirable health outcomes in our communities through the use of prudent interdisciplinary resources.

During the last decade, reimbursement arrangements in the health care enterprise have increasingly changed from fee-for-service to some type of externally managed care. However, virtually all managed care plans tend to shift financial risk from payers to health professionals. This transfer of financial risk has the potential to invite ethical conflicts by way of creating a tension between economic availability and clinical care considerations bearing on patient care, patient rights, and advancing the knowledge base of the health care professions. The purpose of the ethical guidelines is to set forth the positions of the National Academies of Practice on certain of these pertinent issues.

I. Professional Commitment to Patient Needs Must Remain the Prime Concern

Patient-focused care has the potential to be threatened by economic pressures to abbreviate the utilization and scope of professional services. While mindful of economy and efficiency in health care services, an ethically based patient-practitioner relationship should admit no unreasonable diminution of the professional's commitment to the patient's need and care consistent with accepted standards of clinical care.

It is the position of the National Academies of Practice that it is unethical to compromise a patient's needs and quality care concerns to satisfy financial objectives. The patient's right to appropriate care must not be diluted by economic pressures. The benefits offered by all health care providers should

- provide access by the patient to appropriate professional services
- meet with patient satisfaction
- avoid contamination by an overly rigid adherence to clinical guidelines such that the practitioner's decision making is hampered
- provide delivery by uniquely trained personnel, such as medical specialists and other professionals trained in delivering psychosocial services, when the complexity of the patient's condition requires the knowledge base and expertise beyond those of the primary care provider

The rationale for these positions derives from a patient or consumer-focused value that has remained constant in the historical evolution of Western ethics, is reiterated in contemporary health professional codes of ethics and can be found in current regulatory statements such as the Patient Rights Standards of the Joint Commission on the Accreditation of Healthcare Organizations. Health professionals must refrain from subordinating the patient's welfare to economic mandates thereby potentially creating an incursion on the patient's rights. The fiduciary role of the provider must be balanced with the patient's needs.

II. Informational Disclosure

Questions frequently arise over whether the practitioner has an ethical obligation to present reasonably considered clinical options for care and services regardless of those economic restrictions or contractual prohibitions, such as "gag rules," that may be dictated by the patient's insurance or managed health care plan.

It is the position of the National Academies of Practice that all reasonable clinical options for care and services, consistent with sound and accepted clinical standards, should be presented to the patient and that the practitioner should not be deterred through gag rules or otherwise constrained to present only those options for care and services that are covered by the patient's policy or plan.

The rationale for this position inheres in the patient's right of informed consent as a service consumer. This right entitles the patient access to information whose scope may exceed that allowed by the health insurance policy of health care plan. The patient's rights of informed consent also repudiates attempts to restrict patient-provider discussions to the plan coverage.

III. Teaching and Research in Patient Care

A clinical environment that includes teaching and research functions traditionally has represented a hallmark of health care delivery. Teaching and research functions are quintessential ingredients in the advancement of knowledge about the patient's needs and the deployment of sophisticated services. With pressures to produce utilization efficiencies and fiscal economies, managed care arrangements may conflict with teaching and research functions. The values of teaching and research, which are enduring in the advancement of science, must not be lost.

It is the position of the National Academies of Practice that demands for increased economy and efficiency in the health care environment should not be allowed to conflict with teaching and research functions. Such demands risk retarding the advancement of knowledge and training in the health sciences and are of consequential importance.

The rationale for this position inheres in the ongoing necessity of scientific research to realize patient-centered achievements. These beneficial goals require an unremitting effort not only to train but to advance the knowledge base of health care professionals.

IV. Confidentiality

The confidentiality of patient data in clinical encounters is a primary concern. Although utilization review and quality assurance are customary and appropriate functions in every health care environment, these activities should not breach the confidentiality of patient data. Safeguards must be adopted when persons engaged in utilization and quality assurance reviews have access to patient files.

It is the position of the National Academies of Practice that utilization studies and quality assurance reviews are appropriate functions in an efficient and effective health care system. However, safeguards must be adopted, codified, and implemented to protect the privacy and confidentiality of patient data and the practitioner's clinical material. Confidential information can be disclosed only with the patient's consent except in instances where withholding that information poses unreasonable and foreseeable harm to the patient or identifiable others.

The rationale for this position is founded on the patient's autonomous right to control sensitive personal information. It is further based upon an historical recognition in the Oath of Hippocrates, and corroborated throughout the centuries, of the enduring value of preserving confidentiality in order to enhance mutual trust and respect in the patient-provider relationship.

V. Prevention

While direct care based upon episodes of illness, disease, or disability is always appropriate, concerns about preventive services as an integral part of clinical care should be of utmost concern to all practitioners.

It is the position of the National Academies of Practice that every health care enterprise should acknowledge the critical importance of the teaching and inculcation of prevention as well as the need for competently delivered patient care services.

The rationale for this position derives from the ethical principle of beneficence, which recognizes the desirability of preventing illness and disease and promoting health among all persons and communities. The principle of autonomy argues for the informed patient's right to initiate preventive and wellness measures. This right is dependent upon the patient having access to relevant health information and strategies which are essential ingredients of patient care and services.

Sample Informed Consent Form

C hapter Eight provides a discussion of consent forms and a list of elements that should be addressed. As emphasized in the chapter, forms will differ significantly according to the service (for example, assessment, therapy), the clinician's approach, the legal requirements for the relevant jurisdiction, institutional policies and procedures, and other factors. This appendix presents one possible example of a form for obtaining written informed consent, in this case for a forensic assessment.

Although there are many possible approaches to informed consent for forensic assessment in this area, any consent form must be adapted to the purposes and procedures of a specific assessment, the needs of the patient, the theoretical orientation or approach of the

---

Note: The sample "Informed Consent Form for Forensic Assessment" and discussion that appear in this Appendix have been adapted and amended, with permission from the publisher, from two prior forms (Pope, Butcher, & Seelen, 1993, pp. 197–199; Pope, 1994, pp. 205–210). Copyright © 1993, 1994 by the American Psychological Association. Adapted with permission.

clinician conducting the assessment, any unique circumstances of the assessment, and to the array of relevant legislation, case law, administrative regulations, and professional standards. To meet these requirements, clinicians conducting such assessments may find it useful to have a comprehensive form in their computer's database. The form could have numerous statements relevant to the clinician's most common assessment situations as well as reminders of other topics that may, however rarely, need to be addressed. When planning each forensic assessment, the clinician could duplicate the computer file containing this comprehensive form and then edit the duplicate so that it best addresses the elements of the next assessment. Readers should feel free to utilize some or all of this form for themselves.

It is essential that the clinician review such forms with his or her own attorney *before using the form* to ensure that it is consistent with all applicable (in the relevant jurisdiction) ethical, legal, administrative, and professional standards as well as the approach and needs of the clinician planning the forensic assessments.

It is also essential that the clinician take adequate time to review an informed consent form with the patient who is to be assessed so that the patient understands all aspects of the planned assessments that might substantially affect the patient's decision regarding whether to proceed with the evaluation. It is important to give the patient adequate time to digest the information in the consent form, ask questions, and consider whether or not to consent to participate. Providing the form to the client by mail to read in the privacy of his or her home prior to meeting the clinician for the first time, or scheduling sufficient time at the beginning of an evaluation to discuss the informed consent process, can facilitate truly informed and full consent to the evaluation. It is especially important to clarify that this is not therapy.

Finally, such forms may play an essential role in the process of informed consent, but neither the clinician nor any one else should ever assume that the mere presence of the form constitutes or completes the process of consent. The discussion of the limitations of forms in Chapter Eight is crucial. If the clinician has questions about the patient's capacity to give consent due to age, cognitive impairment, language difficulties, or other factors, competency to consent should first be established.

INFORMED CONSENT FOR FORENSIC ASSESSMENT WHEN RECOVERED MEMORY IS AT ISSUE

Your attorney has asked that I conduct a psychological assessment in connection with your court case. This form was written to give you information about the assessment process. Although I am a mental health professional, this assessment is not therapy. While it may be helpful to you, the goal of the assessment is to answer questions about you and the difficulties you may be having. The assessment will contain four main parts.

In the first part, which may take more than one session, I will be giving you several standardized psychological tests. [Add names and brief description of the tests you utilize.] We will discuss the instructions in detail when I give you the tests. It will be important that you understand the instructions for each test. If you do not understand the instructions for a test, it will be important for you to let me know immediately so that we can ensure that you understand.

In the second part, I will interview you. This interview is likely to take about [fill in number of hours]. We will meet for approximately [fill in number of sessions]. During the interview, I will ask you questions about yourself and ask you to talk about yourself. There may, of course, be areas that you are reluctant to talk about. If so, please be sure to tell me that the questions are making you uncomfortable or that you have reasons for not providing the information. We can then talk about your concerns.

In the next part of the evaluation, I will be reviewing records and talking with people, such as family members, friends, co-workers, physician, clergy, or current therapist whose names I will obtain from you, to get more information about what has happened to you. This is to help me in finding materials that would give outside corroboration to what you have to tell me. A form asking for names and your release for me to contact those people is attached to this informed consent. I will only contact these people with your permission, and will not share information about you during those contacts.

In the fourth part, I will describe my conclusions to you and will review with you the information from the interview and tests. You will have an opportunity to discuss any of the opinions or information that I review with you. I will invite you to comment on the information and on my opinions. This will give you an opportunity to call my attention to any errors in fact or conclusion that you believe I have made and any aspects that you believe are incomplete or misleading. (It is possible, of course, that we may disagree about certain conclusions or other aspects of this assessment.) I may do this by talking with you, or by giving you a written draft, depending on whether the attorney has asked me to prepare a report. If I do prepare a report, I will ask you to review it to be certain that I have no factual errors in the report.

It is important that you be as honest as possible when responding to the items on the standardized tests, providing information during the interview, and writing your response to the assessment. Information that is withheld, incomplete, wrong, or misleading may be far more damaging than if I am able to find out about it now and put it in context in my report or testimony. It is important for us to discuss any concerns you have in this area.

Although I will try to be thorough when I interview you, I may not ask about some areas or information that you believe are important. If so, please tell me so that we can discuss it. I will also discuss with you the best way to recontact me if, once this evaluation is complete, you think of something that you believe it would be important for me to know.

I am a [psychologist, psychiatrist, or other professional title] licensed by the state of [name of state]. If you have reason to believe that I am behaving unethically or unprofessionally during the course of this assessment, I urge you to let me know at once so that we can discuss it. If you believe that I have not adequately addressed your complaints in this area, there are several agencies whom you may consult, and, if you believe it appropriate, you may file a formal complaint against me. One agency is the state governmental board that licenses me to practice: [name, address, and phone number of the licensing board]. Other agencies are the ethics committees of my state professional association, [name, address, and phone number], and national professional association, [name, address, and phone number]. However, you have my assurance that I will try at all times to conduct this assessment in an ethical and professional manner and will be open to discussing any complaints that you have in this area.

Please check each item below to indicate that you have read it carefully and understand it.

- I understand that Dr. _____ has been hired by my attorney, [fill in attorney's name], to conduct a psychological assessment for a case in which [some indication of what topics are at issue in this assessment].

- I understand that I will be asked to talk about myself and about a variety of issues that people may consider relevant to my court case, and I agree to do so.

- I understand that it is important for me to be honest and accurate when answering questions or providing information during this assessment.

- I understand that Dr. _____ may write a formal report about me based on the results of this assessment if my attorney requests it.

- I authorize Dr. _____ to send a copy of this formal report to my attorney and to discuss the report with him or her.

- I authorize Dr. _____ to speak to the following persons as additional information sources for this evaluation.

- I understand that Dr. _____ will provide me with this written report and that I may, if I choose, schedule an additional appointment with Dr. _____ to discuss the results of this assessment.

- I authorize Dr. _____ to testify about me and this assessment in depositions and trial(s) related to my legal case.

- I understand that I may interrupt or discontinue this assessment at any time.

- I understand that even if I interrupt the assessment and it is not resumed or if I discontinue the assessment, it is possible (depending the applicable laws, on rulings by the court, and/or on decisions by the attorneys in this case) that Dr. _____ may be called to submit a report or testify about the assessment, even if the assessment is incomplete.

- I understand that if I disclose certain types of special information to Dr. _____, he/she may be required or permitted to communicate this information to other people. As previously discussed with Dr. _____ , examples of such special information include reports of child or elder abuse and threats to kill or violently attack a specific person.

- I understand that the assessment will be audiotaped or videotaped to preserve an accurate record of what I have said.

- I understand that the audiotaped record of the assessment will be given to my attorney and may become evidence in the deposition or trial(s).

- I understand that the cost of this assessment will be _____ per hour. I understand that my attorney has already signed a contract to pay the fees for this assessment. I agree to these fees.

If you have read, understood, and checked off each of the prior sections, please read carefully the following statement and, if you are in agreement, please sign the statement. Do *not* sign if you have any questions that remain unanswered after our discussion of them or if there are any aspects that you don't understand or agree to; contact your attorney for guidance concerning how to proceed so that you fully understand the process and can decide whether you wish to continue.

Consent Agreement: I have read, agreed to, and checked off each of the previous sections. I have asked questions about any parts that I did not understand fully. I have also asked questions about any parts that I was concerned about. By signing below, I indicate that I understand and agree to the nature and purpose of this assessment, to the way(s) in which it will be reported, and to each of the points listed above.

_____

Signature

_____

Name (please print)

_____

Date

—ᴠᴠ— References

Advice on ethics of billing clients. (1987, November). *APA Monitor,* p. 42.

Akamatsu, T. J. (1988). Intimate relationships with former clients: National survey of attitudes and behavior among practitioners. *Professional Psychology: Research and Practice, 19,* 454–458.

Amaro, H., Russo, N. F., & Johnson, J. (1987). Family and work predictors of psychological well-being among Hispanic women professionals. *Psychology of Women Quarterly, 11,* 505–522.

American Association for Counseling and Development. (1988). *Ethical standards* (Rev. ed.). Alexandria, VA: Author.

American Association for Marriage and Family Therapy. (1988). *Code of professional ethics for marriage and family therapists* (Rev. ed.). Washington, DC: Author.

American Association on Mental Deficiency. (1974). *The Adaptive Behavior Scale: Manual.* Washington, DC: Author.

American Psychiatric Association. (1994). *Diagnostic and statistical manual of mental disorders* (4th ed.). Washington, DC: Author.

American Psychological Association. (1953). *Ethical standards of psychologists.* Washington, DC: Author.

American Psychological Association. (1963). Ethical standards of psychologists. *American Psychologist, 18,* 56–60.

American Psychological Association. (1981). *Specialty guidelines for the delivery of services: Clinical psychologists, counseling psychologists, industrial/organizational psychologists, school psychologists.* Washington, DC: Author.

American Psychological Association. (1987a). *Casebook on ethical principles of psychologists.* Washington, DC: Author.

American Psychological Association. (1987b). General guidelines for providers of psychological services. *American Psychologist, 42,* 712–723.

American Psychological Association. (1987c). *Guidelines for conditions of employment of psychologists.* Washington, DC: Author.

American Psychological Association. (1990). Ethical principles of psychologists. *American Psychologist, 45,* 390–395.

American Psychological Association. (1992). Ethical principles of psychologists and code of conduct. *American Psychologist, 47,* 1597–1611.

American Psychological Association. (1993). Guidelines for providers of services to ethnic, linguistic, and culturally diverse populations. *American Psychologist, 48,* 45–48.

American Psychological Association. (1994). Guidelines for child custody evaluations in divorce proceedings. *American Psychologist, 49,* 677–680.

American Psychological Association. (1996). Statement on the disclosure of test data. *American Psychologist, 51,* 644–648.

American Psychological Association. (1997). *Your mental health rights: A joint initiative of mental health professional organizations.* Washington, DC: Author.

American Psychological Association approves FMSF as a sponsor of continuing education programs. (1995, November–December). *False Memory Syndrome Foundation Newsletter* (E-mail edition).

American Psychological Association, American Educational Research Association, National Council on Measurement in Education. (1985). *Standards for educational and psychological testing.* Washington, DC: American Psychological Association. [Revision in progress.]

American Psychological Association Committee on Accreditation. (1989). Criteria for accreditation, doctoral training programs and internships in *Professional Psychology* (amended version). In *Accreditation handbook* (pp. B1–B18). Washington, DC: Author.

American Psychological Association Committee on Ethical Standards for Psychology. (1949). Developing a code of ethics for psychologists. *American Psychologist, 4,* 17.

American Psychological Association Committee on Ethical Standards for Psychology. (1951a). Ethical standards for psychology: Sections 1 and 6. *American Psychologist, 6,* 626–661.

American Psychological Association Committee on Ethical Standards for Psychology. (1951b). Ethical standards for psychology: Sections 2, 4, and 5. *American Psychologist, 6,* 427–452.

American Psychological Association Committee on Ethical Standards for Psychology. (1951c). Ethical standards for psychology: Section 3. *American Psychologist, 6,* 57–64.

American Psychological Association, Committee on Legal Issues. (1996). Strategies for private practitioners coping with subpoenas or compelled testimony for client records or test data. *Professional Psychology: Research and Practice, 27,* 245–251.

American Psychological Association, Committee on Psychological Tests and Assessment. (1996). Statement on the disclosure of test data. *American Psychologist, 51,* 644–648.

American Psychological Association, Ethics Committee. (1994). Report of the Ethics Committee, 1993. *American Psychologist, 49,* 659–666.

American Psychological Association, Ethics Committee. (1995). Report of the Ethics Committee, 1994. *American Psychologist, 50,* 706–713.

American Psychological Association, Ethics Committee. (1996). Report of the Ethics Committee, 1995. *American Psychologist, 51,* 1279–1286.

American Psychological Association, Ethics Committee. (1997). Report of the Ethics Committee, 1996. *American Psychologist, 52,* 897–905.

American Psychological Association Insurance Trust. (1990). *Bulletin: Sexual misconduct and professional liability claims.* Washington, DC: Author.

American Psychological Association Task Force on Violence and the Family. (1996). *Violence and the family: Report of the American Psychological Association Task Force on Violence and the Family.* Washington, DC: American Psychological Association.

Andrews, B., Morton, J. Bekerian, D. A., Brewin, C. R., Davis, G. M., & Mollon, P. (1995). The recovery of memories in clinical practice: Experiences and beliefs of British Psychological Society practitioners. *The Psychologist, 8,* 209–214.

Author target of false-memories lawsuit. (1994, May 4). *Sacramento Bee,* p. B3.

Bache, R. M. (1894). Reaction time with reference to race. *Psychological Review, 1,* 475–486.

Baer, B. E., & Murdock, N. L. (1995). Nonerotic dual relationships between therapists and clients: The effects of sex, theoretical orientation, and interpersonal boundaries. *Ethics & Behavior, 5,* 131–145.

Bagley, C., Bolitho, F., & Bertrand, L. (1997). Sexual assault in school, mental health and suicidal behaviors in adolescent women in Canada. *Adolescence, 32,* 341–366.

Bajt, T. R., & Pope, K. S. (1989). Therapist-patient sexual intimacy involving children and adolescents. *American Psychologist, 44,* 455.

Baker v. United States, 226 F. Supp. 129 (S.D. Iowa 1964).

Bartlett, F. (1932). *Remembering: A study in experimental and social psychology.* New York: Macmillan.

Bates, C. M, & Brodsky, A. M. (1989). *Sex in the therapy hour: A case of professional incest.* New York: Guilford.

Beck, A. T. (1967). *Depression.* Philadelphia: University of Pennsylvania Press.

Beck, A. T. (1990, August). *Cognitive therapy and cognitive theory: A thirty year retrospective.* Paper presented at the annual meeting of the American Psychological Association, Boston.

Beck, A. T., Kovaks, M., & Weissman, A. (1975). Hopelessness and suicidal behavior: An overview. *Journal of the American Medical Association, 234,* 1146–1149.

Beck, A. T., Resnick, H. L. P., & Lettieri, D. (Eds.). (1974). *The prediction of suicide.* New York: Charles Press.

Bell, B. E., Raiffa, H., & Tversky, A. (Eds.). (1989). *Decision making: Descriptive, normative, and prescriptive interactions.* Cambridge, U.K.: Cambridge University Press.

Benson, P. R. (1984). Informed consent. *Journal of Nervous and Mental Disease, 172,* 642–653.

Bernsen, A., Tabachnick, B. G., & Pope, K. S. (1994). National survey of social workers' sexual attraction to their clients: Results, implications, and comparison to psychologist. *Ethics & Behavior, 4,* 369–388.

Beutler, L. E. (1985). Loss and anticipated death: Risk factors in depression. In H. H. Goldman & S. E. Goldston (Eds.), *Preventing stress-related psychiatric disorders* (pp. 177–194). Rockville, MD: National Institute of Mental Health.

"Biography." (1995). *American Psychologist, 50,* 242–243.

Bird, C. (1927). The influence of the press upon the accuracy of report. *Journal of Abnormal and Social Psychology, 22,* 123–129.

Blau, T. H. (1984). *The psychologist as expert witness.* New York: Wiley-Interscience.

Block, N. J., & Dworkin, G. (1976). *The IQ controversy.* New York: Pantheon.

Blume, E. S. (1990). *Secret survivors: Uncovering incest and its aftereffects in women.* New York: Wiley.

Boice, R., & Myers, P. E. (1987). Which setting is happier: Academe or private practice? *Professional Psychology: Research and Practice, 18,* 526–529.

Boring, E. (1950). *History of experimental psychology* (2nd ed.). New York: Appleton-Century-Crofts.

Borum, R. (1996). Improving the clinical practice of violence risk assessment: Technology, guidelines, and training. *American Psychologist, 51,* 945–956.

Borys, D. S. (1988). *Dual relationships between therapist and client: A national survey of clinicians' attitudes and practices.* Unpublished doctoral dissertation, University of California, Los Angeles.

Borys, D. S., & Pope, K. S. (1989). Dual relationships between therapist and client: A national study of psychologists, psychiatrists, and social workers. *Professional Psychology: Research and Practice, 20,* 283–293.

Boss, K. (1994, September 25). Into the past imperfect: Elizabeth Loftus challenges our total recall. *Seattle Times,* pp. 8–13, 24.

Bouhoutsos, J. C. (1983, August). *Programs for distressed colleagues: The California model.* Symposium presented at the annual meeting of the American Psychological Association, Anaheim, CA.

Bouhoutsos, J. C., Holroyd, J., Lerman, H., Forer, B., & Greenberg, M. (1983). Sexual intimacy between psychotherapists and patients. *Professional Psychology: Research and Practice, 14,* 185–196.

Bowman, C. G., & Mertz, E. (1996a). A bias in the flow of information? *American Bar Association's Judges' Journal, 35,* 13.

Bowman, C. G., & Mertz, E. (1996b). A dangerous direction: Legal intervention in sexual abuse survivor therapy. *Harvard Law Review, 109,* 549–639.

Breland, K., & Breland, M. (1961). The misbehavior of organisms. *American Psychologist, 16,* 681–684.

Brewin, C. R., Andrews, B., & Gotlib, L. H. (1993). Psychopathology and early experience: A reappraisal of retrospective reports. *Psychological Bulletin, 113,* 82–98.

Briere, J., & Conte, J. R. (1993). Self-reported amnesia for abuse in adults molested as children. *Journal of Traumatic Stress, 6,* 21–31.

Brodsky, A. M. (1989). Sex between patient and therapist: Psychology's data and response. In G. O. Gabbard (Ed.), *Sexual exploitation in professional relationships* (pp. 15–25). Washington, DC: American Psychiatric Press.

Brown, D. (1995a). Pseudomemories: The standard of science and standard of care in trauma treatment. *American Journal of Clinical Hypnosis, 37,* 1–24.

Brown, D. (1995b). Sources of suggestion and their applicability to psychotherapy. In J. L. Alpert (Ed.), *Sexual abuse recalled* (pp. 61–100). Northvale, NJ: Jason Aronson.

Brown, L. S. (1988). Harmful effects of posttermination sexual and romantic relationships between therapists and their former clients. *Psychotherapy, 25,* 249–255.

Brown, L. S. (1990). Mapping the moral domain: A review and critique. *The Interchange, 8*(2), 5–6.

Brown, L. S. (1994). *Subversive dialogues.* New York: Basic Books.

Brunch, J., Barraclough, B., Nelson, M., & Sainsbury, P. (1971). Suicide following death of parents. *Social Psychiatry, 6,* 193–199.

Burgess, A. W., Hartman, C. R., & Baker T. (1995). Memory presentations of childhood sexual abuse. *Journal of Psychosocial Nursing, 33,* 9–16.

Burke, E. (1961). *Reflections on the revolution in France.* New York: Doubleday. (Original work published 1790.)

Burt, R. A. (1997). The Supreme Court speaks—Not assisted suicide but a constitutional right to palliative care. *New England Journal of Medicine, 337,* 1234–1236.

Butcher, J. M., Graham, J. R., Williams, C. L., & Ben-Porath, Y. S. (1990). *Development and use of the MMPI-2 content scales.* Minneapolis: University of Minnesota Press.

Butler, K. (1994, September 6). Self-help authors freed from liability; suit involving incest claims continues. *San Francisco Chronicle,* p. A16.

Butler, K. (1995, March–April). Caught in the cross-fire. *Networker,* pp. 25–34, 68–79.

Butler, S. E., & Zelen, S. L. (1977). Sexual intimacies between therapists and patients. *Psychotherapy, 14,* 139–145.

Caffey, J. (1946). Multiple fractures in the long bones of infants suffering from chronic subdural hematoma. *American Journal of Roentgenology, 56,* 163–173.

California Department of Consumer Affairs. (1990). *Professional therapy never includes sex.* (Available from Board of Psychology, 1422 Howe Avenue, Suite 22. Sacramento, CA 95825.)

California Department of Consumer Affairs. (1997). *Professional therapy never includes sex* (second edition). (Available from Board of Psychology, 1422 Howe Avenue, Suite 22. Sacramento, CA 95825.)

Calof, D. (1996, June). *Notes from a practice under siege.* Paper presented at the eighth annual regional conference on Abuse, Trauma, and Disassociation, Washington, DC. (Audiotape available from Audio Transcripts, Ltd.; telephone: 800-338-2111)

Cameron, C. (1994). Women survivors confronting their abusers: Issues, decisions, and outcomes. *Journal of Child Sexual Abuse, 3,* 7–35.

Campbell, T. W. (1994). *Beware the talking cure: Psychotherapy may be hazardous to your mental health.* Boca Raton. FL: Upton Books.

Canterbury v. *Spence,* 464 F. 2d 772 (D.C. Cir. 1972).

Caplan, P. J. (1995). *They say you're crazy: The inside story of the DSM.* Reading, MA: Addison-Wesley.

Casas, J. M., & Vasquez, M. J. T. (1989). Counseling the Hispanic client: Theoretical and applied perspectives. In P. D. Pedersen, J. G. Draguns, W. J. Lonner, & E. J. Trimble (Eds.), *Counseling across cultures* (3rd ed.) (pp. 153–176). Honolulu: University of Hawaii Press.

Cases and inquiries before the Committee on Scientific and Professional Ethics and Conduct. (1954). *American Psychologist, 9,* 806–807.

Cassileth, B. R., Zupkis, R. V., Sutton-Smith, K., & March, V. (1980). Informed consent—Why are its goals imperfectly realized? *New England Journal of Medicine, 323,* 896–900.

Caudill, O. B. (1993, winter). Can psychologists be vicariously liable for sexual misconduct? *Advance,* pp. 17–18.

Caudill, O. B., & Pope, K. S. (1995). *Law and mental health professionals: California.* Washington, DC: American Psychological Association.

Chambless, D. L., Baker, M. J., Baucom, D. H., Beutler, L. E., Calhoun, K. S., Crits-Christoph, P., Daivto, A., DeRubeis, R., Detweiler, J., Haaga, D. A. F., Johnson, S. B., McCurry, S., Mueser, K. T., Pope, K. S., Sanderson, W. C., Shoham, V., Stickle, T., Williams, D. A., & Woody, S. R. (1998). Update on empirically validated therapies, II. *The Clinical Psychologist, 51*(1), 3–16.

Chan, C. S. (1997). Don't ask, don't tell, don't know: The formation of a homosexual identity and sexual expression among Asian American lesbians. In B. Greene (Ed.), *Ethnic and cultural diversity among lesbians and gay men* (pp. 240–248). Thousand Oaks, CA: Sage.

Cheit v. *Farmer.* (1994). Case # 954272 Superior Court of the State of California for the County of San Francisco, Judgment, November 14.

Chiang, H. (1986, July 28). Psychotherapist is subject to suit for breaching privilege. *Los Angeles Daily Journal,* p. 1.

Cobbs v. *Grant,* 502 P.2d 1, 8 Cal.3d. 229 (1972).

Cohen-Sandler, R., Berman, A. L., & King, R. A. (1982). Life stress and symptomatology: Determinants of suicidal behavior in children. *Journal of the American Academy of Child Psychiatry, 21,* 178–186.

Colby, K. (1968). Commentary: Report to the plenary session on psychopharmacology in relation to psychotherapy. In J. M. Schlein (Ed.), *Research in psychotherapy: Vol. 3.* Washington, DC: American Psychological Association.

Cole, M., & Bruner, J. S. (1972). Cultural differences and inferences about psychological processes. *American Psychologist, 26,* 867–876.

Colorado State Board of Medical Examiners v. *Weiler,* 402 P.2d 606 (1965).

Colt, G. H. (1983). The enigma of suicide. *Harvard Magazine, 86,* 47–66.

Committee on Professional Standards of the American Psychological Association. (1984). Casebook for providers of psychological services. *American Psychologist, 39,* 663–668.

Cooper v. *Board of Medical Examiners,* 49 Cal. App. 3d 931, 123 Cal. Rptr. 563 (1975).

Council of Representatives of the American Psychological Association. (1976, January 23–25). Policy on training for psychologists wishing to change their specialty. *Minutes of Council meeting.*

Council of Representatives of the American Psychological Association. (1982, January 22–24). Respecialization. *Minutes of Council meeting.*

Crews, F. (1995). *The memory wars: Freud's legacy in dispute.* New York: New York Review of Books.

Crews, F. (1996). The verdict on Freud. *Psychological Science, 7,* 63–68.

Dalenberg, C. J. (1996). Accuracy, timing and circumstances of disclosure in therapy of recovered and continuous memories of abuse. *Journal of Psychiatry & Law, 24,* 229–275.

Davis, L., & Bass, E. (1994). *The courage to heal: A guide for women survivors of child sexual abuse* (3rd ed.). New York: HarperPerennial.

Davison, G. C., & Neale, J. M. (1982). *Abnormal psychology: An experimental clinical approach.* New York: Wiley.

Dawes, R. M. (1994). *House of cards: Psychology and psychotherapy built on myth.* New York: Free Press.

Dawes, R. M. (1995, January). Book review of "Return of the Furies: An Investigation into Recovered Memory Therapy" by Hollida Wakefield and Ralph Underwager. *False Memory Syndrome Foundation Newsletter,* pp. 11–13.

Detroit Edison Company v. *National Labor Relations Board,* 99 S. Ct. 1123–1132 (1973).

Doe, J. [Pamela Freyd] (1991). How could this happen? Coping with a false accusation of incest and rape. *Issues in Child Abuse Accusations, 3,* 154–165.

Doe, J. [Pamela Freyd] (1994). How could this happen? In E. Goldstein & K. Farmer (Eds.), *Confabulations: Creating false memories, destroying families* (pp. 27–60). Boca Raton, FL: Upton Books.

Dowie, J., & Elstein, A. (Eds.). (1988). *Professional judgment: A reader in clinical decision making.* Cambridge, U.K.: Cambridge University Press.

Drake, R., Gates, C., Cotton, P., & Whitaker, A. (1984). Suicide among schizophrenics: Who is at risk? *Journal of Nervous and Mental Disease, 172,* 613–617.

EchoHawk, M. (1997). Suicide: The scourge of Native American people. *Suicide & Life-Threatening Behavior, 27,* 60–67.

Elliott, D. M. (1997). Traumatic events: Prevalence and delayed recall in the general population. *Journal of Consulting and Clinical Psychology, 65,* 811–820.

Elliott, D. M., & Briere, J. (1995). Posttraumatic stress associated with delayed recall of sexual abuse: A general population study. *Journal of Traumatic Stress, 8,* 629–647.

Ellis, E. M., Atkeson, B. M., & Calhoun, K. S. (1982). An examination of differences between multiple- and single-incident victims of multiple sexual assault. *Journal of Abnormal Psychology, 91,* 221–224.

Erdberg, P. (1988, August). *How clinicians can achieve competence in testing procedures.* Paper presented at the annual meeting of the American Psychological Association, Atlanta.

Ethics Committee of the American Psychological Association. (1988a, October 5–7). *Policy statement.*

Ethics Committee of the American Psychological Association. (1988b). Trends in ethics cases, common pitfalls, and published resources. *American Psychologist, 43,* 564–572.

Evans, J. S. (1989). *Bias in human reasoning.* Hillsdale, NJ: Erlbaum.

False Memory Syndrome Foundation. (1992a, November 5). Information needed in assessing allegations by adults of sex abuse in childhood. *False Memory Syndrome Foundation Newsletter,* p. 5.

False Memory Syndrome Foundation. (1992b). *Legal aspects of False Memory Syndrome.* Philadelphia: Author.

False Memory Syndrome Foundation. (1992c, October 5). What can families do? *False Memory Syndrome Foundation Newsletter,* p. 4.

False Memory Syndrome Foundation. (1993, May 3). Important organizational notice. *False Memory Syndrome Foundation Newsletter,* p. 7.

False Memory Syndrome Foundation. (1994, July/August). How does a person know that memories of abuse were false? *False Memory Syndrome Foundation Newsletter,* pp. 3–4.

False Memory Syndrome Foundation. (1995a). *Amicus curiae brief filed with the Supreme Court of Alabama in the case of McDuffie v. Sellers-Bok* (No. 1940524).

False Memory Syndrome Foundation. (1995b). *Amicus curiae brief filed with the Supreme Court for the State of Rhode Island in the cases of Heroux v. Carpentier (Appeal No. 95-39) and Kelly v. Marcantonio (Appeal No. 94-727).*

False Memory Syndrome Foundation (1995c). *Amicus curiae brief filed with the Supreme Court of Texas in the case of Vesecky v .Vesecky* (No. 94-0856).

False Memory Syndrome Foundation. (1996a, February 1). FMS Foundation Scientific and Professional Advisory Board. *False Memory Syndrome Foundation Newsletter* (E-mail edition).

False Memory Syndrome Foundation. (1996b). Information sheet and order form for "False Memory Syndrome" video. Philadelphia: Author.

False Memory Syndrome Foundation. (1997). *Amicus curiae brief filed with the Supreme Court of Illinois in the case of M. E. H. and D. M. H. v. LH. and OH.* (Appeal No. 81943).

Farberow, N. (1985, May 12). How to tell if someone is thinking of suicide. *Los Angeles Herald Examiner,* p. C9.

Faschingbauer, T. R. (1979). The future of the MMPI. In C. S. Newmark (Ed.), *MMPI: Clinical and research trends* (pp. 380–392). New York: Praeger.

Feldman-Summers, S. (1989). Sexual contact in fiduciary relationships. In G. O. Gabbard (Ed.), *Sexual exploitation in professional relationships* (pp. 193–209). Washington, DC: American Psychiatric Press.

Feldman-Summers, S., & Jones, G. (1984). Psychological impacts of sexual contact between therapists or other health care professionals and their clients. *Journal of Consulting and Clinical Psychology, 52,* 1054–1061.

Feldman-Summers, S., & Pope, K. S. (1994). The experience of "forgetting" childhood abuse: A national survey of psychologists. *Journal of Consulting and Clinical Psychology, 62,* 636–639.

Fernberger, S. W. (1932). The American Psychological Association: A historical summary, 1892–1930. *Psychological Bulletin, 31,* 1–89.

Fernberger, S. W. (1943). The American Psychological Association, 1892–1942. *Psychological Review, 50,* 33–60.

Fink, P. J. (1989). Presidential address: On being ethical in an unethical world. *American Journal of Psychiatry, 146,* 1097–1104.

FMSF Advisory Board Meeting: Where Do We Go From Here? (1993, December). *False Memory Syndrome Foundation Newsletter,* p. 3.

Fraser, S. (1997, January 25). Abuse wars: Whose memory matters? *Toronto Globe and Mail,* p. D14.

Freeman, L., & Roy, J. (1976). *Betrayal.* New York: Stein and Day.

Freud, S. (1952). *A general introduction to psychoanalysis.* Authorized English translation of the revised edition by J. Riviere. New York: Washington Square. (Originally published 1924.)

Freud, S. (1963). Further recommendations in the technique of psychoanalysis: Observations on transference-love. In P. Rieff (Ed.), *Freud: Therapy and technique* (pp. 167–179). Authorized English translation of the revised edition by J. Riviere. New York: Collier Books. (Originally published 1915.)

Freyd, J. J. (1996). *Betrayal trauma: The logic of forgetting childhood abuse.* Cambridge, MA: Harvard University Press.

Freyd, J. J., & Gleaves, D. H. (1996). "Remembering" words not presented in lists: Relevance to the current recovered/false memory controversy. *Journal of Experimental Psychology: Learning, Memory, and Cognition, 22,* 811–813.

Freyd, P. (1992, February 29). Dear friends. *False Memory Syndrome Newsletter,* p. 1.

Freyd, P. (1996, March 1). Dear friends. *False Memory Syndrome Foundation Newsletter* (E-mail edition).

Gabbard, G. O. (Ed.). (1989). *Sexual exploitation in professional relationships.* Washington, DC: American Psychiatric Press.

Gabbard, G. O. (1994). Teetering on the precipice. *Ethics & Behavior, 4,* 283–286.

Gabbard, G. O., & Pope, K. S. (1989). Sexual intimacies after termination: Clinical, ethical, and legal aspects. In G. O. Gabbard (Ed.), *Sexual exploitation in professional relationships* (pp. 115–127). Washington, DC: American Psychiatric Press.

Gandhi, M. K. (1948). *Non-violence in peace and war.* Ahmedabadi, India: Narajivan Publishing House.

Garb, H. N. (1997). Racial bias, social class bias, and gender bias in clinical judgment. *Clinical Psychology: Science & Practice, 4,* 99–120.

Gardner, M. (1993). The False Memory Syndrome. *Skeptical Inquirer, 17,* 370–375.

Garry, M., & Loftus, E. F. (1994, January). Repressed memories of childhood trauma: Could some of them be suggested? *USA Today, 122* (No. 2584), pp. 82–83.

Gartrell, N. K., Herman, J. L., Olarte, S., Feldstein, M., & Localio, R. (1986). Psychiatrist-patient sexual contact: Results of a national survey, I: Prevalence. *American Journal of Psychiatry, 143,* 1126–1131.

Geller, J. D. (1988). Racial bias in the evaluation of patients for psychotherapy. In L. Comas-Dias and E. H. Griffith (Eds.), *Clinical guidelines in cross-cultural mental health* (pp. 112–134). New York: Wiley.

Geller, J. D., Cooley, R. S., & Hartley, D. (1981–82). Images of the psychotherapist. *Imagination, Cognition, and Personality, 1,* 123–146.

Gellman, R., & Frawley, K. (1996). The need to know versus the right to privacy. In T. Trabin (Ed.), *The computerization of behavioral healthcare* (pp. 191–212). San Francisco: Jossey-Bass.

Gibbs, J. C., & Schnell, S. V. (1985). Moral development "versus" socialization: A critique. *American Psychologist, 40,* 1071–1080.

Gibbs, J. T. (1997). African-American suicide: A cultural paradox. *Suicide & Life-Threatening Behavior, 27,* 68–79.

Gibbs, J. T., & Huang, L. N. (1989). *Children of color: Psychological interventions with minority youth.* San Francisco: Jossey-Bass.

Gilligan, C. (1982). *In a different voice: Psychological theory and women's development.* Cambridge, MA: Harvard University Press.

Gilligan, C., Ward, J. V., & Taylor, J. M. (Eds.) with Bardige, B. (1988). *Mapping the moral domain.* Cambridge, MA: Harvard University Press.

Glaser, R. D., & Thorpe, J. S. (1986). Unethical intimacy: A survey of sexual contact and advances between psychology educators and female graduate students. *American Psychologist, 41,* 43–51.

Golding, J. M., Sanchez, R. P., & Sego, S. A. (1996). Do you believe in repressed memories? *Professional Psychology: Research & Practice, 27,* 429–437.

Goldstein, E., & Farmer, K. (Eds.). (1993). *True stories of false memories.* Boca Raton, FL: SIRS Books.

Goldstein, E., & Farmer, K. (Eds.). (1994). *Confabulations: Creating false memories, destroying families.* Boca Raton, FL: SIRS Books.

Goldstein, L. S., & Buongiorno, P. A. (1984). *American Journal of Psychotherapy, 38,* 392–398.

Goldstein, W. M., & Hogarth, R. M. (1997). *Research on judgment and decision making.* Cambridge, UK: Cambridge University Press.

Goleman, D. (1985). *Vital lies, simple truths: The psychology of self deception.* New York: Simon & Schuster.

Goodyear, R. K., & Sinnett, E. R. (1984). Current and emerging ethical issues for counseling psychology. *Counseling Psychologist, 12,* 87–98.

Gossett, T. F. (1963). *Race: The history of an idea in America.* Dallas: Southern Methodist University Press.

Gostin, L. (1997). Deciding life and death in the courtroom: From Quinlan to Cruzan, Glucksberg, and Vacco—A brief history and analysis of constitutional protection of the "right to die." *Journal of the American Medical Association, 278,* 1523–1528.

Gottlieb, M. C., Sell, J. M., & Schoenfeld, L. S. (1988). Social/romantic relationships with present and former clients: State licensing board actions. *Professional Psychology: Research and Practice, 19,* 459–462.

Gould, S. J. (1981). *The mismeasure of man.* New York: Norton.

Greene, B. (1997). Ethnic minority lesbians and gay men: Mental health and treatment issues. In B. Greene (Ed.), *Ethnic and cultural diver-*

sity among lesbians and gay men (pp. 216–239). Thousand Oaks, CA: Sage.

Grundner, T. M. (1980). On the readability of surgical consent forms. *New England Journal of Medicine, 302,* 900–902.

Guthrie, R. V. (1998). *Even the rat was white: A historical view of psychology* (2nd ed.). Needham Heights, MA: Allyn & Bacon.

Guy, J. D., Stark, M. J., & Spolestra, R. A. (1988). Personal therapy for psychologists before and after entering professional practice. *Professional Psychology: Research and Practice, 19,* 474–476.

Guze, S. B., & Robins, E. (1970). Suicide and primary affective disorders. *British Journal of Psychiatry, 117,* 437–438.

Hall, C. S. (1952). Crooks, codes, and cant. *American Psychologist, 7,* 430–431.

Hall, J. E., & Hare-Mustin, R. T. (1983). Sanctions and the diversity of complaints against psychologists. *American Psychologist, 38,* 714–729.

Hallinan v. *Committee of Bar Examiners of State Bar,* 55 Cal. Rptr. 228 (1966).

Hamilton, V. L., Blumenfeld, P. C., & Kushler, R. H. (1988). A question of standards: Attributions of blame and credit for classroom acts. *Journal of Personality and Social Psychology, 54,* 34–48.

Handler, J. F. (1990). *Law and the search for community.* Philadelphia: University of Pennsylvania Press.

Harding, S. S., Shearn, M. L., & Kitchener, K. S. (1989, August). *Dual role dilemmas: Psychology educators and their students.* Paper presented at the annual meeting of the American Psychological Association, New Orleans.

Hare-Mustin, R. T. (1974). Ethical considerations in the use of sexual contact in psychotherapy. *Psychotherapy: Theory, Research and Practice, 11,* 308–310.

Harris, E. C., & Barraclough, B. (1997). Suicide as an outcome for mental disorders: A meta-analysis. *British Journal of Psychiatry, 170,* 205–228.

Herman, J. L. (1992). *Trauma and recovery.* New York: Basic Books.

Herman, J. L. (1994). Presuming to know the truth. *Neiman Reports, 48,* 43–45.

Herman, J. L., Gartrell, N., Olarte, S., Feldstein, M., & Localio, R. (1987). Psychiatrist-patient sexual contact: Results of a national survey, II: Psychiatrists' attitudes. *American Journal of Psychiatry, 144,* 164–169.

Herman, J. L. & Schatzow, E. (1987). Recovery and verification of memories of childhood sexual trauma. *Psychoanalytic Psychology, 4,* 1–14.

Hobbs, N. (1948). The development of a code of ethical standards for psychology. *American Psychologist, 3,* 80–84.

Hoffer, E. (1989). *The true believer.* New York: Harrier Perennial. (Original work published 1951)

Hogan, D. B. (1979). *The regulation of psychotherapists.* Cambridge, MA: Ballinger.

Holroyd, J. C. (1983). Erotic contact as an instance of sex-biased therapy. In J. Murray & P. R. Abramson (Eds.), *Bias in psychotherapy* (pp. 285–308). New York: Praeger.

Holroyd, J. C., & Brodsky, A. (1977). Psychologists' attitudes and practices regarding erotic and nonerotic physical contact with clients. *American Psychologist, 32,* 843–849.

Holroyd, J. C., & Brodsky, A. M. (1980). Does touching patients lead to sexual intercourse? *Professional Psychology, 11,* 807–811.

Hovdestad, W. E., & Kristiansen, C. M. (1996). A field study of "false memory syndrome": Construct validity and incidence. *Journal of Psychiatry & Law, 24,* 299–338.

Hubel, D. H., & Wiesel, T. N. (1962a). Cortical and callosal connections concerned with the vertical meridian of visual fields in the cat. *Journal of Neurophysiology, 30,* 1561–1573.

Hubel, D. H.. & Wiesel, T. N. (1962b). Receptive fields, binocular interaction, and functional architecture in the cat's visual cortex. *Journal of Physiology, 160,* 106–154.

Hubel, D. H., & Wiesel, T. N. (1979). Brain mechanisms of vision. *Scientific American, 241,* 150–162.

Hyman, I., Husband, T., & Billings, F. (1995). False memories of childhood experiences. *Applied Cognitive Psychology, 9,* 181–197.

In the Matter of the Accusation Against: Myron E. Howland. (1980). Before the Psychology Examining Committee, Board of Medical Quality Assurance, State of California, No. D-2212. Reporters' Transcript, Volume 3.

Irwin, M., Lovitz, A., Marder, S. R., Mintz, J., Winslade, W. J., Van Putten, T., & Mills, M. J. (1985). Psychotic patients' understanding of informed consent. *American Journal of Psychiatry, 142,* 1351–1354.

Isherwood, J., Adam, K. S., & Homblow, A. R. (1982). Life event stress, psychosocial factors, suicide attempt and auto-accident proclivity. *Journal of Psychosomatic Research, 26,* 371–383.

Jablonski v. *United States,* 712 F.2d 391 (1983).

James v. *Turner,* 184 Tenn. 563, 201 SW. 2d 691 (1942).

James, W. (1890). *The principles of psychology* (Vol. 1). New York: Dover.

Janis, I. L. (1982). *Stress, attitudes, and decisions.* New York: Praeger.

Jones, E. E., & Korchin, S. J. (1982). Minority mental health: Perspectives. In E. E. Jones and S. J. Korchin (Eds.), *Minority mental health* (pp. 3 – 36). New York: Praeger.

Jones, J. H. (1981). *Bad blood: The Tuskegee syphilis experiment—A tragedy of race and medicine.* New York: Free Press.

Jones, J. M. (1990a, September 14). *Promoting diversity in an individualistic society.* Keynote address, Great Lakes College Association conference, "Multiculturalism transforming the 21st century: Overcoming the challenges and preparing for the future." Hope College, Holland, MI.

Jones, J. M. (1990b, August). *Psychological approaches to race: What have they been and what should they be?* Paper presented at the annual meeting of the American Psychological Association, Boston.

Jones, J. M., & Block, C. B. (1984). Black cultural perspectives. *Clinical Psychologist, 37,* 58 – 62.

Kahn, J. P. (1994, December 14). Trial by memory: Stung by daughters' claims of abuse, a writer lashes back. *Boston Globe,* p. 80.

Kahneman, D., Slovic, P., & Tversky, A. (Eds.). (1982). *Judgment under uncertainty: Heuristics and biases.* Cambridge, England: Cambridge University Press.

Kalichman, S. C. (1993). *Mandated reporting of suspected child abuse: Ethics, law, & policy.* Washington. DC: American Psychological Association.

Keith-Spiegel, P., & Koocher, G. P. (1985). *Ethics in psychology.* New York: Random House.

Kelman, H. C., & Hamilton, V. L. (1989). *Crimes of obedience: Toward a social psychology of authority and responsibility.* New Haven, CT: Yale University Press.

Kent v. *Whitaker,* 58 Wash. 2d 569, 364 P.2d 556 (1961).

Kihlstrom, J. (1994). False memory syndrome. *FMS Foundation Brochure,* p. 2. Philadelphia: False Memory Syndrome Foundation.

Kihlstrom, J. (1995a). Inferring history from symptoms. Internet posting on witch hunt, January 24.

Kihlstrom, J. (1995b). On checklists. Internet posting on witch hunt, January 24.

Kihlstrom, J. (1996). False memory syndrome. *FMS Foundation Brochure* (E-mail version). Philadelphia: False Memory Syndrome Foundation.

King, M. L., Jr. (1958). *Stride toward freedom.* San Francisco: HarperCollins.

King, M. L., Jr. (1964). *Why we can't wait.* New York: Signet.

Kleespies, P. M., Smith, M. R., & Becker, B. R. (1990). Psychology interns as patient suicide survivors: Incidence, impact, and recovery. *Professional Psychology: Research and Practice, 21,* 257–263.

Klerman, G. L., & Clayton, P. (1984). Epidemiologic perspectives on the health consequences of bereavement. In M. Osterweis, F. Solomon, & M. Green (Eds.), *Bereavement: Reactions, consequences, and care* (pp. 15–44). Washington, DC: National Academy Press.

Koffka, K. (1935). *Principles of Gestalt psychology.* New York: International Library of Psychology, Philosophy and Scientific Method.

Kohlberg, L. (1969). *Stages in development of moral thought and action.* New York: Holt.

Koocher, G. P. (1994). Foreword. In K. S. Pope, *Sexual involvement with therapists: Patient assessment, subsequent therapy, forensics* (pp. vii–ix). Washington, DC: American Psychological Association.

Koocher, G. P. (Chair). (1997, August 18). *Symposium: Science and politics of recovered memories.* Presented at the annual meeting of the American Psychological Association, Chicago.

Koocher, G. P., & Keith-Spiegel, P. (1998). *Ethics in psychology: Professional standards and cases* (2nd. ed.). New York: Oxford University Press.

Koss, M. P., Goodman, L. A., Browne, A., Fitzgerald. L. F., Keita, G. W., & Russo, N. F. (1994). *No safe haven: Male violence against women at home, at work, and in the community.* Washington. DC: American Psychological Association.

Koss, M. P., Tromp, S., & Tharan, M. (1995). Traumatic memories: Empirical foundations, forensic and clinical implications. *Clinical Psychology: Science and Practice, 2,* 111–132.

Kovacs, A. L. (1987, May). Insurance billing: The growing risk of lawsuits against psychologists. *Independent Practitioner, 7,* 21–24.

Kramer, M., Pollack, E. S., Redick, R. W., & Locke, B. Z. (1972). *Mental disorders/suicide.* Cambridge, MA: Harvard University Press.

Krupnick, J. L. (1984). Bereavement during childhood and adolescence. In M. Osterweis, F. Solomon, & M. Green (Eds.), *Bereavement: Reactions, consequences, and care* (pp. 99–141). Washington, DC: National Academy Press.

LaFromboise, T. D., & Foster, S. L. (1989). Ethics and multicultural counseling. In P. D. Pedersen, J. G. Draguns, W. J. Lonner, & E. J. Trimble (Eds.), *Counseling across cultures* (3rd ed.) (pp. 115–136). Honolulu: University of Hawaii Press.

Landsberg, M. (1996a, February 4). Incest. *Toronto Star,* p. A2.

Landsberg, M. (1996b, February 11). Beware of false prophets. *Toronto Star,* p. A2.

Langer, E. J. (1989). *Mindfulness.* Reading, MA: Addison-Wesley.

Langer, E. J., & Abelson, R. P. (1974). A patient by any other name . . . : Clinician group differences and labeling bias. *Journal of Consulting and Clinical Psychology, 42,* 4–9.

Langer, E. J., Bashner, R., & Chanowitz, B. (1985). Decreasing prejudice by increasing discrimination. *Journal of Personality and Social Psychology, 49,* 113–120.

Larry P. v. *Riles,* 343 F. supp. 1306 (N.D. Cal. 1972); opinion issued as #C-71-2270 RFP (N.D. Cal. October 16, 1979).

Leavitt, F. (1997). False attribution of suggestibility to explain recovered memory of childhood abuse following extended amnesia. *Child Abuse & Neglect, 21,* 265–272.

Lehner, G. F. J. (1952). Defining psychotherapy. *American Psychologist, 7,* 547.

Lettieri, D. J. (1982). Suicidal death prediction scales. In P. A. Keller & L. G. Ritt (Eds.), *Innovations in clinical practice: Vol. 1* (pp. 265–268). Sarasota, FL: Professional Resource Exchange.

Levenson, H., & Pope, K. S. (1981). First encounters: Effects of intake procedures on patients, staff, and the organization. *Hospital and Community Psychiatry, 32,* 482–485.

Levine, R. J. (1988). *Ethics and regulation of clinical research* (2nd ed.). New Haven, CT: Yale University Press.

Lickona, T. (Ed.). (1976). *Moral development and behavior: Theory, research, and social issues.* New York: Holt.

Lindsay, D. S. (1995a). Beyond backlash. *Counseling Psychologist, 23,* 280–289.

Lindsay, D. S. (1995b, August 14). Letter to Karen Olio.

Lindsay, D. S., & Poole, D. A. (1995, Fall). Remembering childhood sexual abuse in therapy: Psychotherapists' self-reported beliefs, practices, and experiences. *Journal of Psychiatry & Law,* 461–476.

Lindsay, D. S., & Read, D. (1994). Psychotherapy and memories of childhood sexual abuse: A cognitive perspective. *Applied Cognitive Psychology, 8,* 281–338.

Litman, R. E. (1965). When patients commit suicide. *American Journal of Psychotherapy, 19,* 570–583.

A little recent history. (1952). *American Psychologist, 7,* 425.

Livermore, J., Malmquist, C., & Meehl, P. (1968). On the justification for civil commitment. *University of Pennsylvania Law Review, 117,* 75–96.

Loftus, E. F. (1992). When a lie becomes memory's truth: Memory distortion after exposure to misinformation. *Current Directions Psychological Science, 1,* 121–123.

Loftus, E. F. (1993). The reality of repressed memories. *American Psychologist, 48,* 518–537.

Loftus, E. F. (1995, March/April). Remembering dangerously. *Skeptical Inquirer,* pp. 20–29.

Loftus, E. F., & Ketcham, K. (1994). *The myth of repressed memory: False memories and allegations of sexual abuse.* New York: St. Martin's Press.

Loftus, E. F., Milo, I. E., & Paddock, J. (1995). The accidental executioner: Why psychotherapy must be informed by science. *Counseling Psychologist, 23,* 300–309.

Loftus, E. F.. & Pickrell, J. E. (1995). The formation of false memories. *Psychiatric Annals, 25,* 720–725.

Loftus, E. F., Polonsky, S., Fullilove, M. T. (1994). Memories of childhood sexual abuse: Remembering and repressing. *Psychology of Women Quarterly, 18,* 67–84.

Lynn, S., & Nash, M. (1994). Truth in memory. *American Journal of Clinical Hypnosis, 36,* 194–208.

MacNeil/Lehrer NewsHour. (1995). Transcript #5155, February 2.

Mann, C. K., & Winer, J. D. (1991). Psychotherapist's sexual contact with client. *American Jurisprudence Proof of Facts,* 3d Series, vol. *14,* pp. 319–431. Rochester, NY: Lawyers Cooperative Publishing.

Masters, W. H., & Johnson, V. E. (1966). *Human sexual response.* New York: Bantam.

Masters, W. H., & Johnson, V. E. (1970). *Human sexual inadequacy.* New York: Bantam.

Masters, W. H., & Johnson, V. E. (1975, May). *Principles of the new sex therapy.* Paper presented at the annual meeting of the American Psychiatric Association, Anaheim, CA.

Masterson, J. F. (1989, May). Maintaining objectivity crucial in treating borderline patients. *Psychiatric Times,* pp. 1, 26–27.

McCartney, J. (1966). Overt transference. *Journal of Sex Research, 2,* 227–237.

McCauley, J., Kern, D. E., Kolodner, K., Dill, L., et al. (1997). Clinical characteristics of women with a history of childhood abuse: Unhealed wounds. *Journal of the American Medical Association, 277,* 1362–1368.

McCord, C., & Freeman, H. P. (1990). Excess mortality in Harlem. *New England Journal of Medicine, 322,* 173–177.

McHugh, P. (1993a, May 3). Procedures in the diagnosis of incest in recovered memory cases. *False Memory Syndrome Foundation Newsletter,* p. 3.

McHugh, P. (1993b, October 1). To treat. *False Memory Syndrome Foundation Newsletter,* p. 1.

McKelvey v. *Turnage,* U.S. Supreme Court, 86-737 (April 20, 1988).

McNeil, B., Pauker, S. G., Sox, H. C., &Tversky, A. (1982). On the elucidation of preferences for alternative therapies. *New England Journal of Medicine, 306,* 1259–1262.

Mednick, M. T. (1989). On the politics of psychological constructs: Stop the bandwagon, I want to get off. *American Psychologist, 44,* 1118–1123.

Melchert, T. P. (1996). Childhood memory and a history of different forms of abuse. *Professional Psychology: Research & Practice, 27,* 438–446.

Mercer, J. R. (1979). *Technical manual: System of multicultural pluralistic assessment.* New York: Psychological Corporation.

Milgram, S. (1974). *Obedience to authority: An experimental view.* New York: HarperCollins.

Miller, I. J. (1996). Managed care is harmful to outpatient mental health services: A call for accountability. *Professional Psychology: Research and Practice, 27,* 349–363.

Miller, L. A. (1997). Teaching about repressed memories of childhood sexual abuse and eyewitness testimony. *Teaching of Psychology, 24*(4), 24–28.

Mintz, N. L. (1971). Patient fees and psychotherapeutic transactions. *Journal of Consulting and Clinical Psychology, 43,* 835–841.

Mitchell, J. (1993, August 8). Memories of a disputed past. *Oregonian,* pp. L1, L6–L7.

Moffic, H. S. (1997). *The ethical way.* San Francisco: Jossey-Bass.

Monahan, J. (Ed.). (1980). *Who is the client?* Washington, DC: American Psychological Association.

Monahan, J. (1993). Limiting therapist exposure to Tarasoff liability: Guidelines for risk containment. *American Psychologist, 48,* 242–250.

Morra v. *State Board of Examiners of Psychologists,* 510 Kans. P.2d 614 (1973).

Muensterberg, H. (1908). *On the witness stand: Essays of psychology and crime.* New York: McClure.

Murdock, B. B. (1995). Human memory in the twenty-first century. In R. L. Solso & D. W. Massaro (Eds.), *The science of the mind* (pp. 109–122). New York: Oxford University Press.

Murphy, J. M. (1976). Psychiatric labeling in cross-cultural perspective. *Science, 191,* 1019–1028.

Natanson v. Kline, 186 Kans. 393, 406, 350 P.2d 1093 (1960).

Nathan, D. (1992, October). Cry incest. *Playboy: Entertainment for Men, 39*(10), 84–89.

National Academies of Practice. (1997). *Ethical guidelines for professional care in a managed care environment.* Washington, D. C.: Author.

National Association of Social Workers. (1989). *Standards for the practice of clinical social work.* Silver Spring, MD: Author.

National Association of Social Workers. (1990). *Code of ethics* (rev. ed.). Silver Springs, MD: Author.

Neisser, U. (1981). John Dean's memory. *Cognition, 9,* 1–22.

Nethaway, R. (1993, August/September). Whining about abuse is an epidemic. *False Memory Syndrome Foundation Newsletter,* p. 6.

Neuringer, C. (1964). Rigid thinking in suicidal individuals. *Journal of Consulting Psychology, 28,* 54–58.

Neuringer, C. (1974). *Psychological assessment of suicidal risk.* New York: Charles Thomas.

Nimeus, A., Traskman-Bendz, L., & Alsen, M. (1997). Hopelessness and suicidal behavior. *Journal of Affective Disorders, 42,* 137–144.

Noel, B., & Watterson, K. (1992). *You must be dreaming.* New York: Poseidon.

Ofshe, R., & Watters, E. (1993). Making monsters. *Society, 30,* 4–16.

Ofshe, R., & Watters, E. (1994). *Making monsters: False memories, psychotherapy, and sexual hysteria.* New York: Scribners.

Olio, K. (1995a, August). *Conscientious trauma treatment in a contentious climate.* Paper presented at the 103rd Annual Convention of the American Psychological Association, New York, NY.

Olio, K. (1995b, July). *Delayed recall of traumatic events: Politics, validity. and clinical implications.* Paper presented at Delayed Recall of Traumatic Events: Implications for Mental Health Professionals, Burlington, VT.

Olio, K. (1995c). Het voorschrift van Kihlstrom; over de verdenking van seksueel misbruik bij kinderen aan de hand van hun symptomen [Kihlstrom's prescription: On the suspicion of sexual abuse of children on the basis of their symptoms]. *Directieve Terapie, 15,* 194–195.

Olio, K. (1996). Are 25 percent of clinicians using potentially risky therapeutic practices? A review of the logic and methodology of the Poole, Lindsay et al. study. *Journal of Psychiatry & Law, 24,* 277–298.

Olio, K. (1997, December). *A practical guide to trauma treatment: Integrating recovered memory research, legal responsibilities, and clinical realities*. Invited presentation at the Harvard Medical School Conference on Tolerating Complexity: Phase-Oriented Treatment of Trauma and the Challenging Patient, Boston.

Orlinsky, D. E., & Geller, J. D. (1993). Psychotherapy's internal theater of operation: Patients' representations of their therapists and therapy as a new focus of research. In N. E. Miller, J. Docherty, L. Luborsky, & J. Barber (Eds.), *Psychodynamic treatment research* (pp. 423–466). New York: Basic Books.

Pamela Freyd et al. v. Charles L. Whitfield. (1997). Civil Case No. L-96-627 in the U.S. District Court for the District of Maryland, Judge's order dated July 18.

Patsiokas, A. T., Clum, G. A., & Luscumb, R. L. (1979). Cognitive characteristics of suicidal attempters. *Journal of Consulting and Clinical Psychology, 47,* 478–484.

Peck, M., & Seiden, R. (1975, May). Youth suicide. *exChange* (California State Department of Health), pp. 17–20.

Pedersen, P. D., Draguns, J. G., Lonner, W. J., & Trimble, E. J. (1989). Introduction and overview. In P. D. Pedersen, J. G. Draguns, W. J. Lonner, & E. J. Trimble (Eds.), *Counseling across cultures* (3rd ed.) (pp. 1–2). Honolulu: University of Hawaii Press.

Pendergrast, M. (1995). *Victims of memory: Incest accusations and shattered lives.* Hinesburg, VT: Upper Access.

People v. Gomez, App., 185 Cal. Rptr. 155 (August 10, 1982).

People v. Stritzinger, 194 Cal. Rptr. 431 (Cal. September 1, 1983).

People v. Younghanz, 202 Cal. Rptr. 907 (Cal. App. 4 Dist. May 31, 1984).

Perspectives. (1990, April 23). *Newsweek,* p. 17.

Petrie, K., & Chamberlain, K. (1983). Hopelessness and social desirability as moderator variables in predicting suicidal behavior. *Journal of Consulting and Clinical Psychology, 51,* 485–487.

Pezdek, K. (1995, November). *What types of false childhood memories are not likely to be suggestively implanted?* Paper presented at the annual meeting of the Psychonomic Society, Los Angeles.

Pezdek, K., Finger, K., & Hodge, D. (1996, November). *False memories are more likely to be planted if they are familiar.* Paper to be presented at the annual meeting of the Psychonomic Society, Chicago.

Pezdek, K., Finger, K., & Hodge, D. (1997). Planting false childhood memories: The role of event plausibility. *Psychological Science, 8,* 437–441.

Pipes, R. B. (1997). Nonsexual relationships between psychotherapists and their former clients: Obligations of psychologists. *Ethics & Behavior, 7,* 27–41.

Plaisil, E. (1985). *Therapist.* New York: St. Martin's/Marek.

Plato (1956a). The apology. In E. H. Harrington & P. G. Rouse (Eds.), *Great dialogues of Plato* (W. H. D. Rouse, Trans., pp. 423–446). New York: New American Library.

Plato (1956b). Crito. In E. H. Harrington & P. G. Rouse (Eds.), *Great dialogues of Plato* (W. H. D. Rouse, Trans., pp. 447–459). New York: New American Library.

Polusny, M., & Follette, V. (1996). Remembering childhood sexual abuse: A national survey of psychologists' clinical practices, beliefs, and personal experiences. *Professional Psychology: Research and Practice, 27,* 41–52.

Poole, D. A. (1996, February 2). Letter to Karen Olio.

Poole, D. A., Lindsay, D. S., Memon, A., & Bull, R. (1995). Psychotherapy and the recovery of memories of childhood sexual abuse: U.S. and British practitioners' opinions, practices, and experiences. *Journal of Clinical and Consulting Psychology, 63,* 426–437.

Pope, H. G. & Hudson, J. I. (1995a). Can individuals "repress" memories of childhood sexual abuse? An examination of the evidence. *Psychiatric Annals, 25,* 715–719.

Pope, H. G., & Hudson, J. I. (1995b). Can memories of childhood sexual abuse be repressed? *Psychological Medicine, 25,* 121–126.

Pope, K. S. (1979, September). *Undertaking a national survey.* Paper presented at the 87th Annual Convention of the American Psychological Association, New York.

Pope, K. S. (1986, November). New trends in malpractice cases and changes in APA liability insurance. *Independent Practitioner, 6,* 23–26.

Pope, K. S. (1988a). Dual relationships: A source of ethical, legal, and clinical problems. *Independent Practitioner, 8*(1), 17–25.

Pope, K. S. (1988b). How clients are harmed by sexual contact with mental health professionals: The syndrome and its prevalence. *Journal of Counseling and Development, 67,* 222–226.

Pope, K. S. (1989a). Malpractice suits, licensing disciplinary actions, and ethics cases: Frequencies, causes, and costs. *Independent Practitioner, 9*(1), 22–26.

Pope, K. S. (1989b). Student-teacher sexual intimacy. In G. O. Gabbard (Ed.), *Sexual exploitation within professional relationships* (pp. 163–176). Washington, DC: American Psychiatric Press.

Pope, K. S. (1990a). Ethical and malpractice issues in hospital practice. *American Psychologist, 45,* 1066–1070.

Pope, K. S. (1990b). Identifying and implementing ethical standards for primary prevention. In G. B. Levin, E. J. Trickett & R. E. Hess (Eds.), *Ethical implications of primary prevention* (pp. 43–64). Binghamton, NY: Haworth Press.

Pope, K. S. (1990c). Therapist-patient sex as sex abuse: six scientific, professional, and practical dilemmas in addressing victimization and rehabilitation. *Professional Psychology: Research and Practice, 21,* 227–239.

Pope, K. S. (1990d). Therapist-patient sexual involvement: A review of the research. *Clinical Psychology Review, 10,* 477–490.

Pope, K. S. (1992). Responsibilities in providing psychological test feedback to clients. *Psychological Assessment, 4,* 268–271.

Pope, K. S. (1993). Licensing disciplinary actions for psychologists who have been sexually involved with a client: Some information about offenders. *Professional Psychology: Research and Practice, 24,* 374–377.

Pope, K. S. (1994). *Sexual involvement with therapists: Patient assessment, subsequent therapy, forensics.* Washington, DC: American Psychological Association.

Pope, K. S. (1995a, August). Memory, abuse, and strange science: Therapy, forensics, and new research. Award for Distinguished Contributions to Public Service address presented at the 103rd Annual Convention of the American Psychological Association, New York. (Audiotape No. APA9S-245 available from Sound Images, Aurora, CO; telephone: 303-649-1811.)

Pope, K. S. (1995b). What psychologists better know about recovered memories, research, lawsuits, and the pivotal experiment. *Clinical Psychology: Science and Practice, 2,* 304–315.

Pope, K. S. (1996). Memory, abuse, and science: Questioning claims about the false memory syndrome epidemic. *American Psychologist, 51,* 957–974.

Pope, K. S., & Bajt, T. R. (1988). When laws and values conflict: A dilemma for psychologists. *American Psychologist, 43,* 828.

Pope, K. S., & Bouhoutsos, J. C. (1986). *Sexual intimacies between therapists and patients.* New York: Praeger/Greenwood.

Pope, K. S., & Brown, L. (1996). *Recovered memories of abuse: Assessment, therapy, forensics.* Washington, DC: American Psychological Association.

Pope, K. S., Butcher, J. N., & Seelen, J. (1993). *The MMPI, MMPI-2, & MMPPA in court: A practical guide for expert witnesses and attorneys.* Washington, DC: American Psychological Association.

Pope, K. S., & Feldman-Summers, S. (1992). National survey of psychologists' sexual and physical abuse history and their evaluation of training and competence in these areas. *Professional Psychology: Research and Practice, 23,* 353–361.

Pope, K. S., & Garcia-Peltoniemi, R. E. (1991). Responding to victims of torture: Clinical issues, professional responsibilities, and useful resources. *Professional Psychology: Research and Practice, 22,* 269–276.

Pope, K. S., Keith-Spiegel, P., & Tabachnick, B. G. (1986). Sexual attraction to patients: The human therapist and the (sometimes) inhuman training system. *American Psychologist, 41,* 147–158.

Pope, K. S., Levenson, H., & Schover, L. R. (1979). Sexual intimacy in psychology training: Results and implications of a national survey. *American Psychologist, 34,* 682–689.

Pope, K. S., & Morin, S. F. (1990). AIDS and HIV infection update: New research, ethical responsibilities, evolving legal frameworks, and published resources. *Independent Practitioner, 10,* pp. 43–53.

Pope, K. S., Simpson, N. H., & Weiner, M. F. (1978). Malpractice in psychotherapy. *American Journal of Psychotherapy, 32,* 593–602.

Pope, K. S., & Singer, J. L. (1978a). Regulation of the stream of consciousness: Toward a theory of ongoing thought. In G. E. Schwartz & D. Shapiro (Eds.), *Consciousness and self-regulation: Advances in research and theory: Vol. 2.* (pp. 101–137). New York: Plenum Press.

Pope, K. S., & Singer, J. L. (Eds.). (1978b). *The stream of consciousness: Scientific investigations into the flow of human experience.* New York: Plenum Press.

Pope, K. S., & Singer, J. L. (1980). The waking stream of consciousness. In J. M. Davidson & R. J. Davidson (Eds.), *The psychobiology of consciousness* (pp. 169–191). New York: Plenum Press.

Pope, K. S., Sonne, J. L., & Holroyd, J. (1993). *Sexual feelings in psychotherapy: Explorations for therapists and therapists-in-training.* Washington, DC: American Psychological Association.

Pope, K. S., & Tabachnick, B. G. (1993). Therapists' anger, hate, fear and sexual feelings: National survey of therapists' responses, client characteristics, critical events, formal complaints and training. *Professional Psychology: Research and Practice, 24,* 142–152.

Pope, K. S., & Tabachnick, B. G. (1994). Therapists as patients: A national survey of psychologists' experiences, problems, and beliefs. *Professional Psychology: Research and Practice, 25,* 247–258.

Pope, K. S., & Tabachnick, B. G. (1995). Recovered memories of abuse among therapy patients: A national survey. *Ethics & Behavior, 5,* 237–248.

Pope, K. S., Tabachnick, B. G., & Keith-Spiegel, P. (1987). Ethics of practice: The beliefs and behaviors of psychologists as therapists. *American Psychologist, 42,* 993–1006.

Pope, K. S., Tabachnick, B. G., & Keith-Spiegel, P. (1988). Good and poor practices in psychotherapy: National survey of beliefs of psychologists. *Professional Psychology: Research and Practice, 19,* 547–552.

Pope, K. S., & Vasquez, M. J. T. (1991). *Ethics in psychotherapy and counseling: A practical guide for psychologists.* San Francisco: Jossey-Bass.

Pope, K. S., & Vetter, V. A. (1991). Prior therapist-patient sexual involvement among patients seen by psychologists. *Psychotherapy, 28,* 429–438.

Pope, K. S., & Vetter, V. A. (1992). Ethical dilemmas encountered by members of the American Psychological Association: A national survey. *American Psychologist, 47,* 397–411.

Porter, N., & Vasquez, M. (1997). Covision: Feminist supervision, process, and collaboration. In J. Worrell & N. C. Johnson (Eds.), *Shaping the future of feminist psychology: Education, research and practice* (pp. 155–172). Washington, DC: American Psychology Association.

Rachlin, H. (1989). *Judgment, decision, and choice: A cognitive/behavioral synthesis.* New York: W. H. Freeman.

Range, L. M., & Knott, E. C. (1997). Twenty suicide assessment instruments: Evaluation and recommendations. *Death Studies, 21,* 25–58.

Reiser, D. E., & Levenson, H. (1984). Abuses of the borderline diagnosis: a clinical problem with teaching opportunities. *American Journal of Psychiatry, 141,* 1528–1532.

Ridley, C. R. (1989). Racism in counseling as adversive behavioral process. In P. B. Pedersen, J. G. Draguns, W. J. Lonner, & J. E. Trimble (Eds.), *Counseling across cultures* (3rd ed.; pp. 55–78). Honolulu: University of Hawaii Press.

Rivers, E., Schuman, S., Simpson, L., & Olansky, S. (1953). Twenty years of followup experience in long-range medical study. *Public Health Reports, 68,* 391–395.

Robinson, G., & Merav, A. (1976). Informed consent: Recall by patients tested postoperatively. *Annals of Thoracic Surgery, 22,* 209–212.

Robinson, W. L., & Reid, P. T. (1985). Sexual intimacies in psychology revisited. *Profession Psychology, 16,* 512–520.

Roe, C. M., & Schwartz, M. F. (1996). Characteristics of previously forgotten memories of sexual abuse: A descriptive study. *Journal of Psychiatry & Law, 24,* 189–206.

Roediger, H. L. III, & McDermott, K. B. (1995). Creating false memories: Remembering words not presented in lists. *Journal of Experimental Psychology: Learning. Memory, and Cognition, 21,* 803–814.

Roesler, T. A., & Wind, T. W. (1994). Telling the secret: Adult women describe their disclosures of incest. *Journal of Interpersonal Violence, 9,* 327–338.

Rosenhan, D. L. (1973). On being sane in insane places. *Science, 179,* 250–258.

Roy v. *Hartogs,* 381 N.Y.S. 2d 587; 85 Misc.2d 891 (1976).

Saakvitne, K. W., Pratt, A. C., & Pearlman, L. A. (1997). Under the mantle of science. *American Psychologist, 52,* 997.

Safer, D. J. (1997). Adolescent/adult differences in suicidal behavior and outcome. *Annals of Clinical Psychiatry, 9,* 61–66.

Salter, A. C. (1995). *Transforming trauma.* Thousand Oaks, CA: Sage.

St. Paul Fire & Marine Insurance Company v. *Downs,* 617 N. E. 2d 33g (Ill. App. 1 Dist. 1993).

San Francisco Boys Chorus. (September 9, 1994). *Public letter of apology in the matter of Ross Cheit.*

Sanders, J. R., & Keith-Spiegel, P. (1980). Formal and informal adjudication of ethics complaints against psychologists. *American Psychologist, 35,* 1096–1105.

Sarason, S. B. (1985). *Caring and compassion in clinical practice.* San Francisco: Jossey-Bass.

Scarr, S., & Weinberg, R. A. (1976). IQ test performance of black children adopted by white families. *American Psychologist, 30,* 726–739.

Schick, F. (1997). *Making choices: A recasting of decision theory.* Cambridge, UK: Cambridge University Press.

Schloendorf v. *Society of New York Hospital,* 211 N.Y. 125, 105 N.E. 92 (1914).

Schneidman, E. (1975). *Suicidology: Contemporary developments.* New York: Grune & Stratton.

Schooler, J. W., Bendiksen, M., & Ambadar, Z. (1997). Taking the middle line: Can we accommodate both fabricated and recovered memories of sexual abuse? In M. A. Conway (Ed.), *Recovered memories and false memories* (pp. 251–292). Oxford: Oxford University Press.

Schulyer, D. (1974). *The depressive spectrum*. New York: Jason Aronson.

Seppa, N. (1996, April). Fear of malpractice curbs some psychologists' practice. *APA Monitor*, p. 12.

Shapiro, D. L. (1990). *Forensic psychological assessment: An integrative approach*. Boston: Allyn & Bacon.

Shaver, K. G., & Drown, D. (1986). On causality, responsibility, and self-blame: A theoretical note. *Journal of Personality and Social Psychology, 50*, 697–702.

Sherrill, M. (1995, September 1). Warriors in waiting. *Washington Post*, p. Fl.

Siegel-Itzkovich, J. (1996, May 19). You must remember this. . . . *Jerusalem Post*, p. 7.

Sifford, D. (1991, November 24). Accusations of sex abuse, years later. *Philadelphia Inquirer*, pp. 11–12.

Sifford, D. (1992, February 13). Perilous journey: The labyrinth of past sexual abuse. *Philadelphia Inquirer*, p. D6.

Singer, J. L. (1980). The scientific basis of psychotherapeutic practice: A question of values and ethics. *Psychotherapy: Theory, Research, and Practice, 17*, 373–383.

Smith, S. H., & Whitehead, C. I. (1988). The public and private use of consensus-raising excuses. *Journal of Personality, 56*, 355–371.

Social political movement. (1996, May). *False Memory Syndrome Foundation Newsletter* (E-mail version).

Sonne, J. L. (1994). Multiple relationships: Does the new ethics code answer the right questions? *Professional Psychology: Research & Practice, 25*, 336–343.

Sonne, J. L., Meyer, C. B., Borys, D., & Marshall, V. (1985). Clients' reaction to sexual intimacy in therapy. *American Journal of Orthopsychiatry, 55*, 183–189.

Spanos, N. P. (1994). Multiple identity enactments and multiple personality disorder: A sociocognitive perspective. *Psychological Bulletin, 116*, 143–165.

Spence, D. P. (1993, August). *Narrative truth and putative child abuse*. American Psychological Association Division 24 presidential address delivered at the 101st Annual Convention of the American Psychological Association, Toronto, Ontario, Canada.

Spiegel, D. (1997). Memories: True and false. *American Psychologist, 52*, 995–996.

Standards for educational and psychological testing. (1985). Washington, DC: American Psychological Association.

Stanton, M. (1993). S.F. Chorus hit with molestation suit. *San Jose Mercury News,* October 5, p. 5B.

Stanton, M. (1995). Bearing witness (a 3-part series). *Providence Journal-Bulletin,* May 7, pp. A1, A18–A19; May 8, pp. A1, A8–A9; May 9, p. A1, A6–A7.

Stanton, M. (1997, July–August). U-turn on memory lane. *Columbia Journalism Review,* 44–49.

Stanton, W. (1960). *The leopard's spots: Scientific attitudes toward race in America.* Chicago: University of Chicago Press.

State v. *Warnberg.* No. 93-2292-CR, Court of Appeals of Wisconsin, District 4 (1994, March 24).

Stevens, N. (1990, August 25). Did I say average? I meant superior. *New York Times,* p. 15.

Stoltenberg, C. D., & Delworth, U. (1987). *Supervising counselors and therapists.* San Francisco: Jossey-Bass.

Stone, A. A. (1978, March 19). Mentally ill: To commit or not, that is the question. *New York Times,* p. 10E.

Stone, M. T. (1982). Turning points in psychotherapy. In S. Slipp (Ed.), *Curative factors in dynamic psychotherapy* (pp. 259–279). New York: McGraw-Hill.

Stricker, G. (1992). The relationship of research to clinical practice. *American Psychologist, 47,* 543–549.

Stromberg, C. D., Haggarty, R. F., McMillian, M. H., Mishkin, B., Rubin, B. L., & Trilling, H. R. (1988). *The psychologist's legal handbook.* Washington, DC: Council for the National Register of Health Service Providers in Psychology.

Tallman, G. (1981). *Therapist-client social relationships.* Unpublished manuscript, California State University, Northridge.

Tavris, C. (1987, November 1). Method is all but lost in the imagery of social-science fiction. *Los Angeles Times,* Section V, p. 5.

Taylor, L., & Adelman, H. S. (1995). Reframing the confidentiality dilemma to work in children's best interests. In D. N. Bersoff (Ed.), *Ethical conflicts in psychology* (pp. 198–201). Washington, DC: American Psychological Association.

Thomas, A., & Sillen, S. (1972). *Racism and psychiatry.* Secaucus, NJ: Citadel Press.

Thoreau, H. D. (1960). *Walden and civil disobedience.* Boston: Houghton Mifflin. (Civil disobedience originally published 1849.)

Tolstoy, L. (1951). *The kingdom of God is within you* (L. Weiner, Trans.). Boston: Page. (Originally published 1894.)

Truman v. Thomas, California, 611 P.2d 902,27 Cal. 3d 285 (1980).

Tsuang, M. T. (1983). Risk of suicide in relatives of schizophrenics, manics, depressives, and controls. *Journal of Clinical Psychiatry, 39,* 396–400.

Twemlow, S. W., & Gabbard, G. O. (1989). The lovesick therapist. In G. O. Gabbard (Ed.), *Sexual exploitation in professional relationships* (pp. 71–87). Washington, DC: American Psychiatric Association.

Underwager, R., & Wakefield, H. (1991). Cur allii, prae aliis? (Why some, and not others?) (1991). *Issues in Child Abuse Accusations, 3,* 178–193.

U.S. Public Health Service. (1973). *Final report of the Tuskegee syphilis study ad hoc advisory panel.* Washington, DC: Author.

van der Kolk, B. A., & Fisler, R. (1995). Dissociation and the fragmentary nature of traumatic memories: Overview and exploratory study. *Journal of Traumatic Stress, 8,* 505–525.

Vasquez, M. J. T. (1988). Counselor-client sexual contact: Implications for ethics training. *Journal of Counseling and Development, 67,* 238–241.

Vasquez, M. J. T. (1992). Psychologist as clinical supervisor: Promoting ethical practice. *Professional Psychology: Research and Practice, 23,* 196–202.

Vinson, J. S. (1987). Use of complaint procedures in cases of therapist-patient sexual contact. *Professional Psychology: Research and Practice, 18,* 159–164.

Wagner, M. G. (1993). He confronts memory—and alleged molester. *Sacramento Bee,* October 7, p. A1.

Wagner, M. G. (1994). Ex-leader of boys camp held in molest: Charges brought decades later based on "recovered memory." *Sacramento Bee,* July 14, p. B7.

Wakefield, H., & Underwager, R. (1994). *Return of the furies: An investigation into recovered memory therapy.* Chicago: Open Court.

Walker v. City of Birmingham, 388 U.S. 307,18 L ed 2d 1210 (1967).

Walker, E., & Young, T. D. (1986). *A killing cure.* New York: Holt.

Wang, C. (1993). *Sense and nonsense of statistical inference.* New York: Dekker.

Wassil-Grimm, C. (1995). *Diagnosis for disaster: The devastating truth about False Memory Syndrome and its impact on accusers and families.* Woodstock, NY: Overlook.

Watson, J. B. (1939). *Behaviorism (2nd ed.).* Chicago: University of Chicago.

Weiner, I. B. (1988, August). *Can a psychological assessment do what we think it can?* Paper presented at the annual meeting of the American Psychological Association, Atlanta.

Weiner, I. B. (1989). On competence and ethicality in psychodiagnostic assessment. *Journal of Personality Assessment, 53,* 827–831.

Weisman, A. D., & Worden, J. W. (1972). Risk-rescue rating in suicide assessment. *Archives of General Psychiatry, 26,* 553–560.

Westen, D. (1996). *Psychology: Mind, brain, & culture.* New York: Wiley.

Westermeyer, J. (1987). Cultural factors in clinical assessment. *Journal of Consulting and Clinical Psychology, 55,* 471–478.

Wetzel, R. (1976). Hopelessness, depression, and suicide intent. *Archives of General Psychiatry, 33,* 1069–1073.

Whitfield, C. L. (1995). *Memory and abuse.* Deerfield Beach, FL: Health Communications.

Widom, C. S., & Morris, S. (1997). Accuracy of adult recollections of childhood victimization: Part 2. Childhood sexual abuse. *Psychological Assessment, 9,* 34–46.

Widom, C. S., & Shepard, R. L. (1996). Accuracy of adult recollections of childhood victimization: Part 1. Childhood physical abuse. *Psychological Assessment, 8,* 412–421.

Williams, L. M. (1994). Recall of childhood trauma: A prospective study of women's memories of child sexual abuse. *Journal of Consulting & Clinical Psychology, 62,* 1167–1176.

Word, C., Zanna, M. P., & Cooper, J. (1974). The nonverbal mediation of self-fulfilling prophecies in interracial interaction. *Journal of Experimental Social Psychology, 10,* 109–120.

Wyatt, G. E. (1997). *Stolen women: Reclaiming our sexuality, taking back our lives.* New York: John Wiley.

Zaragoza, M. S., & Koshmider, J. W. (1989). Misled subjects may know more than their performance implies. *Journal of Experimental Psychology: Learning, Memory, and Cognition, 15,* 246–255.

─ܥ─ About the Authors

KENNETH S. POPE received graduate degrees from Harvard and Yale and is in independent practice as a licensed psychologist. He has chaired the Ethics Committees of the American Psychological Association (APA) and the American Board of Professional Psychology (ABPP). He is a charter fellow of the American Psychological Society (APS) and a fellow of APA Divisions 1, 2, 12, 29, 35, 41, 42, and 44. A diplomate in clinical psychology, he has authored or co-authored over 100 articles and chapters in peer-reviewed scientific and professional journals and books. His ten books include *The MMPI, MMPI-II and MMPI-A in Court: A Practical Guide for Expert Witnesses and Attorneys* (with J. Butcher & J. Seelen); *Sexual Involvement with Patients: Patient Assessment, Subsequent Therapy, Forensics; Law and Mental Health Professionals: California* (with B. Caudill); *Recovered Memories of Abuse: Assessment, Therapy, Forensics* (with L. Brown); and *The Stream of Consciousness: Scientific Investigations into the Flow of Human Experience* (with J. Singer). He taught courses in abnormal psychology, psychological and neuropsychological assessment, and professional standards of care at the University of California, Los Angeles, where he served as a psychotherapy supervisor. His prior experience also includes serving as clinical director and psychology director in both private hospital and community mental health settings. He received the APA Division of Clinical Psychology Award for Distinguished Professional Contributions to Clinical Psychology, the Belle Mayer Bromberg Award for Literature, and the Frances Mosseker Award for Fiction. He received the American Psychological Association Award for Distinguished Contributions to Public Service, which included the following citation (*American Psychologist*, 1995, *50*, pp. 241–243):

> For rigorous empirical research, landmark articles and books, courageous leadership, fostering the careers of others, and making services

available to those with no means to pay. His works include nine books and over 100 other publications on topics ranging from treating victims of torture to psychometrics to memory to ethics. His pioneering research has increased our understanding of therapist-patient sex, especially in the areas of effects on patients, tendencies to deny or discount risks, factors enabling known perpetrators to continue or resume not only practicing but also abusing patients, and approaches to prevention. As the title—*What Therapists Don't Talk About and Why*—of his acceptance talk for the Division 12 Award for Distinguished Professional Contributions to Clinical Psychology suggests, Pope's research frequently addresses concerns that are relatively neglected because they tend to cause anxiety, such as therapists' feelings of anger, hate, fear, or sexual attraction toward patients, or therapists' own histories of sexual or physical abuse. He frequently declines compensation for his work to advance psychology in the public interest. This is evident in his recent book, *Sexual Involvement with Therapists: Patient Assessment, Subsequent Therapy, Forensics,* published by the American Psychological Association. Pope waived all royalties for the volume in order that it might be sold at reduced price and be more readily available and useful. His integrity, good will, humor, and tireless work in the public interest represent the finest ideals of our profession.

MELBA J. T. VASQUEZ received her Ph.D. degree in counseling psychology from the University of Texas, and is a psychologist in independent practice in Austin, Texas. She served on the APA Ethics Committee, the APA Ethics Committee Task Force for Revision of the 1981–1990 Ethical Principles, and the APA Board of Social and Ethical Responsibility. She currently serves on the APA Policy and Planning Board and the APA Ethics Committee Task Force for Revision of the 1992 Ethics Code. She served as director of internship training at Colorado State University and the University of Texas, and as senior psychologist at the University of Texas's Counseling and Mental Health Center. She has taught graduate courses in ethics, counseling and psychotherapy, and multicultural issues in psychology. She has published numerous journal articles and book chapters in the specialty areas of ethics, ethnic minority psychology, psychology of women, supervision, and training. She has served in various leadership capacities of the American Psychological Association, including chairing the APA Board for the Advancement of Psychology for the

Public Interest and the APA Board of Professional Affairs. She was elected to serve as president of APA Division 35, Psychology of Women, for the 1998–1999 term. She is a fellow of the American Psychological Association, holds the diplomate from the American Board of Professional Psychology, and has received numerous awards, including the APA Centennial Award for Early Career Contribution to the Public Interest, the Southwest Texas State University Hispanic Alumni Award, and the APA Minority Fellowship Award for Teaching and Training.

～ Name Index

~~~ Subject Index